To Donna
with love
from Irene and Carl
Oct 10, 1994

HOLOCAUST
REVISITED

By the same authors

OF HUMAN AGONY

HOLOCAUST REVISITED

By
Irene and Carl Horowitz

SHENGOLD PUBLISHERS, INC.
New York

Library of Congress Catalog Card Number: 94-065120
ISBN 0-88400-172-5
Copyright © 1994 by Irene and Carl Horowitz
All rights reserved

Published by Shengold Publishers, Inc.
18 West 45th Street
New York, NY 10036

Printed in the United States of America

ACKNOWLEDGMENTS

The authors wish to express their appreciation to Anna Dichter, George Lee and Wilhelm Dichter for their contributions to this book. Their names have been displayed in the corresponding chapters. They are friends or family of authors Carl and Irene.

These chapters are written by them based on their experiences which are unique. They illustrate life during the Holocaust under the Germans and in Russia.

New York, October 24, 1993

PROLOGUE

This book is a continuation of a previous book entitled "Of Human Agony," which was also written jointly by Irene and Carl Horowitz. It describes their lives in the United States after the war. Even though their life eventually became normal after a period of adjustment in their new country, memories of the Holocaust haunted them. They talked about it constantly. There was hardly a meeting of two or more survivors in which the conversation didn't turn to that subject. After only a few minutes of casual conversation, someone would start to recall the war. It seemed as if they were destined to revisit the Holocaust over and over again.

Many of their decisions, both large and small, were strongly affected by what had happened to them during the war. Although the pain of losing their loved ones softened with time it never fully abated and they never forgot them.

Having survived, they felt a strong sense of obligation and purpose. They felt that their story should be recorded permanently for future generations. When people in the future read it, they wanted them to know not only that six million innocent people had died; they wanted them to feel the individual pain of each victim.

And to those who cast doubt upon the existence of the Holocaust for whatever reason or with whatever motive, this book, along with many others, would bear eternal witness to what really happened.

New York, October, 1993
Irene and Carl Horowitz

Chapter 1

Roth's Mountain

June 29, 1993

Carl was opening the mail one morning at work. Irene stood beside him. This was their usual routine. Carl noticed a large, bulky envelope with an unfamiliar foreign address. Inside it were photographs and a letter. At first he thought it was an advertisement.

All of a sudden, he saw a photo of his hill in Zniesienie. He could not believe his eyes. "Irene, look, it's Zniesienie!" he yelled. He looked again and saw more pictures of the hill where he and his family had lived before the war. He read the letter.

Dear Carl:

I must apologize for my delay in replying. The weather has been bad and I could not take pictures. On the first nice day I went with my wife, following your directions. We saw some really beautiful places where we had never been before.

We found No. 35 Starozniesienska Street right away and spoke to the woman owner, who has lived there since 1946. A couple (Polish–Ukrainian) had lived there before, but they left for Poland. I asked her about the Roth's house and she immediately told me where it was and how to find it. We went 300 meters, turned left, and after some 30–50 meters we were on top of the hill. The view from there was beautiful but, alas, there is no house there. There are only the ruins of its foundations. I asked in the neighboring houses but nobody knew anything because they had moved in after the war, and the house was already gone. But everybody calls it the Roth's Mountain, even the children.

I took pictures along the path, which I identified on the back; maybe they will remind you of something.

Now we are awaiting your arrival. I will gladly help you retrace the road that has changed so much over so many years. We will try to make your stay here a pleasant one. If you have any wishes in connection with your trip, please call us.

Best regards to you and Irene,

Olek.

Olek, who lived in Lvov, had been in New York a few months earlier visiting his friend George. After he had left, Carl asked George to write to him asking him to go to Zniesienie and take pictures of Carl's house.

Now Olek had sent him the bad news. The house on the hill was not there anymore. Carl cried, but he had mixed emotions. On the one hand, he was sad that the house was gone. On the other hand, he was glad that nobody lived there. It would break his heart to see other people living in his house. And he would feel awful if it were neglected and dirty. This way, nobody had it.

But Irene saw the whole thing differently. "Look, Carl," she said, "they call the hill 'Roth's Mountain.' Did they call it that before the war?"

"No, I never heard that name before."

Irene thought aloud: "They must have loved your grandfather very much if they called the place by his name after his death."

Carl made copies of the pictures and sent them to his brother Leo. Leo called as soon as he got them. "Carl, is the house still there?" Carl avoided answering him. "I don't know, the pictures don't show it, but it may still be there," he said.

Now Carl wanted very much to go to Lvov, but he wanted to go with Irene. He wanted to show her his beloved Zniesienie and the place where he had lived with his family before the war. But Irene had resisted his pleas for a long time.

Meanwhile, a trip was being organized by their friend Felicia in Miami. It appealed to Carl because it included Lvov and Boryslaw. It was to be a group tour and several of their friends who had been born in Boryslaw and neighboring Drohobycz were joining in. That evening after supper, Irene said to Carl, "You can go to Lvov."

"And what about you?" asked Carl. "I cannot go," she answered. "It is hard for me to travel with my arthritis." But next morning, when Carl got up early as usual, Irene was not asleep. She turned to Carl and said, "I've decided to go to Lvov with you." Carl couldn't believe his ears. He was so delighted he kissed her face and hands.

The next day he told Leo and his cousin Herta about their plans. Leo wasn't home but his wife, Hilda, asked him for a few days to talk it over with him. They finally decided not to go this year.

Herta said she would go and a few days later told him that her daughter Ruth was going too.

Carl became very emotional. He would cry without any reason, although he hadn't cried since childhood. He talked to Herta more than ever before.

"You know, Carl," Herta said during one of these conversations, "when we go to Lvov we should find a place from which we can see our hill best."

Carl thought for a minute and said, "When we reach the bridge over the railroad tracks, we will stop and get out of the car, we should have an excellent view of the mountain from there. It is about 1 mile from our house and the view is not obstructed by anything."

That night Carl had a dream. He dreamt that he was going to Zniesienie. But when he reached the bridge it was cemented over and they could not go through. Somehow he got there in a roundabout way. And the house was there.

Next, Carl called up his Aunt Fela in Israel. He told her about the trip and asked her to join them, offering to pay all the expenses.

"I cannot go, I don't have the strength for it," she replied. She was now 84 years old.

Carl had his fears about going to Lvov but he kept them to himself. He didn't want Irene to change her mind. Lvov was now in Ukraine. Before the war it had belonged to Poland. If Poland was an underdeveloped country by western standards, Ukraine was ten times worse. And he always remembered Uncle Ed's two brothers, who had visited Lvov from Belgium to see their parents shortly before the war. When the war broke out, they got stuck there. The borders were closed and they could not go back to Belgium. They perished, killed by the Germans.

But in spite of his fears, Carl felt an irresistible force pushing him to go. True, there was no war in Ukraine now. Communism had collapsed and many people were going there to visit their birthplaces.

But they were Jewish, and there was a rabidly anti-Semitic organization in Ukraine. What would happen if they went to Zniesienie and were met with sticks and axes? That had happened to Anna's husband Michael (Anna is Irene's sister), when he returned after the war to the town in which his first wife and child had perished. The villagers would not let him enter the house in which his family had lived before and been killed by the Germans. The local people probably feared that he was coming back to claim his property.

Carl didn't want anything back. He just wanted to see the place where his family had lived once more.

He had an idea. He would have a monument erected on the site where their house had stood. Irene liked the idea. Together with Fela and Herta, they composed an inscription for the monument. It would be in Ukrainian and English and would read:

THIS PLACE IS CALLED ROTH'S MOUNTAIN BECAUSE MICHAEL ROTH LIVED HERE WITH HIS WIFE ESTHER AND THEIR CHILDREN, SUSIA, AMALIA, MEYER AND DONNA AND THEIR FAMILIES FROM 1908 TO 1942. IN LOVING MEMORY FROM THEIR FAMILY. WE EXPRESS OUR WARMEST GRATITUDE TO OUR NEIGHBORS OF STARE ZNIESIENIE FOR THEIR COMPASSION AND KINDNESS DURING THE WAR YEARS 1941–42

It was true. The local population had never done any harm to the Roth family during the war. On the contrary, whenever there was a threat of a night raid on their house by the Germans, their neighbors (the Panczyszyns) warned them about it and offered to let them spend the night in their orchard. They would sleep in the small arbor in the garden. Carl thought about this often. There were probably anti-Semites among their neighbors, but the elders of the village must have forbidden them to do any harm to the Roth's.

Leo and Herta each offered to pay one-third of the cost of the monument.

Chapter 2

Warsaw and Cracow

July 20, 1993

Carl, Irene and their two daughters, Alice and Terry, took a trip to Poland and Ukraine. It was an emotional journey for Irene and Carl. They had left Poland almost fifty years ago and had never gone back. Irene had seen her home town after the war because she had been liberated there, but Carl had never gone back after being liberated in Cracow in January 1945.

When Irene and Carl decided to make the trip to their home towns in Ukraine, they told their daughters and asked if they would like to come. "We are asking you to come with us," Irene said, "but don't feel bad if you decide not to go." She didn't mention it again.

A few days later Terry called and said: "What's with the trip."

"It's up to you, Terry," Irene answered. "You're welcome to join us if you like."

"I want to go," Terry answered.

Irene was glad that Terry had decided to go with them. After all, they were going to the place where her parents were born and grew up. Terry would see where their roots were. Irene thought it would be good for them to make this trip together, and would bring them closer to one another. Terry was a good companion and she liked to travel; this would give her a chance to see this part of the world.

A few days later Alice came and said, "I want to go; I don't want to be left out of it." So the four of them boarded a Delta Airlines flight in New York on July 18, 1993 to take this important trip together. The first stop would be Warsaw.

The flight from New York to Warsaw was uneventful. They stopped over in Berlin and, after another hour in the air, landed in Warsaw. They were in a group of thirteen people traveling back to their childhoods. After registering in the Holiday Inn, they went on a tour of the city by chartered bus.

The city was clean and well supplied. In the two or three years since it had thrown out Communism, the country sprang up almost to western standards from the extreme poverty of before. True, prices were high and many could not afford luxuries, but the people were well dressed and certainly did not look undernourished. Service in the hotel and in the stores was quick and efficient.

The group took a guided tour of the city with an emphasis on visiting Jewish places of interest: the Rappaport memorial, the Umschlagplatz and the Jewish Cemetery. The guide, an English-speaking Pole, talked tactfully about the Warsaw Uprising and the suffering of the Jews. He refrained from boasting about Poland's help during the war. This was a controversial subject, Carl thought, and would have caused a lot of resentment between the visitors. The guide evidently knew this. Although the Poles thought they had helped the Jews during the Warsaw Uprising, the Jews knew otherwise.

At the cemetery, the Jewish attendant explained sadly, "Here is a cemetery with 250,000 graves, God saved them from the Germans, but he let 400,000 people die here. There were that many Jews in Warsaw before the war the largest concentration of Jews in one city, and now there are only three hundred old people left. There are no young people."

The group continued to the Polish parts of the city. The guide's voice now became less guarded and very enthusiastic. "We are now approaching the Tomb of the Unknown Soldier. Would you like to see the honor guard?" People on the bus got up hesitantly and went to see it, not wanting to hurt the guide's patriotic feelings, Carl thought. He and Irene stayed on the bus. Irene had difficulty climbing up and down the high steps of the bus. A few minutes later, the group came back. They were visibly shaken. A woman had shouted at them, "Here you are again, you dirty Israeli Jew bastards! Why don't you drop dead!"

"And what did you do?" Carl asked. "We told them to drop dead themselves."

Carl tried to minimize the incident. He was surprised that it had happened. The group looked like ordinary American tourists, not like orthodox, bearded Jews in caftans. But the Polish people somehow recognized Jews even through the heavy layers of American civilization, language and dress.

Carl said to Irene, "We must concentrate on the positives. We must forget what happened fifty years ago. It is time to mend fences. Somebody has to make the first step. And if they cannot do it, we should."

On the way back to the hotel, Carl's cousin Herta said, "Do you think I should call Ala?"

"Of course you should," Carl answered instantly. Ala, a Christian, had lived with Herta's Aunt Fela and they were responsible, to a large extent, for Herta's survival. They had kept Herta in an apartment for two years and taken care of her, endangering their own lives. Hiding a Jew was punishable by death during the German occupation.

In the evening, the group went to a restaurant called Bazyliszek. They sat down at a table in a room decorated with the armor of knights from Polish history. The food was served elegantly: matjas herring, red Polish borscht and a choice of trout or duck. Carl was watching the door, waiting for Ala to arrive. Herta had called and asked her to meet them there. Suddenly, Herta jumped up and ran to the door. A pleasant-looking middle aged woman was standing there. Herta embraced her. It was Ala. Carl expected her to look old, but she did not. She had a young face and a pleasant smile. Carl went over and kissed her. He had always liked Ala like a sister. She had known that he was Jewish, which in itself was a crime in German eyes.

Carl was often a visitor in their apartment on the fourth floor of 4 Kremerowska Street (Ala had insisted that it was Kremer Street). He didn't know how to begin.

"Remember, Ala our snowball fights?"

"Yes, I remember many things," she answered.

He looked at her close up.

"You look very young," he said.

"I am older than you," she answered. "I am seventy-one."

He was surprised.

They spent the evening talking and Carl hardly touched his food. The whole room was watching them. Alice turned to Irene. "Was dad in love with her?" she asked. "No, he was not," Irene answered, "but his brother Leo was."

Their friend George got up and toasted to Ala, a person who had helped the Jews so selflessly during the war. Everyone applauded. Carl knew that he should have done this himself, but he didn't know if she would appreciate it. Helping Jews in Poland during the war was not applauded by other Poles now.

Carl took Ala's address in Warsaw and tried to figure out how to help her. She was living in retirement and was probably getting very little money. The family took her home and they parted, kissing each other. Afterwards, Herta said, "You know, Carl, I am impressed by how well she dresses. And she lives in a good area, not far from the American Embassy. She looks well and she still has that impish look in her eyes. She was very good to me during the war; I think I will send her $100 a month." Carl said, "I will do the same."

The next day was Tuesday. Carl and his family went to Cracow. Irene had a date with her friend Irene P. from Boryslav. She was the daughter of the family T., who had helped Irene during the war. They were to meet in a restaurant at 12 o'clock. They traveled by train early in the morning. Alice went with another group to Auschwitz.

Meanwhile, Irene and Carl shopped in Sukiennice. At 12 o'clock they went to the Noworolski Café in Mariacki Square to meet Irene's schoolfriends Irka and Tytus. Their parents, Mr. and Mrs. Tabaczynski, had helped hide Irene (see "Of Human Agony"). They waited an hour and, as they were about to leave, Irene saw three people who could fit their description. (The third person was Irka's daughter Lucyna.) They had been waiting inside and had almost missed their friends. Their reunion was very emotional. They talked for a long time and reminisced. Irka's sister Basia, with whom Irene had been very close, had died several years ago. Irene missed her classmate, who had helped her a lot during the war. Lucyna, her niece, was a lot like her old friend.

That evening, Alice came back from Auschwitz visibly shaken. "The sight of the piles of shoes, clothing, eyeglasses; I imagined a living person in each pair of shoes. It is awful." She talked hesitantly and quietly, almost in a whisper. Alice had also seen the crematoria and the gas chambers.

The next day they boarded the plane to Lvov. Carl thought about the last two days. He felt like crying and tried to hold back the tears. He didn't even know why, because there were no specific thoughts in his mind. They were now leaving Warsaw. They had mixed emotions about Poland. Carl resolved not to think about his grudges against the Polish people and what they had done to him and his family during the war.

Chapter 3

Boryslaw

After a 35-minute flight, the group landed safely in Lvov. Olek Reichman was waiting for Carl and George. After a short greeting and a long wait at the customs office, Carl had a chance to talk to Olek. He paid him for the pictures he had sent him. Olek said enthusiastically, "Carl, I got a permit for the monument and I brought you a small replica of it." In his excitement, Carl pushed Irene, twisting her knee. She was in a lot of pain. Carl forgot about everything else. He felt terribly guilty.

They proceeded by bus to Truskawiec, with rolling, fertile land, thousands of cows, and farmers in simple clothes. A few old cars could be seen on the road. As they approached Drohobycz, a town next to Boryslaw, one could feel the excitement in the air.

The group registered at Hotel Beskid in Truskawiec. The "most elegant hotel in town" was impressive on the outside but modest inside, even compared with the Holiday Inn in Warsaw. The red tape was at its best and keys to the rooms could not be gotten even though the rooms were ready. Felicia, the trip organizer, finally lost her temper and started to scream, "I want the keys to my room and I want them now!" The attendant called the manager and said something in Ukrainian. Felicia did not understand it but she heard one word: "Israelis." Now she really got mad and said, loudly, "We are Americans, not Israelis, and I want the keys to my room now!"

This worked like magic, and the keys, lying idly in a box, were given out to the tired travelers in a few minutes. The food was served in small portions, but after Carl gave the waitress a generous tip the amounts and quality improved greatly.

They got up from the table, Irene walking with difficulty. "What should we do now?" she asked. They had planned to rest after the trip but Carl had other ideas.

"Let's go to Boryslaw," he said, "I want to see every place where you lived." Irene agreed immediately, in spite of the pain in her knee. They got a small bus and took off with Alice, Terry and another couple who were also interested in seeing their house.

"Let's see the Pushmans' house first," said Irene.

"Where is it?" asked the driver.

"At the end of Truskawiec; I will show you,"

They drove over a busy country road, stopping occasionally for herds of cows. But when they reached the place, the house was not there. They drove a little further and Irene thought that the house on the right might fit the description. They approached it and asked about the Pushmans. The middle-aged woman did not know them. Instead, she started to tell them about her troubles with the authorities. They listened patiently to the end and left convinced that it was not Pushman's house.

Next they went to see the house where Zenek's sister had lived. An old, sick woman lived there with her son in a house much in need of repairs. They knew the young man, Andrew, having met him in Zenek's house half a year ago, where he was visiting in New Jersey.

As Irene listened to the woman, Carl took video pictures to show Zenek after getting home.

They then drove to Boryslaw, where, after some searching, Irene located her grammar school. The boys' school was still standing, but she could not find the girls' school. She was disappointed.

"Irene, let's find the house where you lived," said Carl. The constant climbing in and out of the bus was difficult for her.

"Let me see; I cannot find it." Irene looked intently to the left and right. "It must be somewhere here," she said uncertainly. But there was an obstacle in the street and they could not get through.

"Let's go around it," suggested the driver. They had to take a large detour and were in the process of getting lost when Irene suddenly noticed a church.

"Here, it must be here!" she exclaimed. "And this was a cemetery," she said, seeing a single cross in a large, open field. Using the church as a reference point, they got back to the same place but on the other side of the obstacle.

"Here, here it is!" cried Irene. The driver stopped the bus and she jumped out, forgetting her bad knee. She ran down the hill with Carl following her. And there it was. A large wooden house in relatively good condition. "This was our house!" cried Irene. A pleasant-looking older woman walked towards them.

"Please don't be afraid," said Carl. "My wife lived here years ago and she just wants to see it." He was speaking in broken Polish and

Ukrainian, knowing that she would not understand English. The rest of her family, a granddaughter with an infant in her arms, were now looking at them.

"Would you like to come in?" asked the older woman politely.

"No, I just wanted to see the outside," said Irene.

"Yes, we would like to come in," Carl contradicted her. He hadn't traveled halfway around the globe to miss this opportunity. They went in.

The apartment consisted of a small anteroom, a kitchen, a living room and a bedroom, all in a row. One had to go through each room to get to the next. The rooms were modestly furnished but clean, with crystal and porcelain filling a glass cabinet in the living room. The rooms looked warm and homey.

"Yes, this was our bedroom, our living room, our kitchen," Irene kept saying.

They stayed for a while, and Carl listened politely to the woman, who told him how Sheva Weiss (the speaker of the Kneset in Israel), who had been a child at the time, had walked out of his hiding place with his family right after the end of the war, dirty and unkempt. But the next day they were clean and shaven. For that entire time, nobody had known that they were hidden right next door in a dugout.

Carl thanked the woman for her kindness and they went back to the car. Irene rested her head on the back of the seat before her and cried. Everybody had tears in their eyes.

July 22, 1993

It was raining very badly. The group's bus proceeded to Bronice. They got out on the side of the road and walked along a dirt road into the woods. After about half a mile, they reached a clearing. A large monument was standing there. The dedication was covered with black fabric. There were a few speeches and an emotional tribute to a Ukrainian named Sniatynski, who had hidden Jews during the war. Here, during the German occupation, hundreds and perhaps thousands of innocent men, women and children had been killed and buried.

It was now raining so badly that Carl could not take any pictures. The camera had gotten completely wet and he was afraid it would stop working altogether.

They went by bus to Boryslaw. There, under the slaughterhouse, thousands of Boryslaw Jews were killed by machine gun during the war. Milo's son Romus, 2½ years old, was killed by the Germans and thrown into a mass grave.

Carl got a candle from an older man and let Irene light it at the large black monument erected to commemorate the dead. Numerous members of the Ukrainian government, including the Mayor of Boryslaw, were present and delivered speeches. They spoke of innocent men, women and children killed there during the war. They admitted that some Ukrainians had participated in the killings. They promised to work hard so that these tragedies would not be repeated, and were eager to build friendly relations with the Jews and the Jewish state.

Carl turned around. Zenek's nephew Andrew, whom they had seen the day before, was standing there. Tears were flowing down his cheeks. Carl was deeply moved. This young man was atoning for deeds done not by him but by his countrymen, proving that there was still goodness in the human heart and hope for a better world.

July 23, 1993

Irene awoke with a terrible pain in her knee. After taking an analgesic, she started to feel somewhat better, but she decided to spend the day resting in her hotel room. It was pouring outside and it would be impossible to walk anyway. But when Andre, the guide, came to the dining room ready to take them to Boryslaw, Irene got up and was ready to go.

"Where should we go?" asked the guide.

"To my first home," Irene answered at once. So they went there for the second time.

They entered the pharmacy and found it to be the same as it was fifty years ago, although the owners had changed. Then they returned to Irene's house and again examined every detail carefully. Alice and Terry watched their mother's reactions with fascination.

"Where do we go next?" asked Andre.

"To the cemetery," said Irene.

After searching for a while and asking older people where it was, they found the place. The cemetery was covered with asphalt, but one part had been left uncovered and had a black monument in the middle. There was a chain fence around it with a Star of David at each pole.

There was an inscription in Ukrainian and English, stating that a Jewish cemetery once occupied this spot. Carl, remembering Anna's request prior to the trip, started to recite the Kaddish (prayer for the departed).

From there they went to find Irene's high school. There were a number of schools, but none fit her description. Suddenly, the driver exclaimed, "There's an old school behind this building."

"Yes, yes, that's my school!" Irene cried in excitement. And there it was, an old school behind a new building, resembling a respectable Swiss chalet. Irene looked at it for a long time and cried. Then it started to rain again and they returned to the hotel.

Chapter 4

Irene Goes to Boryslaw

July 21, 1993

Our group arrived in Truskawiec. The weather was chilly and it was drizzling. I had lost my umbrella. The hotel was very disappointing. Electricity must have been very expensive because the lobby was dark and depressing. There was a strange odor and the attendants were slow. However, when they found out we were Americans, not Israelis, they began to work harder and soon we had our rooms.

We had come to Truskawiec by minibus from Lvov. We were picked up at the airport where we waited 2 hours to be checked out. As soon as we entered the bus, a young man named Andre told us that he would be our guide and would take us everywhere.

Lunch was ready. They served a small platter of cold cuts and a plate of vegetables. The bread was excellent, as were the tomatoes, just like the tomatoes of my youth. When the weather cleared I felt a strong desire to go to Boryslaw. Carl encouraged me, so we, Alice, Terry and Andre took the bus to the town where I was born and lived for twenty-two years.

I asked the driver, Igor, to stop at the edge of Truskawiec, hoping to find Pushman's house, where I was in hiding during the war. We approached a family who were working outside their house and asked if they knew or had heard of Pushman. They hadn't. We rode slowly and I looked around, but the house wasn't anywhere to be seen. What had happened to this good house? I was very disappointed.

I had never seen the house from the outside. I would come to hide there after dark and leave after dark, and I didn't know what it looked like. But it didn't matter: all the one-family houses had disappeared. In their place were three-story houses, very primitive and painted pink, housing several tenants.

Now we proceeded to Truskawiec, a suburb of Boryslaw. The night before we left New York, Zenek called us. He felt very jealous, being unable to travel because of a bad leg. He gave me the address of his house after I asked if he wanted a picture of it. So we moved on in our minibus and came to Tustanowice. We found the house right away. I stood in front of it while Carl and the girls took pictures. Suddenly someone came out. To my surprise, it was Zenek's nephew Andre, whom I had met at Zenek's house in New Jersey. He was very happy to see us; he knew we would be in the area. He asked us in, but I felt uncomfortable about going in. However, after a few minutes, his mother (Zenek's sister) came out to see us.

I had a strange feeling. This was the house of my ex-boyfriend. I had never seen it before now. I couldn't even go near it during the war. I introduced myself to his sister and wondered if she knew who I was. Carl was nearby taking video pictures all the time.

I spoke with the woman about Zenek and about herself. She told me about her illness and difficulty she had breathing. This was the house from which Zenek stole bread and flour and potatoes to bring us because we were starving. Only recently, he had told me that his mother had known he was taking the food out but had pretended not to see. I thank her for it; we needed it badly.

We got back in the car and continued to Boryslaw. I didn't recognize anything. Boryslaw as I knew it didn't exist. When we came to Zielinski Street, I wasn't even sure this was it. We started to look for my house and, before we knew it, we were on the bridge. This bridge, which was sort of the center of town, had been cemented. The river beneath it, our Tysmienica, wasn't visible. Now I knew where I was.

"We have to turn back," I said to the driver. "We have gone too far." The driver turned around and I saw a big sign in Ukrainian: "Poczta" (Post Office).

"This can't be our Post Office, it was so much bigger!" I exclaimed. We stopped some people and asked them about it. Yes, it was our "Poczta." It looked much smaller, but there it was, standing next to "Dom Robotniczy," which had been converted to an apartment house. We stopped to inspect it. "Milo left for the army from here," I said, "and we stood across the street to say good-bye." Resia with Romus, Andzia and I. My mother couldn't bear to watch him go.

Now I knew how to get go to my house; I had walked that way a thousand times. It was a long walk, but by car it took a few short minutes.

I asked the driver to go very slowly, which was no problem as we were almost the only car on the road. I looked around; nothing was familiar. Then I saw it. "There it is!" I cried. The driver stopped the car.

The pharmacy was still there. Let me wait a little longer; first I'll go into the pharmacy, I thought. "Let's go in here," I said. My heart was beating fast. I had grown up next to that pharmacy. A friend's father had owned it, and here I was, fifty years later.

It looked the same inside; not as white or full of medicine, but everything was in the same place.

Inside there were three people, a man and two women. When I told them that we were from America and that I had once lived next door, they got excited. They let us take pictures and posed for them too. I bought Valerian drops before we left.

We were now standing on the street at the top of the hill running down to my house. How short it was! I remembered it as being much longer. I used to run down this hill; now, Carl had to help me down so that I wouldn't fall.

But there it was in all its "splendor"—my house on 3 Sternschuss Street Now it was No. 13.

We started to take pictures. The house had aged the way I had aged, by fifty years, but it stood proudly before me as if it wanted to say, "You see, I am still alive, like you. I survived."

The people who lived in the house came out and I went over and told them I had lived here many years ago. We meant no harm. They insisted that we go in. Slowly, I entered the house where I was born and had lived for many years.

I saw the same little hall where my father had locked Milo up in a pantry because he refused to get dressed up on Yom Kippur to go to the synagogue. I stepped over the threshold and I was in the kitchen, the kitchen where my mother had prepared and served our meals.

I began seeing ghosts. I spoke to the people who were living there, but I saw my mother by the same stove, my father making wine for Passover, and Andzia and Milo. And there I was, a very young girl at the table eating Kali-kase and bread and butter.

In the dining room I remembered every piece of furniture that had been there and my mother's shiny floor, which she would polish dancing on her feet. And I saw the white bed where I had slept and where my mother had spent six weeks with me when I had scarlet fever.

I walked over to the window and saw Lena, my best friend. She had not been allowed in because of my illness, so she stood under the window to keep me company. And I saw the stone ovens on which my father had warmed my quilt before I went to bed so that I would feel warm right away.

It was all the same. In my mind I didn't see any furniture or people; this was my house as I remembered it. Only smaller.

My heart beat fast. Carl and Terry were taking pictures. Carl asked me questions and I answered them automatically. But in my heart there was a storm. I couldn't believe I was there, in Boryslaw, in the home where I had lived with my family. Who was I? The girl of fifty years ago who had gone through the Holocaust, or a woman who had come back to revisit her past?

All of a sudden, I wanted to leave. My memories were too strong to share with the strangers living there. We said good-bye and I gave them some money for the baby.

We continued down the hill to Marian's house. It was much closer than I remembered. We didn't go inside. The weather was awful—rainy, cold and muddy. I didn't remember July being like that when I lived there. The summers had been beautiful and sunny.

Terry took some pictures of Alice and me in front of Marian's house. I started to feel depressed and wanted to go on. I looked for the field where I had spent many hours during my summer vacation playing ball. The game was similar to baseball but there was no pitcher. The player would throw the ball in the air, hit it and run through the bases. But there was no field. Houses had been built over it. I felt a sense of personal loss. I looked once again at the place where I was born and had had a happy childhood. Carl and the girls were very sympathetic and supportive. "Let's go," I said. "Let's go back."

I had accomplished part of what I had come for. I had seen my home; it was there, waiting for me. I missed Andzia and Milo; they should have been there with me.

July 22, 1993

This was the morning of the day designated for the memorials in Drohobycz and Boryslaw. We had been hoping for better weather, but it was just plain miserable.

We got into our buses and proceeded to Drohobycz–Bronice. Everyone was very somber. Little Jewish flags were distributed which we attached to our lapels. There were buses going into the woods, where the large monument commemorating the victims of the Nazi persecutions stood. Next to it was a smaller monument to be uncovered after the prayers and official ceremonies. I felt sad watching the crowd. Everyone had a plastic for his head, as it was pouring cats and dogs.

I returned to the bus early, wet and afraid to catch a cold. Alice, Terry and Carl stayed to the end.

Then we went to Boryslaw. This was where Romus, my nephew,

lay buried in a mass grave. Many other members of my family lay there too. The Germans would shoot them under the slaughterhouse and bury them right there. We went to the monument. There were flowers and candles waiting to be lit. Carl got a candle and gave it to me to light for Romus. I had difficulty at first but someone helped me. Carl said Kaddish for Romus. A rabbi spoke. Then he prayed and a group of ten stood around saying Kaddish for the victims of the Nazis. Afterwards someone started to sing El Mole Rachmim.

There were hundreds of people; it was impossible to see how many because their umbrellas were in the way. It looked like a forest of umbrellas. It was a sad and unusual sight. I remembered having seen a picture of a funeral that looked something like that.

My friend Zenek's nephew came to the memorial with two umbrellas. This saved us from getting soaked. There were police all around. Now the Mayor of Boryslaw was speaking. He was humble and repentant. He spoke of people helping the Germans kill the Jews. He spoke of the thousands of women and children who lay here in a mass grave and said that it should never happen again. There were others from the city committee who spoke in the same vein. I thought to myself, at least they admit that they did wrong.

The weather got worse, if that was possible. A man came over to me and said, "I have someone here who wants to meet you." I looked at the man standing next to him. He took off his glasses and asked, "You don't recognize me?" No, I didn't. "I am Wilek Sandman," he said.

"Oh my God!" We fell into each other's arms. My good friend Wilek. He lived deep inside Russia. He had gone into the army in 1940 and never returned to Boryslaw. I was thrilled to see him and he felt the same. In the next few days he came to see me a few times. He told me about his life and asked about mine. It was wonderful to see him. Who knew if I'd ever see him again? I met more friends from the past. These meetings sweetened the bitterness of the occasion.

The ceremony came to an end. All of us were soaked through and through. We returned to the hotel. There were more memorials to commemorate but it was impossible to go in this weather.

That night, in the hotel, we had a dinner for everyone who had attended the ceremonies, people from Israel and the United States together. What a day!

I couldn't wait to go back to Boryslaw. My leg hurt a lot and so did my back. I couldn't let this interfere with our trip. Here we were in

Boryslaw and I couldn't walk? But I took some medicine that helped reduce the pain. Herta joined us, as she wanted to see my house.

Boryslaw was only 7 kilometers from Truskawiec. We stopped at my house. At first we thought that no one was home, but the door opened and the young woman came out holding her baby in her arms.

"Come in," she greeted us warmly. I was grateful to her. Carl explained that we were leaving the next day, and I wanted to see the house once again. When we went in, we could see that she had thought we might be back. The house was very neat and clean. Herta looked around, exclaiming how nice it was. She should have seen it when we lived there.

Once again we went through the rooms. I started to get a feeling of detachment once more. Who was I? I had lived here and I remembered so much, yet I had the feeling that another me had lived there, not the person I was now. How strange it was.

We thanked her and bade good-bye to the young woman who so generously let us into her home. As we were leaving, she ran after me and gave me a vase, a lovely blue vase with flowers on it. I was moved to tears. "Thank you very much," I said and tearfully left, probably forever.

There were many other places I wanted to see, but first I had to go to the cemetery where Bronek was buried.

The rain got worse and we were scarcely protected by the umbrellas. I showed the driver the way and, after a little confusion (it was hard to recognize where we were; everything looked different) we found the place where the cemetery had been. Now it was all cemented over. The only thing standing there was a monument saying that this once had been a Jewish cemetery. There was a wreath of flowers at the foot of the monument. I don't know who put it there.

We stopped the car and walked over to the monument. Carl was saying Kaddish for Bronek's soul. I felt like crying out, "He was so young and handsome, why did he have to die?" Bronek was 35 years old when he died in 1944. He had been such a wonderful man. Carl asked me to say something and I cried and spoke for Andzia and for my brother-in-law, Bronek. I loved him so.

We left the cemetery to try to find the house where Andzia and Bronek had lived, but to no avail.

Now we went down the main street (Panska Street) which would take us to the house where we had lived all together during the war, the house we had left only to go to the ghetto, the house where I saw my mother for the last time.

The main street looked so different. There were no more stores or cafés or private homes—everything was gone. The only thing that I recognized was the gate of Dr. Teicher's house. The house itself wasn't there anymore. I recognized my area immediately. There was the "Reiterzug" across the street and here was the yard leading to my house. I saw our windows, the same windows from which we watched the first pogrom and at which we spent a whole night watching and listening to what was going on across the street at the Reiterzug. The same windows from which we saw my father coming out of the Reiterzug with a bloody band around his head, returning to us from the pogrom alive.

We walked over to the door. A young man came out to see several people approaching his home with cameras. We promptly explained that we had come from America, that I had lived in his house and would very much like to see it. Now several people came outside.

The word "America" is like magic in this part of the world. It opened doors for us everywhere.

The people didn't speak English but we spoke to them half in Polish, half in Ukrainian and they let us into the house.

It was a three-bedroom apartment divided by a small hallway. On the right side of the hall the door led to two bedrooms. During the war our whole family of eleven had lived there. The first room to the right had been occupied by Milo and Resia, his wife, and the baby Romus. They were married in 1940 and immediately moved in with us. In the second bedroom lived Andzia, Bronek and Wilus, their son.

There was a reason for our living together. When the Russians occupied eastern Poland in 1939, they felt that many people had too much room in their homes and assigned other families to live with them. To avoid this, my parents gave up their apartment and moved in with Andzia, who had three bedrooms. Each bedroom was occupied by one family, who shared a kitchen and bathroom. On the left side of the hallway, a different family lived in the kitchen and the bedroom where I had lived with my parents.

Now the rooms were occupied by a large family with children. They had built a stove in one of the rooms in order to be able to cook.

I looked around. Everything looked so familiar and yet so strange. During the Russian occupation I was happy, and my memories of the house were very good. I was in school, a teenager with many friends and activities. My family was well and I had no worries except for the little problems every teenager has: boyfriends, school, etc. The two years between September 1939 and July 1941 were good ones.

On July 1, 1941 the Germans came to town at the outbreak of the war between Germany and Russia. Everything changed very rapidly. I was a Jewess, a member of the race persecuted by the Germans. All of a sudden, I was not the person I had been only a few short days before. My gentile friends were no longer my friends, my family was worried all the time, there was no more school and no more normal life as I had known it.

That all happened while I lived in this house.

Now I looked around and remembered only the tragic things that had taken place while I lived there. I walked into Andzia and Bronek's bedroom and remembered the first pogrom. Their windows led to the yard where it had taken place. Through them I had seen the crowd gathered in front of our house, shouting, hating. Some of them had sticks and were beating the Jews they led into the Reiterzug. I remembered myself and my father being taken from the house into that place. I remembered us sitting at those windows during the pogrom, watching all day and all night, hearing the screams and moans coming from inside the Reiterzug. I felt like crying and I wanted to leave.

We went to the other side of the house, where I had lived with my parents and where the kitchen had been. The kitchen had been the gathering place for the family. We ate there, we spent evenings there talking about the situation we were in. Friends and neighbors would come to visit and discuss over and over again what was happening to us.

This kitchen witnessed so many gatherings, heard so many bitter words and saw so many tears. Now I stood there and remembered these things with sorrow.

Carl was talking to the family who lived there and Terry was taking pictures. Herta was there, participating fully in my memories.

I couldn't take any more and I walked out. I stood on the steps, the same steps from which my mother waved to me when I went into hiding during the big pogrom. I never saw her again. She was taken away by the Germans to a death camp, Belzec, together with five thousand people. One-third of the Jewish population was destroyed in that particular pogrom.

I survived in hiding; when I came back, my mother wasn't there anymore and I was never to see her again.

Now, standing on the steps, I could see her smile of encouragement and her hand waving good-bye to me. My mother, whom I had loved and adored, was no more. She had been the best mother, had never done wrong to anybody. She used to help people and her family, even when she couldn't do it easily. She was the best human being I knew. Why did this have to happen to her? To her and millions of other innocent people? How could we let these things happen?

I started to cry and left the steps. Now I saw all the houses in the yard, so familiar to me and yet so strange. The big house where the Reiterzug people had lived. My mother was supposed to have been hidden there, but at the last minute they backed out. And the house where my mother had been hidden by the neighbors and from which they took her because another neighbor had pointed out the hiding place to the police.

I cried and remembered. I didn't want to go back to this house ever again. Too many painful memories were attached to it. It is fifty years later, but the pain is still there.

Chapter 5

Zniesienie

They traveled to Lvov in a small bus on July 24 and, after 2-hour ride over a country road full of potholes they arrived at the Grand Hotel. They unpacked and went down for a snack in the restaurant. It turned out to be a sumptuous meal, elegantly served.

Then they went for a walk in town. Carl showed them the beautiful buildings with the pride of an owner. The city was beautiful indeed. It had imposing cathedrals, churches, parks, the Grand Opera, avenues full of stores and thousands of people walking around. Irene exclaimed, "This is really a beautiful city. I like it very much."

"Let's go to Zniesienie!" Irene said. Carl could hardly hide his impatience. Off they went in two taxis. Carl, Irene and Herta were in one and Alice, Terry and Ruth went in the other. On the way, they passed Carl's high school. Carl told the driver to stop the car and ran out towards the school door.

He entered the empty building and ran through the corridors. A young man stopped him.

"What are you doing here?" he asked in Polish.

"I went to this school fifty years ago and I would like to see it again," Carl answered.

The young man smiled, "Go right ahead."

Carl ran through the corridors. The classrooms were closed, as was the gym. Carl turned left and saw the backyard. It was the same as before; nothing had changed.

His eyes filled with tears. So many sweet, happy moments and memories. Classes, lessons, fights with other boys during the breaks, running around in the yard—all these things went through his mind.

They continued along Zolkiewska Street (now Bohdan Chmielnicki St) to the Baczewski Liquor Factory. But all the roads leading to Zniesienie were closed by big steel gates, exactly as in the dream he had had a few days before the trip.

"The plant has expanded so much that all the roads here are closed," explained Olek, who had gone with them.

"So how did you get here before to take those pictures?" asked Carl.

"We went a different way," he answered.

Olek led them to a side road parallel to Starozniesienska Street, as Carl exclaimed "I know this!" every time they passed a familiar place. Suddenly, the "tserkev" (Ukrainian church) appeared out of nowhere. Soon they turned into the alley leading to Roth's Mountain. The cars stopped. "Now you'll have to walk," said the driver.

Terry took pictures. She wanted a record of everything she saw. She followed Carl with the camera wherever he went.

They walked up the hill, with Carl easily recognizing the familiar features under a heavy layer of wildflowers and weeds. When they reached the top of the hill, Irene exclaimed, "This is much more than I expected." She turned to Herta, "The view from here is so beautiful. Carl was unable to explain it fully to me. I love this place."

Carl ran from one end of the hill to the other. The house wasn't there. In fact, no building remained. There were grass and weeds everywhere. After a while, they started to walk down. An old man was cutting grass. Carl approached him and said, "I come from America. I lived here fifty years ago. Do you know anything about this hill and the people who lived here?"

"No, I came here after the war," replied the man. "But I've heard about the owner of the hill. He was a really good farmer." Carl felt a soothing balm on his heart. Many years ago, when he was a child, a man had told him, "Your grandfather is not a farmer, he is a Jew. It had hurt him very much, but he felt that his grandfather was being vindicated now by this simple statement of another man.

He saw an older woman sitting on a bench in front of her house. Her name was Jadwiga. Carl asked her about the house as Alice took the video camera from him and started to tape. Carl was too emotional to do it himself. He was anxious to get as much information as he possibly could.

"No, I don't remember, but there is Maria, who lives not far from here; my granddaughter can take you to her," said Jadwiga. "But my husband lived here before I did and he used to tell me a lot about Roth's Mountain before he died. He used to tell me about the people living there and about the owner, Mr. Roth." When asked what had happened to the house on the hill, she said that she did not remember. She seemed to be hiding something, Carl thought.

They found Maria, a small, older woman with whom Carl quickly found common ground. She had been born in 1912 but did not look her age. She told him a lot about all the people whom she had known.

Most of them were dead. Their friend Genek was alive and had visited there a few months earlier. He was now living in West Germany. He had two cars and was doing well. His sister, Janka, lived in the city on Warsaw Street. When Carl mentioned how handsome he had once been, the old lady replied, "He is now bald and fat."

They kept reminiscing and she said, "I knew Mr. Roth. Everybody respected him. He helped the neighbors when they needed something. He owned the hill and land around it. He had ten cows and two horses. There were a lot of people working for him."

Carl gave her some money, which she refused at first, but she was persuaded to buy something for her family. "I want to give you some fruit from my garden," she said. She filled a bag with apples, cherries and currants (Carl's favorite berries). He promised he would come to see her again.

Now he went to Genek's house. He walked into an alley opposite the entrance to Roth's Mountain. An old woman was sweeping the yard. Carl approached her and said, "I am looking for Genek Vertyporoch. Do you know anything about him?"

"Oh yes, I knew him and his family. But his parents died and the house doesn't exist anymore. Genek lives in West Germany. He was here but he said that he wasn't going to live here anymore." Her information was similar to what Maria had said. She also described Mr. Roth: "He was a nice man. He always said, 'Good morning, Mrs. Skalka, how are you today?' He had a large farm with a lot of cows and servants."

Now Carl remembered the woman. She was Lusia, the sister of Marian, with whom Carl's brother Mark had been very close. They had gone to school together. Mark had been Mr. Skalka's assistant; Marian's father was a painter. He had liked Mark and praised him for his ability to match colors. The family had always invited Mark over on Christmas and Easter, and he had raved about the wonderful food they served.

It started to rain heavily and the group returned to the hotel.

Mark Twain once said that when he went back to his childhood home as a grown-up man, it seemed to be much smaller. Carl found just the opposite. The buildings in the city, especially the Opera House, seemed huge and Roth's Mountain was vast. And the notion that "you can't go home again," was not true.

July 25, 1993

They spent the morning in Lvov, where they went to the "Ukraine" fleamarket next to Zielona Street and bought a few odds and ends. There were thousands of people walking between two rows of peddlers. Each held pitiful merchandise in his hand.

They had been taken there by Olek, who warned them to leave their cameras, pocketbooks and jewelry at home because the place was full of thieves. "Keep your money in your pocket, and one hand inside the pocket." They were relieved when it was over after about an hour of walking.

In all fairness, the amount of crime in Ukraine was very low. They left their cameras and valuables in their rooms and nothing was ever taken. And in the Waly Hetmanskie, an equivalent of Central Park, one could see couples and single people walking late at night.

Later they went to an artists' square on Teatralna Street and bought some paintings.

The next morning Carl said, "I don't want to go back to Zniesienie anymore. We were there yesterday and that's good enough for me. We had a good experience and I want to leave it that way." But in the afternoon, when Andre came with a minibus, Carl changed his mind. The sun was shining and he wanted to see Zniesienie in full daylight once more.

As they boarded the bus, Carl got vary anxious. He wasn't sure how to get to Zniesienie. First, he didn't know how to get to Zolkiewska Street, because changes had been made there, and second, he didn't know how to go around the Baczewski factory. There, all the approaches to Zniesienie were closed.

The bus driver was not from Lvov and everybody depended on Carl, a born Lvovianite, for directions. Somehow he managed. Again he passed his high school. His daughters wanted to see it (they had gone in a separate taxi on the first trip and hadn't stopped there). The school was closed, but the attendant, hearing that he had gone there fifty years ago, let them in. This time Carl didn't cry.

He managed somehow to retrace the road around the Baczewski factory and soon they were back on Roth's Mountain. The sun shone bright and the place looked beautiful. The panoramic views were magnificent in every direction, starting on the left with Czartowska Skala (Devil's Rock) to the east, proceeding to the forests of Kaiserwald (which were bare when Carl lived there) to the south, Lion's Mountain, Wysoki Zamek (High Castle) and the city to the west and, finally, New Zniesienie now fully developed, to the north. (It had been all arable fields and pasture lands back then).

A man of about 50 and a young man of 20 came over and watched the group. Carl became nervous, but Andre and the driver would defend them against muggers, he reasoned. In fact, the older man was Jadwiga's son. He came over and introduced himself. His name was Yaroslaw. Carl showered him with questions about his house and grandfather in broken Polish and Ukrainian. The man knew a lot about Roth's Mountain from his father (Jadwiga's husband). He talked about what a fine man Mr. Roth had been, how he had helped out his neighbors, and how large and wealthy the farm had been.

There had been cows and horses, a lot of land and servants. The man spoke with respect and without envy.

From what he said, Carl could piece together the story of their house after they had left it in December 1941 by order of the Germans. It had been occupied by German anti-aircraft artillery and tanks during the last years of the war. In August 1944 the Russians came and dug in their tanks. For several years they used the mountain for military exercises. Then they left and the hill had been empty ever since.

Later, city employees came with a bulldozer and leveled everything to the ground planning, to grow vegetables. But this came to nought because, before they could collect the harvest, it was stolen by somebody. So they gave up the idea.

The house, ruined by the rumbling of tanks and artillery, crumbled to the ground. It was looted after the Roth family left during the German occupation. The local people took whatever they could, hauling away roofing tiles, wood and furniture that the family could not take to the ghetto because of lack of space. Even Yaroslaw's father, by his own admission, took part in the looting.

Carl was not angry. These were poor people and the house had been uninhabited. If they hadn't taken it, someone else would have. As long as they had lived there nobody had touched them during the pogroms. There had been some teenagers before the war who had called Carl a "dirty Jew," and he had fought them over it. During the German occupation they could have taken revenge by plundering and killing the Roth family without punishment. This is exactly what happened in other places. But here it didn't take place. Maybe, Carl thought, the village elders or the priest had told them not to touch his family. He didn't know.

It was getting late and they had to return to the hotel. This time, Carl decided to go back through New Zniesienie, where the small ghetto used to be. (The large ghetto had been in the Kleparow section inside the city proper.) He knew this way better and Herta wanted to see the full view of the mountain from there.

They went through the railroad underpass. During the war they had moved to the ghetto through this underpass unmolested by the German police, who probably hadn't known of its existence. At other passes to the ghetto people were beaten, robbed of their meager possessions, or sent straight to the death camp in Belzec.

Now, as they drove further along Nowozniesienska Street, Carl suddenly recognized a house. "This was our house when we lived in the ghetto after being expelled from our house on the mountain!" he exclaimed, and asked the driver to stop. There was a small, one-story structure with four windows facing the street. An outhouse, unmistakable with its bright orange wood, could be seen in the back. Carl stood silently in front of the house. He didn't speak to the people in front, who looked at him with wonder. He saw scenes from the past moving before his eyes: the hunger, the constant fear and then the moment when his mother was taken away for the first time in the middle of the night. He saw his brother Leo kneeling in front of the German soldier, begging him to leave her alone, and he saw himself, a young boy standing in his nightshirt and crying aloud. They took his mother away but she came back the next day. A couple of weeks later she was taken away from a hidingplace in the field. This terrible news was brought to them in the house. This time she did not come back.

Carl was brought back to earth by Irene calling him from the bus. She was worried about him. He slowly returned to the bus, still thinking about those horrible, indescribable days of August 1942 when most of his family and one third of the Jewish population of Lvov (50,000 people) were taken away and sent to their death in Belzec death camp.

The group returned to the hotel and Carl made the final arrangements to build a memorial to his family. He signed a purchase order for a stone to be erected at the entrance to Roth's Mountain. A large arrow was to point towards the hill and the house. He and Olek had agreed upon an inscription.

The next morning they were on a plane back to Warsaw, Poland. While sitting on the Ukrainian Airlines plane, Carl thought about his

Zniesienie and how little it had changed. The new Zniesienie had grown by leaps and bounds and was now three times larger, absorbing arable fields, many of which had belonged to his grandfather.

Old Zniesienie was wedged between the Hills of Kaiserwald (now called Shevchenko's Forest) on one side and the railroad tracks on the other. Even the approach to the city was now closed off completely by the sprawling factory built on the site of the old Baczewski Liquor Factory. There were no roads going there that were suitable for large trucks or buses.

In Stare Zniesienie, time had stood still. People got older and died and children were born. Otherwise, nothing had changed. True, the house on Roth's Mountain didn't exist anymore, but Carl believed that his beloved grandfather had taken it with him to heaven.

Chapter 6

Irene Meets Zniesienie

We arrived at Lvov around noon. It was still raining, but less than on the previous day. The Grand Hotel exceeded our expectations. After the Beskid in Truskawiec, we expected something similar, but to our delight this hotel was as elegant as any hotel in New York.

We had two beautiful rooms, one for Carl and myself and one for Alice and Terry. Both of them had a lovely view of Waly Hetmanskie. The hotel was on Legionow, the best location possible, and the service and food were excellent.

Our trip started well. Even before we had a chance to unpack, Olek and a friend (also Olek) came to see us. He and Carl discussed the monument he wanted to put up in Zniesienie in memory of his family. This took a while. Afterwards, Olek (the second one) offered to take us around the city. Carl was very eager to go; after all he was in Lvov, the city he loved so much.

The weather was improving; finally it stopped raining and we took off on our tour of Lvov. What a beautiful city it was, full of architecturally beautiful buildings and full of parks. I thought of Paris and Rome where we had vacationed in previous years, and thought that Lvov was just as beautiful in its own way. Here, the atmosphere was nicer. People were friendlier.

We walked for a while, taking pictures, and finally I said, "Why don't we go to Zniesienie?" Carl had been waiting for this. "Let's go!" He was full of enthusiasm and anticipation.

Olek took Alice, Terry and Ruth by car. Herta's daughter, Carl, Herta and I went by taxi.

Carl had wanted to direct us, but at one point the road was blocked and we had to go differently. "We always went the other way," he kept saying with chagrin. "It is fifty years later," I remarked. "Things change." Carl wouldn't listen: "I still think we could have gone the other way," he said. But he had to give in if he wanted to get to Zniesienie. In front of us we saw Baczewski's tower and then the famous "cerkiew" that Carl had spoken of so often.

Baczewski had owned a factory that manufactured liqueurs. The place wasn't in operation anymore, but the tower was still there, tall and very visible.

"If we go towards the cerkiew we can't go wrong," Carl said. So we went that way and in a short while we were on a narrow street at the foot of the mountain, the mountain that I knew from so many descriptions, the mountain upon which was his grandfather's farm and house had stood.

"We have to walk from here," someone said. I took a deep breath and looked up the mountain. On its side there was a narrow road going up the hill. Carl was already on it and the rest of us followed. It was easy to walk up and in a minute we found ourselves on top. It was very big, much bigger than I had imagined from Carl's description. He was like a child, running from one side to the other. "Our home stood here," he said, "or maybe here." He asked Herta to help him out. They looked for the spot where the house had stood. But there was no house. Carl cried. His voice cracked and he tried to compose himself. I was a little worried. His words were interrupted by labored breathing. Carl called me over, wanting to share this experience with me.

"Take it easy," I said. "Please take your time." I was afraid that this was too much emotion for him to take. He had waited fifty years for this moment.

"I'm all right," he said, breathing heavily, "don't worry." I tried to stay close to him but it was hard for me to keep up. I couldn't run the way he did. "Look at the view from here," he cried. "This is the way we came home from school." His thoughts ran faster than his words could come out. He and Herta were reminiscing, comparing their memories of the house and the farm.

They must have been very happy when they lived here, I thought. "I wish Poldek were here," Carl said. "I would like to know what happened to the house."

After a while we went down. I was tired and my leg hurt a lot. I got into the taxi, while Carl, Alice, Terry, Herta and Ruth went on to talk to some people who had come out of their houses. A woman named Jadwiga came over to the car and spoke to me. She herself hadn't known Carl's family but her late husband had remembered them well. She told me that he had spoken about Carl's grandfather with respect and affection. He had told her that he was a kind man who had helped his neighbors when he could.

The mountain where the house had stood and where Carl had spent his childhood was now called Roth's Mountain, named after Carl's grandfather. That's what the people had named it and that's how they remembered the mountain. I thought this was a great homage to Carl's grandfather. His name would be remembered forever.

Chapter 7

The Rabbi's Revenge

On a balmy Monday afternoon, July 26, 1993, the group went by taxi to Krakowskie Przedmiescie (The Old City) in Warsaw to do some shopping. They went to the famous Lalka jewelry store and bought some gifts. Then they went to the main square and looked at some books about the Jews. These were now in vogue in Poland. Funny, they had not been very popular when there were three million Jews living in Poland before the war. After resting at an outdoor café and having ice cream and soft drinks, they went to a bookstore, where Alice bought an illustrated book about Poland. Carl could not decide whether to buy an illustrated book entitled "Jews in Poland." The book was large and heavy and he didn't want to carry heavy luggage. But his love of books got the better of him. He quickly ran to a Kantor (money changer), exchanged his dollars for zlotys and hurried back to the bookstore, which was closing in 15 minutes. Carl bought the book and was happy. He intended to give it to Milo as a present. Then he was sorry he hadn't bought two copies, but the store was already closed.

It was getting late and the group were tired. They decided to take a taxi back to the hotel, so they went to a stand and got into the first one. The driver, a slight young man, informed them in a monotone, "The fare will be 120,000 zlotys." They had paid half that amount to get there. "Yes, that's true," he said, as if guessing their thoughts, "but this is a private taxi and we charge twice as much as public taxis."

They were too tired to look for a public taxi and decided to pay the amount he had asked for. On the road, Carl asked as usual about interesting buildings, names of large avenues, churches, statues etc. Suddenly he saw a tall, glass building. "This must be the Marriott Hotel," he said to the driver.

"No, it is not," answered the cabbie, "it is the Golden Skyscraper."

Carl wondered, "Why is it called Golden?" he asked.

"Because it took twenty years to build and people said it cost so much money it could have been made out of gold."

Carl asked, "Why did it take so long to build?"

The driver started to tell the story, "It was the first skyscraper that the Communists wanted to build. But when the building was partially finished, it started to crack and crumble. The engineers said that the calculations were in error and the design was faulty. Now, the land on which the building stood belonged to a Jewish synagogue that had once stood there and which the government had simply appropriated for the building. After several years of unsuccessful work, the building was still crumbling. They gave the job to a Swedish construction company. They in turn worked for several years trying unsuccessfully to finish the building, which was still falling apart. People started to whisper that this was the rabbi's revenge because the Jews had not been paid for their property, so the authorities settled this debt quickly and turned the construction over to an American—Yugoslav building concern. They completed the building in a year and a half and it no longer crumbled or cracked. But the Polish people still talk about the Golden Skyscraper and the revenge of the rabbi who was the head of the synagogue that had once stood there.

July 27, 1993

The Marriott–Warsaw was a beautiful hotel, as modern as any luxury hotel in New York. All the staff members spoke English well and the service was fast and efficient.

Irene, Carl, Alice and Terry went down to the second floor for dinner. They decided to dine in an elegant Italian restaurant on the hotel grounds. A band played Italian songs at the door.

They sat down at their table. The menu had all the popular Italian dishes. They raised toasts. Irene's was the first: "I want to thank you children for the help you have given us on this trip. It has been a difficult time for us and we appreciated it. We are a family and that's what a family is all about: helping each other."

Alice listened intently. Terry twisted uneasily in her chair. Irene continued, "Alice had a difficult time last year and she suffered a lot. We sympathized with her and we suffered too. But she has proved to be a strong person and she has weathered the storm. We admire her for this. She deserves recognition for it."

Now it was Alice's turn to speak. She raised her glass and, looking directly at Irene, said, "This trip is a very important one for me and I am glad that I came. It has made me understand your background better. Telling us about it was not enough. But going with you to all the places we went to gave us a visual picture of how you lived and what you went through. I am glad that I went to Auschwitz. I saw all the horrors that people like you went through. I saw the piles of eyeglasses and shoes, each having once belonged to a living person. I saw the bunks in which they slept on plain wooden boards, four to a bunk. In cold, unheated barracks in winter, they warmed themselves with body heat by sleeping close to each other." Alice stopped, strongly affected by what she had seen.

Irene turned to Terry: "You are so quiet; you haven't said a word." Terry let out a big sigh and said, "We went on this trip to help you."

They now turned to Carl, "You haven't said anything."

"I thought you'd never ask," he said. "There is something I must tell you. Something that has bothered me very much. And on this trip it came back to me. There are three words I never said to my mother and they were, 'I love you.'" Here Carl paused for a while. He remembered his mother sitting at the sewing machine and working, trying to supplement their meager income. It was Mother's Day and he had bought a box of candies for her. He approached her but he didn't have the courage to give it to her. There was a certain barrier between parents and children fifty years ago. His mother, also, had never shown him affection openly, even though he knew that she loved him.

Terry interrupted his thoughts. "Deeds count more than words," she said.

"Yes, it may be so," replied Carl, "but you should tell your loved ones that you love them. How much would I give now for the possibility of telling my mother, of giving her that sweet sensation."

Alice said, "You feel guilty and you should deal with it."

Carl answered emphatically, "I don't want to go to a priest, rabbi or psychiatrist to get absolution. I want to go to my grave with this feeling. It is a part of me."

Irene said, "Your father feels that it is important to say, 'I love you' to your family. He always says it to me, and he says it to you, too."

Two weeks later, on August 10, the employees of the Polymer Company threw a surprise birthday party for Carl. He was 70 years old.

Chapter 8

The New Beginning

1948 was an important year for Irene and Carl. It was the year they came to the United States to start a new life.

After they got married in Poland in 1946 they left for Germany, where they lived for two years and attended college. Carl studied chemistry and Irene studied medicine. They received their visas to the United States at the end of 1947. After living through the German and the Russian occupations and then spending two years in Germany waiting for their visas to the United States, they were both thin and tired. However, at the age of 24, these things didn't matter. As their boat, *Marine Tiger,* neared the New York port, the couple stood on deck looking with amazement at the Statue of Liberty. Their hearts beat strongly with apprehension and the expectation of a new life and a new beginning.

Carl and Irene arrived in New York Harbor in January 1948 during a severe winter storm. They were met at the pier by his aunt, Helen Viener, who took them home to her apartment on Simpson Street in the Bronx. She was Carl's father's younger sister and had emigrated with her husband to South America before the war. During the Second World War she came with her husband and three children to the United States and settled there permanently.

As soon as greetings were exchanged, Aunt Viener told Irene and Carl that there had been a telephone call from a Mrs. Yardney inquiring about their arrival. "Do you know who this Mrs. Yardney is?" she asked. "She left a telephone number and asked you to call her as soon as you could."

Carl looked at Irene; they were both puzzled. "No, we don't know anybody by that name. As a matter of fact, we don't know anybody in the USA." Then they forgot the subject.

It was difficult to get a taxi. The weather was very severe and there was a lot of snow on the ground.There were hundreds of other people waiting for cabs at the pier where our young couple had arrived. Finally Aunt Viener decided to take them home by subway. This was quite a new experience for the couple. Their bags were pretty heavy, but they didn't even notice, with so much excitement and so many things attracting their attention. After about an hour they arrived on Simpson Street. They climbed the stairs to the second floor. The door was opened by a pretty young woman about 20 years old.

"This is Ida, our older daughter and,"—here she pointed to an approaching girl—"this is Jean, our youngest daughter."

Carl and Irene were given a small room with a bed, where they were to stay for the next two weeks. After they cleaned up a bit they were asked to join the family for supper.

They were asked many questions. Since they didn't speak English, Carl's aunt had to translate so that her daughters could understand what they were saying.

After a while, Irene asked if she could return the call to the mysterious Mrs. Yardney. When she did, the person on the other end of the line, hearing who was calling, started to speak in Russian. She explained that she was related to Irene's brother's new wife Dita. Milo had written to her and asked her to get in touch with Irene when she arrived in New York.

"So here I am," the lady said, "and I would love to meet you and your husband. Please come to see us." She gave Irene her address and asked them to come to dinner the following weekend.

Carl's aunt told them about her family's experiences in South America, where they had struggled before coming to the States. They couldn't get a visa and, finally, after a number of years, she and her family had come here. They opened a photography studio in Harlem and worked very hard until the war began in 1941. During the war, families were separated and people were eager to have pictures taken to send them to their sons in the Armed Forces abroad. This was a lucky break for Carl's uncle and the business became very successful.

The family had three children. Leo, the oldest, had been a soldier in the Army. While in Italy he had met an Italian girl, fallen in love with her and married her. This was much to the discomfort of his parents, since the girl was Catholic and, at that time, mixed marriages were rare. The two daughters, Ida and Jean, were still living at home.

The next evening Aunt Viener and her family took Irene and Carl to Times Square. Their first impression was unforgettable. Back in 1948, the place was entirely different from the way it is today. Thousands of elegantly dressed people strolled up and down the avenue, whose neon lights changed night into day. There were hundreds of advertisements, such as a huge picture of a man with a cigarette in his hand blowing smoke from his mouth under a sign that said, "I'd walk a mile for a Camel." There was a huge waterfall running from the top of the building, framed by a large statue of a naked man on one side and a naked woman on the other, all brightly lit with neon lights. There was a huge Peanut Man waving his cane and Maxwell House Coffee dripped from a huge coffee pot into an equally large cup. And last but not least, there was the Times Building, showing the news in large "moving" letters made of electric light bulbs.

Finally, Aunt and Uncle Viener treated Irene and Carl to a show at Radio City Music Hall. They admired the beautiful lobby and lounges while waiting in line for the movie. They sat in plush seats and listened to an "American Symphony" by Copland, played on the organ. Then the Rockettes danced, fifty or more girls kicking up their shapely legs with perfect coordination. After the show there was a new movie, "I Remember Mama." Who could forget that heart-rending story about "Mama's Bank Account" made into a movie? It was indeed a treat. Irene and Carl had seen many cities in Europe and had seen many shows, but this one topped them all. It was like a dream world.

On Sunday, Irene and Carl took the subway to Manhattan, where Mr. and Mrs. Yardney lived. They got off at 86th Street. Mrs. Yardney opened the door, and they walked into a large and sunny living room. A grand piano stood in the corner of the room. A young girl of about 10 was playing it. "This is Maya, our daughter," said Mrs. Yardney. "By the way, call me Sana. After all, we are sort of related." A little while later, Mr. Yardney walked in, holding a pipe in his mouth. He introduced himself and asked Carl what he intended to do now that he was in New York. Carl answered that he wanted to continue studying chemistry.

"Good," said Mr. Yardney. "When you finish school, come to me. I own an electrochemical battery company and we can always use a chemist."

They sat down to dinner. Irene and Carl enjoyed themselves. The conversation was in Russian. They were asked many questions about their experiences during the war and were given advice that was both kind and intelligent.

Finally, the time came to go back. The couple said good-bye to their hosts and took the subway back to the Bronx.

Irene knew that she would have to work in order to help Carl finish school, but didn't really know how to go about getting a job. She went with Carl to the Joint, a New York Association for New Americans, and asked for help. They were told to go to HIAS, the Hebrew Immigrant Aid Society.

After two weeks at Carl's aunt's house, the young couple was told to find an apartment and move out. They sublet a room from a Hungarian widower on Charlotte Street in the Bronx. Charlotte Street was a black neighborhood with only a few white people living there. Yet it was safe even late at night. The streets were full of strollers and nobody was afraid to stay out late. Food and fruit stands were open, displaying all kinds of summer fruit even though it was winter.

While in Germany, Carl had received a scholarship from the Hillel Foundation. He went to their offices in New York. The person in charge, Mrs. Rapkin, told him that although his scholarship was for South Dakota, there was no chemistry department there. He could stay in New York, but the scholarship would be cut in half to a total of $117 a month. The Foundation supplied him with schoolbooks, a suit, an overcoat and shoes. They also provided medical care. Carl enrolled at City College, where the tuition was free, and began his studies. The money he received from the Hillel Foundation went into the bank, saved for a rainy day.

The couple went to HIAS (Hebrew Immigrant Aid Society) looking for help for Irene, who wanted to study medicine. The office was in downtown Manhattan, on Park Row. The weather was freezing cold and the pair had to stop every few blocks and warm themselves in the hallways. When they finally reached their destination, they were told that studying medicine was out of the question. There was no possibility that Irene would be admitted to medical school. The people at HIAS suggested that she train to be a nurse. Irene didn't want to be a nurse. Instead, she was sent to work in a sewing company in Brooklyn, a two-hour subway ride from the Bronx.

When Carl and Irene got home, the window to the fire escape was wide open; they saw immediately that someone had been in their apartment. A rope was hanging from the roof, used by the burglars to lower themselves. A note hanging from the end of the rope said, "Sorry we couldn't leave you anything, because you are even poorer than we." They laughed. It happened to be the truth, They had absolutely nothing. They had come to New York with two suitcases. One of them contained a silver coffee set, a present for Carl's aunt, and the other one contained all their belongings. They also had $18.

Carl attended City College in the evening. As a non-resident he was not admitted to the day session. Irene was working during the day and, as she arrived home from work, Carl was leaving for school. They would sometimes meet in the hallway if they were lucky. By the time Carl came home from school, Irene was fast asleep. She had to leave the house at 6:15 A.M. in order to be at work at 8:00. They could only spend time with each other on the weekends. Irene's health, since the war, was not perfect and she could not work at the pace expected of her.

Irene's job was hand-finishing men's suits. One day she asked another girl how many suits she finished in a day. "Twenty-five," was the answer. When Irene saw that she could finish only three suits, she quit. Her next job was in a zipper factory. The manager took her to a machine and explained, "All you have to do is put a zipper in and press the machine pedal." Oh, that's easy, thought Irene and started to work. It was easy at the beginning, but soon she saw that she had to press the pedal 10,000 times a day, which made the work extremely hard. Yet she persisted, especially because everybody was very nice to her and the owner, realizing her capability and mental potential, suggested that she eventually open a similar shop in partnership with him. Most of all, she needed the money.

The owner of their apartment made advances to her while Carl was at school, so they moved. They found a single room on Aldus Street in the Bronx, which they sublet from an elderly Jewish lady named Bessie. The room was so small that the bed filled most of it, and anybody entering would literally fall onto it. There was also a tiny table at the window where Carl studied.

Bessie was a good-natured older woman and tried to help them as much as she could. When Irene wanted to invite some friends on their anniversary or some other occasion, Bessie offered them the use of her living room. However, Bessie was kosher and, fearing that Irene would not cook the right food, she offered to prepare it herself. Irene didn't mind that at all, since Bessie was a good cook and Irene's culinary experience was practically nonexistent.

The couple developed close ties with this gentle woman. They were very lonely, as their relationship with Carl's relatives had become strained. Carl's uncle resented the fact that he went to school instead of working. "You carry your suitcase under your arm and pretend that you are somebody, but you are really a 'kaptsan (beggar)'!" he shouted. "Who do you think you are? When we came here we had to work our fingers to the bone. There was no thought of going to school." And when Carl explained that he wanted to study chemistry at

Columbia University, his aunt said, "What are you talking about? My daughters tried to get into Columbia and were not admitted. Only the children of the wealthiest two hundred families are accepted. If you go there they will kick you in the behind and throw you right out."

Carl was very upset by his family's attitude. They were jealous and did not wish him well. He didn't want anything from them, but their moral support would have meant a lot to him.

He applied to Columbia University and was accepted to the day session. This meant he could take more credits and complete his studies sooner than at City College, where he could only study at night. Also, Columbia gave him credit for his studies in Germany, which would shorten his studies by almost a year, an important consideration given their financial situation. However, there was a new problem. While City College was free, the tuition at Columbia was high at $360 a semester, a large amount of money for them at the time. Irene and Carl sat down to figure out if and how they could do it. Irene suggested that she keep working in the factory and support them both, while Carl's scholarship would go entirely towards tuition at Columbia.

A difficult period in their life began. On Mondays, Carl would go to school with 10 cents in his pocket for the subway fare to school and back. Irene had 5 cents, just enough to pay for one way on the subway. She was paid $30 a week on Mondays, so she had enough for the fare back home. But her health was failing and one day, coming home from work, she passed out on the subway. From that day on, Carl brought Irene to the factory and then continued to school. But this couldn't go on for long and Carl urged Irene to try to get a job in an office.

"They will never hire me," she pleaded. "I don't know the language and I don't know anything about office work." But Carl insisted, "Please try, I'm sure that they will hire you."

"Yes, they will hire me and the next day they will throw me out." But she knew that he was right: she couldn't go on the way she had been anymore. She went to a doctor, who told her she was very anemic and should stop working at the factory. He prescribed iron pills.

The following Sunday Irene copied down the addresses of firms advertising for office help in the newspaper. She didn't have much hope, but she needed another job desperately.

The next morning she went for an interview at Hubshman Factors, a financial firm in Manhattan. It was the first place she had gone to and she was hired right away. It was the season before Christmas and the company hired twenty inexperienced girls for the temporary job of writing end-of-the-year statements. When the holiday rush was over, the company laid off nineteen and kept Irene. She was diligent and conscientious, and everybody in the office liked her.

Irene was too embarrassed to speak to other people. Her English was very limited, since she couldn't go to school. She spoke German to her supervisor, but it was several months before she had enough courage to speak in English. Then there was great excitement among the girls in the company. They whispered, "She talks, she talks!" They had thought she couldn't speak any English at all.

Irene was very happy working there. She stayed there for three years and eventually worked herself up to the position of secretary to the manager of the entire office—quite an achievement, since the office employed about thirty girls.

A new problem developed. Carl had constant stomach aches and an x-ray revealed that he had a duodenal ulcer, probably the result of malnutrition during the war. The doctor recommended a bland diet, so while everybody else ate meat or appetizers, poor Carl had to eat steamed cereal and cooked vegetables. But once in a while, when invited to visit friends or at a party, he loaded up his plate with goodies he was not allowed to eat. Then Irene would say, "May I have your plate, Carl? I like what you've got there." She would eat it so that he wouldn't hurt himself. This was typical of Irene. She was always ready to help and do anything for the people she loved with tact, without hurting anybody's feelings. Yet she did not hesitate to tell Carl the truth, straight to his face, if she didn't like something that he did.

Chapter 9

The New Beginning (Continued)

One day, the doorbell rang. It was Sunday and both Irene and Carl were home. Irene opened the door. A young blond man was standing in the corridor. They looked at each other for a moment and then Irene exclaimed, "Mundek!" The young man screamed, "Irka!" and they threw themselves into each other's arms. Marian, because that was his name in English, had been Irene's neighbor in their hometown, Boryslaw, and the brother of Lena, Irene's best friend. Irene was especially fond of Marian, who was a little younger than she; they had grown up together.

She showered him with questions, "How did you survive? How come you didn't get in touch with me earlier? How did you find me and what happened to Lena?"

Marian tried to answer each question: "I found out your husband's name and tried to find your married name in the telephone directory. There were many people named Horowitz, but I picked this one and got lucky.

"I was taken from our town to the concentration camp in Plaszow near Cracow, and then to the notorious Mauthausen concentration camp. The Germans didn't give us anything to eat during the transport in freight cars and people were dying of hunger."

They listened with sadness as Marian went on.

"In Mauthausen the Germans put us in work battalions and gave us so little food that many people died of hunger and exhaustion every day. Finally they left us for dead, and when the Americans came and liberated us, I was a skeleton weighing 80 pounds. An American Jewish soldier took pity on me and placed me in the army hospital. For a long time in the hospital, I was half-dead. I thought that all the Jews in the world had been killed and that I was the only Jew who had survived the war.

"After I recovered, my American friend put me on a ship in the Merchant Marine and I sailed all over the world. I have no entry visa to the United States, but our ship landed in New York and we got passes to go to the city. That's why I had been able to visit my benefactor in Brooklyn and see you."

He told them that his sister Lena had also been taken to a concentration camp, where she perished with many others. Irene started to cry. Even though she had expected this news, she became very sad and began to reminisce about her friend. Then she told him the story of her own survival and they cried and hugged each other for a long time.

Finally the day came when Hilda and Leo, Carl's brother, arrived from Germany. Leo had graduated from the Munich Polytechnic Institute and was now looking for a job. It took him four months to get work, and meanwhile Hilda found an apartment in the Williamsburg section of Brooklyn for $36 a month. She also found a four-room apartment in an adjoining building for Irene and Carl; it was fifth-floor walk-up. The rent was only $30 a month. They bought old furniture from the janitor in the basement, paying 50 cents for a kitchen table and a dollar for a bed.

The two couples, living so near to each other, grew close. They shared their meager resources and enjoyed small pleasures of life. They would spend their weekends together, taking long walks; having no money to spend, they enjoyed things that didn't cost anything.

For example, one day, when they had gone to the HIAS in New York, Hilda suggested that they walk home: "We can save the subway fare. It's not too far, I can see the Williamsburg Bridge from here." The subway fare was 5 cents. They were on Fourth Avenue and Eighth Street in Manhattan and the Williamsburg Bridge seemed deceptively near. But when they started to walk, the bridge seemed to move away with every step they took. Finally, after three exhausting hours in the summer heat, they arrived home. They never repeated this experiment again, even though they had saved a total of 20 cents on the subway fare.

The people who lived in Williamsburg were very poor, but they were friendly and ready to share whatever they could. For example, there was Jack, who liked to gamble on horses. Every Friday he would try to convince someone to take him to the racetrack, since he didn't have a car. Then there was Estelle, his wife, who worked hard to support him and their teenage daughter, since all Jack's earnings had been spent on the horses. There was Heddy, who had no willpower at all and spent most of the money her husband earned buying unnecessary items she saw advertised on television. There was also Molly, who had illegal card games going on in the apartment across from Hilda's. When the games were over, she served food to the players and sent the leftovers to Hilda via the clothesline.

Some gypsies lived in the abandoned stores around the corner. They were totally uninhibited and one could watch their entire lives through the display window. As poor as the neighborhood was, it was safe to walk at night; there were no robberies and no muggings. For 50 cents you could get a ticket to the movies. Also, for that amount you could get a free dish or some other gift and could see a feature film on Broadway in Brooklyn, often at the same time that it was playing on the other, more famous, Broadway. As people got caught up in the action, you would occasionally hear a gift dish drop to the floor and break amid the laughter of the audience. One day, Irene and Carl happened to see a movie with a strange-sounding name—"The Wizard of Oz." They fell in love with it.

During the hot summers, without air-conditioning in the apartment, Irene and Carl often picnicked and slept on the roof of their apartment house.

Shopping for clothes was accomplished through a peddler, who would sell you a garment for $7 on installments, payable at $1 a week. The peddler would climb the five floors each week to collect the payment.

When Christmas 1950 and New Year's 1951 came, somebody always made a party to which everybody on the block was invited. This time, Irene and Carl, who had recently moved in, wanted to invite everybody. They didn't have any furniture yet, so they went to a store in the neighborhood and bought a couch and two easy chairs for $150. The problem was that the store could not deliver the pieces in time for the holidays. So they all carried the furniture on their backs for several blocks to the fifth floor of their building.

The party began in Irene and Carl's apartment. After a few drinks, they and their guests went to visit the neighbors. Jack had lost his shoes somewhere, so Carl and Leo took two brown paper bags and tied them around his feet. He then ran around the hallways in the paper bags along with the rest of the people, to everyone's delight. It was a miracle that he didn't catch pneumonia in the bitter cold of the hallways. They went to Heddy's apartment and Leo, who was quite tipsy, danced with all the girls. His coordination was a little off and he broke a few pieces of furniture that were in his way. But nobody minded; these people really knew how to have a good time. The party ended in Hilda's apartment, where little Alexander, their son, barricaded himself under the table and from there watched the party in bewilderment.

When everyone sobered up somewhat, they exchanged gifts. Alexander got a Lionel train set which Leo, Mark and Carl had bought together for $30. This was a lot of money for them, but they had wanted to give the little boy something special. However, as they started to assemble the trains for him, Jack walked in and gave the boy a set of cards with the pictures of famous baseball players, which had cost 30 cents. Alexander started to play with the baseball cards and didn't even look at the train set, while the three brothers assembled the set and played with the trains.

Irene and Carl would remember their life in Williamsburg with nostalgia. They knew their present situation was only temporary, that eventually they would be able to leave this poverty behind. However, the other people living there were unable to do so. They were destined to spend the rest of their lives in the poverty of Williamsburg.

Irene and Carl stayed in touch with Bessie and visited her from time to time. Bessie's second husband had died and, as his widow, she applied for Social Security benefits. But her husband's children from his first marriage petitioned against her receiving any money. They claimed that she had not been a good wife, and that for the last several months their marital relationship had been very bad. The case went to court and Irene and Carl were called in as witnesses, since they had lived at that time in Bessie's apartment. After the husband's daughter testified against Bessie, Irene and Carl were asked by the judge, "Was Bessie a good wife to her husband?"

"Yes," they answered.

"Did she live with him? Did she take care of him when he was sick?"

They answered these and similar questions in the affirmative. When the court session was finished, the judge announced, "Mrs. Bessie Margolies is entitled to Social Security payments, and my judgment was based on the testimony of Mr. and Mrs. Horowitz, who testified so convincingly in her favor. They seemed to me to be telling the truth."

They were indeed telling the truth and they were glad that they could do something to help the poor woman who had helped them when they first came to America.

Carl was now a student at Columbia University. He was amazed at the difference between the European and American educational systems. In Germany, for example, the emphasis was on theory and on chemistry. In the United States the stress was more on the practical aspects of the subject. Also, one was required to study other subjects, such as mechanical engineering, civil engineering, economics and the humanities. The relationship between professor and student was relaxed and informal, something unheard of in Germany. Carl was impressed by the fact that the instructors called him by his first name and took an interest in knowing his name. In Germany the teacher was next to God himself. He never knew the students' names, and when he called them out from the register he addressed them by their last names only. The American students were friendly and tactful, and quick to compliment Carl on his progress in learning English. They never laughed at his pronunciation or his foreign accent. On the other hand, in Germany, the moment you said something in the classroom, you heard the whispers, "Auslander, Auslander (foreigner)."

The Dean of Columbia University at that time was General Eisenhower. Carl remembered this name well from the war. When he was in the concentration camp, he once listened to a forbidden foreign transmission in the radio repair shop. The penalty for listening to a foreign radio transmission was death. Yet people hungry for foreign news and tired of the German lies were willing to take this chance. The announcer said that General Eisenhower had proclaimed that any German who harmed the prisoners in the concentration camps would be brought to justice after the war and tried before the War Tribunal. For days afterwards, Carl was in a state of euphoria, hoping that this would help save their lives, and General Eisenhower became a hero and an idol.

And now one day, as he was sitting in the classroom with an empty seat next to him, General Eisenhower himself walked into the room. After greeting the teacher, the General looked around, searching for an empty seat. Seeing the one next to Carl, he approached, shook hands with Carl and sat down next to him to listen to the lecture. After the class ended he shook Carl's hand again and walked out of the room. All the students were envious of Carl's distinction and jokingly advised him not to wash the hand which had touched the hero.

When he was in the concentration camp, Carl had never dreamed that one day he would see General Eisenhower and shake his hand. He was overcome with emotion.

Carl graduated from Columbia University in June 1950. He worried about getting a job. Some of the students who had graduated a year before him were still looking for work. It was hard to get a job then, especially for a professional. However, having graduated with a B.S. in Chemical Engineering, he had accomplished what he had set out to do. He and Irene decided to take a vacation.

Irene's friend Tess, who had studied medicine with her in Germany, invited them to her house in Orlando, Florida, where she was now living with her husband Abe. Carl and Irene spent an unforgettable two weeks there. They visited Cypress Gardens, the St. Augustine Singing Tower and many other beautiful places. While they were vacationing, a telegram bringing good news came from Mark, Carl's younger brother, who was living with them in New York. A job offer for Carl had arrived in the mail. Irene and Carl were very happy and they celebrated with Tess and Abe. The future began to look bright.

Carl began work immediately upon their return from Florida and brought home his first week's salary of $65. Adding to this the $55 that Irene was making, they felt like millionaires.

It was the eve of Yom Kippur and Jews everywhere were preparing for this most important holiday. Irene was making the holiday dinner when she suddenly felt a terrible pain in her abdomen. At first she thought that she had eaten something that had upset her stomach, but the pain grew so severe that she couldn't bear it and Carl decided to call a doctor. The doctor refused to come on the holiday. Finally, Carl convinced him that something was very wrong and he came to the house. He examined Irene briefly and gave her a shot of morphine to quiet the pain. As soon as the doctor left, Irene passed out; when she came to the pain was as strong as before. The next day was Yom Kippur. They went to a hospital and the doctor told her to go home and rest. He couldn't find anything wrong. Irene was getting weak and her pain was increasing.

Carl was desperate; he didn't know what to do. He thought of Irene's friend Rafael and called him. Rafael had studied medicine with Irene in Munich and was now working as an intern in Beth David Hospital in Manhattan. When Carl told him the story, Rafael asked him to bring Irene to the hospital immediately. The doctor in the emergency room, seeing that she was in terrible pain, gave her another injection of morphine before Irene could tell him what had happened after the first shot. She went into shock again. They couldn't figure out what was wrong with her. She was now near death and the doctors decided to perform an exploratory operation immediately. Carl was crying, "Irene, please don't die. Don't leave me. I don't want to live without you!" They took her to the operating room.

The operation revealed that she had an ectopic pregnancy and was bleeding internally. She had lost a lot of blood and needed a large transfusion. Even that didn't go smoothly. A young intern was trying unsuccessfully to insert a needle in Irene's vein. After several stabs, Irene ran out of the room. It turned out that he was using the wrong blood type and the blood kept congealing. He could have killed her.

After the operation she recovered slowly. Fortunately, some of the young doctors had been her schoolmates and took good care of her in the hospital. After her release, Carl took her home. He had to carry her to the fifth floor because she was too weak to walk. She was now convalescing at home and got very depressed. Carl tried to cheer her up, but to no avail. Friends tried too, but it didn't help. When the weekend arrived, friends came to visit. One of them brought an accordion and started to play Irene's favorite old tunes. Somehow this helped her to break out of her depression. She sat up in bed and started to sing along with the music and, after a while, she cheered up and got out of bed. She took control of her life again. She realized how unfair she had been, ignoring Carl's quiet despair and helplessness. What had happened to her was nobody's fault and she had to deal with the situation she was in now. This meant do everything possible to have a child. After the operation she had been told that she could not have children. This had been a shock to them since both of them loved children and wanted to raise a family. But the reality was not what they had expected. For the time being, Irene decided to get well. Then she would go to the doctor and try to do something about having a child.

Carl loved her very much and was happy to see her healthy again. He told her that she mattered more to him than having children; having her as his wife was all that mattered.

There was a meeting of psychiatrists in the United States in the early 1960's to determine how much damage the war had done to survivors of the Holocaust. To their astonishment, they found that the majority of survivors had adapted well to their new environment. They had pursued their ambitions and their goals in life as if nothing had happened to them. There was only one thing that differentiated them from other immigrants. Survivors stuck together and talked about their war experiences incessantly. They were constantly afraid that something terrible could suddenly happen to them. They went to high school and college or found jobs. They were determined to make something of themselves. But they never forgot life before they had come to the United States.

Carl and Irene fit into this pattern. Carl followed college with postgraduate studies in chemistry. Irene worked in an office for several years. They met people who became very close friends. They were American-born but they found a common language with Irene and Carl and their lives moved along the same paths. They also had many friends from Europe. In time, their surviving families came to the United States and joined them.

Chapter 10

Grand Hotel

One day Carl and Irene went to the HIAS. As new Americans, they had to go there once in a while to take care of formalities. This time, as they were sitting in the large hall waiting to be called in, Irene noticed a young man accompanied by a young woman. They spoke to each other and looked in Irene and Carl's direction.

"Carl, I know him," Irene said. "He's from Drohobycz. He used to come to visit my neighbors." Now the young man got up and came over. "Excuse me," he said, "are you from Boryslaw?" He knew who she was and she knew him too; these were formalities.

Now the young woman came over to join them. They all shook hands and introduced themselves. The names of the other couple were George and Gisella (Gisa). The four sat down together and a lifelong friendship was born. They made arrangements to see each other during the coming weekend.

Irene and Carl visited George and Gisa in Manhattan. They had a great time together. Since none of them had any family in the United States, they needed each other. It was July 4th and they decided to go away together. This was to be the second vacation for Irene and Carl since they arrived in America.

A friend at work had told Irene about a hotel in the Catskill Mountains, the Grand Hotel in Parksville, New York. Carl had an old car and the four decided to go to this hotel for the July 4th weekend.

The Grand Hotel was an inexpensive resort. On Friday evening during their July 4th vacation, in the casino of the Grand Hotel, the entertainer was a hypnotist. "Put your hand on the chair and concentrate on your index finger. It will rise up without your will," he commanded. After a while he said, "Now, the people whose fingers rose, please come to the stage."

Several vacationers approached the wooden planks at the end of the casino. They got onto the stage, on which several chairs had been lined up beforehand. The hypnotist told them to sit. "Fall asleep!" he commanded.

A young blond woman fell asleep instantly. The hypnotist approached her, "You are now at your high school graduation. You have just graduated. March and sing your high school anthem!"

The young woman obediently marched on the stage, singing. Irene watched her with amusement. She was fascinated by what she saw. In the row behind her, a young man was laughing uncontrollably. Irene looked back, annoyed, but he continued to laugh. The whole audience was having fun. After the performance, there was dancing.

The next day Irene was walking on the hotel grounds when she spotted the young woman who had been hypnotized the night before. She was dressed in a white tennis outfit. Her blond hair and white dress gave her a very fresh appearance. Irene was drawn to her. Being very curious about how it feels to be hypnotized, she went over to her and said, "Excuse me, would you mind telling me how you felt last night during the hypnosis? I've never been hypnotized and I would like to know."

The young woman was surprised at being approached so directly. She said, "I don't remember anything."

The two young women exchanged a few more words and the woman in white said, "By the way, my name is Shirley."

"I am Irene. I'm pleased to meet you."

Then they parted.

The Grand Hotel had a very nice swimming pool; after lunch most of the guests gathered around it, swimming or just sunbathing. Irene, Carl and their two friends went there too. While Irene and Giselle went into the pool, Carl and George sat on the lawn by the pool and started a game of chess.

When Irene got out of the pool and went back, she noticed a third man standing over the men, watching the chess game. She recognized him from the evening before as the one who had been laughing so loudly during the hypnotist's act.

He looked at Irene and said, "I would like to play the loser." They all laughed. "My name is Paul," he said.

Carl asked, "Why were you laughing last night at the casino?"

"I laughed because my wife Shirley is shy and she would never had done what she did if she hadn't been hypnotized. It struck me as very funny. Besides," he continued, "she fell asleep so fast because she had played cards all night." He started to laugh.

"Where is she?" asked Irene.

"Oh, she is playing pinochle with the men. She loves to play cards and men like to play cards with her because she is a good player."

"What about you?" asked Irene.

"I play cards but I don't gamble like Shirley. She can go day and night playing pinochle or poker."

Irene said, "It would be nice if she could join us." Paul laughed, "Don't even try. She would never leave a card game."

Irene got up, "I'll try. Where is she?" She felt very playful and courageous. She would try to get Shirley away from the card table. Paul laughed loudly now. "She is in the card room near the dining room. Good luck."

Irene covered up her bathing suit and left.

As she walked into the card room, she felt her courage leaving her. There were many tables and card players, and the mood was intense. She stopped at the threshold. These people are gamblers, she thought. But she had accepted a challenge. Her eyes moving slowly, she located Shirley at one of the tables. Irene walked over and stood beside her. All the players looked up curiously. Had something important happened? One didn't just interrupt a game in progress without an important reason, but Irene didn't know that. She had never seen gamblers involved in a card game. Seeing all their eyes on her, she felt that she had explain.

"Excuse me, Shirley," she said, "your husband has joined us at the pool and we would like you to join us too."

Shirley couldn't believe her ears. Who was this woman who was making such a ridiculous statement so innocently, she wondered.

A lot of money was involved in the game. These people were heavy gamblers.

She suppressed a smile. "I cannot leave now. I am in the middle of a game."

But Irene was not about to give up now. To her this was just a game.

"Please come, they are waiting for us."

Shirley saw that it would be hard to get rid of this young woman, so she said, "I can't go now, but I promise that my husband and I will join you for the show in the casino tonight."

"OK," Irene said, "but I am going to hold you to it." Shirley watched Irene as she left the room. She felt a strong attraction to that young woman.

That night, Shirley and Paul came to the show in the casino and the couples spent the evening together. They had such a good time that they stayed up late into the night talking.

Shirley told them the story of her life. She was the daughter of a well-to-do owner of a vacuum cleaner store. Her mother, Gertrude Flicker, was from a small town in Poland, not far from where Carl was born, a *shtetl* (Yiddish small town) called Megerow. Gertrude had a friend named Willie who was courting her. After a fight, they broke up but he had left his umbrella at her house and had to come back for it. They made up, got married and emigrated to the United States, where they had two daughters, Shirley and Ceil. Shirley was a rebel; from her earliest childhood she would go to Coney Island and play all the games. She especially loved a game called Fascination. It involved gambling, and she acquired a taste for it, although it may have been in her nature anyway. There she met Paul, a handsome Jewish–Italian boy, and they fell in love.

Paul came from a poor family. His father, Frank, was Italian, a handsome, short man. His mother was a Jewess from Poland. They had three children, Olive, Paul and Joey. But their love began to sour when Frank started to make his own whiskey during Prohibition and became an alcoholic. He made money selling the whiskey and would come home totally drunk. He fought with his wife and terrorized the children. Slowly, he became estranged from his wife. One day, driving while drunk, he was in an accident that disfigured his face. When whiskey was legalized, Frank lost his source of income and could hardly support his family.

Paul and Shirley got married and took an apartment near her mother's store. Both of them worked there. Shirley became a superb salesperson and Paul dreamt of the big business deals that were going to make him rich. He wanted to be a millionaire by the age of 40.

After the weekend Carl and Paul returned to New York, and the women stayed for another week at the hotel. They moved into one room, which was much cheaper. Shirley wanted to know everything about her new friends.

"Irene, how do you say, 'You are my best friend' in Polish?" she asked. Irene told her, "Ty jestes moja najlepsza przyjaciolka."

"But I cannot say that. Please write it down phonetically."

Irene wrote on a piece of paper, "Tee yestes moya naylepsha pshiyatsulka."

Shirley pasted the piece of paper on the bathroom mirror and practiced the sentence till she got it perfect. Then she amused her new friend by saying in Polish the only sentence she knew.

Meanwhile, the men met in the city after work. Paul invited George and Carl to his and Shirley's apartment on Avenue J in Brooklyn. It was a nice place, neatly furnished, but there was not much to eat and Paul wanted to serve something to his new friends. He took a whole salami out of the refrigerator.

"I am sorry but that's all I have," he said. He was embarrassed, but

George asked, "Do you have a knife?" Paul gave George a knife and took a bottle of vodka from the cabinet. He poured three glasses. George cut the salami into three pieces and said, "Bottoms up."

They drank the whole bottle of vodka, ate the salami and got drunk. After that they met every evening after work and became close friends.

When Friday evening came, they went back to the country. Carl had an old jalopy, a 10-year-old Chrysler, which occasionally conked out and had to be pushed. But this didn't bother them. They were eager to get back to their wives.

They found the women in a state of euphoria. They had had such a wonderful time together. They made all kinds of plans, how they would spend more weekends together in the city and how they would see each other as often as possible after work.

Paul was very charming. He invited the group and other hotel guests for pizza at an Italian restaurant. Irene and Carl ate pizza for the first time in their lives and they loved it. Shirley entertained everybody with jokes and imitations of various dialects.

These are two of her favorite jokes:

> A moron is shaving in front of a mirror when the mirror suddenly falls down. He looks at the empty space on the wall and says to himself, "Oops, I cut my head clean off."

> A man sees a woman hitting her son with a loaf of bread. The next day he sees the same thing. On the third day he sees the same woman hitting the boy with a cake. Curious, he asks her, "Why are you hitting your son with a cake?" To which the woman replies, "Because today is his birthday."

Each joke would be followed by a roar of laughter from the appreciative audience. But it wasn't the joke alone that caused the laughter, it was Shirley's delivery that was so funny.

After the weekend, they all returned to New York. They didn't want to part, so they stopped in the city and went to the movies. They saw Dostoyevsky's "Idiot" and "Crime and Punishment." Shirley fell asleep during the program. Afterwards they walked around the city late into the night. They found much pleasure in each other's company and seemed drawn to each other by an irresistible force.

Two worlds had come together in these three couples; they liked what they saw in each other. Finally they went home just in time to prepare for the next day's work, Shirley and Paul to Brooklyn, Irene and Carl to Queens.

Chapter 11

East Meets West

Carl and Irene got home and started to prepare for bed. It was Sunday, 10 o'clock at night, and they had to go to work the next day. Irene had begun to set her hair in curlers when the doorbell rang. They looked at each other: Who could it be at that hour? They opened the door and, to their surprise, they saw Shirley and Paul were standing there. Shirley was holding a box in her hand. "I thought you could use a toaster, so I brought you one," she said and held the gift out towards Irene. There was laughter in her eyes. "Would you like to go for a ride? The night is so beautiful."

"Now?" Irene was shocked. "Tomorrow is work; we have to get some sleep." But as she was saying this, she was removing the curlers from her hair. Carl laughed. "OK, we'll go for a little ride."

Shirley and Paul had come in their old delivery truck. Everybody squeezed into the front seat and they left. They talked and sang songs. Irene sang in Polish, the only language in which she could sing. At first, Carl was embarrassed to sing in a foreign language in the presence of born Americans who didn't understand them. When he saw that Shirley and Paul were humming along he lost his inhibitions and joined the chorus. His withdrawn nature, conditioned by years of hiding and distrust, was gradually giving way to trust in these wonderful, open and friendly people. It was well into the morning when they finally said good-bye and went home to sleep.

After that they were inseparable. They saw each other every night of the week and stayed up till the early hours of the morning. They ate dinner together in a wonderful little Italian restaurant called Carolina in Coney Island, and Paul taught them how to order dishes they had never heard of before.

"First you order baked clams as an appetizer" (Shirley interjected, "make sure that they are Little Necks"); "then a Caesar's salad. After this, you order pasta. You can have either spaghetti with white clam sauce or ravioli with cheese. For the main course, you can have veal parmigiana or zuppa di clams. And we will order one serving of mushroom sauté for all of us."

The food was delicious. Paul insisted on paying. He was generous and knew that Irene and Carl couldn't afford it.

After dinner they would play miniature golf or just stroll in the Coney Island Amusement Park till late, and then Paul and Shirley would take Irene and Carl home.

Sometimes they went in the evening to the Pizza Parlor on 86th Street in Brooklyn for pizza and a coke. The place had tables with sun umbrellas in the front yard. The setting sun, with the view of Coney Island Amusement Park in the background, had an almost enchanted appearance. The combination of pizza and coke tasted delicious to these new immigrants, who still remembered vividly the horrors and hunger of the war.

The couples spent weekends together. On Fridays, Carl and Irene would go to Shirley and Paul's apartment straight from work. Meanwhile, Shirley would buy all kinds of appetizing such as white fish, sturgeon, smoked carp and pickled herring. She prepared a home-made spring salad consisting of sliced fresh cucumbers, radishes and scallions. She also bought expensive fruit out of season, such as strawberries, nectarines, blueberries and honeydew melons. The table she set would have tempted the most demanding gourmet. And since it was Friday night, with no work the next day, they sat up talking all night long and into Saturday morning.

After a late breakfast, they would follow their impulse—take a ride to Albany, for example. Once there, they would decide to go to the movies. They saw "The Man in the Gray Flannel Suit." It started at midnight at night and ended at almost 3 in the morning.

The women were very tired. Shirley said, "Let's sleep over in a motel." They stopped at a roadside inn and went in. "Do you have a couple of rooms?" Paul asked.

"Yes, we do."

"How much are they?"

"Thirteen dollars a room."

Carl and Paul looked at each other: "Maybe we should keep driving to New York."

The women teased them about this incident for a long time, "For your own wives you wouldn't spend that kind of money to go to a motel." But they said it with good humor and everybody laughed wholeheartedly whenever they told the story.

Sometimes the couples were invited by Shirley's mother, Mrs. Flicker, for Friday night dinner. It was very much like the Sabbath dinners they had eaten in Poland at their parents' houses.

Mrs. Flicker lived in an apartment above the vacuum cleaner store with her husband Willie. Both her daughters were married. Ceil was married to a truck driver, also named Willie.

For dinner she would invite her daughters and their husbands and sometimes other members of her family. She had several married sisters whom she was helping out. The dinner usually began with chopped liver served with finely grated radish mixed with chicken fat. The second dish was "gefillte fish," which was prepared by grinding up carp and pike and mixing them with pepper and matzo meal. This was then shaped by hand into medium-sized balls and boiled in water. It was served with a jelly prepared from cooked onions and gelatin. After this came two main courses: chicken soup and boiled chicken. But this was not the same chicken broth that was served in the restaurants. It was prepared by boiling a chicken with flanken (a special cut of beef), carrots, a whole onion, with the froth continually skimmed off during the cooking to remove the unpleasant taste. The soup was served with hot noodles. The remaining hot meat was served with red horseradish and boiled potatoes. Challah (Jewish white bread) was served for those who liked to supplement their meal (as if there was not enough food on the table!) Challah always had to be there. The Sabbath dinner without it would be incomplete.

For dessert she served a compote prepared by cooking dried prunes, apricots and sugar. Mrs. Flicker was an excellent cook, and even though she ran the store single-handedly, she still had time to cook and bring up her children.

Shirley adored her mother and loved her father. But her parents did not get along very well. Mrs. Flicker was a capable and energetic businesswoman and provided well for her family. She even managed to accumulate considerable wealth. Her husband Willie, on the other hand, played a secondary role in their household.

Shirley and Paul loved each other very much. They worked together, they struggled together and they strove together. Paul was proud of Shirley, who was a very capable businesswoman. He was proud of her attractiveness and, after a full day's work together, they still had plenty to talk about. They had their plans for the future, their dreams of success and their love for each other. Shirley simply adored Paul.

Neither couple had children. Shirley had a hormone imbalance and Irene couldn't bear children after her operation.

The relationship between the two couples was exceptional. There was no dissonance or jealousy. Shirley and Irene loved each other. Carl, who had had few friends in his life, became very close to Paul, and eventually Paul became his best friend.

Like everybody else, Shirley and Paul had plenty of problems, but they never discussed them in company and never burdened other people with them. In a group, they could detach themselves completely and participate fully. They appeared to be the most carefree and happy people. Both were very generous. Whether it was a restaurant or a movie Paul was always the first one to pay, and he insisted on it. Irene and Carl thought their new friends were the most wonderful people in the world.

They neglected almost all their other friends, some of whom eventually, impressed by Paul and Shirley's charm and personality, joined the group, including Giselle and George, Marian and Blanche and Joe and Elaine. Now they were all waiting impatiently for the summer, and making plans to return to the Grand Hotel to capture the magic of last summer. This time they made reservations for two weeks at the rate of $47 per person a week, including food. Shirley also invited her father Willie and Paul invited his business associate Jack.

More of their friends, who had heard about the wonderful time the couples had the previous summer, came to stay for a few days. The owners didn't have enough rooms and put them all into one room, not wanting to slight Shirley and Paul, whom they liked very much. Finally, their friends wound up eight in a room, with Jack and Willie sleeping in one bed.

Jack, a young man three times divorced and a very flirtatious person, would get up in the morning and go out looking for adventure. One day he spotted two young girls riding horses and started to make provocative remarks. The girls got angry and started to pursue him on horseback, while Jack ran away as fast as he could. Soon the whole hotel and all the guests were watching the show from the windows and front porch, laughing and encouraging one side or the other.

Jack ran breathlessly into the tennis court and closed the gate. One of the girls got off the horse, opened the gate and continued the pursuit. In desperation, Jack took off his jacket, stretched it out, and fended off the attack like a toreador facing a bull in the arena.

All the guests were now laughing hysterically, and who knows what would have happened to poor Jack if the hotel's help hadn't come to the rescue and extricated him from the hands of the enraged girls.

Our two couples, Shirley and Paul and Irene and Carl took two adjoining rooms in the newly built addition to the hotel. They wanted to be close together and spent most of their waking hours together in one or the other room. The four of them would get up at 6 in the morning to play tennis. This was the best time to play, as the sun wasn't too hot yet. That unforgettable summer, the hotel held a tennis competition for all the guests and Carl, Paul and Irene became finalists. Irene played Carl and won. Now only Paul was left. Paul was a very good and aggressive player and Irene didn't expect to beat him. But the inconceivable happened. She won the game and became the tennis champion of the Grand Hotel. It was a wonderful feeling and she cherished the memory forever.

After tennis, the two couples would go down to the swimming pool and swim until it was time to change for breakfast. Their appetites after these exercises were enormous, and the hotel didn't make much money on them. Carl ordered two portions of everything and Paul would laugh at him. He had never seen anyone eat so much. Afterwards he would ask Carl to go with him to the scale to see who was thinner. Paul was much thinner at that time and this made him happy.

"Let's play strip poker," Shirley suggested one afternoon. In this game, whoever lost had to take off a piece of his clothing. Carl, who was a poor card player, soon found himself wearing only his shorts. Shirley was down to her panties and brassiere. Then Carl lost again and, not wanting to undress completely, ran out of the room into the hotel corridor. Paul locked the door and Carl ran frantically up and down the hall, looking for a cover. Unable to find a hiding place and afraid that some of the hotel guests might find him half-naked, Carl knocked urgently on the door. Paul opened it obligingly and poured a pail of water on Carl. Everyone laughed heartily.

The next day at lunch, Paul was sitting in the main dining room with Shirley when Carl appeared with a garden hose and sprayed him with water. Other people joined in and soon everybody was splashing water on each other and laughing, having a good time.

On Friday and Saturday there was dancing in the casino of the hotel. Everybody would get dressed in their best clothes for the occasion. On those nights the band would play till 2 A.M. On one such evening the hotel had a dance contest and Willie, Shirley's father asked Irene to dance a polka with him. They won first prize. It was wonderful as Willie was in his sixties at the time.

Like everything else, those two weeks came to an end and it was time to go back to work. When they returned to New York, Irene and Carl had to move out of their apartment in Queens because of a disagreement with their landlord. He objected to their inviting friends over, to their walking too noisily or even talking loudly. They moved to the Bensonhurst section of Brooklyn.

Chapter 12

Gathering Of the Survivors

Gradually, members of Carl and Irene's family who had survived the war came to live in the United States.

Herta, Carl's cousin, came from Europe with her husband Pelek and little daughter Ruth. After living for a while with her aunt in East New York, they also moved to Bensonhurst, near Irene and Carl. They became very close friends. Pelek, having worked in the diamond business in Belgium, developed a diamond saw with superior qualities and needed diamond powder to manufacture it. He came up with the idea of collecting the floor sweepings of diamond-polishing places and recovering the diamond powder from it. Since Carl was a chemist, he asked him to help solve the problem.

After some experimentation, Carl decided on extracting the diamond powder by destroying all the organic and inorganic matter with sulfuric acid. One weekend, Carl and Pelek filled a tank with a large amount of floor sweepings, which Pelek had obtained free from diamond polishers, and they poured sulfuric acid over it. A chemical reaction started slowly, at first, then, with gathering momentum, a foamy, foul-smelling froth started to rise in the tank. The smell of rotten eggs caused by the formation of hydrogen sulfide started to waft over the apartment and then through the whole house. The neighbors began to complain, "Gas, we smell gas!" As the odor became more intense, they complained louder, "Somebody call the police, there must be a gas leak somewhere!"

Seeing that they could get into trouble, Carl and Pelek grabbed the tank, put it in the car and drove it to a deserted lot, where they poured the whole thing out. This was the end of their budding diamond-recovery business, but they became close friends. Eventually Pelek succeeded in realizing his dream and opened his own business.

Although they had met Pelek briefly in Poland Irene and Carl now had an opportunity to get to know him better. He was a caring and wise young man and both Irene and Carl loved him dearly. They especially loved the way he celebrated the Jewish holidays. Several days before Passover Pelek would buy all kinds of cakes and wine and, after the meal, he would lead the whole family in singing and dancing around the table, with all the participants holding hands. It was something that Irene and Carl had never seen before and they enjoyed it tremendously.

Pelek was deeply rooted in the Jewish tradition and he was keenly aware of Jewish problems. He came from a wealthy, very religious Jewish family in Poland. He had met Herta in high school and fallen in love with her. Then the war had separated them. He survived the war as a Christian and although a teenager, helped his whole family survive. He never boasted about his achievements during the war but one could sense that he was quite a hero. Herta survived the war hidden by her Aunt Eva, who lived on Christian papers and saved the lives of quite a number of people including Carl.

After the war, Herta met Pelek on the street in Cracow. She was an orphan. She had lost her mother and her brother in the Holocaust. By then Pelek was a successful businessman and a very handsome young man. He proposed to Herta and she accepted. They got married and emigrated to Belgium. There, Herta gave birth to Ruth. In Belgium Pelek learned the diamond business, specifically the use of industrial diamond powder. The Belgian authorities were unhappy with the activities of the refugees, and one day Pelek found that his safe in the bank had been confiscated by the government. Seeing that he couldn't do business in Belgium, Pelek decided to emigrate. They came to the United States.

Irene's brother Dr. Samuel (Milo) Mandel was now living in Israel. After the war he learned the horrible truth about his family, and he dreamt of being reunited with his two sisters, the only survivors of their large family. He married an Israeli girl, Dita, and for a while practiced medicine in Israel. He was able to visit his sister Anna in Poland, thanks to the high position and influence of Anna's husband Michael, but could not see Irene as long as she was in Germany. After Irene came to the United States, he applied for a visa and eventually got an invitation from an American hospital to come and work as an intern at $100 a month, which was very little.

Milo came to the United States on the famous American liner, the Independence. Irene had last seen him in 1941, before he went to Russia. He had been recruited into the Russian Army and left Boryslaw before the Germans entered. He was spared the Holocaust but he lost his wife and child during the war.

There was a big age difference between Irene and Milo, and Milo had always treated Irene like a child. Although she had resented this, there was little she could do about it. He made fun of her and she couldn't stop him. She knew that he loved her, but it wasn't enough. Irene wanted to have a mature relationship with him, but this had never happened.

Now Milo was coming to the United States to see her. Twelve years had passed since she had seen him last. There had been a war, and much of their family was lost; she, Irene, was 30 years old. She wondered about Milo and anticipated his arrival with great uncertainty. She tried to tell Carl about her brother. She said that he was very handsome and had a good sense of humor, but she stopped there. She couldn't describe his character or nature. After all, she didn't know him that well. He had left home when she was very young; after that, he was rarely home. Most of the time he was in Prague or Bologna, where he studied. On his vacations, he spent all his time at his fiancé's home.

Now Irene thought about their relationship and how it would develop. The day was freezing. On a cold day in January 1953, Carl and Irene went to the dock to greet Milo's boat. They arrived very early; the boat had already docked at Pier 84. It was a long time before the passengers began to disembark. They had to go through Customs first. Finally they began to leave the ship. Milo was nowhere in sight. After a while Irene became worried. "Where is he?" she said. "Almost a hundred people have come downstairs. Let's go to the baggage area and look for his suitcases." They did, and, since many people had already removed their luggage, they found Milo's easily.

"Thank God," Irene said, "he is on the boat, but where is he, what happened to him?" They tried to get some information but were told to wait.

"There are still many people on the ship," an official told them. "They are being cleared through customs and your brother is probably among them. Don't worry, he will come down soon."

Hours passed; it was now late in the afternoon and it was beginning to get dark. Carl and Irene were freezing.

Finally they saw Milo coming down the stairs. He saw Irene and waved to her. She wondered if he was as anxious as she was. They embraced each other with great intensity. Milo pushed Irene away and looked at her at arm's length. "I can't believe it, you are all grown up," he laughed. "You were so young when I saw you last."

Milo's luggage was nearby so they went straight to the car. They tried to carry on a conversation ,but there was a lot of emotion between them and they didn't know where to start. The twelve years that stood between them had been the hardest years of their lives. They didn't want to talk about them now—it was too painful a topic—but it was difficult to skip over them as if nothing had happened. Therefore, they asked about Milo's trip, about Dita, his wife, and similar things.

At home, Irene had prepared a special dinner in her brother's honor. She busied herself heating it up and this gave her a little time in which to compose herself. The dinner was quite a hit with Milo, but it was the dessert he liked most. Irene had made a delicious cake made with lady fingers, melted chocolate and whipped cream. Milo had always loved sweets, and this cake delighted him. They had wine with the meal and slowly, the atmosphere grew more relaxed.

For the next three months Milo lived with Irene and Carl. Irene and her brother developed a new relationship based on deep affection and respect. Carl and Milo took a real liking to each other and became friends for life. Finally Irene had a member of her family nearby.

Irene, Carl and Milo couldn't get enough of each other's company. They spent every evening reminiscing and remembering the time when they were still home and carefree.

Chapter 13

Making Friends In A New Country

A new couple moved in next door to Irene and Carl. Joe, a survivor of the concentration camps, was Irene's second cousin. He married Elaine, a Brooklyn girl. All the friends were invited to their wedding. There were no parents of the groom or of his friends, the survivors. Their parents had all been killed by the Germans during the Holocaust. After the ceremony, the couple said good-bye to everyone and left for their honeymoon. But to everybody's surprise the newlyweds showed up at Shirley's apartment a few hours later. "We missed you and didn't want to miss the fun," they explained with embarrassment. Everybody hugged them and wished them all the best. They left for their honeymoon the following day.

Irene and Carl met members of Shirley's and Paul's families. There was Irwin, the joker. He was tall and very thin. With his red hair and freckles, he could easily have passed for an Irishman, but he was Jewish. One day Irwin went to an appetizing store and asked for some smoked fish.

"You have to take a number," said the salesman.

"But there is no one except me," answered Irwin.

"You still have to take the number," insisted the salesman.

OK, thought Irwin, I'll play the game your way, and he took a number from the dispenser.

"Give me your number," the salesman said.

"Oh no, you have to call out my number," said Irwin innocently.

The fuming salesman started to call out, "One, two, three. . . ."

Irwin stood motionless until the man got to his number. "Here I am!" he hollered and gave him the slip of paper.

One day he called Giselle up on the phone during a city-wide water shortage and, in a serious voice introduced himself as a city water inspector: "Miss, we are investigating water abuses. How often do you take a shower?" Afraid of being penalized, Giselle answered, "Only once a week." To this Irwin answered, "Lady, you smell." Or he would call Shirley's mother, Mrs. Flicker, and say, "Miss, we are from a radio station. If you can sing the national anthem, we will give you a prize." When Shirley came home, her mother was singing, "O say can you see. . . ." Shirley interrupted her, "Mom, it is Irwin, he is playing a joke on you." But the old lady continued to sing. When she finished and there was no prize, Shirley said, "Mom, I told you that it was Irwin."

"Yes," answered clever Mrs. Flicker, "I thought so too, but I sang just in case it wasn't."

Shirley loved to play jokes on her friends too. On Halloween she painted her face, put on Paul's jacket backwards and went trick-or-treating to Joe's. Meanwhile, children were constantly knocking on Joe's door until he lost patience: "The next time a child comes to the door, I'll push him so hard, he'll fall," he told Elaine. The next "child" was Shirley. She knocked on the door, bent down to appear smaller and said in a childish voice, "Trick or treat!" Joe didn't recognize her and gave her a shove. Shirley started to fall back, laughing. "Get lost, or I'll push you again!" hollered Joe, while Shirley kept repeating, "Joe, stop it, it's me, Shirley."

Shirley had such a reputation as a prankster that when Blanche, her friend, got a call from a radio station asking her to answer a simple question to receive a prize, she said, "Shirley, I know it's you, you can't fool me." The announcer said, "Lady, who's Shirley? Just answer our question and you'll get a prize." "I know that you are playing a joke on me, Shirley," Blanche insisted. The announcer finally gave up. The next day, Blanche said to Shirley, "I know that was you." "What are you talking about?" asked Shirley. After being told the story, she assured her friend that she hadn't played a joke on her this time, but her friend never believed her.

One weekend, as Irene and Carl were sitting in their apartment, Shirley walked in carrying a large package. "I got a box of toilet paper on sale," she announced triumphantly. They were in a playful mood. Somebody grabbed a roll of toilet paper and threw it across the room. The roll slowly unwound itself into a trail of paper tissues. It looked so funny that they took one roll after another and threw them at each other as they laughed.

Shirley prepared a big surprise for her best friend Irene. Irene's thirtieth birthday was coming and she secretly invited her brother, Carl's family and all their Polish friends to her house. She told Irene and Carl that she and Paul were taking them to the theater that evening. They met them downstairs in the hall of Shirley's house and she said she had to go to her apartment for a moment; would they mind going with her? When they entered the apartment it was completely dark. All of a sudden the lights went on and, to their surprise, everybody they knew was there. Friends and relatives started to sing, "Happy birthday to you!" as Irene and Carl stood there dumbfounded.

Shirley had prepared plenty of food and drink although she and Paul were making very little money at the time. She had bought the best appetizing in Brooklyn. There were all kinds of smoked and pickled fish, salads and cheeses. There were also fresh, crispy bagels, "bialys" and onion boards. For dessert she had bought the most expensive fruit out of season. Everybody had a wonderful time and Shirley's parties became events that everybody looked forward to.

Now Shirley arranged one of her big schemes. She spoke to the owners of the Grand Hotel, Max and Rose Schmidt, asking them to quote a price for the summer for herself and Irene, and Paul and Carl on the weekends. The Schmidt's asked for $45 per couple a week, but it was still too high for Irene and Carl.

"Please tell Irene and Carl that the price is $35 and I will take care of the rest," Shirley said. "And please keep this conversation secret."

Then she told Irene and Carl, "Listen, I talked to Max and Rose Schmidt and they are willing to give us two rooms for the two summer months along with food on Saturdays and Sundays for $35 a week per couple. To make it more credible, she added, "They feel that we are very lively and create a good atmosphere, and give them good publicity." Irene and Carl swallowed the story, hook, line and sinker. Now both couples waited impatiently for the summer.

Carl had been working for a year for a small company on Long Island. The owner was a retired businessman who was working on a new mica product. He insisted that he was doing this to fill up his time and didn't need to increase his business. Carl quickly realized that there was no future there for him and began to look for another job. He saw an ad in the New York Times for a company called Yardney Electric, which was looking for electrochemists. He applied and was hired at a starting salary of $130 a week, a big improvement over the $65 he was making. The owner, Mr. Yardney, called him in. He was a short, stocky man with a red face and a pipe in his mouth. "My vice-president, Martin Kagan, was against hiring you, but I decided to give you a chance. By the way, my wife told me that your wife Irene is a sister of Milo's, who married my niece Dita."

It was the same man who had told Carl three years ago to study electrochemistry when he came to the United States.

Mr. Yardney came from France, where he had gotten a degree in mechanical engineering. He had been born in Russia and emigrated from there to Palestine. There he was stabbed with a knife by Arabs and left for dead. He recovered miraculously and went to study in Paris. After he completed his studies in France he met a French inventor, Professor Henri Andre, who showed him his new silver–zinc battery, five times more powerful than the conventional lead–acid battery. They agreed that Mr. Yardney would try to sell the invention in the United States, while Andre would try to sell it in France. Yardney emigrated to the United States with his wife and two small children, Maya and John. He tried to sell the invention, but without any luck. His rent was three months in arrears when he left for Washington to try sell the battery to the military. The general in charge of purchasing was away and would be back in three days, so Yardney, with no money for a hotel, waited for three days and nights in the general's waiting room. When the general finally arrived, he was so impressed that he gave Yardney an initial order of $800,000 to manufacture the new batteries for the government. This was the start of a very successful business; Yardney rented a floor on Chambers Street in New York and hired a small staff. Two years later, when Carl joined the company, he had twenty-five people working for him and the company was growing rapidly. He put Carl in production, assembling the batteries. He thought that it would be good to start him at the very bottom.

There was a chemist working at Yardney's named Dr. Meyer Mendelsohn. He was small of stature and unimpressive in appearance and speech. He had a heavy German accent and he always smoked a cigar. But when he spoke, people listened to him. He was a very clever man and an excellent research chemist. Carl immediately fell under his spell. He asked Mr. Yardney to assign him to work with the doctor but he wasn't the only one who admired little "Meyer der Weise" (a nickname that referred to another Mendelsohn, described by Theodor Lessing as "Nathan der Weise").

It was fascinating just to watch this man work. He would hold a beaker with one hand, stir its contents with a glass rod, and chew a cigar, the ashes occasionally falling into the beaker. He would murmur to himself, "I'm oorking and oorking and nobody cares, nobody wants to use my inventions and nothing happens." But things did happen. His inventions were highly valuable to the company and found immediate application in the production of the batteries, prolonging their useful life and improving their performance. They also found applications in unrelated fields, such as bactericidal products and protective coatings.

Once Dr. Mendelsohn got sick and Carl went to visit him. Irene, who had prepared a pot of chicken soup, went along. They found the doctor in a Dickensian setting: a large single room with a bed, table and a couple of chairs. The walls were covered with bookshelves from floor to ceiling. Even though he had a severe cold, he was in excellent spirits, full of wit and very hospitable. He had had nothing to eat and the chicken soup was greatly appreciated.

Irene was persuaded by Carl to quit her job at Hubshman to work at Yardney's. Now they could travel together and would both work for Mr. Yardney, who was expanding the company and looking for extra people. She felt bad, leaving Hubshnan's. The people there were very nice to her and liked her very much. They were sorry that she was leaving and asked her to come back whenever she would wanted.

Irene was a very beautiful young woman. Carl was very proud of her. She was 30 years old, but looked much younger. When one of the office girls was getting married, she went with two of her co-workers to a beauty parlor to have their hair done for the wedding. The three women were about the same age, but the owner of the parlor looked at them and pointed at Irene, saying, "I know. You are the bride." Then, pointing at one of her companions, she said, "and you are the bride's mother." Finally, pointing at the third girl, who was heavyset, she said, "and you are the bride's grandmother." The girls never forgave Irene this incident, although it was obviously not her fault.

Herta, Carl's cousin, was brought into the company by Irene and started to work as a secretary to the production manager, Mr. Zarovich. Soon she became indispensable and he consulted her on everything. She ran the whole department for him and Zarovich walked around telling everybody she was "Golova" (brains). Zarovich was a Russian, an extremely handsome man in his sixties with gray hair. He reminded one of an old Russian aristocrat. However, he had a very short temper and would holler at his subordinates for the smallest insubordination. His face would get red as a beet and Herta was afraid that he would have a heart attack. She spoke to him about this during one of his quieter moments. "Hertochka," he called her endearingly, "next time you see me holler, interrupt me under some pretext. Tell me, for instance, 'Mr. Zarovich, you have to repark your car' and I'll stop screaming." They agreed on this scheme.

The next day, Mr. Zarovich started screaming again at the production foreman. Herta came over and interrupted him politely, saying, "Mr. Zarovich, you have to repark your car." Zarovich turned to her, surprised, and yelled out, "What are you talking about! I don't have a car!" At that point Herta realized that when Mr. Zarovich got excited, it was impossible to reason with him.

The company moved to a large building on Leonard Street in

downtown Manhattan, which it had bought for less than $1 million dollars from J.P. Stevens, a large textile-manufacturing company. The company now employed close to a thousand people and it occupied all five floors of the building. When Christmas came, Mr. Zarovich organized a wonderful party with plenty of food and drink and a band. Mr. Yardney got a lot of gifts from the employees and was drinking heavily. Finally he got up on the podium and tried to give a speech, but he became annoyed with a young technician named Max, who laughed constantly during his oration. Mr. Yardney turned to him and said, "You are laughing and interrupting me; you're fired!" The room got very quiet. Carl was worried because Max, who worked for him, was a good worker and he didn't want to lose him. But Max was not afraid. He climbed to the podium and, facing the owner of the company, said, "This is a free country and if I want to laugh or say something I will do so and nobody can forbid me to." Everybody started to applaud him and Yardney turned red as a beet. One of the women from production went up to the podium and said, "Mr. Yardney, can I have a dance with you? You promised to dance with me." The band started to play and the incident was quickly forgotten. Max was not fired and he became Yardney's favorite. Many years later he became a vice-president of the company.

Irene and Carl were invited often to Mr. Yardney's house, as they were distantly related. Besides, Yardney loved to talk about his business even during the weekends. On one such occasion, as they relaxed after dinner at the fireplace in the large family room, Mr. Yardney said, "People in my company hate me."

Irene asked, "Why do you think so?"

"Because I yell at them even for small mistakes."

"Well, then why do you do it?" she asked.

"I do it because I cannot catch them making big mistakes, but I want to maintain discipline."

It was true. Yardney would call an engineer or a manager into his office and would scream at him and humiliate him in front of the whole staff.

Now Irene said, "Mr. Yardney, you just got some beautiful gifts from your employees at the Christmas party. Do you think they would have done that if they hated you?"

The company's lawyer, Dr. Simon, who was also present at this conversation, said, "Irene, you are not only beautiful, but you are also clever."

Carl enrolled for graduate studies in chemistry at night at New York University. It was difficult. After a full day's work he would travel by car to the School of Engineering, which was in the North Bronx, and eat a quick supper in the school's cafeteria. After two hours of classes, he would drive home to Brooklyn, a 1-hour drive, and get home at 10 P.M. He had to get up at 6 o'clock in the morning to go to work the next day. But he was determined to get a Master's degree in chemistry.

His ulcers became aggravated from hard work and other pressures, and one weekend evening, while dancing at a party, he fainted right in the middle of the floor. He was taken the next day to the Beth El Hospital in Brooklyn, where Irene's brother was doing his residency under the famous Dr. Bela Schick, the inventor of the Schick test for diphtheria. Carl was released from the hospital after one week, but Irene decided to quit her job and take good care of him. Again she felt that she should sacrifice her own interests for those of her husband.

Irene's sister Anna still lived in Poland with her husband Michael and son Wilus. Michael occupied a high position in the Polish government and he didn't want to emigrate, even though Anna and Irene missed each other terribly. Irene wanted her sister to visit New York. This was very difficult, as Poland was Communist and didn't allow anybody to leave the country. Finally, through Michael's connections, Anna got permission to leave Poland. However the United States consulate refused to give her an entrance visa. Irene wrote a letter to her congressman and senator trying to get permission for her sister to come to the United States on a visitor's visa. Not even Polish boats were allowed to dock in New York harbor. Finally, in 1957, after several visits to the authorities and a long wait, Anna got her visa. She left on a Polish ship, "Stefan Batory," on its way to Quebec. Irene was excited beyond description. She hadn't seen her sister for twelve years. Shirley lived through this excitement too and insisted on traveling with her best friend to Quebec. She knew how to do things in style. She reserved a room in the best hotel in Quebec, Chateau Frontenac, even though she didn't have much money. She ordered room service while waiting for the boat to arrive, and the friends enjoyed being together. But most of all they enjoyed the anticipation of seeing Anna.

Irene lay awake all night. She remembered her childhood, when Anna took her along on dates or walked her to school. She recalled the war and the horrible things that had happened to both of them and their family. Finally, she remembered the moment she left Poland and said good-bye to Anna. She was afraid she would never see her again. Irene cried on and off until daybreak. She got up and was dressed at a very early hour. When Shirley got up, she saw Irene's distress and tactfully acted as if she didn't notice it. She listened as Irene tried for the *n*th time to describe Anna. She called for a taxi to take them to the boat. It was a very cold day, but Irene didn't feel it. She was warm with expectation. When the taxi came to the harbor, the two young women saw the "Stephan Batory" standing there, waiting for them.

It took a while before Anna emerged, but she finally appeared on deck and slowly came down the stairs. She never took her eyes off Irene. They walked towards each other with tears in their eyes and embraced with all their hearts. They cried and laughed and kissed each other for a long time. Shirley, who was standing on the side, touched by the scene, called for a cab. The three of them went back to the hotel, where they waited till it was time to board the train to New York.

When they got to the hotel they were hungry. Shirley ordered steak to be brought to the room with all the trimmings. When Anna saw the steak, she thought that one of them was for all three of them. She had never seen that much meat for one person. She really enjoyed it and loved steak ever after.

Carl started for the train early, in plenty of time. It was 7 o'clock and the train was supposed to arrive at 9 A.M. All of a sudden he found himself in the middle of a tremendous traffic jam on the Belt Parkway. The cars simply couldn't move at all. He was desperate. Under these conditions he knew that he would never be able to meet Irene and Anna on time at Penn Station. He put on the radio. There was a subway strike and everybody going to work had taken his car. Traffic was moving at a snail's pace and he arrived at the train station at 11 A.M. Irene, Anna and Shirley were still there. They were worried but they knew about the subway strike. Irene was united at last with her family, or with what was left of it after the Holocaust, and she was very happy. Carl, seeing the happiness in Irene's eyes, was happy too. He loved her very much. She was a sensitive, compassionate and loving person, always there for him and her family and friends.

He was happy Anna had come. He liked her very much. And Anna was happy to be with her sister. She had brought her beautiful gifts from Poland, mainly porcelain. The three of them spoke constantly about their life in Poland.

"Anna," Carl said one day, "you went through the war with a small child, you should tell your story for your grandchildren. One day they will want to know."

Anna was excited about this idea. It took her a long time, however, to put it on paper. Finally she did.

Chapter 14

Anna's Story

Childhood.

I was born in Boryslaw in southern Galicia, which at that time belonged to Austria. I was the second child; my brother Milo was two years older. I was a sickly child. My parents were very young; my mother was 21 years old at the time.

In 1914, the First World War broke out. My father was taken to the army and my mother, with two small children, was evacuated to Vienna. The earliest time that I can remember was when I was 4 years old in a kindergarten in Vienna. I was a good student and the teacher told me to recite a poem at the Christmas party. I got a beautiful plate full of apples as a present. My brother didn't get anything. He pushed me and the plate fell down and broke. I cried a lot.

Milo was very wild and always showing that he was older by pushing me and sometimes even hitting me. But I knew that he loved me very much.

We stayed in Vienna till the end of the war and in 1918 we returned to Boryslaw. When I started the elementary school I didn't know any Polish, but I quickly learned.

My father was the head bookkeeper in an Austrian company, making very good money, and our childhood was very happy. We always had everything we wanted. I always wore beautiful dresses. A few years later, the headquarters of the company moved to Vienna and my father lost his job.

When I was 6 years old, my mother gave birth to a girl named Poldie. She was a beautiful little girl with blond hair and blue eyes. She was also very smart. But one day she became sick with scarlet fever and she died a few days later. This was a terrible shock to our family. My mother couldn't take it for a very long time. She was depressed and sick. The doctors couldn't help her. But two years later she gave birth to a little girl and named her Irene. We all loved her, although she was a crybaby till she was 9 months old. But she was beautiful and very smart.

My parents gave us the best education one could get. We were given piano lessons by the best teacher in town. We took them twice a week, and every Saturday we had music theory. The teacher told us about every composer and his work. Each year we gave a concert and every student played a long composition by heart; the teacher gave awards for that. We also took Hebrew lessons and studied Jewish history. Both of us, my brother and I, spoke fluent Hebrew.

When we finished elementary school, we went to gymnasium, which was very costly. It was a private school and the only one in our town. Although tuition was very high, my parents wanted to give us the best education. We had the finest teachers one could have.

When my father lost his job, we all had a very difficult time. I went to high school and my brother did too. We had to pay a high tuition which was very hard for my father. But he wanted his children to be educated. We also went to Hebrew school and took piano lessons. My parents struggled a lot, but nothing was interrupted. While at high school we worked a lot, because the teachers demanded a lot from us. But we also had a good time; we had parties and dances and a lot of friends.

Our family was a big one. My mother had three sisters and we had two grandmothers. My father had five sisters and two brothers. All of them were married and had children. It was a close family.

My father couldn't get a job, so he opened a hardware store which didn't prosper. After a few years he went bankrupt. Luckily, he found a good job, but he had lots of debts to pay. When I was in the higher grades in school, I tutored younger children and was well paid.

Meanwhile my brother Milo finished high school. My father's dream was that Milo would become a doctor. A Jew couldn't go to the university in Poland to study medicine, so my parents sent him to Czechoslovakia to study. But this was very expensive. We all struggled to help my father. The money I made went for Milo's studies.

When I was in the last year of high school, I met a man named Bronek and I fell in love with him. He was the most gorgeous man in town. He was six years older than I, and I was still at school. He had a very good job and lived with his mother, a widow. It was a beautiful family, very intelligent and good people. I dreamt of marrying him and so did all the girls in our town.

We went out for three years, and finally he told my parents that he wanted to marry me. I was the happiest person in the world. Bronek had a very good nature, never moody, good and loving. His mother, Minnie, loved me very much too. We got married three months later.

My parents bought me the most beautiful wardrobe and my father ordered a hand-made bedroom set for me.

We went to Zakopane for our honeymoon. We loved each other very much. After ten months I gave birth to a boy; his name was Wilhelm. My parents and my brother Milo were crazy about the little boy. He was brought up in luxury and love. After one year, Bronek got sick and developed tuberculosis. We took him to the best clinic in Lvov. At that time they didn't have much medicine for this disease. The best doctors helped him and after six months he came home. Throughout these six months I went to visit him in Lvov every week. It was 100 kilometers away. It took 3 hours by train. I took the express train called Lux-torpedo. I was 23 years old at that time. Bronek felt good. I did not worry about catching tuberculosis; I was only afraid for my little son. Willie was a very good child, beautiful and very smart. He grew up in a house where everything was done for him, and he got a lot of love and attention.

Three years after I married, my mother-in-law died. It was a shock for all of us.

In June 1939, I won a lot of money playing the lottery. I took my whole family—my mother, Irene, Willie, my brother Milo and his fiancée Teresa (Resia for short)—to one of the best resorts in Poland. We spent one month there and all of us had a very good time.

Russian Occupation

On September 1, 1939 war broke out between Poland and Germany. After a few days the first German tanks arrived. The Germans started to persecute the Jews immediately. But after nine days the Russians entered our town. On the basis of a pact between Molotov and Ribbentrop, they left this part of Poland to the Russians. The Russians immediately began introducing the Communist system. I had an apartment consisting of three rooms and a kitchen. We were only three people, so they wanted to move us to a very small apartment. My parents and my brother moved in with us, so everybody had one room. The kitchen was shared by everybody, and here we gathered there in the evenings to talk. Life was not easy. Food was rationed in small amounts and we had to stand in line in front of the stores to get it. The peasants would bring food to town in exchange for clothing, linens, etc.

Although Bronek had the same job as before, the price of food was about ten times higher.

Milo finished medical school and started working as a doctor. Irene was in high school and she was happy there. They had a lot of parties and shows and she loved it.

In January 1940 Milo married Resia, a cousin of Bronek's. She was a very nice girl whom everybody loved. In January 1941 she gave birth to a little boy named Roman (called Romus). He was the most beautiful little boy and very good too.

Before the war with Germany broke out, the KGB (Russian secret police) came and told us not to stand at the windows and never to open them. We had to put wooden blinds in the windows, but Bronek made a little hole in them and watched through it. Covered trucks were bringing in people who were taken to the basement. We heard the sound of shooting afterwards. This happened every night.

German Occupation

In June 1941 war broke out between Russia and Germany. It was 4 o'clock in the morning. Milo was immediately drafted into the Russian Army as a doctor. Romus was 6 months old when he left. Resia was very upset and so was my mother. Milo was her beloved son.

The Russians began to leave and the last of them set all the oil wells on fire. Boryslaw was burning; you could see parts of the wells in flames, flying through the air. The men went to the roofs with pails of water, afraid our house would start to burn. It was a horrible night. The Russians left but the Germans were afraid to enter the town because of the fire.

They entered on July 1 1941. You could tell immediately that something bad was going to happen, and on July 3 the first pogrom took place. Peasants and local people ran through the streets with sticks, and some of them with axes.

The First Pogrom

One day during the German occupation, I saw fear in the eyes of my son and my mother. Suddenly the door opened and two boys came in. They took my father and me and said, "You, Communists, go and wash the people you have killed!"

They took us to the place across the street. A lot of cadavers were lying there. They left me alone but led my father to the bodies. I saw him take his shirt off and wash them. Then I heard a voice behind me,

"You, please take my arm and come with me." I didn't know what he meant, but I had nothing to lose, so I did what he had told me to do. He took me outside and said, "Run home!"

I ran but the crowd started to hit me. Somehow I reached my house. While I was running, I saw two boys take my sister Irene. Mother saw me running and unlocked the door. Behind me stood two Germans. One of them said, "If you are the chosen people, where is your God?"

The mood at home was terrible. My mother was crying and my son was shaking. A few hours later a friend brought my sister back. But my father was still gone. Night came and it was fearful. We heard shooting that did not stop, and we were sure that my father was no longer alive. But the next day at 12 o'clock we saw him coming back. This pogrom took the lives of four hundred people.

After the First Pogrom

The pogrom left an unforgettable impression on us. Now we knew what to expect. My husband Bronek was dismissed from his job and so was my father. Bronek looked for work, but they would only hire him to carry heavy pipes. As I have mentioned, he wasn't healthy, but he had to do this or the Germans would have taken him away. At that time the concentration camps had not yet built, so they took the Jews to the woods and shot them.

Food was very hard to get; we traded our clothing and linens and got very little food for it. Hunger reigned over our town. You could see people who were swollen and dying in the streets. The winter of 1941–42 was very cold. Heating gas was not available to the Jews and warm clothes were impossible to come by. People would give away their last shirt to get something to eat. There was a pogrom in November 1941 and all the old and sick people were taken away and shot in the woods. The Germans started to ration the food, but they gave very little. We lived on Adolf Hitler Street. The building across the street, where the KGB used to be, was now occupied by the Reiterzug (mounted police). They caught Jews on the street, beat them, poured water on them and made fun of them.

Still, life had to go on, although it wasn't easy. My son Willie was in constant fear, remembering the pogrom. He was also hungry, as were all of us. My mother, once quite heavy, lost a lot of weight and was wearing clothes she never dreamt she could wear.

Spring of 1942 was very bad. Even more people were dying of hunger. The Germans collected from the Jews all their furs and metal objects and sent them to Germany for the army. We didn't know what was going on in the world; they took the radios away. Anyway, we had not been allowed to listen. We gathered in the kitchen and discussed the situation very quietly. Resia's parents and brother, who was blind, had moved in with us. So there were four families living in that apartment.

By the end of July 1942 we could tell that something awful was about to happen. Everybody was looking for a place to hide. The Reiterzug promised to hide some of us, but not children. My sister's friend Koppel found a place for Resia, her son and me and my son. My father was at work place and Bronek, my mother and Resia's mother had to go to the Reiterzug.

We left at night, thinking that everybody would be safe. Meanwhile, the Germans in the Reiterzug changed their minds, so my mother, Resia's mother and her brother went to a neighbors house where there was a hiding place.

The Third Pogrom

On the morning of August 6 the third action broke out. The Germans took everybody they could find. Sick people were shot on the spot. After one and a half days they stopped. I wasn't sure what had happened to my husband and my mother. I left Willie in the hiding place and went to see. At home I found out that my mother and Resia's mother and brother had found a place to hide, but the owners wouldn't let Bronek in because his cough could betray their whereabouts. Meanwhile, the Germans started shooting again and taking people away. I didn't go back, but stayed with Bronek in our house. I heard the Gestapo breaking the window, but the Reiterzug saved us by telling them that this was their private apartment. We stayed in the basement for a day and a half without food, full of fear. The next day, around noon, we heard my father's voice telling us to open the door. We came out of the basement, opened the door and my father told us that one of our neighbors had shown the Germans where my mother was hiding and the Germans had taken all of them to the railroad station and shipped them to the Belzec death camp. They took around six thousand people of Jewish descent.

There were fifteen thousand Jews in our town before the war, but a lot of them had run away to Russia before the Germans came. After the war I found out that Belzec was a camp in which the Germans shot and then burned Jews. Not one person came back alive from that camp.

Now three people were missing from our house. It was very hard to accept being without our mother. We all took it very hard. I was the oldest woman, 28 years old. I started to run the household.

In October 1942 they told us to move into the ghetto. Our belongings were very meager by now, so we put everything in a small wagon and two people carried it.

Life in the ghetto was even worse than before. Food was rationed in very small portions and the peasants were afraid to come to trade in anything. I forgot to mention that, when we lived on Hitler Street, a Polish woman had come to buy something from me. She had liked me and said that, if I was in trouble, I should come to her and she would hide me and my son. It was a kind gesture.

In October another action took place. Bronek, my son and I went to hide at Mr. Turow's. He put us in a barn loaded very high with hay. We stayed there for three days. At night he brought us a few cooked potatoes and some apples. I paid him with two suits of Bronek's.

When we came to the ghetto my father was there and he told us that he had been taken to the Umschlagplatz (gathering place), but that his boss, Mr. Beitz, had removed him from the transport. Mr. Beitz was an assistant director of the oil trust. He was a nice man and he protected the Jews as much as he could. In November 1942 the Germans started a new action. My husband was at work and so was my father. Irene, my son I and ran away without dressing; there was no time. We just threw on our coats. It was a miserably rainy day. We ran over a small bridge above the Tysmienica River, which separated the ghetto from the Aryan side of the city. The Germans started to shoot at us from the Jewish side. We were running in the rain and mud. My son Willie was begging me, "Mother, let them shoot us, I have no more strength to run." I took him in my arms and ran as fast as I could, and so did Irene. I passed the road to my former house and ran into the basement of one of the buildings. We were wet and hungry. Suddenly a woman came in; I knew her well. When she saw us, she brought hot tea and bread and a blanket to cover us. She went to the gates of the ghetto when the Jews were returning from work and told my husband, where we were.

He arrived late at night and took us about 15 kilometers to the house of the woman who had promised to help me when I was in need.

She was very nice and she took us in. But she was very poor. She lived with her father, who was also a very nice man. I lost my shoes in the mud on the way.

The next day we moved to the city. Bronek and my father were still working and living in the ghetto. This action lasted a whole month. They took mostly women and children and also older people. People who worked were left alone.

In February 1943 another action took place. I was running to the ghetto to help Bronek and my father when this action again caught me in the ghetto. Again, I ran away and went to my hiding place. This time they took people to a place near the slaughterhouse and shot them on the spot. This action lasted for three days.

I was still going to the ghetto and, in May 1943, the Germans surrounded it. This was the liquidation of the ghetto. My husband built a hiding place in our apartment, so I remained there with a lot of people who knew about it. We were eighteen people in a place maybe 6 by 6 feet. We heard the Germans come into the apartment and rip up the floors and walls, but fortunately they moved a little couch to the opening of the hiding place and covered it. so we survived. At night my husband found an opening in the fence surrounding the ghetto and I ran to my hiding place. Three Polish women saw me running. They showed me to the Germans who were watching the ghetto. They started to shoot, but I ran so fast that not one bullet reached me. I got back safely.

After three days of liquidation, the working people were moved to an "Arbeitslager" (labor camp). Resia was in that camp and her son Romus, 2½ years old, was given away to hide with a Polish family with seven children. I went to see Romus on his birthday. I was taken there by Koppel. I hadn't seen him for a long time, not since he had been placed in hiding with a Christian family. He was a beautiful boy with blond hair and blue eyes. When he saw me he got up on my knee and wouldn't budge. He sat there during my entire visit. He looked at me intensely, as if trying to recognize me. Finally he called out, "Aunt Anna!" When I was leaving Romus started to cry and wouldn't let me go. He followed me with his eyes and called my name until I disappeared from view. I heard him crying from far away.

A woman neighbor who saw Resia went to the police and reported that a Jewish child was being hidden by this family. Romus was taken away by the police. I didn't know about it at the time. Later, Bronek told me about it accidentally during a conversation. A friend who had also been arrested as a Jewess had seen Rommie at the police station. The poor child had been running from one person to another. He didn't understand what was happening. The next day the police took him away and shot him at the slaughterhouse, where the Germans and Ukrainians were carrying out mass executions of the Jews.

When his mother, Teresa, found out about what had happened, she lost her will to live. She kept repeating, "What will I tell Milo when he comes back?"

That is why I hate the Germans and the Ukrainians and I will never forgive them for what they did.

In June my landlady told us to leave because she was afraid. It was 1 o'clock in the afternoon. I took Willie by his hand and went to my father's workplace. When he saw us he almost fainted. He put us in a little shed, where we spent the night and the next day. During the night two watchmen passed by us and I heard them say, "He thinks we don't know that a Jewish woman and a boy are around here."

"We'll find her," the other one said.

In the morning my father went to work. He came where we were and told us that he had found a place for us with a woman "Volksdeutsche" (of German descent), and that evening she took us in. She was a nice woman, but the watchman denounced us to the Gestapo and they came with dogs and looked for us everywhere. The woman's brother was a Gestapo man himself. When they came to her door, he told them that the apartment was his sister's. This saved our lives. But the next morning she told us to leave because the Gestapo would return, and she showed us where to go.

That day, Governor Frank was supposed to visit. Security was heavy, but somehow nobody recognized us and we got to our new hiding place. We stayed in that house for two weeks. After that, the brother of my former landlady, the Gestapo man, came and asked us for money. Otherwise, he said, he'd take us to the police. We didn't have any money, so we had to move out.

My father found us another place and we left at night. The new place was a small room in an attic, 3 by 5 feet.

The Jewish situation in the labor camp got worse. The Germans started to select people who were weak. My husband wasn't feeling well, so he decided to stay with us. He was very sick with tuberculosis. My son was 7 years old at the time and I was afraid that staying in a small room would be bad for him. But we didn't have a choice, so I slept with my husband on a very small couch and Willie slept on a wooden shelf attached to the table. There was a window in the attic, but sometimes the sun shone into it, so we couldn't go near it out of fear that somebody would see us. Willie spent most of the time lying on his shelf, trying to read by combining the letters of the alphabet that we had shown him. He had never gone to school. Because he never used his legs, his muscles became very weak and he could hardly walk. Also, food supplies were very low. We only had a small piece of bread for each day. Because of the conditions, my husband's health deteriorated. My father tried to visit us as often as possible, which wasn't easy, and he brought us whatever he could. One day I said to him, "Father, before I die, I would like to have a cup of coffee and a roll and butter." A few days later, he brought me a little coffee in a small bottle and a piece of roll with butter. Where he got it, I don't know. Everybody got a bit of it.

In November 1943 my husband came to our hiding place to stay with us. His health was very bad. The tuberculosis spread and he coughed constantly. I still believed that the war would end and that doctors would help him. But he got worse every day. I was afraid for my son; tuberculosis was very contagious. But there was no other way; we had to stay together in this small room without air or food.

The winter of 1943–44 was coming to an end. The Germans had been defeated in Russia and had started to withdraw. On April 1, 1944 they were about to leave Boryslaw. My father was still in the labor camp. I begged him to come and stay with us, but he said that he had a good hiding place. The Germans didn't leave because the Russians stopped 80 kilometers from our town; on April 14 the Germans surrounded the camp and rounded up everyone there, including my father. I was told by my landlady, who had seen the Jews surrounded by the Germans and marching to the railroad station. At night I stood at the window waiting for him, hoping that maybe he had escaped, but in vain.

My husband's health kept deteriorating. He was afraid that he would die and that we'd be thrown out of the place. He begged me to let him out, but I was afraid that he would die on the street or the Germans will shoot him. I just couldn't do it, so we lived in constant fear.

One day I got a letter from my sister Irene, who was hiding elsewhere. She begged me to come visit for a day so she could see that I was alive. She wrote that she couldn't stay alone. She would send somebody to pick me up.

It wasn't easy to go, because somebody might recognize us as Jews. But I decided to go to see her. I missed her very much; we had always been close. My husband and I discussed what I should do. I was afraid to leave him and, on the other hand, I loved my sister and was afraid that she would hurt herself. Bronek said, "You must go see her."

"But how can I leave you?" I asked.

"I'll manage." he said. "Go and take Wilus with you. Come back the next day."

It was a very long walk, about 10 miles.

A few days later, on May 2, 1944, a friend of my sister's came to get me. Willie wanted to go with me and Bronek wanted me to take him, but he couldn't walk; how could I? My sister's friend said that he would carry him, so we decided he would come.

We left. It was a beautiful day. I hadn't been outside for a long time. I breathed in the fresh air. My friend carried Willie and we looked at each other with fear. Suddenly we heard the sound of an alarm. People fled the streets in fear, but we kept going. Planes were flying and we heard the sound of bombs exploding, but we were not afraid. The streets were empty. The place we were going to was 7 miles away, at the outskirts of Boryslaw. We arrived there late at night. It was inside a well in a large garden. Getting in there was difficult. The hiding place had been dug above the water and the entrance was covered with large stones. Somehow we got in safely. Irene and I fell into each other's arms and cried together for a long time. We hadn't seen each other for a year and a half and had missed each other very much. My son reacted the same way. The next day the landlord came and said that the only bomb had fallen on the house where we had been hiding. They had found my husband hanged. He had been very sick and couldn't have lived much longer, so he probably had taken advantage of my absence to end his life. The house where he had been was destroyed. I was in shock.

I looked at Wilhelm. I knew he understood what had happened, but I was unable to speak to him and explain the tragedy. I just embraced him and held him fast to myself. I was alone and I would have to raise my son. I had to be strong.

But I couldn't stop crying for days. I blamed myself for leaving Bronek. Irene tried to calm me, explaining that I had saved the life of my child and myself. After a few days, I began to understand that I have to live in order to bring up my son.

Wilus never said a word. But I know what he went through and how he suffered. Irene tried to help him; he was only 8 years old. She told him stories about his father. But the danger we were in helped all of us a lot.

Wilus didn't say anything for many, many years. Only a few years ago he began asking questions.

The landlord hadn't known that I was there, and when he found out, he wanted me and my son out. Irene's friend gave him a lot of money for us and left himself so we could stay there. The place was very small; we could only sit and food consisted of a slice of bread and a potato daily. We stayed there for three months and, on August 6, 1944, after a night of shooting and bombing, the Russians entered our town.

Irene and I had only one dress left between us, so she went to her friend, asking to stay there and to get a dress for me. Our apartments had been taken over by strangers, along with our furniture and belongings. We didn't know where we were going to stay. When Irene returned with a dress for me, I left the hiding place together with my son, going nowhere. My son had been in hiding for two years. When we left, it was August and the sun was strong. He swelled up. I helped him to walk, but mostly carried him. On the way I met a friend of mine, who told me that my cousin had found a room and was waiting for me. She also gave me 50 rubles. My cousin Anna had survived by hiding, but she had lost both her parents. We held each other for a long time; we couldn't believe that we were alive.

The room was big, but completely empty, so we slept on the floor without bedding. But we were free. Since I had nothing, I went to look for a job and got one in a cafeteria as a waitress. My son outgrew his pants and shirt. I got an old dress from a friend and my cousin, who was a seamstress, made him pants and a blouse.

It was now September 1944. Willie was going to school now; he was 8 years old. I asked his teacher to test him, and he was put in the third grade. He was very capable and a very good student. I worked during the day and at night I baked rolls to sell early in the morning. Working as a waitress was too tiring for me because, coming out of hiding, my legs were very weak. I started to look for another job and got one as an assistant bookkeeper in the gas company. The salary was very low. One day, as I was going to sell my rolls, I met my old schoolmate Michael, who was an engineer. He told me that he had been in Russia during the war and had returned to find out what had happened to his family. He found out that his child, 1 year old, had been taken away by the Germans and killed. Later, his wife had been taken to a synagogue along with other Jewish people, and the Germans had set the building on fire. Everyone had burned to death. His mother and two sisters had been killed and his brother and another sister had been taken to Auschwitz. Michael had been in love with me in high school, but I hadn't paid any attention to him at the time. Now he proposed to me.

I spoke to Irene about it and she said, "Don't think about yourself; you have a child to support and Willie needs a father."

We were married on November 16, 1944 by a rabbi.

Chapter 15

The Russian Saga: George's Story

One day Carl and George were sitting in the garden. It was a beautiful summer day and the air was full of birds chirping. An aroma of honeysuckle wafted over from the bushes with each breeze. It was very peaceful. "George, please tell me about your life in Russia during the war," said Carl. "I know so little about this chapter of Jewish suffering." George was more than happy to tell Carl about his adventures:

The flamboyant General George Patton of the U.S. Third Army once said to his troops, "You will be able to tell your grandchildren that their grandpa, instead of shoveling manure in Iowa, rode with Patton to victory."

I, however, would like to tell my grandson(s) that I managed to do both: I shoveled manure, not in Iowa but in the Kolhoz Kirova, a village of Atchit in the region of Krasnoufimsk, province of Sverdlovsk, in the Ural Mountains and instead of riding with General Patton I rode with General Rokossovsky, not exactly alongside him but as a soldier of the First Polish Army, a part of the Second Ukrainian Front.

It all started on June 22, 1941 in the town of Drohobycz in eastern Galicia, Poland. As a rule, 16-year-old boys sleep rather soundly and I was no exception. On this memorable morning, my mother shook me, trying to wake me up. "Listen, listen! Do you hear this?" There was a tone of urgency in her voice. Being half asleep, all I heard was the heavy distant sound of thunder, not unlike a summer storm.

"Storm, so what?" I always liked a storm. Usually I would open the windows and inhale the fresh, ozone-filled air coming from the garden that surrounded our small house. By 1941, after two years under the Soviets, we were no longer living in the large apartment house in the center of the town that had once belonged to my grandparents, but on the outskirts of town in the primarily Polish and Ukrainian section.

"No, my son, this is not a storm. I think this is war," said my mother.

For a moment I couldn't comprehend what war she was talking about. Poland, despite its gallant stand in September 1939, had lost the war to the Germans and the entrance of the Russian Forces on September 17, 1939 had unfortunately sealed her fate. Our native town of Drohobycz was certainly a prize for any attacking or defending army because of its oil refineries, salt mines and the headquarters of the 7th Podhalan Regiment. Whoever tried to capture the town tried to capture it intact because of its immense strategic value, whether it was the Austrians in the First World War or the Germans in 1939.

As a matter of fact, the Germans had come to Drohobycz briefly in mid-September, greeted wildly by the Ukrainian population. They were soon replaced by the Red Army.

"Mom," I said, "surely now, in 1941, the Germans wouldn't be stupid enough to start up with the Russians. "The 'mogutchya,' the all-powerful Red Army, would crush them in two weeks. Even Napoleon tried and did not succeed."

I tried to calm my mother, saying that the heavy bombardment we were hearing was most likely a training exercise.

"No, my dear, these are not maneuvers, this is a real war."

Both my parents had lived through the 1914–18 period and my father had served the Kaiser during that time. So they could tell the difference.

I grabbed my crystal radio, and sure enough there was an announcement. The cowardly Germans had attacked the peaceful Soviet Union and the brave Red Army had repelled the fascist invaders. Units of the Red Army were entering territory previously held by the Germans.

"You see, mom and dad, there is nothing to worry about. Such a war can't last long. As we talked, in came our neighbor, a Polish woman whose son had a new Telefunken radio and was able to "catch" London.

"Dear friends," she said, "the Germans are deep into Russian territory with 100,000 Russians killed or captured, and they are going unopposed all the way to Moscow."

The situation was truly confusing. The population of our town was equally divided between Poles and Ukrainians, with the Jews usually trapped in the middle.

With the death of Jozef Pilsudski, the de facto ruler of Poland, the situation of the Jews became more and more difficult, and yet, when war broke out on September 1, 1939, many Jews, including doctors, volunteered to serve in the Polish Army, only to be rejected by the Poles. ("After all, we can win the war without Jewish help," they said.)

With the war lost, Drohobycz became a part of the Western Ukrainian Republic. The Jews of the town, always choosing the lesser evil, preferred the Soviets to the Germans. However, a number of Jews openly declared their pro German feelings. Most of those Jews had gone to German schools, served in the Austrian Army and preferred the company of "cultured" Germans to the simple, uneducated masses ("Fonnie Goniff" they called the Russians.)

During the First World War my uncle Joel managed to save the life of Count Kurt von Schuschnigg, the future premier of Austria. For his bravery he had been awarded the Iron Cross. No German would dare touch such a person. (My uncle, his wife, two children and a grandson were later killed by the Nazis.)

Conflicting reports and wild rumors added to the total confusion and soon panic overtook the town's population, except for the Ukrainians, who were awaiting their liberators. The Ukrainians wanted to pay back the Poles and the Jews for all they had suffered at their hands.

The Soviet radio spoke of victories but the beaten and totally disoriented units of the Red Army were moving east rather than west as the radio proclaimed.

Some members of our family talked about joining the fleeing Russians to avoid a pogrom. My uncle Abe, who held a high position in the administration, decided to leave town together with his pregnant wife Helen and their 11-year-old daughter Lilly on the fourth day of the war. He mentioned to us that he could also arrange a place for our family on the last train leaving the city for Russia. We were faced with a dilemma: to go or not to go.

My mother rejected the idea of leaving home because my younger sister Edith was vacationing with our Aunt Ethel in nearby Boryslaw, and my mother was not about to leave her child behind. Besides, who was going to take care of the house? She strongly urged my father and me to join Uncle Abe in fleeing the city. After all, the war would only last two to three weeks at the most. The Germans might make the men dig trenches, and so forth, but they would leave women and children alone, just as they had during the First World War.

At the time this seemed to make perfect sense. My parents decided jointly that my father and I would join Uncle Abe and his family in taking the train out of the city. We started to pack, taking enough for an extended weekend only. I took my schoolbag and a backpack filled with a few changes of underwear, my knickerbockers and, of course, a few pairs of white socks (the height of fashion at the time), heavy but comfortable shoes ("Bergsteigers") and I was ready for the adventure. Having read Karl May, Henryk Sienkiewicz, Dumas and many Russian classics, I was eager to see mysterious Russia with my own eyes. Tenderly I embraced and kissed my mother good-bye, solemnly promising to write and to be back as soon as possible.

Had I known at that time that I would never see her and my sister alive again, I would never have left town. Who knows—maybe my mother's premonition saved my father and myself from the Holocaust.

Packed, we started to walk towards the main railroad station. (Drohobycz had three stations.) It was quite a walk from our house, but my father and I loved to walk. Often during previous summers my father had insisted that we walk to the neighboring resort town of Truskawiec, much to my displeasure, as my friends rode in taxis or buses.

As we made our way towards the railroad station, a horse-driven carriage stopped near us. It was mother, who had hired "droshke" in order to see us off and say good-bye to our Uncle Abe and Aunt Helen, with whom we were to share our Russian odyssey.

The driver, who was in a rush himself, got us to the station within minutes. Bedlam of unimaginable proportions greeted us. There stood a long train "echelon" crammed with yelling and screaming people, babies crying, dogs barking and soldiers shouting orders. Every wagon seemed to be filled to capacity, with some people even sitting on the roof.

We walked along, trying to locate our Uncle Abe and his family. Luckily we spotted him standing next to a militiaman.

"These are my relatives, they are coming with us," he said to the soldier guarding the wagon that was reserved for members of the administration. Since many people did not show up, we had plenty of room to stretch out. We had barely managed to put our meager belongings on the racks above our heads when we heard a long whistle and an announcement that the train was about to pull out.

Once again, tearfully, I kissed my mother and again asked her to join us, but to no avail. My Uncle Abe embraced my mother and, while shaking her hand, slipped her a few gold coins.

The heavily loaded train started to move very slowly and my mother got off. She stood there crying and we kept waving. As the train picked up speed, her silhouette became smaller and smaller, finally disappearing at a bend, never to be seen again.

My Uncle Abe was an unusual man. Although of medium height he was powerfully built, with an engaging smile. He was in his mid-thirties and had all the qualifications of a born leader. Somehow, in his presence, everyone felt safe.

He had married my father's younger sister Helen and had been a very successful businessman in prewar Poland, trading in timber. He had often traveled to Czechoslovakia and other countries. Highly polished and always elegantly groomed, he came from a rather modest family, but made up for his lack of education with native intelligence, a quick wit and sheer force of personality. According to rumor he had not one but two mistresses in town at the same time. Whenever my Aunt Helen got wind of this, it cost him another fur coat or piece of jewelry.

Aunt Helen, who came from an old, quasi-aristocratic Jewish family, had lived in the center of town, and at one point in her life had aspired to be a diva at the Vienna Opera. Indeed, she did have a very melodic voice, but unfortunately, not good enough for Vienna. Therefore she settled and married Uncle Abe.

My parents and I had always been very fond of Uncle Abe, and I came to love and respect him deeply during the next, very difficult, years.

The train moved slowly towards the old Polish–Russian border, stopping at each station, with some people getting off but more and more trying to get onto the already overcrowded train.

With the militiaman still guarding our compartment, we were comfortable and could buy bread, milk, fruit and the occasional bottle of vodka needed to grease the palms of the "nachalstvo."

My uncle realized that sooner or later some additional people would be forced upon us, so at the next station he spotted a Jewish couple with a daughter of a similar age to our Lilly and asked them to join us. They were, of course, very grateful and I even more, because no self-respecting 16-year-old boy from the gymnasium wanted to play with an 11-year-old girl.

From now on I roamed through the train and stations thus meeting a classmate of mine, Regina W., a beautiful girl with long blond braids. Half of our class was in love with her and here I had her all to myself. What an extraordinary stroke of luck!

The train made frequent long and unexplained stops, leaving the main tracks in order to let military convoys pass. They were full of soldiers going to the front or, every so often, military hospital trains filled with wounded and suffering soldiers. At every station a team of N.K.V.D. police checked our papers. Uncle Abe was well prepared.

His papers identified him as a "nachalnik" or leader. There were so many stamps on those papers that the police would simply salute and return them.

Later I found out that all those impressive papers were written by my uncle and the stamps were from his office. I am quite sure that no other people on this globe had greater respect for stamps than the Russians.

A few days later, deep in the Soviet Ukraine, we came under air attack by German war planes. People ran in all directions, trying to hide under nearby trees, ravines or under the train itself.

The German pilots had clearly seen civilians running around, but that did not prevent them from shooting anything that moved. I ran quickly towards the bushes with my father right behind me. Turning around I saw my Uncle Abe lying down, shielding his daughter with his own body.

The bullets were "stitching" the road, but luckily we escaped unharmed. Many others weren't so lucky. The planes left and the train started to move again, leaving many dead and wounded behind. At the next station many people got off, scared by the air attack, and I didn't see my blond friend again. (I located her thirty years later alive in Israel.)

With the lack of proper sanitation facilities and clean water, dysentery began to affect most of the passengers. My father, an old soldier, somehow always managed to obtain water. The summer was exceptionally hot, with cloudless blue skies. Throughout the trip my father kept himself immaculate, washing himself with cold water in summer or winter. (His idea of fun was to ask me to take off my shirt in the winter and to wash myself with the first snowfall so as not to be afraid of the cold. I hated this and so did my mother, fearing pneumonia. Little did I know how well it prepared me to later withstand temperatures of -53 degrees C.)

I don't remember who first discovered lice on us. We all had lice, in our clothing, in our hair, under our arms, lice everywhere. It was frightening to comb one's hair because of the white, ugly creatures moving on the black comb.

Wherever possible we would boil our clothing while going to "banias"—Russian saunas located for that purpose near every railroad station. Nothing ever helped. I am convinced that we left our own lice there and picked up somebody else's. The lice were to stay with us for the duration of our trip and then some.

We kept zigzagging through Russia, changing trains from time to time, always ahead of the advancing German Army. At every station I would manage to send a postcard or letter home. To this very day I don't know if any of my letters ever got through.

By mid-July we had crossed the majestic River Volga and continued to move towards the Ural Mountains that separate Russia from Asia.

Upon finally reaching the city of Sverdlovsk, we were assigned to work on a collective farm called Kolkhos in the village of Atchit, a couple of hundred kilometers from the city itself. We went by train to the smaller city of Krasnoufimsk, and from there we were picked up by a "troika" (a wagon pulled by three horses).

The wagon driver was a 12-year-old peasant by the name of Volodia Vatolin. As it turned out, my father and I were billeted in his mother's house located on Pushkina Street #26. I greatly admired our driver's skill in making sure that all three horses pulled the wagon in unison. My uncle and his family were given an empty house diagonally across the street from "our" place.

No one ever told us what had happened to the previous owner of that empty house.

We were the first war refugees ("biezhentsy") to reach Atchit, but not for long. More and more people started to come, mostly Russian Jews from Byelorussia.

Volodia dropped off our relatives and their belongings. They were better prepared than we were, having taken along some warm winter clothing. Then he took us to his house.

Nobody had asked the Vatolin family if they wanted to accept Jewish refugees. The Party had given them an order, so we had a room to live in. Pushkina Street was a typical unpaved village street, lined with log cabins. Poland, in comparison to Germany, France or England, was a backward country. The village in which we stayed was still in the 18th Century at best. There was no electricity and no running water; some of the more "modern" houses had privies outside their homes; ours did not even have that. Volodia, prior to returning the horses to the Kolkhoz's barn, introduced us to his mother, Valentina Nikolaevna Vatolina and his sisters Katia and Natasha. During the entire introduction Valentina Nikoaevna was busy in delousing her daughter's head, using a knife to kill the lice. Our conversation was interrupted by the snap snap sound of lice being killed.

"Dobropozhalovat—Welcome to our house. I will be back in a

minute and then I will put some tea in the samovar."

From a shelf she took down an old samovar made in Tula, still showing emblems of tsarist Russia. Burning coals from a large baking oven were put into a pipe in the middle of the samovar. She then quickly added some fresh coal, took off one of her boots and started to pump air into it like a blacksmith. I watched the entire procedure mesmerized.

Within minutes the tea was ready and the daughters set the table. From a locked cupboard Valentina Nikolaevna took out a very large home-baked bread, and with the same knife she had used to kill the lice cut the bread into large slices.

Back home I would probably have vomited by this time, but after traveling for six solid weeks through Mother Russia I was sufficiently hardened and sufficiently hungry not to pay attention to the demands of hygiene. The niceties of clean food and elegant surroundings can only be afforded on a full stomach. If you are hungry nothing but food matters.

Yet old habits did not die easy. I gave my father a look, he understood perfectly. He said very quietly, "Eat, just eat."

The bread with jam was delicious; so was the hot tea.

A few minutes later I could hardly keep my eyes open. Noticing that, Valentina Nikolaevna suggested that we retire to "our" room. The room had two crudely made beds; the mattresses were sacks filled with fresh hay. A contraption resembling a chest of drawers completed the furnishings. An old icon stood in the corner, adding to the Russian atmosphere.

It was the first time after traveling almost six weeks through the vast expanse of Russia that we had been able to sleep not on trains or in railroad station waiting rooms, but in beds.

We slept as only tired people can sleep. We were so exhausted that we did not feel the armies of bedbugs covering our bodies, which we quickly discovered in the morning.

My father and I declared open war on the bedbugs. We started to clean, pouring boiling water on the beds and changing the "mattresses," and though we considerably reduced their numbers, they were never totally eliminated. I am sure that when God said that the meek shall inherit the earth, he surely had in mind the indestructible bedbugs.

The next morning we reported to the "predsiedatiel," or boss of the collective farm, the Kolkhoz, named after comrade Kirov.

It was the peak of summer and everybody young and old worked from sunrise to sunset.

My father was assigned to a "brigade" charged with building an additional barn. My uncle, on the other hand, was sent to harvest the wheat using a scythe. He was the best. As a young man he had managed a large farm for a Polish aristocrat and was familiar with every phase of agriculture. He pointed out to me how neglected the horses and cows were. He had never seen livestock in such poor condition.

A team of men and women were sent to cut the wheat. The fastest and strongest cutter would be put in front. A few steps behind, another person cut and from there a whole line of cutters spread tangentially cut the wheat. The last cutter usually another fast one, would set the pace and woe to the person ahead of him if he or she did not move fast enough.

Someone would start a "chastushki" (folk song) and the whole group joined in, forgetting the monotony and drudgery of this hard labor. Behind the cutters another team, mostly women, would tie the wheat and load it with pitchforks as high as they could on wagons pulled by horses.

I was told to bring another horse and wagon. The order was simple enough, but being the son of a merchant I had not been around horses very much and had no idea of how to get a horse to pull a wagon. What confused me even more was the Russian equipment, unlike anything I had seen in Poland.

Frustrated and ashamed, I asked an old Russian peasant guarding the barn how to proceed. He looked me over, noticing my knickerbockers and what used to be white socks, and my Polish accented Russian. He understood my dilemma.

"Smotri! (Look)," he said, "first you back the horse up to the wagon and then you put on this "chomut" (horse's collar), a yoke you turn around, then you put on a "duga" (wooden horseshoe-shaped shaft) from the left side and fasten it to the pole beside the horse. Finally, you put on this miniature saddle, which supports the yoke. Remember, if you put the yoke on too high you will choke the horse, and if you put it too low it will rub against his neck, so pay close attention, do it right. Spare the horse and, above all, promise me you will feed the horse before sitting down to your own meal."

That promise I always kept.

Within a couple of weeks I was almost half as good as the 12 year old Volodia.

My aunt managed to stay home despite constant pressure from the management to go to work on the farm. The fact that she was pregnant in her 5th or 6th month did not make any difference to the "nachalstvo."

They kept pointing out that Russian women worked in the fields up to and including their 9th month of pregnancy and many times after giving birth on the field they would continue working a couple of hours afterwards. My Aunt Helen did not have any ambition to compete with these Russian "Stachanov" women.

For a piece of jewelry she managed to obtain a statement from a "Felcher" (a nurse acting as a doctor in the village). From that time she was left alone to take care of her daughter and the house.

Every chance I got I would go to the Post Office to mail registered letters to my mother, hoping against hope that somehow, some of my letters would get through. The clerks in the Post Office knew me well and when one day one of the clerks said that there was no sense in writing, the other female clerk said good naturedly "Pust on pishet k mamie." Let him keep on writing to his mother.

Did any of my letters ever reach my mother? Who knows? I only knew that the 2 or 4 weeks of our exile would change into years.

The war kept intensifying. Despite the constant propaganda about the Red Army's victories, reading between the lines we fully understood that the Germans had reached Moscow. The situation was desperate and yet my gut feeling was that Hitler would share the fate of Napoleon who also started the war against Russia on the 22nd of June. The war was felt in the village too. More and more men were drafted into the Army and some of the members of their families started to receive death notices.

Towards the end of 1941 almost all the able bodied men were drafted as were some women, among them the oldest daughter of our landlady.

The already cut food rations were cut in half again.

The brilliant, dry autumn suddenly gave way to heavy, cold rains and early frost.

As a result of a pact made with Stalin and General Sikorski forming a Provisional Polish Government in exile my father, my uncle and myself were not conscripted into the Red Army much to the disappointment of the local draft commission.

The local population was much better off than the refugees. Most of them had some livestock, goats, chicken, potatoes and vegetables stored in the basements of their houses. They also had warm clothing, fur coats "shubas," fur hats "ushanka" and the most precious possession, the felt boots "valenki" that kept their feet warm in the coldest of weather.

Wood used for cooking and heating was in abundance since we were surrounded by the thick Ural forest but the wood had to be cut during the early summer so as to give the wood a chance to dry otherwise it was very difficult to light.

The kolkhoz gave us some used clothing because we could not go to work without appropriate winter clothing and our landlady gave me an old pair of patched up "valenke" the best gift of them all.

The food became very scarce. My father bartered his pocket watch for a "pud"—16 kilograms of potatoes and that, of course, did not last too long either.

We managed to eat three meals a day but without meat or butter we were constantly hungry and I who turned 17 in the meantime had a rather healthy appetite.

One day a "troika" driving quickly past our house ran over a duck belonging to our neighbor, crushing it totally into the mud that reached the axles of the wagon.

Next morning the temperature fell to -10 degrees C. freezing all the mud and the duck in it.

I told my father about it pointing to the spot where the duck met its untimely death. My father without a word went out and dug out the duck.

"Papa, how can you eat this taken from Blote?" I said, using a popular Yiddish word for mud.

"Don't worry my son, by the time I'll finish with it you will lick your fingers."

Indeed I licked my fingers "Blote" or not "Blote."

On rainy days I would watch out through the window for ran-over ducks or geese but they disappeared entirely.

The winter made its appearance in all its majestic and frightening fury. The temperature dropped to -53 degrees C. and it was bitter cold.

Faced with the possibility of freezing to death, we had no alternative but to steal the ready cut wood belonging to the villagers. Stealing might be a very strong word, but if you say it in Russian "na levo" it becomes almost respectable. We would leave out the initialed pieces and take a few from each pile not to make a visible dent in the pile.

The winter was long, cold and very difficult. My father who was 48 years old at the time was considered too old for active duty in the Polish Army and therefore was conscripted into the Russian Labor Battalion and sent to Chelabinsk to work in a tractor factory. There he met other Polish Jews and to supplement his meager earnings he started to deal in "Machorka" a rough cut tobacco. Soon after he started to send some money and occasional food or clothing packages.

Both my uncle and I refused the induction into the Red Army waiting for the Polish Army to claim us, however, the Poles weren't to happy with so many Jews willing to join the Legion. Thus we were left in limbo for another 6 or so months.

In the meantime many things happened to our family, none of them pleasant. My uncle, a strong man tried to lift a fully loaded wagon with his back, to repair a broken axle, just like Jean Valjean in Les Miserables but this time my uncle got an aggravated hernia.

At his next pre-induction medical examination he was permanently removed from active duty and from work in the Kolkhoz. He was assigned to be a night watchman for the local bank and Post Office.

With so many men leaving the Fire Department for the Army I was ordered to join the local fire brigade.

Comrade Ivanov, the Fire Chief, was an ethnic Tartar and a fanatic party member. My first day as a fireman was pleasant enough. I was issued a new, black "robashka" with golden epaulets, leather belt, heavy cotton padded parka called "foofayka," padded pants and the luxury of them all, a brand new pair of long boots. What's more, in my size.

I was overjoyed with my new wardrobe and could hardly wait to show it off to my uncle and aunt.

Their first comment on my new attire was, "You do look like a typical "Moskal" (a Polish derogatory term for a Russian). Personally I couldn't care less how I looked; I had clean, warm clothing, free of lice, so far.

Chapter 16

The Russian Saga: George's Story (Continued)

My uncle suggested that I move in with them since my father was away and I gratefully accepted.

It took me only a few minutes to collect and bring my belongings across the street; of course, I said "do svidania" to Valentina Nikolaeva and her kids. She was a good, simple peasant woman who lived through some incredibly hard times.

Later I found out that her husband whom she respectfully referred to as "choziain" was arrested during the mid thirties and sent north. She never heard from him again.

It must have been very difficult for her to bring up three children in a society where a woman was considered almost a beast of burden. Without a husband she was a nobody.

I would visit her from time to time and there was always tea for me. If not tea then just hot water "kipiatok" with a few drops of milk. Sugar was totally unavailable.

My first few weeks in the Fire Department were spent on all kinds of exercises, such as how to link water hoses or how to climb ladders without injuring yourself. The idea was to keep the knees outside the ladder so as not to hit the rungs on the way up.

Above all my duties consisted of feeding and grooming the horses used to pull the fire extinguishing apparatus and a hand pump. With feeding and grooming went also the barn.

There was a fire engine mounted on a truck, nice and shiny but mostly inoperative. The village of Atchit still lived in the era of horse dominance.

While doing those chores I also had guard duty. I was posted on a 3 story tower. There were very few telephones in the entire village. The village itself was small and built of wood. Sometimes large fires occurred.

Chief Ivanov was fond of saying "Bez dyma niet ognia" (Where there is smoke there is fire.) He would repeat this several times daily using the local dialect. Instead of the word "niet" he would say "nietu." Everyday I had to haul fresh drinking water for people and horses because the Fire Department, as the entire village, had no running water.

The source of supply was the nearby river with its crystal clear water. In the summer it was easy enough but in the wintertime it was complicated by the fact that the ice covered the river and each morning I had to hack through the ice to reach the water with a long stick attached to a large pail. 20–25 pails would fill a large wooden barrel laying horizontally on a sled. The ice 20 cm. thick would support the weight of the barrel, wagon and the horse, not to mention the driver.

While I was hauling water, my aunt managed to deliver a little bouncy girl named Ilana.

With a new baby at home food became a burning issue. A large diamond ring was exchanged for 2 "puds" (32 kg.) of flour. We were all happy about it. After all you can't eat diamonds, as my uncle would say. "Don't worry Helen, if we ever get out of here I'll buy you even better stones." A promise that he eventually kept.

I never knew how many different dishes could be made out of flour. From home baked bread to macaronis, pierogis, soups, sauces. I was fascinated by my aunts culinary talents.

The winter seemed to never end with snow permanently blanketing the village. Many a night while on duty I would observe from the tower the quiet, peaceful village; the smoke they emitted from the chimneys would go straight to the sky which was littered with millions of shiny stars. The peace of the night would only be interrupted by the barking of dogs and the howling of wolves in nearby forests.

I did not mind the night watch, dressed in a long fur coat "shuba." I had the time to think and to reflect.

After the watch I had a glass of "kipiatok," boiled water with a few drops of goat milk that some of the women on the force would share with me. By this time most of the firemen were women.

The "bathroom" was just an outdoor hut, unheated and that, of course, presented a problem of another kind because of each "deposit" that would freeze on top of another thus reaching the seat itself, so sooner or later someone would have to remove the frozen apex.

Chief Ivanov asked for volunteers to clean the outdoor privy. There weren't any. However, when he offered a bonus in the form of half a glass of sugar (about 4 oz.), I was only too glad to do it because we had no sugar at home.

I brought the priceless sugar home never mentioning how I obtained it. The sugar was only for my Aunt Helen who was breast feeding the ever hungry, ever screaming Ilana.

The spring although delayed, started to show some signs of visiting our village too, but it was still very cold. The ice still covered the river although some cracks started to appear on the monolithic surface.

I went on with my chores of bringing daily water, failing to notice some loose patches and just kept filling up the wooden barrel located on the wagon. Suddenly I heard a loud crash and the ice under the combined weight of partially filled barrel, wagon and the horse, broke and we all fell into the icy river.

Like a giant brace the cold water embraced me squeezing the air out of me. While the horse tried desperately to reach the bank of the river, the wagon and the barrel were pulling the horse down.

My screams for help alerted some fishermen and they came to the rescue. My only thought was to save the horse. I did not have a kingdom to give for the horse, I was only afraid that if I lost it, due to my "negligence" it would be Siberia for me.

Still in the water I freed the horse from the confinement of the equipment. The freed horse started to climb out of the water towards the bank while I held on to his tail.

By this time some onlookers helped to pull the wagon and the barrel out of the water, some other people brought some hay and an old blanket. I dried the horse pulling the blanket on the shivering horse while I was completely soaked. By the time I reached the Fire Department my clothing resembled an ancient suit of armor.

Members of my crew seeing me in this condition gave me some old clothing and plenty of hot water.

Whether it was the iron constitution of the young or my nervous energy or extra adrenalin flowing, I did not catch double pneumonia, not even a sniffle. I just waited till my clothing dried (it shrank a bit) and went home afraid to mention the capsizing of the wagon.

The bread was rationed and as the war progressed the rations were constantly cut. I always brought my share of bread home. The share would be a thick slice of bread that was supposed to last a whole day. The bread, whatever quality, was always delicious. My problem was that sometimes when the bread was weighed a small piece might be added to reach the appropriate weight. That small piece I must confess was eaten up immediately or on the way home. I just could not resist.

Living with my aunt and uncle was a unique experience because I learned the true meaning of family love, in some very difficult and trying circumstances.

It is very easy to be good and even generous in time of plenty, but it is very tough to share the last piece of bread with someone who is not even your child.

Hunger is the most degrading and humiliating experience. Luckily I never experienced real HUNGER. I was hungry and there is a world of difference.

My uncle was truly a remarkable person. As many times as he came home from work, dead tired, his first question to his wife was if I ate already. From a playboy husband he turned to be the most considerate and the most understanding husband.

All the cooking was done in a long, almost 12 feet, baking oven and to light such an oven was an art. One had to start a fire at the far end of the oven and gradually add pieces of wood till a steady fire took place.

The cooking pots were moved by a long stick with a horseshoe like ending. Pots had to be lifted or gently pushed near the flame.

My Aunt Helen being a lady in pre war Poland never in her life had seen such a stove and having had servants, very seldom would come into the kitchen all together. Trying to cook in such a long oven she would sometimes knock over pots containing the very precious food. She would then cry uncontrollably.

My uncle much to his credit never reproached her and many times he would walk kilometers just to light the oven for her.

Maybe he felt guilty for taking her away from a life of luxury in Drohobycz to a primitive life in the Urals.

Of course, neither he nor anybody else knew at the time that that move saved all our lives, almost all. A tragedy soon struck our family. Our little cousin Lily while playing with other kids obtained an infection and very high temperature.

One of the village doctors, a Jewish refugee from Latvia, was very pessimistic about the case. She was hoping that in the city of Krasnoufimsk needed medicine might be gotten.

The distance from our village to Krasnoufimsk was exactly 26 km. I knew that because I'd covered that distance by foot many times, but this time my uncle managed to borrow the fastest horse from comrade Bezimienny, the chief of the Kolkhoz. My uncle gave him a wrist watch which Bezimienny did not accept and simply said, "Idi, spasay svoyou dotch." Go and save your daughter.

I took that horse and mercilessly ran it to Krasnoufimsk's apothecary. Luckily they had that medication. Elated I turned around and kept whipping the poor beast all the way back.

When I arrived with the medicine the horse was foaming. I gave the medicine to my uncle and then attended the horse before returning it to Bezimienny. Despite all our efforts and prayers our little Lily died just 4 days later of high fever. We were devastated. The irony of it was the fact that we ran away from Hitler only to lose a member of our family so far away from front lines.

There was no Jewish cemetery in Atchit and my uncle did not want to bury her in the town's cemetery.

We picked an isolated place near a large birch tree overlooking the village and I started to dig the grave. It took me the entire day to do it because the ground beneath 5 or 8 cm. of snow was frozen solid. I had to chip it off centimeter by centimeter crying doing it. My uncle stood nearby dressed in a Talith. I never expected for him to be so religious. Russia or no Russia he would pray every morning.

We finally buried our cousin in a simple pine board coffin. On the top I erected a wooden heart with a metal arrow going through it. Thus Lily remained for ever buried in the vastness of Russia.

The news of Lily's death spread throughout the Jewish refugee community. Our home became the center of all "Poliacks" living or passing by, as more people were released from Gulags.

My uncle became the unofficial and later the official head of the Polish community. He and my aunt were very much liked by the gentile Poles as well as the Polish Jews. People were made welcome with a cup of tea or "kipiatok." Among the released were also members of the Polish aristocracy and Polish intelligentsia. These people arrived in unspeakable rags and instead of leather shoes they would wear sandals "lapties" made from the bark of a tree.

By this time we started to receive more clothing from England. They were British Army uniforms dyed deep green. These uniforms were sheer delight. Once dressed in them we could spot another Pole from afar.

In addition to former members of Polish Administration or Government on their way to join General Sikorski's Army, there were also some hardened Polish criminals and murderers released from the Russian prisons.

At that time we did not know that the Soviets managed to deport from the Western Ukraine and Byelorussia (which comprised 50% of pre war Polish territory) almost 500,000 people.

A significant part of these deported people were also Jews accused of being "speculants," kulaks, landowners, business people and members of the clergy.

My uncle and aunt were able to communicate and establish a good rapport with everyone, which explained their popularity.

With members of the intelligentsia they would speak in highly cultural Polish and one would think that they were in some elegant Polish salon instead of a small wooden house.

One day two Polish "gentlemen" found their way to our home. They were, as we found out later, convicted murderers. The older one Stasiek was built like a professional wrestler in his early forties. Whoever encountered Stasiek usually moved aside. The younger one Antek was in his late twenties or early thirties, tall and very handsome. One of his arms was badly mangled, it looked as if it had been bitten by dogs. Every time they came they would elegantly click their heels and kiss my aunt's hand.

Nothing was ever missing from our house after they left. To the contrary, we started to have meat, chickens, veal, extra potatoes and bread on a regular basis. They would "organize" or raid at night villagers or unguarded Kolhozes.

We ate well but always with the door closed.

Stasiek was soon inducted into the Polish Army since he held the rank of sergeant only to die later in Italy on Monte Cassino. Every time I hear the song, "Czerwone maki na Monte Cassino" (Red poppies on Monte Cassino) I think of Stasiek.

Antek remained and under my uncle's tutelage he prospered living with a "soldatka," a young wife of an army officer who was at the front.

In the meantime I was working alternating between the Kolhoz and the Fire Department. From time to time we would be called to extinguish fires and since houses were built out of wood they burned like matches. Mostly we prevented fire from spreading further. Once dousing a burning house with water I came across what I thought was a piglet; unfortunately it was a small child burned to a crisp.

The time flew and my aunt gave birth to a boy by the name of Chaim named after her brother. In the early stage of pregnancy she talked about having an abortion due to very difficult and uncertain times but uncle managed to persuade her to do otherwise.

Writing letters and waiting for replies became my obsession and therefore I was very much surprised to receive a letter from an unexpected source. It was from the local N.K.V.D., the much feared secret police, requesting my presence at 10 A.M. on the next day. An "invitation" to N.K.V.D. was always considered a bad omen. My conscience was clear and I was sure there was some kind of mistake.

I put on my English army uniform, took all my papers attesting to Polish citizenship and went to face the "Natchalnik" Pavlov.

After several hours of uninterrupted interrogations I was accused of having two bread ration cards, which was a serious crime under #58 statute of the U.S.S.R. criminal code. While I was denying the charge and loudly protesting my innocence my hair was shorn and I was jailed.

To this day I believe that it was pressure put on my uncle whom the N.K.V.D. wanted to turn into an informer ("Stukach").

I was put into a cell with other people accused of every possible crime. My uncle managed to send me some food and a warm sweater. A few days later a convoy was formed and I was included.

We walked the same 26 km. to Krasnoufimsk, the road I knew so well. We walked 5 people abreast holding each other's arm as per instruction, constantly warned by the guards, "Shag v pravo ili v levo schitaetsa pobieg, prinimayem cruzhie." " A step to the right or left will be considered an attempt to flee and we shall shoot." Nobody ever thought of running away.

From time to time we would rest kneeling on a snow covered road. Eventually we made the railroad station in Krasnoufimsk in the middle of the night. I suppose the NKVD preferred to transport prisoners at night so minimum of citizens would see the masses of people sent to jails.

After what seemed like eternity, we finally boarded the infamous Stolypin's train (named after the Tsar minister Stolypin who wanted to solve the Jewish question by deporting a third of the Jews from Russia, a third to forced assimilation and the remaining to be killed). This train on the outside looked like an ordinary train but inside were cages like in a zoo but instead of animals they kept people. On average 10 people were put to each cage. An hour or so after the train pulled from the station the guards started to distribute food which consisted of very salty herrings and bread.

I was just about to eat my bread with herring when an old-timer "blatnoy" warned me, "Don't eat the herring because you will be very thirsty and the frigging guards won't give you any water."

It made perfect sense although I hated to part with the herring. I gave my herring away and later I was very glad that I had listened to the voice of experience. Other prisoners either too hungry or who couldn't think ahead, ate the herrings and their cries for water were heard throughout the night. I was also advised not to address the guards as comrades (tovarishch) but as citizens, because prisoners were not comrades to the guards ("goos svinye nie tovarishch").

My advisor was a "blatnoy" or a member of the Russian criminal underworld and as such commanded and received respect from prisoners and guards alike. Noticing my British uniform he asked me who I was. I told him I was a Pole. I surely looked like a Pole and surely considered myself a Pole and I doubted very much if he considered my religious beliefs.

After a long train ride we got off at Sverdlovsk, the capital city of the region, at night again. We marched to a giant jail. After processing procedures I was assigned to a large room with about 50 prisoners. We slept on a cement floor. There were no mattresses or bedding. A small electric lamp enclosed in wire mesh was hanging high from the ceiling lit both day and night.

A gigantic, always overflowing pot served as a chamber pot for the entire room. The "tradition" was such that all newcomers with the exception of "blatnye" were put next to the stinking pot.

I was as green as my uniform and I was told by the "starshyi" boss of the cell to lie down next to the pot "parasha."

"Oh no, this fellow is with me!" I turned around to see to whom the voice of authority belonged and spotted my "herring adviser" from the train. "That is another story"—said the "starshyi" whose name was Vania. He simply ordered another two fellows to move instead. My protector and I had room far away from the "parasha." In the Soviet jails the "Blatnye," the real criminals and not the political prisoners, rule. They literally exercise the power of life and death over the rest of the prisoners.

If a "Blatnoy" liked your boots or shirt you had better give them to him with a smile if you valued your life.

Slightly beneath the "Blatnoy" in pecking order were people with special talents like singers, magicians and story tellers or interpreters of dreams. These were people that kept other people from boredom, fights or depression. Some of these singers had magnificent voices singing beautiful, haunting songs such as the prerevolutionary song:

> Sizhu ya za reshotkoy v tiemnitze syroy
> Vskarmlionyi na volie oriol molodoy
> (I sit behind bars in a wet dungeon
> Brought up in freedom young eagle)

or another song very popular at the time about Kostia the Sailor or about Moorka, a female traitor.

The singer never had a more appreciative audience. We were certainly quite "captivated."

I found my "specialty" that made my life almost bearable. I could tell stories based on books I have read and, of course, interpret dreams. The Russians were and are quite superstitious. I could always tell these poor souls that water or birds always meant freedom. I believed in good dreams only and as a result I was in demand sometimes rewarded by a piece of bread or tobacco. Every so often I would be awakened by the guards and led to be interrogated. Walking those long corridors I had to face the wall if another prisoner was walking in my direction.

It was a simple but effective method of preventing prisoners from seeing each other or communicating.

My so very experienced "advisor" told me how to handle the interrogating officers in order to get a minimum sentence, which in my case he guessed to be "just" 10 years (a "tchervoniets"—named after a 10 ruble note) and that one can do even standing on one foot.

Respectfully I have listened to his lessons, however, I did not plan to spend 10 years in a Siberian vacation spot and therefore I kept telling my interrogators that I am a Polish citizen and that they have no right to keep me after Stalin HIMSELF signed an agreement with "OUR" General Sikorski and who are they to defy comrade Stalin. I told them also that I won't sign any papers even if they would kill me and what's more I was sure that my Government was looking for me and there will be hell to pay.

Russians have a fear of authority and if you speak with conviction in your voice they might even listen to you with respect. Whether it was my "Chutzpah" or some directions given from higher up, the result was that 6 weeks later I was sent back to Atchit for court appearance.

My "advisor" could hardly believe it; he wished me good luck and I was on my way back supervised by a single NKVD agent in civilian clothing. My trip back was rapid by comparison with my departure and I found myself in the same cell.

The authorities must have notified my relatives that I was back because within hours I had fresh clothing and food which I shared with people in my cell. The fresh clothing was extra welcome because I spent 2 months wearing the same outfit.

Next day after signing an affidavit that I'll be back for trial I was released. I ran home as fast as I could. Never did the sun look so good, never was the air so fresh, never were girls so pretty.

My uncle, aunt and little cousins gave me a hero's welcome but first I had to go to a Russian sauna "Bania" and later I ate and ate.

My uncle had some interesting news for me. Captain Pavlov of NKVD was no longer in command. A new man took over and he was a local man whose sister worked in the same bank where my uncle was employed as a night watchman.

Through this woman a deal was made. My uncle gave her for Captain's wife, a beautiful gold wrist watch belonging to my Aunt Helen, with a clear understanding that the trial be postponed at least for 6 months. Deal or no deal my uncle did not trust the "Fonie-Goniff." He said to me:

"Listen, now is your opportunity to run away. Try to reach Chaliabinsk where your father is working. Perhaps he can arrange for you to work there too. If you stay here the NKVD will get you sooner or later."

Seeing the logic of his suggestion I packed my old back-pack with a minimum of clothing but a maximum of "Zwiebak" dried bread. I tearfully said good-bye to my dear uncle, aunt and two little cousins. I was back on so very familiar road to Krasnoufimsk.

Before leaving we made up a code that my aunt would write me to my father's address. If she would include the words that, "Aunt Rose sends her love" it would mean that Reds are looking for me.

So here I was again on the same road in the middle of the night too busy with my own thoughts to pay attention to a pack of wolves running parallel to the road. To scare them away I used up a couple of precious matches to light a bark from a birch tree and to curse them in Russian. By that time I acquired a rather rich vocabulary because the wolves understood me and disappeared into the wilderness.

I arrived at the station at early dawn and luckily there was a train leaving for Cheliabinsk in a short while. The problem was that I did not have a ticket or special papers permitting me to travel and there was no shortage of Railroad Militia checking people's papers.

My fresh green British uniform made me more visible but the Militia did not pay any attention to me because they were used to seeing Poles with transfer papers. Not having any papers I could not afford an encounter with Militia. Seeing a young woman loaded with all kinds of packages I took a chance of asking her for help.

"Listen, I have to go to Chaliabinsk to see my old and sick father. If you help me I will carry all your packages and I have some food enough for both of us." She readily agreed and I grabbed all her packages and followed her waving her papers into a crowded train. Her papers worked like a charm because nobody bothered to stop or check those papers.

Every seat was taken and the only place where I could hide was under the seats.

God bless the Russian women and their wide and long skirts. Every time the inspection team would enter our compartment my angel would spread her legs slightly covering me entirely.

Somewhat uncomfortable but happy as a lark I have reached the large, industrial town of Cheliabinsk.

It was quite a walk to the Tractor and Tank Factory where my father worked. I located his dormitory and his bunk and proceeded to wait for him to finish his shift.

Tired I fell asleep only to be awakened by my father's kisses and embraces. We were soon surrounded by mostly middle aged Polish Jews who were only too glad to help my father in hiding me.

After a few days of trying to be invisible it became apparent that a solution had to be found.

The solution arrived totally unexpectedly in a form of a tall. redheaded man by the name Wowek Tepper whose sister Anna married my father's younger brother, Izio. It was a most joyful reunion.

The last time we had seen him was back in Drohobycz in 1940 when he was conscripted into the Red Army. He left his pregnant wife and his parents there. Prior to the outbreak of hostilities he would often visit his sister Anna and her son Otto. We lived nearby and I would join them in all kinds of games. At that time he was 30 years old and quite a successful timber merchant like my Uncle Abe.

Shortly before the 1939 war he fell in love with a very beautiful girl, the only daughter of one of the wealthiest Jews in town. The young lady was a chemical engineer.

So when Wowek asked the father of the young lady for her hand in marriage, as was the custom, the old man told him, "What, do you want to marry my daughter? Your father is selling leather to shoemakers and you have the nerve to ask me for my daughter? Never! Never!"

Well, the war broke out and the Russians came in and "liberated" the old man's properties and monies. Wowek did marry her after all.

He was a type of man who didn't take no for an answer.

Miraculously he was with us in Cheliabinsk, dressed in an elegant long leather coat and soft leather boots "na garmoshku."

"What on earth are you doing in Cheliabinsk?" he asked me. That is a very good question and I proceeded to tell him how I came to be in town.

"No problem! I will take you with me to Ufa in Bashkiria. Don't worry about papers either, I will take care of it."

He was right. For a thousand rubles and 8 glasses full of "machorka" Russian tobacco he obtained for me all the necessary travel papers "komandirovochnoye udostvirienye."

Having the proper credentials we traveled in splendor allotted to big shots only, so called "Bolshye shishki."

Ufa, the capital city of Bashkiria, was quite a distance from Cheliabinsk. We reminisced about the past and wondered about the future. After living in a backward village and spending a couple of months in jail, I was certainly not prepared for the most luxurious apartment I had ever seen in Russia. Persian Bukharin carpets were on the floor, oil paintings on the walls, crystal, silverware, a rare samovar all complemented the hand-carved furniture. Small wonder that Wowek's brother Arthur, who also lived in Ufa, had taken the maiden name of their mother for fear of being associated with Wowek and his dealings. His favorite expression at the time was, "I am not a sub-lieutenant but a senior speculator."

The more crooked and dangerous the deal the better Wowek liked it. I think he got more satisfaction from sheer danger than from the rewards. Thanks to his entrepreneurial spirit, we lived like tsars. Two days after my arrival in Ufa he took me to a performance of "Swan Lake" at the Bolshoi Theater.

Life is full of paradoxes. A few weeks after sitting in jail I was watching a most enchanting performance.

Wowek worked as the supply master and purchasing agent for a meat-processing plant. If anyone stole as much as a small sausage, he or she could spend years in jail. Naturally, Wowek did not bother stealing mere sausages. He would literally take half a pig and hide it under his long coat, and then walk through the gate with a big smile on his face. The guards knew him, but from time to time they stopped him inquiring what he had under his coat. He would say, "Polovina kabana" (half of a pig) and by the time the guards had stopped laughing he'd be on his way home.

With all that food I finally managed to put some meat on my skinny bones. One day I received a letter from my father with a coded message from my uncle that the N.K.V.D. were making inquiries about my whereabouts. Although I doubt if they could have found me in Ufa, I decided not to take no chances. When I heard an announcement on the radio that all Polish citizens must report to the Polish recruiting station, I did not hesitate and went right over to present my papers.

The medical examination was a farce. They didn't even look at me. Men who looked sick were also accepted. I am sure the doctors had a quota to fill because I heard one of them say, "If they can walk, they can carry a rifle."

I was told to get ready the very next day for the swearing-in ceremony and to be shipped at once to a boot camp. The arrangements suited me perfectly. What I did not realize was how hard Wowek would take the news that I was joining the Polish Army. He was heartbroken.

"Why did you do it? Are you 'meshugeh?' Is that why I carried you halfway across Russia, for you to leave me?" It was really very painful for me to see this big and wonderful man cry, but the die was cast.

Again I packed my belongings. This time, however, I was almost elegantly dressed. Tearfully I said good-bye to my dear benefactor.

Chapter 17

The Russian Saga: George's Story (Continued)

I duly reported to the induction center and waited for my group to leave for the railroad station and the train that was supposed to take us all the way to Sumy in the Ukraine.

While waiting to be shipped out, I heard my name being paged. It was Wowek, who had come to see me off, bringing with him another gift. It was a very large loaf of bread, at least the size of two bricks. If the gift had been pure gold it couldn't have been more welcome. Only people who had been really hungry in their lives would appreciate such a gift.

A rag-tag bunch of civilians, all speaking Polish, made their way to the station and eventually we boarded a cattle train with about twenty men in each wagon. With every turn of the wheel I felt I was finally coming home. Asleep, I dreamt that the wheels were saying, "Do domu, do domu, do domu, home, home, home. . . ." After a few days we reached our destination, the town of Sumy, where our army unit was forming.

The railroad station resembled a beehive, with thousands of men and some women milling about in total chaos. Finally, Russian and Polish officers started to divide the mass of people into groups according to their ages. Young men with some education were assigned to anti-aircraft artillery, that is where I found myself.

Seeing that the fellow in charge of our group had trouble communicating, I offered him my help, which he gratefully accepted. At the time I did not know his rank, but eventually he became our C.O. for a very short time.

Making order out of this Tower of Babel was not exactly easy. People spoke Russian, Polish, Ukrainian, White Russian and Yiddish. While the Slavic languages were somewhat similar, there were idioms and expressions that left some people bewildered.

I spoke all these languages with equal ease and was soon put in charge of a group of ninety men, whom I led to a nearby barrack.

The same afternoon I met the four platoon leaders assigned to our group. These "podporuczniks" (sublieutenants) were still in the Russian uniforms of "mladshiy lieutenants," the Russian 90-day wonders out of Frunze Military Academy. Later on another officer joined our unit on a temporary basis. He was a senior lieutenant, a Russian veteran of Polish descent by the name of Zyniel. He was the senior officer, he constantly reminded us, but we were told to expect the arrival of the company commander.

We had not yet receive any uniforms, military equipment or weapons, but bit by bit we began to get Polish uniforms, and by the time we finally put on our four-cornered military hats we had also received our company commander, a Soviet Ukrainian named Lieutenant Nikita Kirilovich Didenko.

Technically, Senior Lieutenant Zyniel outranked Lieutenant Didenko but the latter was the C.O. The difference in rank was a sore point between those two men, but because Lieutenant Didenko was a party member, I found out later, he was given the position if not the rank. The rank followed soon anyway.

I became indispensable and was billeted with the officers in a private house. My sudden power and that respect of the men from the ranks hit me like champagne on an empty stomach. Here I was, basically a quiet mama's boy, yelling and screaming in three languages, giving orders right and left.

But I began to love the army. When an opening for a chemical instructor was available, I volunteered, and while everybody else was going through the tough basic training I attended classes dealing with chemical warfare and gases such as mustard, Iprit and Luisit.

A few weeks later I was a full-fledged instructor. After distributing gas masks and making sure they fit properly, I took platoon after platoon to a makeshift gas chamber to introduce them to the dangers of gas attack. Even though we were using only tear gas, there were always some fatalities due primarily to men who did not believe tear gas was dangerous. But usually, after coughing for a few minutes, they would learn the lesson of the day.

My prestige, if not my rank, soared. Every army in the world has mechanisms by which some soldiers either "disappear" or remain in some kind of limbo. I found myself in such a position, being directly responsible only to the Chief Chemical Officer (a Jewish Ph.D. from Lodz) and indirectly attached to my company.

If it suited me, I would report to my company commander that I was wanted at the Divisional Headquarters or the other way around. As a result I had plenty of time in which to roam the countryside and the nearby villages for those things that complete a soldier's life.

Within three months we had become, though still green, a formidable fighting unit itching to get to the front to fight "Fritzes." Stripes were given to the more able and enterprising soldiers, and I found myself the recipient of two of them.

Then, in the early spring of 1944, the picnic ended; we received our marching orders. The entire regiment including the 37-mm artillery pieces and the 2½ ton American trucks, was loaded on flat platform wagons.

The soldiers were jubilant; they sang spontaneously the Polish National Anthem, "Jeszcze Polska nie zginela" (Poland shall not perish) and the very popular "War oh war, what kind of lady are you that the best looking guys are running after you?"

We did not have to run after war. It came to us soon enough in the form of an air raid by German Stukas.

The German pilots did not realize that, instead of a troop-training train, they had stumbled into an anti-aircraft unit. Even before the alarm was sounded, some of the crews had opened fire, recognizing the silhouettes of the German planes.

One out of three planes was shot down almost immediately. The other two turned around and disappeared into the clouds.

A loud "hooray" lifted the troops' morale. Crossing the old Polish–Russian border, many a soldier wept openly, kneeling down and praying loudly. Deeply moved, I wondered whether I would ever see my mother and sister again.

Our unit was posted briefly on the defense of a military airport near the city of Lublin, where British and American planes occasionally landed. Only Russian troops could get near those gigantic planes.

By October 1944 we had reached the Polish city of Praga; only the Vistula River separated us from the capital of Poland, Warsaw.

In Praga we came under repeated air attacks by the German Luftwaffe and lost some good men, including the best-liked Lieutenant Porucznik Borysewicz.

Senior Lieutenant Zyniel was still with us, utterly disliked—in fact, deeply hated. The men vowed to kill him as soon as we reached the front. After the Liberation of Warsaw on January 17, 1945 we moved towards the German city of Kolberg on the Baltic Sea. There Senior Lieutenant Zyniel was killed during a street fight, but by a bullet that hit him from behind. There was no inquiry.

Soon after, in early May, our unit, a part of Rokossovsky's Second Ukrainian Front, moved towards Berlin itself, and the war ended for us near the River Elbau, not very far from American forces.

Returning to Poland I met the surviving members of my family, but regretfully my mother and sister were not among them. I found out later that my mother had been shot by a Ukrainian SS man. I was told this by my Aunt Anna, who said as a solace, "At least she did not suffer much." My sister Edith was drowned near Stuthoff along with a boat full of Jewish inmates. Ironically, I had fought for the cities of Kolberg and Stettin, not very far from Stuthoff. When my relatives decided to leave Poland in 1945 I simply joined them, deserting the Polish Army and leaving behind my Polish uniform, which I had worn so proudly for almost two years.

I was the second Jew to go AWOL; shortly afterwards the Jewish soldiers started to leave the Polish Army officially or unofficially by the hundreds. The war was over, but anti-Semitism was not. We, the Jewish soldiers, did not owe Poland anything.

The surviving four members of my family and I illegally crossed the Polish–Czech border and later the Czech–German border, and on October 10, 1945 we reached the displaced persons camp Foehrenwald UNRRA Team #106 near Munich in Bavaria.

We spent almost three years in Foehrenwald awaiting our visas to the United States. Had our American relatives sent the affidavits for us airmail, we might have been in the D.P. camp for only a year. It was just a matter of 4 cents: regular mail 3 cents and airmail cost 7 cents. Our mail came via regular mail. By that time there were hundreds of thousands of people waiting for their quotas. My relatives, tired of waiting, decided to go to Israel, where they prospered. I finally reached the land of my dreams, the United States of America.

As of this writing some forty-three years later, my father and my Uncle Abe have been dead for twenty-two years. I lost both of them in the same year, even though my uncle was ten years younger than my father. I miss them both.

My Aunt Helen lives in Israel, quite advanced in years. Every couple of years I manage to visit her in Tel-Aviv. Her first question is always, "Do you remember Atchit?" How well I remember it!

My benefactor, Wowek, also lives in Israel, quite well off, and still very spry; his red hair has turned gray. He has the same spirit and is still willing to take any trip into the unknown and make any deal as long as it is challenging and, of course, profitable.

My Atchit cousins live in Israel and Guatemala.

Once we lived in Drohobycz for generations and now we are all spread throughout the world, in Israel, the United States, Guatemala and Australia.

There is no one left from our family in Drohobycz; only the stones are witnesses to the fact that we lived there once upon a time.

I am going to preserve those sweet memories and maybe, just maybe, one of these days I will take my grandson or grandchildren to Drohobycz to show them their roots.

To be fully objective about my Russian odyssey I must use a Russian proverb, "Rossiya komu to mat a komu to blad"—"Russia to some might be a mother and to some a whore."

To me she was both.

Gefilte Fish and Hand Grenades

I really adore gefilte fish, especially when it's made from carp with lots of onions and peppers, horseradish (the white kind), well-chilled vodka and a piece of fresh-baked Challah. It is a dish fit for a king.

But what about grenades? I do not want to jump the gun (I mean the grenades), so I'll say that I personally have great respect for them.

The Bible says, "He who comes to slay you, slay him first." After all, the Bible wasn't written by fools. This makes perfect sense to me because if you are dead, you cannot kill anybody.

You will see the connection between these two completely dissimilar objects and, what is more, their perfect compatibility if you listen to the rest of the story. Our story took place in war-torn Eastern Poland in September 1944, shortly before the holiday of Rosh Ha-Shana, the Jewish New Year. As luck or the fortune of war would have it, I found myself in the Polish 1st Division of the First Polish Army, in a 37-mm anti-aircraft artillery unit assigned to the defense of an airport near the city of Lublin.

In our unit, besides me, there were only three Jews. Two fellows came from the capital city of Warsaw and both were named Yuzef (Joseph), and the other one, like myself was "pure" Galician; his name was David and my nickname was Olek.

At this time the front itself moved about 30–50 kilometers further west, leaving us safely in the hinterland.

Like soldiers the world over, we spent all our free time searching for food, whiskey (especially the home-brewed type called "bimber") and, of course, girls, girls and girls.

I don't want to give the impression that we didn't get much food.

On the contrary. But after having soup for breakfast, soup for lunch and soup for dinner, it was no wonder that we were constantly looking for something else to augment our "diet." Lining up for chow was never my idea of fun. They would hold out the army's "menazhka," a sort of heavy-duty 2-quart pot with a handle that in an emergency also served as a helmet or washbasin, depending on the situation.

The company's cook either gave you soup from the top, which was mostly hot or lukewarm liquid, or, if he liked you, would put the ladle deeper into the cauldron and come up with meat and potatoes. I think it was the Russian General Kutuzov who said in 1812 that army cooks should be put against the wall and shot after six months of service. I am sure that anyone who has been in the army would agree.

As I have already said, we had our fill of soup. The bread was the consistency of clay, but if one was hungry enough, it seemed like sachertorte.

We also got front-line rations of 100 grams of vodka, or approximately half a glass. The problem with this was that your appetite was just whetted. It was enough to keep you sober but not enough to get you drunk, so you looked for vodka diluted with eau de cologne or even gasoline.

As far as girls were concerned, nothing much mattered to a 19-year old lad; they could be young or old, fat or skinny. Women in general are fascinated by uniforms, Polish women in particular. Whether it was their "patriotic" duty, my well-tailored uniform or above-average looks, or perhaps my innocent face that still had never felt a razor, or the irresistible but true "You are my first"—Eros did not overlook me. While one cannot eat all the food in the world or drink all the vodka or sleep with all the women, I certainly gave it a good try.

Like Jason and the Golden Fleece, we would go to the nearby villages trying to buy, barter or "organize" (euphemism for stealing) things that we needed. David, whom we called "rabbi" (owing to the miniature Torah scroll he always wore, which once had even stopped a bullet), announced that the Jewish Holidays were coming; if we could "organize" some fish, he would prepare the very best gefilte fish for us.

Hearing from some local people that in the neighboring village of T. there was a farmer who kept carp in his pond, we proceeded on foot to the farm, licking our lips in anticipation of David's culinary art.

It was a gorgeous, sunny day, perhaps best described as the "golden Polish autumn." The sun was so intense, the fields full of birds and insects in a state of agitation; everything gave us the feeling that our paradise was about to end. Unburdened by weapons, we covered the 5–6 kilometers in no time. There, on top of a small hill, stood an old house, complete with wishing well and stork's nest. To the left of the house was a large pond half-surrounded by white birch trees and weeping willows. It reminded me of a picture postcard. It was as if the war and the armies going back and forth had overlooked this island of peace and serenity.

As we approached the house a medium, stockily built farmer came out. Recognizing our Polish uniforms, his face broke into a smile as he appraised us shrewdly.

I was about to greet this man in the traditional Polish peasant way—"Lord's name be praised"—when our friend David asked the farmer outright if he had any fish for sale.

In Polish the word for fish is "ryba" and for carp is "karp" both words having the letter "r." David had grown up in a strictly Orthodox Jewish family and Polish was his second language. While his Polish was fluent enough, it carried a distinct Jewish intonation, with a guttural "r" that was the object of many anti-Semitic jokes. David also had a large, slightly crooked nose and a stooped figure dressed in a poorly fitted uniform. Armies the world over have uniforms in two sizes, either too small or too large, but David's uniform must have been extra large.

It didn't take the farmer a second to identify David as a Jew, and he said, imitating the Jewish sing-song, "So you want fish for Shabbos maybe?"

"Yes," answered David, not realizing that the farmer was poking fun at him.

"I do not have fish for kikes," said the farmer. "However I would be glad to sell some to you gentlemen"—addressing the rest of us.

"No, thank you," I said. "You see, we are kikes as well."

The farmer turned pale and, using his "aristocratic" Polish said, "In that case I am sorry but I don't sell fish to Jews." This time, however, he used a polite word to describe us.

Having said that he just turned around and went back to his house as fast as he could.

Now, I thought, this fellow needs a lesson in good manners, and since we had come to get fish, we just did not want to leave empty-handed.

Four young fellows could easily beat up a middle-aged man; that would not be a contest, yet it would teach him a lesson he wouldn't soon forget. The general directive to all army troops was to be polite to the civilian population, however, I was privy to the information that our unit would be moved within 24 hours or less. On the double we went to the barracks, this time leaving our friend David behind.

We took some hand grenades and, for good measure, our submachine guns. Taking off the round barrel-like magazine containing seventy-two bullets, I replaced it with a banana-type clip containing only thirty-six bullets. The round barrel magazine was not only very heavy, but also very uncomfortable on a long marches. The banana clip, when attached to the gun, rested comfortably on the back, allowing complete freedom of movement.

Thus equipped, we ran back to the farm. Whether by design or by chance, the farmer was at the pond.

His face was ashen white. I had an eerie feeling that the farmer knew we would be back. The game was up.

"Jesus, Maria!!! What are you sirs going to do?" he said, trembling. Now we were no longer kikes or even Jews. Now we were Sirs.

"Oh, nothing at all," I answered. "You know that we came here before to get some fish for the Jewish Holidays; do you think we can have some?"

"S-s-s-ure," he answered quickly.

"And how much can we get?"

"As much as you would like, sirs," His eyes were resting on my submachine gun and on the two white stripes of my epaulets.

"That is exactly what we had in mind. After all, you as a Pole, wouldn't turn hungry Polish soldiers away, would you?"

"N-n-n-o, I wouldn't."

"We didn't think so!"

Out of the bags that were supposed to house anti-gas masks came the grenades. Almost simultaneously, three grenades hit the pond, disturbing the majestic, mirrorlike surface. Accompanied by a tremendous explosion, three geysers rose towards the azure sky like three gigantic upside down crystal chandeliers momentarily suspended in mid air, each droplet of water diffusing the sun's rays into millions of small rainbows. Hardly had the three columns of water had a chance to get down when fish by the dozens deafened by the noise, came up, their white bellies gleaming in the September sun.

The farmer, like Lot's wife, had turned into a pillar of salt.

"In case you are thinking of talking to the 'Kommendatura' (M.P.), just imagine what these "eggs" can do to your house."

We weren't worried about the farmer; he would remember us as long as he lived.

Walking back to the base I reflected about what had happened. Here I was, a Jew whose forefathers had lived in Poland even before 966, the year that Poland accepted Christianity; his relatives had ridden with Berek Joselewicz and Kosciuszko and marched with General Haller. The fact that I could recite verbatim pages and pages from Adam Mickiewicz, Henryk Sienkiewicz or Juliusz Slowacki did not mean a thing to the farmer. Not even my tunic, adorned with decorations, had made any impression on him. From the moment I told him that I was a Jew, all his Polish "refinement" simply disappeared; he looked at me as if I had leprosy. I stood there naked.

While I personally did not want to hurt the poor fellow, my friend Joseph would have cut him down without blinking an eye. Still, it did feel reassuring to have my finger on the trigger. Had the situation been reversed, I'm sure we would be like the fish. We arrived back at the base loaded with fish, but we had hardly a chance to eat them before we were ordered to move out, something that was happening more and more often. We were only too happy to carry them out because they were bringing us closer and closer to the hated capital city of Germany.

The enormity of the tragedy that was befalling the Jewish people was still unknown to us in September 1944. We all hoped that further west, behind the Vistula River, we would find our relatives and friends alive. Alas, as we moved in a westerly direction our hopes kept dimming, and eventually the evidence of mass murder on a scale unparalleled in the annals of history became inescapable.

Was it a coincidence or by design that most of the concentration camps were built on Polish soil? Only with the cooperation of the native population could the Germans have been able to identify every Polish Jew. If not the majority, then a very large minority, of the Polish population participated in denouncing the Jews to the Gestapo. Had one Pole in ten hidden a Jew, nobody would have been killed. The sad truth is that not even one Pole in a hundred saved his fellow citizens who were Jewish.

To a great extent my Polish uniform, which I was so proud of, protected me from attack.

After the liberation of Warsaw on January 17, 1945, our unit went as far as the Baltic Sea, then south to Berlin and eventually to the River Elbe. Both of the Josephs, who were from Warsaw, found that no one had been left alive in that city. Their vengeance upon the Germans was total and merciless. The story of our "fishing expedition" became known throughout the unit, including our C.O. As a Russian he had no love for the Poles or vice versa. At the end of the war he contracted syphilis from a German fraulein and had to be sent to the hospital. His parting words to me were, "You are such a nice fellow; if only you weren't Jewish"; he used the polite Russian word, "Yevrei."

Well, Nikita Kirilovich Didenko, if you are still alive, I am a nice fellow not despite being a Jew but because of it. As for gefilte fish, I still like it very much and intend to eat it until I am 120.

Chapter 18

A Christmas Story: George's Story

Late in the autumn of 1944, units of the elite First Polish Army approaching from the east reached the Prague suburbs of Warsaw, the capital of Poland. The beautiful Vistula River not only separated Prague from Warsaw proper, but also divided the warring parties: the Russian Third White Army with some Polish units on the east, and the Germans on the west side of Warsaw. We shall leave it to the historians to determine whether Stalin wanted to "bleed white" the uprising Poles under General Bor-Komorowski or whether the halt was really precipitated by considerations of logistics and the desire to shorten the lines of communication.

Perhaps it was the combination of these two factors that brought the company of the 37-mm anti-aircraft artillery to Inzynierska Street (Street of Engineers) by the very large yard of the Mechanical Engineering School. The place had been well chosen strategically because it was near the Kerbedzia Bridge and the Wilenski railroad terminal.

In a relatively short time the 37-mm artillery pieces were well dug in and properly camouflaged. The 37-mm gun had several advantages over its heavier "sister," the 88-mm gun, because of its ability to change standard tracing bullets into armor-piercing ones. It thus became a formidable anti-tank weapon, simple in design but ultimately quite effective. Across the street from the 37-mm artillery stood a row of three- and four-story buildings in amazingly good condition, as if ignorant of the devastation of the surrounding area.

There are two things, more than anything else, that gladden a soldier's heart: to have the support of the local population and the sight of an enemy fleeing. The Polish population greeted the Polish Army with open arms and showered them with flowers, cigarettes and occasionally bottles of homemade brew ("bimber"). Indeed, it was the experience of a lifetime to have been present at the liberation of Prague, as the adulation of the people was completely overwhelming, with hugs, kisses and tearful smiles for all.

In vain one looked for a Jewish face; alas, there were none to be found. The Jews were simply gone. From time to time one could hear someone remark, "At least Hitler did one good thing: he killed all the Jews."

Perhaps if these people had known that these remarks were being uttered in the presence of another Jew, they would have been more careful. Somehow their idea of a Jew didn't quite coincide with that blond slim youth of 19 wearing the well-tailored uniform of the Polish Army and the insignia of his exalted rank of staff sergeant on his chest. Instead of the eagle symbol of Kosciuszko's Army (the eagle resembled an oversized chicken), he wore the honest-to-goodness proud eagle of the prewar army, albeit minus the crown.

His mannerisms and speech identified our 19-year-old hero as a native of Lvov (Lemberg), one of the old Polish bastions of nationalism and, coincidentally, the center of a large Jewish population. The high reputation of people from Lvov was reflected in their fine manners, quick wit and intelligence, which were not lost on a certain young lady who lived with her family on Inzynierska Street.

It must have been her long eyelashes and deep black eyes that attracted Olek Litwin's attention. Krystyna Kobinski was, he thought, a curious combination of the a biblical Rachel and contemporary Spanish senorita. Because of his position as an instructor, rather than because of his rank, Olek managed to see Krystyna quite often.

It is one of the ironies of wartime (or maybe its compensation) that every minute might stretch into an hour or lead to a call to battle, all of which makes the soldier most attractive. Surely, the moments spent listening to records on an old-fashioned hand-wound record player with a charming young woman belong to the happiest times in one's life. Once safely inside an apartment with darkened windows, one could and did let the war go to hell and lived for the precious moment. Only while changing the popular "szlagiery" could one hear the heavy shellings and occasional German propaganda over the loudspeakers ("Dear fellow countrymen, the Vistula is frozen, come right over"). Olek, being in love, was quite oblivious to the "golden Polish autumn" that gave way to the bitter cold winter that, in 1944, came rather unexpectedly (or, as the joke at the time went, was brought by the Russians).

It is an old Polish tradition to invite soldiers home for a big and festive Christmas Eve meal. Olek was "officially" invited to the Kobinskis for Christmas. As he had claimed that he was too busy to attend midnight mass, he could not very well have refused the Christmas invitation without arousing suspicion. Thus, at the appointed hour, he knocked at the door and was admitted to a brightly lit and tastefully furnished room. In a corner of the room stood a Christmas tree in all its splendor, gaily decorated, and somehow mocking the ugliness of the war. Olek put under it the few modest gifts he was able to obtain for the members of Krystyna's family and a bottle of vodka for her father, whom Olek had never met.

For Olek, a Jew, the Christmas holiday and its customs were somewhat alien. While wondering how to act or what to say on such a solemn occasion, his thoughts were interrupted by a friendly "Greetings and welcome!" from Mr. Kobinski, who had entered from the living room quite unnoticed. Olek clicked his heels smartly and gave Pan Kobinski a military salute. Mr. Kobinski was in his late forties or early fifties, of medium height and with slightly graying hair. While Olek had no doubt that Mr. Kobinski was an ethnic Pole, he was quite puzzled. Was it his black hair, his slightly crooked nose or the name Kobinski, which might have been shortened from the typically Jewish Jakobinski, that added to his curiosity.

Wondering if he was in the presence of brethren, Olek was invited to a seat of honor at the head of the table. The table was set magnificently, with a hand-embroidered tablecloth with matching napkins, elegant dishes and silverware, and, above all, an unbelievable array of food the likes of which Olek had not seen in a very, very long time. As delicious course after course was served, including a large variety of fish, many toasts were raised to the final victory.

Towards the end of the meal Mrs. Kobinski, Krystyna and her younger sister Irena left the dining room for the kitchen, leaving Olek alone with Mr. Kobinski. It was one of those rare moments when certain things become crystal clear when Olek addressed Mr. Kobinski with a single word, the password of the Jewish underground, "Amcho? . . . ."

"Yes," Mr. Kobinski replied, "Amcho."

Further conversation was interrupted by the smiling and excited ladies of the Kobinski household, who brought the dessert. Mr. Kobinski put his finger on his lips. The rest of the evening was spent singing carols, which every Polish child knew by heart.

At midnight Olek bade his charming hosts good-bye and reported back to his unit. Shortly afterwards it was put on full alert and the beginning of the liberation of Warsaw had begun.

On January 17, 1945 a completely destroyed Warsaw was finally free. Olek's unit kept moving steadily westward towards the heart of hated Germany. After capturing Berlin, they continued all the way to the Elbau River and the historic meeting with the American Armed Forces, where the war finally ended for Olek.

Olek never managed to see the Kobinskis again. Who knows? The Kobinskis might now be worried about Mr. Walesa or their Israeli grandchildren on a kibbutz. Olek survived the war, but every time afterwards he lit the Chanuka menorah it took him just a little longer to light the last candle.

The Furlough

With the jubilant, yet so sad liberation of Warsaw behind us, our unit of 37-mm anti-aircraft artillery kept rolling west, pulled by those magnificent 2½ ton American GMC trucks. All roads leading west seemed to be jammed with soldiers from the Russian and Polish armies in all kinds of military and civilian transport, including captured German equipment and horse driven carriages. Tired, dirty but smiling drivers displayed signs that read, "Na Berlin," (Towards Berlin). Every kilometer brought us closer to the old border separating Poland from Germany. There was a distinct smell of victory in the air.

After a brief stay in the Polish city of Poznan, we kept moving and moving. Nothing could have stopped the gigantic pincers reaching for the heart of Germany. The closer we got to Germany the better the roads were. Since every army runs on its stomach, we had to stop every couple of hours for refueling and for the mess kitchen to catch up with the rest. The food was very simple, but to the young and always hungry crews it tasted delicious, even if it was soup three times a day.

As a top kick and chemical instructor, my responsibilities were many from Logistics of the unit to directing and submitting plans to headquarters each time our company dug in and camouflaged itself, leaving visible the long and slender barrels of the guns, which looked like deadly cobras with extended necks.

While the overall responsibility for the company belonged to the company's commander, an ethnic Russian, I discovered early during our unit formation in Sumy (and I was sure headquarters knew it too) that the C.O. Captain Nikita Ivanovich Didenko was totally unqualified and at best semiliterate. His Polish was, of course, nonexistent. He had some redeeming qualities that I indeed envied: he could outdrink and out-curse anyone around. Admittedly, the Russian language is very rich, but to curse for 4 to 5 minutes without repeating himself even once was surely a sign of a genius.

His great talents, coupled with native, peasant shrewdness, kept Captain Didenko a C.O. He certainly knew how to delegate responsibility and being the product of a couple of years of Polish gymnasium qualified me as "gramotny" or well educated. So it was small wonder that I was given the captain's map, which he kept in a square leather case dangling from his side, and unable to read German maps or any other maps, I found myself leading the entire outfit.

During the day, driving, although often interrupted by false alarms about Germans being just ahead of us or right behind us and occasional equipment breakdowns, was passable, but driving at night was very difficult and extremely dangerous. Masked headlights emitted just enough light to see about 30–50 meters ahead. Sitting in the front cabin of a truck with our driver from Lvov on my left and the snoring C.O. on my right, somehow we kept going. Then the weather changed suddenly and a thick fog reduced the visibility to zero.

Unable to contact headquarters, we were forced to stop and pull off the road, forming a semicircle, posting guards and prohibiting smoking or making fire. It was a bone chilling night. In the morning the fog slowly lifted, exposing a small cluster of farms and homes.

An armed patrol was dispatched towards this small village and everybody else got ready to leave at a moment's notice. A few minutes later the patrol returned carrying bread and canned fruit. The soldiers were smiling broadly and told us triumphantly that the homes belonged to German bauers. For the first time we found ourselves inside Germany, without having realized that we had crossed the old border at night.

Having finally contacted divisional headquarters and finding our coordinates, we were issued new orders directing us northwest toward the city of Stettin on the Baltic Sea. The Germans were in full retreat, yet they were putting up a struggle, slowing down our advance, especially in Pomerania.

We had seen less and less of the German Luftwaffe and had therefore been ordered to change the 37-mm anti-aircraft ammunition from tracer to armor-piercing type, thus becoming an anti-tank artillery unit as well.

We moved, dug in and moved again. The trenches and bunkers became shallower and shallower because nobody wanted to dig regulation-size holes and the officers were not enforcing the rules, knowing that the units would soon be on the move.

One night I became the inspecting officer of the guards and my duty was to check the posts at regular intervals. The password was changed every 24 hours and all the officers and noncoms were familiar with it. I would walk over to each gun emplacement, being challenged by the soldier on guard duty.

At about the third post everything was very quiet; nobody stopped me. As I walked up closer, I noticed that the guard was soundly asleep, holding his rifle between his legs. The poor bastard hadn't heard me coming at all. I removed his rifle and moved back 50 meters, hiding the rifle in the bushes. Having done this, I returned and proceeded again towards the sleeping guard, this time whistling and loudly waking him up.

"Halt! Who goes there?" he called out.

"A friend," I said, giving him the password of the day.

"Come closer and be recognized."

Of course we knew each other well, but we had to go through the procedure.

Having returned the guard's salute I asked him what had happened to his rifle. Shock and disbelief registered on his face.

"Well, my friend, you must have been asleep, and had the Germans come during the night, we would all have been butchered! Surely you know, corporal, that the punishment for sleeping on duty is that you will simply be shot."

I had to teach this anti-Semite a lesson. Although he was always extremely polite towards me personally, he was most obnoxious with the other three Jewish soldiers of our company, who didn't have my rank or position.

I knew this and, from time to time, I would give our corporal Grudzinski some extra KP duty or pushups on a muddy field, and once even an hour of "pod-Karabin," or holding a rifle at "present arms" position for a solid hour on a rainy day.

This time I had a chance to "nail" him for good. Having finished my rounds I went to my bunker to get some sleep. A few hours of sleep left me totally refreshed and ready to face another day of army life.

I usually started the day with some form of exercise. As I stood in front of the bunker I heard shots being fired. Right next to me stood a pail containing drinking water; the bullets hit it and water started to pour out. Even then I didn't realize that I was directly in the line of fire. Something tapped me lightly on the chest and I managed to catch a hot, obviously ricochet bullet on the brass button of my uniform, flattening it completely. Thank God for brass buttons!

I sounded an alarm and the entire battery opened fire in the direction of the rifle fire coming from the nearby bushes. After a few minutes of concentrated fire, nothing remained of the bushes or the three German soldiers hiding there. A quick check through their pockets revealed only some stale bread, perforated by bullets, family pictures and what appeared to be an old condom. There was also a Luger with a slightly damaged handle, which I immediately pocketed. Whether the sight of dead enemy soldiers sharpens one's appetite is an open question, but having had so much excitement I realized that I was simply hungry and went back to my bunker for some hot tea and bread with marmalade. Barely had I bitten into the bread when several noncoms of my unit, led by my very close friend Kazimierz Jazlowiecki, came to see me.

"Olek, do you really want to court-martial Grudzinski for sleeping on duty? He was very tired and has a wife and two children; please let him off this time."

"Forget it, the bastard could have had us all killed. As soon as I finish my breakfast, I shall make out a full report and send it to divisional headquarters!"

My friend Kazik knew only too well why I was doing this. He himself had told me several times about Grudzinski's anti-Semitism. Suddenly I noticed a figure standing in the door of the bunker. It was Grudzinski himself. He knelt down, grabbing and kissing my boots. "Please spare me," he begged.

I realized that only a few minutes ago I myself had been spared by God.

"I'll let you go this time, but if I ever catch you asleep on duty again I'll cut off your balls! Is that understood? And remember for the rest of your shitty life that a Jew gave you your life back! Dismissed!!!"

There was a collective sigh of relief because everyone knew only too well my reputation for sticking to the rules.

Being a Jew in the Polish Army, one had to be tough and even more Polish than the Poles themselves; that included having shiny boots at all times, razor sharp creases in one's pants and a clean collar.

There were few handshakes and everybody left the bunker. My thoughts were interrupted by mail call.

Mail call is always more welcome than food. The few soldiers lucky enough to get mail from home would take their letters and read them back in the privacy of their bunks or bunkers. Lately I had been getting mail on almost a "regular" basis. My father would write from an ammunition factory in Cheliabinsk, in the Ural Mountains, and my Aunt Helen would write often from the Ukraine. The fortunes of war had separated our family. My father was deep in Russia, my mother and sister were living under the German occupation and I was in the army.

I cherished those letters and read them many times. They were the threads that connected me to my tomorrows. This time, in addition to my "regular" letters, there was a letter from Lublin, Poland. I tore it open and, to my astonishment, I found that it was from my Uncle Izio and Aunt Anna on my father's side. It was the first time I'd been told that my uncle and aunt had managed to save themselves by hiding from the Nazis in our native town of Drohobycz. The letter was long and very painful; it described in detail the tragic news of our family.

In the privacy of my bunker I cried uncontrollably. Right then I decided to go see them in Lublin, war or no war, with or without permission. Clutching the letter in my hand I went to see my C.O. This time, instead of addressing him in Polish as required, I switched to Russian, telling him about the letter and my desire to see my family.

"My dear fellow, believe me, I know what you and your people are going through; but this is war and I can't let everybody go see their families. Besides, I need you here too much. However, it looks as if we are going to stay here for a few weeks to guard the nearby airfield. If you can get permission from divisional headquarters, I can let you go for three or four days, but only if you give me your word of honor that you will be back."

Hearing this I simply hugged him and kissed him on both cheeks.

"Spasibo"—"Thank you very much, Comrade Captain. I won't disappoint you, I promise."

I saluted him sharply and while doing an about-face, I thought about my next step. Using the pretext of going to divisional headquarters to file present disposition plans, I took with me two bottles of recently "liberated" cognac, hoping to see Major Wolodkiewicz, the division's Chief of Staff, whom I knew rather well. Unlike many other Russian officers attached to the Polish Army, Major Wolodkiewicz was highly intelligent, soft-spoken and sensitive. I didn't have any problems reaching the major.

"What brings you here with that troubled expression on your face?"

I told him about the letter and what it would mean to me to see my relatives. Without a word, he picked up a document written in Russian and Polish—an authorization to visit general headquarters in Lublin.

"Here," he said, "go and see your family. I am writing down only the date of your departure, and you mark the date when you wish to return. I know that you will be back."

"Thank you very much, Major; I have given Captain Didenko my word that I'll be back within three to four days."

"Then good luck," he said, affixing all the necessary stamps and signatures.

"Major, I have brought you a small token of my appreciation," I said, giving him two bottles of priceless French cognac.

"I would have let you go with or without these bottles, because you really deserve this furlough, but thanks just the same."

I ran back to my unit as fast as I could. My C.O. couldn't believe his eyes when I showed him the papers.

"I must admit, you fellows really know how to manipulate people."

I wasn't about to argue with him, but simply told him that I was going to catch a ride to Lublin the first thing tomorrow. He didn't cherish the idea of letting me go but like an ancient Pharaoh, he had to comply with higher powers.

"Don't worry, Captain, I'll be back."

Leaving the C.O.'s post, I went to my own bunker singing the very popular song, "Przepustka to najpiekniejsze slowo swiata" ("Furlough is the most beautiful word in the world"). The news of my emergency leave spread like wildfire. My buddies came to congratulate and wish me well, giving me letters to hand deliver in Lublin. Among the well-wishers was the "King-Chief" cook Szymanski, bringing a very precious large can of Oscar Meyer meat products. I quickly packed a few of my personal belongings and, from a crocodile leather valise I took out a suit for my uncle, a couple of silk dresses for my aunt and an elegant diamond and platinum cocktail ring. All these items were war trophies called "szabr" "liberated" whenever possible, along with the ever-present bottle of vodka. The German Luger hidden in the small pocket of my backpack and a submachine gun completed my "luggage." Thus equipped I asked my driver Tad to drop me off at a nearby major highway in the direction of Bydgoszcz in Poland. After a few minutes I spotted a large Russian truck coming my way. I raised my hand but the truck kept on moving, so I positioned myself in the middle of the road waving my gun. The truck came to an abrupt stop.

"You stupid, frigging Pollack! Do you want to get yourself killed?"

"No, comrade Senior Lieutenant," I said recognizing his shoulder pads. "I need to get to Lublin to army headquarters. Here are my papers."

"Who needs your stupid papers, do you have some vodka?"

"Yes, I do."

"So why didn't you say so? Get in the back and let's go."

Hands appeared from under the tarpaulin-covered lorry that lifted me from the ground as the truck started to move. There were four other Russian soldiers in the truck.

"Look, fellows! This Pollack has a chicken as an emblem on his hat." He was right, of course; the metal eagle of the Polish Kosciuszko Army resembled a chicken more than an eagle.

"What can you do; such is a soldier's life," I said, pulling out a bottle of vodka and passing it around, including to the senior lieutenant sitting in the cabin. In no time at all one of the soldiers took out an accordion and soon I joined them in singing the rhythmic "Katiusza," the very sentimental "Dark is the night" and my favorite, the majestic "Officer's Waltz."

It was dark by the time we had reached the city of Bydgoszcz. We were stopped by the Russian military police looking for deserters and I was checked by the Polish police, known as "Kanarki" because of their yellow scarves resembling canaries. I asked them where I could spend the night and was advised to just knock on any door and ask for a place to sleep. My traveling companions were directed to a school; I walked a block or so and knocked rather loudly on a door of a small frame house. The door was opened by an "elderly" Polish couple; he must have been around 45 years old and she was in her early thirties. Of course, to a 20-year-old lad everybody over 30 is old.

They were visibly frightened upon seeing a soldier brandishing a submachine gun in the doorway, but recognizing the Polish uniform they gave a sigh of relief and broke into smiles. "Lord's name be praised," I said. "Forever and ever," they answered, inviting me in.

"I came to ask you for a place to sleep; you won't be bothered and I have bread which you are welcome to share."

"Please, sir, it is our privilege to be of service to our Polish soldiers. We are Jan and Janina Szczepanscy. You will sleep in our bed and we'll sleep in the other room."

After one look at the heavy down comforter I forgot about objecting to their offer. I hadn't slept on a bed like that for a very long time. Taking off my army overcoat and putting down my things, I sat down with my host and hostess to a simple meal of bread, potatoes and ersatz coffee. I expressed my thanks and went to bed, putting my pistol under my pillow. I asked the Szczepanskis to wake me up at dawn. As I covered my head with the comforter I barely heard Pani Janina say to her husband, "Look at that poor tired soldier." I didn't feel poor. I felt rich being in such a bed and never have I slept better. It was still dark outside when Pan Jan woke me up saying that it was time for me to get up. They prepared a breakfast for me that included a real egg—a luxury indeed. I ate hurriedly and thanked them for their real Polish hospitality, and I promised to stop by on my way back from Lublin. As I left the lady of the house made the sign of the cross, blessing me on my voyage. I don't know how they would have reacted had they known that I was Jewish.

Hitching on several different trucks I was able to get to the city of Lublin late that day. The first passerby I asked directions to Mickiewicza Street told me, "You're on it." A few more blocks and I had reached the building where my uncle and aunt lived. Before I knew it, the door was opened and there stood my Aunt Anna, not as tall as I remembered her from childhood. Her beautiful copper-red hair was mixed with gray, her slightly freckled face had deep lines, but her smile was still there.

We fell into each other's arms kissing and hugging, while my uncle waited for his turn. He looked much older; the war years under the Germans had aged him considerably, and the loss of their only son, I later found out, had left indelible marks on their faces and souls.

We sat down and talked and talked. I shed bitter tears on hearing about the fate of my mother and sister.

"You don't have a mother now and I don't have a son. You'll be our son," said my aunt, holding me close. I had loved her even as a child. My first skates, skis and box camera had been her gifts. She had always had time for me and was interested in my school life and activities. I had often played with her son, who was a bit younger. My uncle loved me too, but he couldn't show it. Perhaps he thought it wasn't a manly thing to do. Physically and mentally exhausted, I fell asleep, not knowing who undressed me and put me to bed. I dreamed that I was back home in Drohobycz and that the war had just been a nightmare. When I woke up my aunt was sitting nearby: "I heard you crying last night; come, get dressed. Uncle has gone to the market to get fresh rolls," she said.

I put on my army pants, boots and shirt, which had two dangling laces instead of buttons, and went to the bathroom. Unlike many apartments, this one had indoor plumbing. I had just washed my face—I still didn't shave because the peach fuzz I had was hardly worth it—when I heard a commotion and arguing coming from the parlor. Still holding the towel, I noticed two men in coats and hats. I was about to say something about wearing hats in the parlor when one of these "gentlemen" barked at me, "Your papers!!!"

I didn't like being addressed that way in general and by civilians in particular.

"Just a second, sirs, my papers are in my jacket."

"Go and get them, and make it snappy!"

"Yes, sir!" I said, returning to the bathroom and putting on my uniform, making sure my pistol was visible, and grabbing my faithful submachine gun, which luckily I had left in a corner of the bathroom so it would be out of the way. Walking back to the parlor, I slowly released the safety catch. The metallic click really shook them up.

"Well, gentlemen, which papers would you like to see?"

"Oh no, sir, we made a mistake; please forgive us."

"Hold it right there, and don't move."

My aunt had told me that the Polish police had a habit of "shaking down" Jews from time to time, accusing them of speculation so that they could be paid off: "Before we had Nazis and now we have Poles playing Nazis." Their papers identified them as members of the municipal police.

"Well, gentlemen, I am a "Frontovik," I said, using a Russian word for frontline soldier, "and my cousin is a colonel in the military police. If I ever find out that you have bothered my family again I'll make sure you spend the rest of your life keeping the white bears company. Is that understood? About face and forward march!"

I knew how brave and strong some Poles were when it came to the Jews. I didn't have a cousin in the military police, but just the promise of a Siberian vacation sufficed. My aunt, who hadn't lost her sense of humor, said, "What a performance; you even had me convinced."

As we talked and laughed, my uncle came in carrying fresh rolls and a piece of kielbasy. When told about our guests he was very worried. I assured him that nothing would happen to them. As a matter of fact, they lived in Lublin for another year before moving to the city of

Lodz, and nobody ever bothered them again. Now my aunt prepared breakfast and I took gifts out of my rucksack, having forgotten to give them the previous evening. The suit fit my uncle perfectly, the dresses needed alterations, the Oscar Meyer can of meat was a big hit and, as a special gift, I gave my aunt the diamond cocktail ring.

"My darling! I can't accept this ring."

"Auntie," I said, "the Germans took everything from you; what are you worried about?"

"Not because of that. I'll keep this ring for your wife; when you get married, it will be hers."

I didn't remember when I had laughed so hard.

"Listen, I am 20 years old and I've got to go back to the front. Besides, I don't want to get married." (Years later, when my aunt found out that I had gotten married in the States, she indeed sent the ring from Israel, where they had settled.)

When we finished breakfast my Aunt Anna said, "I noticed that you have lost a filling in your front tooth. Let's have it fixed; there's a dentist living next door."

I pleaded with her to forget it; I even promised that I'd fix the tooth the first thing after the end of the war.

The dentist fixed my tooth standing on only one foot because the other was used to operate the drilling machine. Who in my unit would believe that I had spent part of my furlough sitting in a dentist's chair?

The time flew. When the time came for my return, my aunt washed and pressed my shirts, darned my socks and baked some cookies. My uncle gave me a bottle of "bimber." We were all crying, as we said our good-byes.

"Will I ever see you again?" I asked.

"Yes, you will, we promise you."

Thus reassured, I walked quickly, trying not to turn around. With so much military transport around, I had no problem getting a ride all the way to Bydgoszcz, where I had spent my first night away from the unit. I easily located the house of Mr. and Mrs. Szczepanski. I knocked gently this time and Pani Janina opened the door, welcoming me like an old friend. She quickly prepared some food and said, "I'm sorry, but you can't stay here overnight because I am all alone. My husband went to a nearby village to see his sick mother. It wouldn't be proper."

"Proper or not proper, I am not about to start looking for another place to sleep in the middle of the night. Don't you prefer my company to that of a dozen Soviet soldiers? Besides, a good Polish soldier will be here to protect you."

There were wholesale rapes in the town. Polish women were terrified of the Tartars. (Anybody with slanted eyes was a Tartar.)

Her scruples suddenly disappeared. "Oh no! Please stay; you can sleep in the same bed by all means."

She didn't have to ask me again; I undressed and went to bed. A few minutes later Pani Janina came in from another room dressed only in a homespun nightgown and carrying a kerosene lamp.

"I only came to say goodnight," she said, putting out the light and slipping under the down comforter to join me.

"Janino," I said dropping the "Pani" for "Mrs." "You forgot to say your prayers." (I was joking.)

"Oh, my prayers have just been answered," she said removing her nightgown. Needless to say, I didn't get much sleep that night, but in the morning I felt totally refreshed, and after a brief but tender goodbye I started on my trip back to the unit.

I rejoined my company in six days rather than the four promised to the C.O. His first words to me were, "Where have you been, you son of a bitch?"

"On my furlough, Nikita Ivanovich. Major Wolodkiewicz gave me six days, so go and argue with him!"

I could be very impertinent, but only if there wasn't anybody else around. We understood each other so well All right, because we needed each other to survive.

"Davolno, get moving. Tomorrow we move again."

Chapter 19

Just Another War Story: George's Story

May 8, 1988 marked the forty-third anniversary of the end of World War II. For many, this was only a historical fact, but for those who lived to see the victors vanquished, it was a landmark in their lives.

On a sunny day in April 1945, Olek Litwin got into a street fight in Kolberg, on the Baltic Sea. One could still hear the staccato sound of automatic fire ricocheting off burned out buildings, the thunder of 85-mm artillery, see the skies covered with blue-black blankets of smoke, smell the air saturated with a mixture of spring and death.

"Forward! Let's finish Fritz!"

"Herrrraus Haende Hoch!"

"Hitler kaput!"

"Hey Stasiu, here comes a Fritz with his hands up."

"Nicht schiessen, bitte, nicht schiessen."

"Just look at them. Are they the same Krauts? Must be."

Thus the men of the third Company pressed forward from floor to floor, from building to building, from street to street: the twins, Stanislaw and Zbigniew Skoczylas, Jozef Szymanski, Kazimierz Jazlowiecki, Olek Litwin, Tadeusz Kierod and Waclaw Zakoscielny.

Wasn't there supposed to be a Jew among them? Yes, but which one? Some said that Olek is a Jew. But he couldn't be; he was 100% Polish. He was blond, spoke Polish very well and drank like a fish. Had you ever seen a Yid who could drink vodka? Of course not. This guy was as pure as the rest of us. But them why didn't he ever go to confession? Of course he was a Kike! Still, why worry about a single Jew? Hitler killed off plenty of them. If Olek was still alive, good luck to him. Remember, he saved Tadek's life, so even if he was a Jew, he was "our Jew."

"Our Jew" ran as fast as his legs could carry him, hugging buildings and watching out for telltale smoke. In his hands he held an automatic pistol (one can see the same gun at the West Point Museum, marked "Primitive but effective weapon of World War II"), as he worried about the bullets left behind.

"Quick! Let's check out this three story building." He hoped the twins were covering him; Stasiek and Zbyszek were good guys. It would be so easy to get shot, climbing the broken stairway. Nobody was upstairs; let's check out the cellar.

"Hey, Olek—throw a grenade just to be sure."

"Good idea. Out of my way, here it goes."

After the smoke had cleared the entrance to the cellar, Olek slowly entered, step by step. Suddenly he fell into something sticky. Afraid to strike a match, he put a finger in the liquid. No, it wasn't possible; he was up to his knees in honey! No longer afraid, he struck a match and saw six large wooden barrels slowly oozing honey.

The city of Kolberg fell, and the men were ordered back into those magnificent American trucks. Direction: Berlin, the heart of Germany. A long convoy of trucks moved south on the autobahn. Olek, completely exhausted, barely heard the men singing. "We are young" to the melody of "Lily Marlene" and the song about the Uhlans and the girls and widows who ran after them. No lullaby had ever sounded sweeter.

A sudden jolt and their truck came to a halt. Olek quickly reached for his gun, but there was no cause for alarm. In front of them was a long column of civilians, some pulling little wagons and displaying flags of the allied nations. Belgian, French, British and Yugoslav banners waved in the sun. Olek noticed a young man in his early twenties wearing a pajama-like suit. Something about him was disturbing. He jumped off the truck and approached him. The man, just liberated by the Russians from a concentration camp, Oranienburg, was trying to get back to Poland to look for his family. "Amcho?" asked Olek.

"Yes, I am," answered the man.

They embraced each other warmly, but there wasn't time for a longer conversation. Rushed by the officers, the men had to board the trucks.

"Wait just a minute!" From the truck, hidden underneath the gas masks (there was a rumor that Fritz might use gas as a last resort and Olek was a chemical instructor) emerged a large tin of Oscar Meyer Exclusive and an elegant crocodile leather valise containing war booty—civilian suits, shoes, shirts, etc. Then he took out a folded black top hat and threw the valise to the man standing near the truck.

"Hey Olek, what the hell do you need the hat for?"

"I want to enter Berlin in style."

The column proceeded rapidly towards Berlin, occasionally strafed by a lone Messerschmitt 109 or Focke Wulfe 110, which were themselves chased by a swarm of Russian and Polish "Stormoviki."

So this was the capital of Germany? House after house was destroyed. And was this the famous Allee Unter den Linden, now better known as Allee Unter den Bomben? Olek removed his army hat and put on his top hat, uncorked a bottle of cognac, took a long swig and sang as loud as he could, "Das ist der schoenster Tag in meinem Leben" ("This is the best day of my life"), the song Schmidt and Jan Kiepura had made so popular. There were no bravos from the long line of captured Germans marching slowly towards the east.

But there was no satisfaction in seeing the destroyed capital of hated Germany or in seeing her armies crushed. Sadness overwhelmed him. Olek knew that, sooner or later, this city would be rebuilt, but no one could give back life to those who had died.

The unit moved towards the River Elbau and its historic meeting with the American Army. For reasons known only to the Russians, no Polish soldiers were allowed near the Americans. But there was no problem obtaining the "rubashka" of a Russian soldier. How big they were; how well fed and dressed these "chocoladniks" were.

Using his intuition, Olek found a Jewish sergeant from Brooklyn. "Don't worry kid," he said. "I'll find your uncle in Williamsburg". . . and later he did.

Lo Tirzach! Thou Shalt Not Kill

We recently celebrated the anniversary of the Warsaw Ghetto Uprising. Although the following story, as told by a friend, much decorated veteran of the elite Polish First Division of the Polish Army, is not specifically about the uprising, it sheds an interesting light on the Polish Jews who participated in the liberation of Warsaw on January 17, 1945.

In September/October 1944 the units of the Second White Russian Front liberated Praga (the eastern part of Warsaw) and halted along the Vistula River, which divides Praga from Warsaw proper. Historians seem to agree that the Red Army had enough momentum to pursue the retreating German Army further without stopping for the supposed reason of "shortening logistic lines." According to some versions, Stalin was so infuriated by the premature uprising of the Polish Home Army (A.K.) under General Bor Komorowski that he decided to let the Poles "bleed white." The Germans were then able to return to Warsaw and literally destroy the entire city, capturing many combatants, among them a small number of Jews, who somehow survived.

Shortly after the liberation of Warsaw, a friend of mine spent the night on the western outskirts of the city in a small peasant hut. The place was overcrowded with soldiers and a few civilians because of the sub-zero temperature typical of Poland in the winter. Sitting in a corner of the hut, he wrote a letter to his father, who at that time was in a forced labor factory in Cheliabinsk, Ural. My friend wrote about how lucky and privileged he was to be taking part in the liberation of the capital city of Poland. As he wrote, he witnessed the reunion of two Polish sisters who had been separated by the warring armies. It was a most tender scene. After many hugs, kisses and tears, one of the sisters said, "The only good thing Hitler did was to kill all the Zhidow (kikes)." Upon hearing these words my friend got to his feet and screamed as loudly as he could, "How dare you! I am one of those Zhidow who liberated you, but you won't live to see it!" And he grabbed for his submachine gun.

Everyone got out of the line of fire, leaving the two sisters huddled together. He tried to cock his weapon, but the gun, which had never malfunctioned before, jammed. "Please don't" begged one of the sisters, falling to his feet and kissing his muddy boots. "Please, Sir, don't kill her; she doesn't know what she is saying. For God's sake, don't kill her!"

Unable to control himself, he ran out of the room, crying bitter tears. There in the cold Polish field he understood the lesson he had learned in Cheder, "Lo tirzach" (Thou shalt not kill). Jews were not meant to be murderers.

After George finished his story, they sat for a long time in silence, each one deep in his and her thoughts.

Chapter 20

The House

The two couples, Shirley and Paul and Irene and Carl, began to make plans for the future. They wanted to live near each other so that they could be together as much as possible. After many trips to different neighborhoods, they finally found something they liked, a row of attached brick dwellings on Fillmore Avenue in Brooklyn. Paul said, "We can buy two adjoining houses, have the wall between them removed and put a large glass aquarium in between. That way we can see each other through the glass."

The houses were not far from the vacuum cleaner store owned by Shirley's mother, where Paul and Shirley worked. Shirley didn't have enough money for the house. She was paying $55 rent for her apartment on Avenue J and would have to pay $90 a month towards the mortgage on the house. Paul wanted the house very much. "Look, Shirl," he said, "we'll save money on rent." To which Shirley replied, "You always tell me to buy this or that to save money. Frankly, I can't afford to save any more." But her mother gave them $10,000 towards the purchase of the house, which made the mortgage payments as small as possible. The house cost $18,800. Irene and Carl were also very eager to buy a house. They had saved as much as possible and were able to come up with $1800, just enough for a down-payment. Mrs. Flicker, Shirley's mother, offered to finance their mortgage privately.

Thus, the two couples moved into their new houses. They couldn't get adjoining houses, but they were separated by only three houses and could practically roll out of bed and be with each other.

The houses were sturdily built, two-story brick buildings with full basements. There were large front yards, which gave privacy to the front verandas. The front door led to a small foyer, a large living room to the right and a kitchen straight ahead. To the right of the kitchen was a dining room. A staircase in the foyer led to three bedrooms upstairs. In the back of the house was a small yard. The houses looked cheerful on the outside and were full of sunlight inside. A large living room window faced east, receiving sunlight in the morning, and the kitchen and dining room faced west, getting the sun in the afternoon.

Their first week there, Carl was awakened by loud noises. Looking out the window, he saw, to his surprise, a young couple playing tennis on the street in front of the house. Paul had invited them to visit his "house in the country," so they had brought their rackets and, on Sunday morning, started playing tennis right there.

Paul and Shirley rapidly expanded Mrs. Flicker's vacuum cleaner business. Paul bought a truckload of vacuum cleaner hoses and, having no place to put them, asked Carl to keep them in his basement. Carl agreed. In the middle of the Jewish High Holidays, Paul and his workers were busily washing the dirty plastic hoses in a portable swimming pool in his backyard.

This could not last very long; Paul rented larger quarters and started a mail order business. He and Shirley worked very hard and the future started to look promising.

There were amusing complications that arose in their house. Shirley had gotten a dog, a gentle-looking Collie. She put food on the table for supper, as Paul was expected home from work any minute, and the dog climbed onto a chair and ate everything. When she tried to chase him away, he started to growl; Shirley got scared, ran to the basement and screamed for help. The dog had to be given away.

Irene had had new carpets installed and Shirley and Paul came to see them. They brought along the new, young dog they had just acquired. All of a sudden Paul got up in the middle of the conversation, saying, "We have to go home, Shirley!"

They left quickly, to Irene and Carl's surprise. They could not figure out how they had insulted their friends.

A few minutes later they noticed an unpleasant odor in the house. The dog wasn't house-trained and had soiled the new carpet. Carl called Paul and asked for an explanation, but Paul was laughing so hard that he couldn't even talk. So Carl started to laugh with him. He and Irene tried to clean the carpet, but although the smell came out, the spots remained. Fortunately, they were under a table and not readily visible. Paul was so charming that nobody could stay angry with him.

The dog was very nasty. When there were guests, Paul had to lock him up in the closet. His friend Joe once tried to hang his coat up, and when he opened the closet door, he saw a ferocious beast standing there growling and snarling at him as if ready to bite. Joe was scared out of his wits, while Paul was laughing hysterically.

Paul was not really mean. He was eager to please anybody he met and give the shirt off his back to anyone in need. Carl needed only to say that he liked an article of clothing that Paul was wearing, and Paul would take it off immediately and insist that Carl take it.

Shirley was also very generous, but Irene was proud and wouldn't take gifts readily. Then Shirley got a dog Irene liked from the first minute she saw it. Without a moment's hesitation, Shirley gave her the animal. Its name was Sticks, and it was the most loyal and devoted animal one could imagine. The dog was a small mongrel with short brown hair, a mixed terrier and very intelligent, as mutts tend to be. Irene got very attached to him and took him everywhere, even to the Grand Hotel in the summer. The owners, who liked Irene and Shirley very much, pretended not to see the dog in their room. They treated Irene and Shirley like royalty.

Soon after they bought the house, Carl got very sick. It was a few days before the Jewish holiday of Rosh Hashanna, the Jewish New Year. A new couch was delivered to their house and Carl tried to help bring it up to the second floor. He may have aggravated a chronic ulcer condition.

At night, on his way to the bathroom, Carl fainted. When Irene called the doctor, he was taken immediately to Beth El Hospital (now called Brookdale). A checkup revealed that he had a bleeding ulcer and was losing blood rapidly. His hemoglobin fell to 30 percent and he was near death.

The doctors recommended an emergency operation. A gastrectomy was performed, leaving Carl with a fraction of his stomach. Paul stayed with Irene during the long wait, trying to calm her and talking all the time. After the operation Carl was taken to the recovery room. Irene's brother Milo, who was resident in that hospital, took her to the cafeteria, as she had hardly eaten anything. While in the elevator Milo saw someone he knew. "How's business?" Milo asked.

"Not so good," was the answer.

When they got out of the elevator, Milo turned to Irene and said, "See, you have nothing to worry about. The man I was talking to was the undertaker." This was Milo's sense of humor. At the most difficult times he could always find a way to cheer people up. Carl especially enjoyed his sense of humor and always laughed at his jokes.

Not everybody escaped the undertaker that day. The convicted spies Julius and Ethel Rosenberg were less fortunate. Their bodies were brought to the morgue nearby for burial by their families.

After staying a while in the hospital, Carl was taken home to convalesce. The doctor recommended six weeks' rest at home and Irene prepared a bed in the living room so that he wouldn't have to climb the staircase to the bedroom. She quit her job in order to take better care of him. Milo worked for the HIP Medical Group. He came to the house every afternoon to care for Carl and give medical advice. He assured them that the operated-on stomach would stretch back after a while and Carl would be able to eat and drink everything. However, at the moment his stomach capacity was so small that he could eat very little. He lost a lot of weight. But he recovered quickly and was impatient to go back to work. He hated to sit idly home all day.

Things were slowly getting back to normal. Irene and Carl were very happy except for the fact that Irene couldn't have children and she wanted one badly. She had gone for various medical treatments in order to conceive, but without success. It was 1958 and Irene was now 35 years old; they realized that their chance to have children was quickly slipping away.

Chapter 21

Carl's Birthday Party

It was a hot summer night in the Catskill Mountains in August 1958. Irene, Carl, Shirley and Paul were staying at the Castle Bungalow Colony near the Monticello Race Track. Shirley liked to gamble and often went there with Paul. Once in a while, they took Irene and Carl with them and made reservations in the restaurant overlooking the races and they watched them while eating dinner. Shirley and Paul liked to do everything in style; when they took their friends out there was nothing they wouldn't do to please them. Sitting at the dining table and watching the races, with the sun setting and the evening moon slowly rising, was really enchanting.

Their friends Joe, Elaine, George, Gisa and several other couples were staying down the hill at Spector's Bungalow Colony. There were Latzie and Ruth and their teenage daughter. Ruth, a survivor of the Holocaust, was an exceptionally pretty young woman and had once even been offered a chance to go to Hollywood. She had married Latzie in a D.P. camp in Germany when she was only 16. She soon became pregnant and had a daughter, Ilona. They emigrated to the United States and Ruth became sick with tuberculosis. She had to go to a sanatorium. Her mother took care of the growing child. When Ruth came back cured, her relationship with her husband had deteriorated. She was a German Jewess, while Latzie was a Hungarian Jew. They had different backgrounds and levels of intellect, with Ruth reading a lot while Latzie was mainly interested in business.

Then there were Richard and Irene. Richard had graduated in dentistry from the university in Munich and Irene and Carl knew him well, though they had never been close. Irene was a very beautiful woman and had even won first prize in a beauty contest given by the Jewish community in Munich.

It was Carl's thirty-fifth birthday and Irene decided to make him a party. She prepared food and drinks in the bungalow colony downhill and everybody had a very good time. Carl had a few drinks and quickly got drunk. Paul and he had dared each other and other friends to show who could drink the most. Then they filled their glasses with vodka and said, "Bottoms up!" Now Carl sat in a garden chair holding an unfinished glass of whiskey in his hand.

Suddenly a pretty young woman sat on the armrest of his chair. It was Ruth, Latzie's wife. Carl was flattered by her attention, though he didn't care for her. But Irene became furious. She thought that Ruth was sitting on Carl's lap and she asked Shirley to leave with her. They returned to their cottage in a rage.

Carl noticed that Irene was missing and went looking for her. Someone told him she had gone home. He found Paul and the two drunken men, holding plates of food high like waiters in a restaurant, started to walk unsteadily up the hill. Walking with their plates above their heads, they started to laugh hysterically.

Irene heard them laughing and getting closer. She got into the car to leave. Upon seeing this, Carl lay down across the road. Irene started the car and began to drive slowly towards him, at which point Paul jumped into the car and stopped her.

They all went into the bungalow, where they lay down on the beds and watched the ceiling, which seemed to be rotating. Paul's teeth were chattering, while Carl began to feel queasy. He went to the bathroom and started to throw up. Irene run after him and, seeing that his head was approaching the water in the toilet bowl, grabbed him by the hair. She spent most of the night holding his head up by the hair over the toilet and swore never to make him a birthday party again.

The beautiful Ruth did leave her husband, but not for Carl. She ran away with Richard the dentist. Ruth left her husband and daughter Ilona and Richard left his wife, the beautiful Irene, and his son. Latzie, who loved Ruth very much, died a few years later, a broken and lonely man. Ilona, their daughter, who was as beautiful as her mother, committed suicide by jumping into the Thames River in London at the age of eighteen. Many people were affected and a series of tragedies resulted from these two broken marriages.

Chapter 22

The Children

Like Irene, Carl wanted a child, but he knew that Irene could not have one and accepted the fact. He was busy with work and school and his life was very active. He was working towards a Master's degree in chemistry.

Irene had also enrolled in college and received partial credit for her studies in Germany. She intended to get a B.A. in biology. However, this did not fully occupy her, and she thought all the time about having a family of her own. She had a very good doctor and he did everything possible to help her. One day he called to ask her and Carl to come to his office. He said, "I am sorry to say that all our attempts to open Irene's fallopian tube were futile. She cannot conceive. There may be a slight chance that, if she underwent a major operation, her tube could be opened. But even then there is no guarantee."

He saw Irene's eyes water; her disappointment was obvious. He continued, "It is a shame that it had to happen to you; you would make wonderful parents." He paused. The couple saw that he wanted to say something else but was hesitant. Finally the doctor said, "Please forgive me for being so outspoken, but I feel that there is a child out there who would be very lucky to have you as parents. There is an agency in Manhattan." He wrote the name on a piece of paper and gave it to Carl. "Think about it. I am sorry I cannot do more for you."

The couple left. They walked to the car in silence. In the car Carl said, "Don't worry, Irene, we will have a full life. I love you and you are more important to me than having children. We will arrange our lives accordingly."

Irene didn't answer. She was on the verge of tears and didn't want to show her deep sadness. She thought that maybe she should go through with the operation. The doctor hadn't held out much hope but maybe. . . . No; she thought of her last operation. It had taken a very long time to recover and she didn't want to be disappointed again. She would have to accept this fact of life.

When Anna came from Poland to visit, she brought regards for a couple in Queens; they all went to see them. They were a nice couple; during the conversation they mentioned that they had recently adopted a child through an agency, the same agency the doctor had mentioned to Irene and Carl. Th couple were ecstatic about the baby; they finally had a family after twelve years of marriage.

That night Irene said to Carl, "Maybe we should think about adopting a baby?" Carl's reaction was negative. "No," he said "we'll manage without children." He was so firm about it that he left no room for discussion.

The next day, when Irene told Anna about this conversation, Anna said, "Why don't you go to the agency and register with them and see what happens. You can always refuse a baby if Carl doesn't change his mind."

They went to Manhattan the following day and Irene registered with the adoption agency. She didn't say anything to Carl.

A month passed and one day Irene got a letter addressed to them both from the agency. With shaking hands she opened it. In it was an invitation for Irene and Carl to call for separate appointments in connection with her application. Now she had to tell Carl the truth. His reaction was surprising. He accepted the fact and was willing to cooperate. They called up the agency and made their appointments.

On the day of the appointments Irene met Carl in the city. She was called into the room of the social worker first. Her name was Mrs. Kundrat. She explained that this was a preliminary appointment and didn't mean they would get a child. There would be several appointments and a visit to their home before a decision was made as to whether to allow them to adopt a baby. "Please don't build up too much hope; there are ten couples waiting for each child and they are screened very carefully," she cautioned.

Mrs. Kundrat asked Irene many questions about her childhood and her present life, about her marriage, health, etc. At the end she told her that she would be called for another interview in about a month.

Carl was called into her office next; Irene hadn't even had a chance to tell him anything about her talk with the social worker. Only after Carl's interview could they exchange their impressions. Thus began the process of adopting a baby. They wondered what the future held in store for them.

It was a very exciting time. They visited the adoption agency several times during that year. They were interviewed separately and together. Mrs. Kundrat came to visit them at home and made sure that, if they got a baby, there would be a separate room for it and that the conditions were right. Irene checked the mail constantly in the hope that there would be some word from the agency.

Finally, after a whole year, they received a phone call from Mrs. Kundrat. She said, "Mrs. Horowitz, we have good news for you. The agency has decided to let you and Mr. Horowitz adopt a baby. The baby was born two weeks ago; it is a girl. We would like you to come and see her. When can you come?"

Irene sat down; she couldn't speak.

"Are you there, Mrs. Horowitz?"

"Yes, please forgive me. We can come today."

Mrs. Kundrat laughed. "No, not today, but if you can come Friday it will be convenient."

"Oh yes, we will be there."

She hung up and called Carl. He was excited and overjoyed. This was Wednesday; they could hardly wait for Friday.

On Friday the two of them went to the adoption agency to meet Mrs. Kundrat. "Let's go to the foster home where the baby is."

They arrived at the home about 45 minutes later and were taken to a room where the baby lay in a carriage. She was a tiny little thing, so beautiful. They didn't move. After a moment the baby opened her eyes. She smiled, or so they wanted to believe. Later they were told that it was only a grimace, but they wanted to believe it was a smile.

"The baby is healthy and seems to be content," Mrs. Kundrat said. "Would you like to hold her? What a question! But Irene was afraid to pick her up.

"Don't be afraid," said Mrs. Kundrat, babies don't break easily." Irene bent down and picked up the child who would finally make her a mother. Tears fell down her face. Her happiness was complete.

Mrs. Kundrat watched them. "We will leave now. Go home and prepare for your baby." Carl asked if they could have lunch together to discuss the particulars. She agreed.

Over sandwiches she told them a little about the baby's background and asked what they wanted to name her. The couple said that since both their mothers' names started with the letter "A," they had decided to name the baby Alice. Mrs. Kundrat was taken aback. "The baby was named Alice at birth; you won't have to change anything. I believe she was truly meant for you." They laughed. After they took Mrs. Kundrat back to her office, they went home to prepare for the new addition to their family. They went on a wild shopping spree for infant's clothes, furniture and dozens of other things the baby needed. They could hardly wait to take her home. Finally the day came. They picked up the social worker in the city and continued on to the foster home. They brought the baby home and were greeted by all their neighbors with well wishes and gifts. Everyone was excited and wanted to see the baby. The only one that was not happy was their dog Sticks. The next day he came home with a broken leg and had to be taken to the animal hospital. Carl had never heard of a dog breaking his leg. He thought that Sticks must have done it deliberately out of jealousy of the baby.

Now their lives changed completely. It revolved entirely around the baby. Irene was a born mother: she knew exactly what to do and Carl watched her in amazement. Irene busied herself with her chores with the expertise of an old pro and wanted to do everything herself. When the baby cried at night she was the first one to run to the nursery, change the diapers or clean up the baby. She gave her all her love and attention.

They named the baby Alice Joy for the joy she had brought into their home.

Shirley and Paul wanted to have a child too. Shirley had a hormone deficiency and could not have a child of her own. Inspired by Irene's example, they adopted a child too. It was also a girl, and they named her Betsy Irene. The baby had been born with a dislocated hip and had to be kept in a cast for many months at the beginning. She was visibly uncomfortable in the cast. However, she didn't cry, she only moaned and sighed.

Now both couples were extremely busy in their new roles as parents and could not see each other as often as before. Also, they could not go out as freely as they wanted. Shirley hired a black woman to help her with her chores. Her name was Gladys and she was an extraordinary person. She took over all the work in the house, cooked, cleaned and took care of the baby. This left Shirley free to pursue her favorite pastime, which was going to the racetrack. Specifically she loved the trotters. She once said to Irene and Carl, "When I was a young girl an uncle took me to the trotters. When I saw the horses pulling the two-wheel carriages and the jockeys driving them and racing around the track, I thought it was beautiful. Since then I have been in love with the trotters."

Shirley loved to gamble. She would go to the $100 window until, one day, the Daily News printed a picture of her with the caption, "Who is this blonde at the one-hundred-dollar window?"

Once in a while Shirley won a large amount of money. When this happened, everybody who heard about it would run to the track, hoping to win too, and, of course, they lost. Paul was not a gambler, but he played along with Shirley. When they had some money he even bought some racehorses and would take Carl to the stables to talk to the jockeys, probably in the hope of getting some tips.

Irene became completely involved in bringing up Alice and neglected her best friend. The fact that the child was adopted didn't matter to them, although the agency had advised them to inform the child about it as early as possible. They decided to follow this advice and were never secretive about it. As soon as Alice could understand, they told her too. She ran up to everybody and told them proudly, "I'm adopted," not really understanding what it meant.

Alice was an unusual girl, full of charm and personality. She created a special atmosphere that made people love to be around her. Carl loved to hold her on his arm for hours and she loved it too. He imagined her grown, as his companion. He imagined how proud he would be of her. Meanwhile, however, she got so used to falling asleep on his arm that she would not go to sleep any other way. The moment he put her in her crib she would wake up crying. He had to pick her up until she fell asleep again. Finally Irene and Carl decided to break her of this habit. The next evening they put her in her crib and left the room. Alice screamed and started to cry. Meanwhile her parents held each other's hands in order not to give in. Alice kept crying for an hour, until she finally got tired and fell asleep. The next night this procedure was repeated and Alice cried for only half an hour before falling asleep. On the third night she only cried for 15 minutes, and after that she went to sleep without her father's shoulder.

One night they were awakened by unusual noises. They ran into Alice's room. There she was standing in her crib, happily smearing her excrement all over it, on the nearest wall and herself. Carl almost fainted, but Irene grabbed the child and put her in the bathtub. She spent most of the night cleaning up the baby and the mess in the room.

On more peaceful occasions, however, it was a pleasure to watch Irene bathe the baby. She prepared warm water in a small basin, undressed her and placed her in the bath. Alice was plump and well fed. She had almost no neck and looked like a couple of sausages connected together. As Irene soaped her thoroughly from top to bottom, Alice chirped happily in the water. She loved to play in the water. Irene rinsed off the soap with a sponge and lifted her out, saying the Polish nursery rhyme, "The water has lost and the baby has gained."

She wrapped her in a towel and dried her gently. Then she applied a heavy layer of zinc salve to her underarms and other areas. The baby had very sensitive skin and got rashes easily. She also caught cold easily and was often sick. Fortunately, Irene's brother Milo was now a practicing pediatrician and visited Irene every day. His professional help and moral support were indispensable.

Irene relied on Milo for so much that it occasionally created comic situations. Once Milo gave her a book describing what the child should be doing at every age, week by week and month by month. Irene followed the child's development with this book in her hand. When Alice didn't start to do something she was supposed to do, Irene got worried. She would ask Milo to explain and he would say, with his usual sense of humor, "The baby didn't read the book."

Once Carl came home from work and found the following drama unfolding before him: Alice was crying. Herta, who was there on a visit, was holding her, trying hard but unsuccessfully to calm her down. Irene was on the telephone, saying, "Operator, please connect me with Doctor Mandel; his line is busy." The operator said, "I can only do that in emergencies."

"Then, please interrupt his conversation, this is an emergency." Finally, she reached him: "Milo, the baby is crying, she must be sick. What should I do?"

"Maybe she is hungry; why don't you feed her?" answered Milo.

"I fed her only 3 hours ago; you told me to feed her every 4 hours."

Eventually she fed her and the baby stopped crying.

Alice was growing up quickly and Irene started to think about adopting a second child. "A child should have a brother or a sister. It will be important for her now and in her adult life," she said firmly to Carl, and he saw the logic of it.

This time the adoption agency was more than happy to fulfill their request. They knew their background and the social worker visited them to see how Alice was doing. She was very impressed and promised to recommend them to her office.

Thus, after more than two years since the first adoption, they were informed that they could have another child. Again they were taken to a foster home to see the baby. This time it was a 6-month-old girl who had recently had chicken pox.

They liked her very much and, on their second trip, they took her home. On the way to their house, they tried to get friendly with her but the child seemed aloof and suspicious. Finally Carl took a bunch of keys on a chain from his pocket and slowly jingled them in front of her. She smiled for the first time and took an immediate liking to Carl.

They named her Terry Jacqueline in memory of Milo's first wife Teresa, whom Irene had loved very much. She had been killed by the Germans in the last days of the war. They had loaded all the prisoners onto a boat, sent it to sea and torpedoed it. All the prisoners, including Teresa, perished.

Milo told Irene to be especially careful with Terry, but Irene had a hard time in the beginning, since Terry was set on eating the way she had in the foster home. She refused to eat eggs or drink milk, which were essential for her health, and would spit out the food. The only way she would accept food was as a liquid cereal in a bottle with a large hole in the nipple.

However, under Irene's experienced care Terry grew quickly and soon surpassed Alice in size. She was a blond, robust little girl and very friendly; Alice was a delicate girl with dark hair. Both girls were very pretty. The house was always full of their voices and laughter. When Carl came home at night he was almost torn between his two daughters. They both wanted his attention. Irene was put aside in the evenings; they had their father.

Chapter 23

Clare And Artie

Now that Irene had two daughters she realized how different children could be. Terry was much more secretive than Alice. Alice liked to share her experiences, but Terry didn't unless she was sure that she had accomplished what she wanted. A typical example was puzzles. Alice liked to put puzzles together with Irene and mastered this art very quickly. She was an expert at the age of 3. Terry would sit down in the corner of the room with her puzzle so that nobody could see what she was doing. She worked hard and was very happy when she finally achieved her goal. Both of them were bright and a joy to be with.

They played well together. Alice, being the older one, set the tone for their games. Her friends twins Ruth and Beth were always on hand and Terry played with them too. Even though she was two years younger than they she was mature enough to keep up with them and they liked to having her around.

Terry grew beautifully. She was tall and mature for her age, perhaps because she wanted to keep up with her sister and the twins.

Carl enjoyed his daughters very much and gave them all the time he could afford. They in turn loved to be with him. He played games with them and made them laugh. He was not much of a disciplinarian, and Irene had to handle that when it was necessary.

At 14 months, Alice was a delightful child, very lively and always full of ideas. She already spoke well and liked to play with dolls. She also liked to color with crayons and could spent much of her time absorbed in that.

"Mama," she would say, "do you like red or green?"

"Green," Irene would answer.

"Why green?"

"Because it is a pretty color."

"Red isn't pretty?"

"Oh, yes, it is pretty too."

"And I like green too," Alice would say. "I will color the horse green."

Alice was able to busy herself with anything she enjoyed doing for hours at a time. Irene was able to clean the house or prepare dinner while Alice played with a toy. She made sure the child was in the same room so she could watch her. This baby had come to Irene late in life and she was the most important thing to her. Taking care of Alice was Irene's biggest pleasure.

Carl worked in Manhattan and was home by about 6:30 in the evening. Alice would wait for him at the door. As soon as he came in she took him by the hand and wanted him all to herself. He was more then willing to cooperate.

In the meantime Irene would put the final touches to dinner. Carl changed his clothes, washed up and they sat down to eat. Alice would nibble, as she had already eaten her dinner. She kept them company and then it was time for her to go to bed.

In the afternoons Milo would come to visit. He worked in Brooklyn and, after his office hours, he had to stay on call. Instead of sitting in the office he came to Irene's house; his office called him there with messages.

Irene would make him lunch and good coffee, which he liked. They were very close and he was good company. The arrangement suited both of them. Alice loved Milo too. He was very patient with her and played with her all the time.

Often Shirley came by for a little while to say a quick hello. She worked during the day, but she always found a few moments for a visit.

One day the bell rang; Shirley was standing on the porch. She said, "We have new neighbors; they are just moving in. The woman is young and very pretty and they have children about Alice's age."

Irene was interested. She knew that a house on the block had been sold, it would be very nice to have little children whom Alice could play with. She went out to the porch and looked towards the house, two houses away. The people who were moving in must have been inside.

A few days later a neighbor, Zelda, told Irene about the new neighbors. "They are a young couple and they have twin girls 14 months old. Imagine, they are exactly Alice's age and girls too!" Zelda said. "Now you won't have to worry about finding children for Alice to play with."

"We will see," Irene answered, "when we meet these new people," but she was excited at the prospect of having someone new on the block.

She met Clare and Artie a few days later. They seemed very nice and likable. Little did she know at the time that her relationship with Clare would turn into a lifelong friendship.

Irene didn't work. She was very content with her present life. In the morning she would clean up and prepare dinner. At around 10:30, she dressed Alice and they went for a walk, Alice in a stroller.

On this particular day, as Irene was pulling the stroller down the stairs, she noticed her new neighbor Clare on her porch, with the little girls running back and forth. Irene walked over and stopped in front of Clare's house.

"How are you doing in your new house?" she asked.

"OK, I guess. There are so many things to take care of. Artie tries to take care of everything, since my hands are full, as you can see." She pointed to the twins. Both girls held on to Clare's dress, apparently a little shy and fascinated with the lady and the little girl.

Irene laughed. "I can imagine that it isn't easy for you. I have one child and I am busy all the time. How do you manage to feed them?" she asked.

Clare smiled. "Artie helps when he's at home; otherwise it is quite a job. It is better now that they are older. When they were babies I tried to feed them at different times."

"Why don't you sit down?" Clare suggested.

Irene was glad to. She liked the young woman. She took Alice out of the carriage and went up the steps. This was the beginning of their friendship. The little girls, Beth and Ruth, were adorable and they both fell in love with Alice.

The women established a routine. After the usual morning chores they would meet outside and stay together either on Clare's or Irene's porch. The girls played together and were no trouble. Meanwhile the two young women got to know each other. They were both warm, sensitive people and they had a lot to talk about.

Clare wanted to know about Irene's war experiences and they spent many hours talking about that time in Irene's life. Clare was very sympathetic. They felt very comfortable with each other. They had similar backgrounds and were more or less on the same intellectual level. Their relationship grew closer every day.

Shirley was a little jealous. She and Irene had many friends, but till now she had been in a special category. Now her friendship with Irene was threatened by this new person.

Shirley was right. Irene did feel very close to Clare. The two women needed one another. They had the same interests and enjoyed doing things together, and they lived near each other, which made everything even easier. Their children got along very well, which drew them even closer together.

Irene loved Shirley and didn't want to hurt her. She was very careful about how she talked to her about Clare. Somehow she managed to keep up these two relationships without complications. Shirley and Clare were very different and Irene had to balance between them all the time.

This wasn't too hard. Shirley worked during the day, when Irene was with Clare, and Irene always found time for Shirley in the evenings or during the weekend. In Shirley's presence Irene was always laughing and enjoying herself. She had a great gift for creating a good time.

Clare was much more serious. She was someone that Irene could talk to and listen to. She could talk to Shirley, but by nature Shirley was light and funny. Irene was happy with both of her friends and she loved them both.

After Alice went to sleep Irene had time for herself. Carl would stay home and she was free to do whatever she wanted. After dinner she would go shopping, visit Shirley or spend time with Clare. Artie was very good with his children. They were not good sleepers like Alice and stayed up till all hours. Artie didn't mind. He gave Clare the freedom to do what she wanted.

Often in the evening, Clare and Irene went out to Kings Highway, which was a very nice shopping area. They would have ice cream or go to dress shops, or sometimes just window shop. They had a wonderful time together.

One day Irene asked Clare if she had been born in the same house her parents lived in now. To Irene's amazement Clare said, "I wasn't born in the United States, I was born in Belgium."

"What?" Irene was shocked. "I took it for granted that you were born here!"

"Not at all," Clare answered. "I came here when I was 5 years old."

"Tell me about it."

They sat on Irene's porch as it was getting darker. It was a beautiful summer evening. The two women sat till late in the evening talking about Clare's childhood and youth.

"My mother sent me to America with her sister and my aunt on one of the last ships leaving Europe in 1940. She couldn't leave Europe because she didn't have a visa to the United States. My Aunt Hilda got a visa to America because she registered in time, together with my Aunt Regina. My mother never registered. I was born in Belgium and, as a Belgian citizen I didn't have a problem in obtaining a visa; I suppose that there was no quota set on Belgian immigrants to the United States.

I was 5½ years old at the time and didn't really know what was happening. I remember our arrival at the New York port. I had been sponsored by distant relatives, Jack and Tessie, and they were supposed to pick me up at the port when I arrived. To this day I am not sure why they didn't come to the port.

We waited for them but nobody came. I couldn't leave the port without legal guardians, so I was sent to Ellis Island. My Aunt Hilda wouldn't let me go by myself, so she came with me."

Clare was visibly distressed. These memories were so vivid that she had to try to put her thoughts in order.

Irene remembered when she herself had visited a friend who had come to the United States illegally and had been sent to Ellis Island. She remembered the buildings and the large halls, with all the people crowded into them. She could almost picture Clare, the little girl of that time, in those surroundings and a cold shiver came over her.

She said quietly, "How long were you there?" Clare looked at her strangely. She was so lost in her thoughts that she had probably forgotten about Irene. Now she came back to reality.

"I was there a few days. Tess and Jack didn't come for me till Friday. I don't know why it took them so long."

"And then?" Irene asked."

"They took me to their house." Clare had tears in her eyes. "I spent six and a half years there." She was clearly upset. Irene could see her struggling with her emotions.

"Don't talk about it anymore," Irene said. "We'll talk about this some other time."

"No, I want you to know. I don't talk about this to anyone, but I feel very close to you and I would like to tell you about that part of my life.

"The house Jack and Tess took me to was very nice. Jack was a dentist and he did very well. They had two children—Estelle, who was about 9 or 10 years old, and Morton who was about 7 or 8."

"Were you close with them?"

"Estelle was just there; I had very little to do with her. My relationship with Morton was closer. He treated me better, sort of like his younger sister. I used to wear his shoes when he outgrew them."

"His shoes? Why? Didn't you have your own shoes?"

"No, I had to wear his shoes and I hated it. I was ashamed but I had no choice. I went to school from there. I called Tess and Jack Mother and Father. I didn't want to be different from other children. I never told anybody that they were not my parents."

"And your father? Where was he at that time?"

"My father was here in New York. He lived in Manhattan in a furnished room and we lived in Brooklyn. He worked and couldn't take care of me. He would come to visit me every Sunday. Later, when he moved to Brooklyn, he came often in the evenings, late, to spend a few minutes with me. I agonized every time he left me.

"Shortly afterwards my father enrolled in the army and was sent off to Europe. I stayed at Jack's house till the end of the war and longer."

"When did you see your mother again?"

"My mother came here in April 1946 as a war bride. I was 12 years old at the time. They bought me a new outfit and we went to meet my mother at the pier. I will never forget that day as long as I live. I brought her flowers. I recognized her immediately when she came down and ran to her. My father came down behind her."

"And you lived happily ever after?" Irene was relieved that Clare was together with her parents again. "Not really," Clare said. "I had to go back to Tess and Jack for another two weeks until our house, which my father had bought, was ready."

"It was too much for me to accept. I cried well into the night. When I finally went to my parents house after those endless two weeks I walked in and kissed the walls."

Clare stopped, exhausted. Her cheeks were red and her eyes were full with tears.

Irene took her around and hugged her. It was dark and the hour was late. "I'll see you tomorrow," she said to Clare. "Try not to think about it anymore tonight."

"I'll sleep better tonight. It took a big load off my chest, talking to you."

Irene was very busy and happy these days. She and Carl finally had Alice and Terry. Nothing was too hard for her. She handled the cleaning, cooking, shopping and cared for the children. She had found a purpose in her life in raising a family. The girls were very good but, being two years apart, it was getting a little difficult to watch them. Irene, being a perfectionist, overdid it. Everything had to be just right.

She had time for everything except herself. Running after the children all day and doing all the chores, she started to lose weight. Her old cough came back. When she went to the doctor he told her to take time out during the day to rest, but that was easier said than done.

Alice napped during the day but Terry didn't sleep day or night. She would wake up in the middle of the night and try to wake Alice. Terry had a bad temper but, as time went by, she became more secure and behaved much better. Alice got along with her little sister very well and tried to help Irene take care of her.

Irene and Clare usually met around 12 o'clock. They would eat at a local luncheonette just to break the routine. Afterwards, they stayed together until it was time to start dinner.

Sitting on the front porch, while the girls played near them, they talked about their lives, about current affairs, about everything that went on around them. "Do you realize, Irene," Clare said on a beautiful, balmy afternoon as they watched the children play, "that this is a wonderful time for us."

"I would even go further than that," Irene answered. "I would say that this is the best time in my life. I am at peace with myself. I enjoy every moment and I am grateful for this. My life is fulfilled. This is what I always wanted: to have children. I hope the time goes slowly; I would like this to last forever."

"Unfortunately, it will end," said Clare, "but let's enjoy it while we can. This time belongs to us."

Often in the evenings after dinner and after the children were in bed, Shirley and Paul would come over to visit Irene and Carl. On Sundays Shirley made southern fried chicken and home-made french fries, which, for Irene and Carl, was a real feast. The men always talked about Polymer Company, which was slowly growing. The women had a lot to discuss.

Then there were George and Gisela. George came from Drohobycz, a town near Irene's home town in Poland, Boryslaw. They knew each other because George's relatives had lived near Irene, and George would come to visit them. They were children at the time and had little to do with each other. They met again casually in Germany and then in New York. Now they were close friends.

Chapter 24

Starting A Company In 1963

Carl knocked impatiently at the door of Paul's new house. He was clearly agitated. "Paul, I am in trouble, you have to help me!" he cried.

"What happened?" asked Paul.

"Well, your friend Jack went to my company and told our salesman that I am working for you in the evenings and on weekends. You know how possessive Mr. Yardney is about his employees. If he finds out that I'm working on the side, he'll fire me."

Mr. Yardney considered his employees his soldiers and ruled them with an iron hand. He liked Carl very much and Carl knew how Yardney would react. It was not uncommon for him to call an employee to his office and humiliate him in front of the entire staff.

Paul had heard many stories about Carl's chemical inventions at Yardney's and had tried to convince him to leave his job as research director, a position Carl had taken over after the death of Dr. Mendelsohn, his mentor and the previous director of research. Paul wanted Carl to start a chemical company with him, but Carl was not ready. Finally Paul was able to convince Carl to do some research for him on the side.

Carl's first invention was a bactericidal treatment for vacuum cleaner bags to eliminate odors coming from the vacuum cleaners. The product did so well that competitors became worried; one of them, Jack, simply went to Yardney and denounced Carl. Fortunately, the man to whom Jack spoke was Carl's friend and he didn't report it to Mr. Yardney; but he did tell Carl. And there was always the possibility that sooner or later Mr. Yardney would find it out.

Paul saw that Carl was very disturbed and promised to help. He went to Jack, who was his competitor, and spoke to him. Paul was a charmer and could convince anybody of the merits of his case. Jack stopped trying to hurt Carl, but the incident engraved itself deeply in Carl's memory.

Paul was now doing very well financially. He decided to move out of his relatively modest house on Fillmore Avenue and was looking for a bigger house. Typically, he came home one day and announced to Shirley, "Honey, I've just sold our house."

"Do you have another house for us?" asked Shirley anxiously.

"No, but we'll find something," he answered confidently.

"Where will we live in the meantime?" she asked. This problem had not entered Paul's mind, and for a while they lived with Irene and Carl.

After a few weeks of intensive searching, Paul found a beautiful mansion not far from where they lived. It had previously been inhabited by the Fortunoffs, the owners of a large department store in Brooklyn. The owners had moved their store to Long Island and decided to sell the house. Paul bought it for $45,000 dollars. It was a one-story structure with many rooms, a huge kitchen, a sunken living room and several bedrooms. A large garden occupying an acre of land surrounded the house, replete with trees, lawns and a playground in the backyard.

Again Paul tried to persuade Carl to go into business with him. He wanted to start a chemical company for Carl where he would provide the financing and Carl would perform the research.

Irene was enthusiastic about the project. "Carl, this is your only chance to become independent in business. Paul can do it now, and he is willing to do it. An opportunity like this may never come again."

Carl wavered. "I am afraid," he kept saying. "Suppose the business does not succeed; what will we do then?"

"You can always go back to work for somebody else," she said confidently. "You don't have a guarantee on your job either."

Carl went to Mr. Yardney and told him that he wanted to talk to him. Yardney, immediately sensing that it was a serious matter, suggested that Carl come over on Sunday to his apartment near Central Park.

That Sunday morning Carl was so nervous that Irene suggested he take a tranquilizer, which he had never done before. He was still pretty nervous when he arrived at his boss's elegant home. He knew the apartment well. He and Irene had been guests of Mr. Yardney and his wife Susan many times. Irene's brother Milo was married to Mrs. Yardney's niece Dita. On their visits, the conversation always centered on the company, Mr. Yardney's favorite subject.

This time, however, Mr. Yardney looked at Carl curiously. He did not expect anything.

"Mr. Yardney, I would like to quit my job," said Carl after they had exchanged the usual pleasantries.

"What do you mean? Do I hear you correctly?" Yardney was visibly shaken.

"I intend to start a business of my own," continued Carl. "It will not be in the area of silver–zinc storage batteries," he added. Yardney's company was completely devoted to the manufacture of these high-power batteries for the United States Government.

Now Yardney looked at Carl with a stony stare, "I will never trust people like you again," he thundered. "You betrayed me."

Carl walked out of his apartment with Yardney's words ringing in his ears. On the next day Yardney called Carl to his office. Several executives were present. Dr. Simon, his legal adviser, began: "Carl, I understand that you intend to leave the company?"

"Yes, I do," answered Carl. He liked Dr. Simon. He thought that the feeling was mutual.

"We have decided to increase your salary substantially if you stay."

Dr. Simon tried to change Carl's mind, but Carl stuck stubbornly to his guns. He felt that once he had told Yardney he was leaving, their relationship could never be the same.

That afternoon Mr. Yardney's son Johnny came over to Carl, who was working as usual in the laboratory. Carl could not sit around doing nothing, even though he was not working for the company anymore. He liked Johnny and he felt that the young boy looked up to him. Johnny spent the whole afternoon with Carl and reported back to his father that Carl's decision was unchanged.

"Paul, what should we call the company?" asked Carl when they met in the evening.

"Maybe we should call it PICS," suggested Paul. Remember, we once wanted to start a company and name it after the first letters of our names: Paul, Irene, Carl and Shirley. We will all be partners, the four of us, right?"

"No we won't," interrupted Irene. "You two should be the only partners. Shirley and I will not interfere. It will be better that way."

Carl thought about the name of the company. At the time he was still studying for his Master's degree in polymer chemistry at the Brooklyn Polytechnic Institute. He, along with many other students, was fascinated by the lectures given by the famous professor Herman Mark, the venerable father of plastics science and industry. Professor Mark liked Carl and often summoned him to his office, where he would show him the latest articles and inventions before they were even published.

Polymer Research Corporation of America: that name seemed to roll off one's tongue. It almost sounded musical. Carl suggested the name to Paul, who accepted it immediately.

There was still the question of Carl's salary; Irene recommended that it be the same amount that he was last earning at Yardney's. Paul would pay all the initial expenses of the company for a year, and then the company should be able to support itself. If not, they would dissolve the partnership.

Paul gave the company a small front store on Coney Island Avenue next to Flicker's Vacuum Cleaners. It was an addition built originally as an expansion of Flicker's. Flicker's was now flying high under the combined leadership of Paul and Shirley and occupied a much larger place. They did not need the small building and it was ideal for Carl. It was new and cheerful. He immediately ordered chemicals for his work although he didn't have any idea what he would be working on. The general plan was for him to invent things and for Paul to sell them.

He missed the busy, electrifying atmosphere of Manhattan. There, people were always rushing and the crowds were exciting, especially on Fridays, when they had just been paid. This was completely opposite to Brooklyn, relaxed in an almost rural atmosphere. He worked hard in the tiny laboratory, but he was alone and felt lonely.

Paul, seeing this, suggested that Frank Peter, Paul's father, keep him company and do the menial chores. Frank Peter was an uneducated man but very friendly. He also liked to drink. He watched Carl mixing chemicals for a few days and then said, "Eh, Carl, why are you doing all this? Let's put up a whiskey still and make drinks. We'll make a lot of money."

"No, thank you," Carl replied. "That would be too dangerous. It's against the law."

Frank thought for a while and then said, "So let's plant tomatoes in the backyard. I know how to grow them that big." Here he cupped both hands to form a large sphere.

Frank Peter had made whiskey during Prohibition and had made a lot of money. Unfortunately, the close contact with alcohol was too much of a temptation for him and he became an alcoholic. It ruined his married life and he was once in a terrible car accident while driving intoxicated. His face had been permanently disfigured. Now, in addition, he wore false teeth. One day he came home completely drunk and tried to make himself a steak. His teeth fell out of his mouth and into the frying pan. Frank didn't notice this until it was too late. By the time he had pulled them out, they were hopelessly bent out of shape. Undaunted, he put them right back in his mouth. When he came to work next day, he looked quite comical and Carl could not keep from laughing out loud when Frank told him what had happened.

On another occasion the telephone rang and Frank picked it up. The person on the line wanted to speak to Paul about business and asked, "Can I speak to Mr. Genoa?"

To which Frank replied proudly, "Speaking!"

Carl saw that no business was coming in and he realized that he could not wait for Paul. He had to generate some business for himself.

Not all his work was wasted. A couple of "clients" did call. One was the owner of a beauty salon. He needed a formula for a shampoo for his salon. Carl prepared the shampoo but, when it came time to pay, the man told him that he had no money. However, he did have two live chickens and offered them as payment. Carl took the chickens and brought them home, upon which Irene threw him out of the house together with the chickens. He had to set the poor birds free before he was readmitted.

One day a baker came to the laboratory with his "project." He needed a floor wax for his business. He, too, had no money. He offered, instead, to bring Carl a "Challa" each Friday. So every Friday Carl brought home a delicious Jewish Challa for the Sabbath.

A number of salesmen visited the company, probably attracted by the big gold sign in the store's large display window. Carl had no desire to buy anything, but he was eager to tell them what he could do. One of them was quite intrigued by his technological abilities and reported back to the management of Burlington Company's Fiberglass Division, known at the time as the Hess and Goldsmith Division.

Carl was invited to the headquarters of this large and respectable company, located on Broadway in New York, and, after a long conversation, was offered a one-year research contract at $2,000 a month. "Just apply your technology to our fabrics," said the vice president, "and we will evaluate the results. We know exactly what we are looking for."

Carl was overjoyed. It was his first research contract and it put the company on a partially independent footing. It was almost a year since the company had gone into business and he had thought they would have to close it down. Paul had already spent $50,000 on the venture and was beginning to have his doubts about the wisdom of proceeding much longer. But this changed everything!

Just before Carl left, the vice president asked, "How many chemists do you have working in your place?"

Carl immediately replied, "We have six."

The vice president nodded approvingly and said, "We would like to visit you and see your company. Is it all right if we come a day after tomorrow?"

Carl panicked. He did not have anybody working with him. Trying to hide his emotions he said, "We would be delighted to have you."

What would he do now? He was angry with himself for having fallen into his own trap. But how else could he have answered? These people could have had second thoughts and changed their minds about giving a contract to a company in which he was the chief cook and bottle washer.

He called Paul from the first public phone, "Paul, what shall we do? We have to present a laboratory with six chemists to a client the day after tomorrow."

Paul thought for a minute and said, "Don't worry. I'll take all the men from my company, give them white coats and let them mix water in beakers while the visitors are there."

Carl replied, "What should we say if they ask what they are mixing?"

Paul, who was enjoying visualizing the whole scenario, answered, laughing, "We'll say that it's top secret."

The show went without a hitch. When the visitors came on the appointed day, the "chemists" in their white coats were busily mixing "chemicals" with glass rods in beakers. After they left, Carl sighed with relief and said to himself, "Now we're in business. Or so he thought.

Chapter 25

Shirley

It was the fourth of July. Every year before July 4th, Irene and Carl packed the car, took the children and went to Monticello to their summer place in Circle Ten, so named because there were ten bungalows built in a semi-circle. Each bungalow was occupied by a family, and they all were friends.

It was a unique colony. People who came to visit envied them. The place was beautiful in itself, consisting of three acres of land with old, majestic trees in the middle. The trees gave shade on the hottest days, while the rest of the meadow was bathed in the light of the sun.

Irene liked to sit under these trees and watch the others who were bathing in the swimming pool or simply lying on the beach chairs trying to get a suntan. Carl had taught her how to swim when they first came to the mountains, but she never really liked the water. Sometimes she put on her bathing suit and went over to the swimming pool just to be with her friends, but after a half hour or so she would leave it.

She was never alone when away from the swimming area. There was always Shirley. She hardly ever swam. She didn't feel well enough. It was hard for her to do anything. She liked sitting on her little porch and watching from there, writing something or having a cup of coffee. Shirley had developed an enlarged heart. She and Irene spent their time talking, joking about everybody, all in good fun. One could never be bored when Shirley was around. She had an inexhaustible number of sayings and jokes, and she never let herself become overwhelmed with her own problems, which were many. She had a wonderful ability to detach herself from them and be open to anybody who wanted to talk to her. And everybody did. Shirley had a special relationship with her friends. She didn't judge anyone. She understood that people came in different sizes with different natures and dispositions. She simply didn't expect anyone to be different from what they were. Sometimes, when Irene was angry with one of them, Shirley would say, "This is Elaine (or this is Blanche or this is Gisa). Irene, you must take people the way they are. We are not perfect either."

Irene listened and learned so much from Shirley. Shirley, who had hardly left Brooklyn, was more worldly and knowledgeable than people who had traveled the world over. She had the natural ability to understand human nature; thus she loved and observed people, but never criticized them or became angry at them. She was a spiritual giant.

Every morning Shirley was the first one in the colony to get up. She had a cup of coffee and then drove to the store for fresh bagels, lox, cheese and tomatoes. By the time people started getting up she was back and the table on her little porch would be bending beneath the most delicious breakfast. There were two pots of coffee brewing. They would not be wasted.

One by one, her friends came in, sit down at the table and had coffee or a bagel. They would leave and others would arrive. Sometimes there would be standing room only on her little porch.

Shirley was a great hostess and everyone felt welcome and comfortable at her place. Elaine was always the last one to arrive. "Here she comes," Shirley would say affectionately. "She finally woke up." Elaine was married to Joe, who was a survivor of the war. He had been in concentration camps and had come to the United States after the war. Joe was from Boryslaw and Irene had known him and his parents before the war. Joe and Irene had been very happy to see each other in the United States and became very close. Joe met and married Elaine when she was 19 years old. She was American-born, an intelligent woman who put up with all Joe's teasing about his American wife with a sense of humor. Irene liked them both a lot and so did Shirley.

Now Elaine strolled down the lawn to Shirley's bungalow. "Come in, come in," Shirley said. "You're sure you are awake?" She laughed, seeing that Elaine was still half-conscious.

"I guess so," Elaine laughed. Nothing ever bothered her or so it appeared. Irene always suspected that Elaine wanted to create this impression and admired her for her ability to keep her temper.

Now the three of them sat drinking coffee and watching the bungalows come to life. Children made noise, doors opened and closed, people went about their daily business.

Shirley said, "Look at this place, isn't it beautiful? I love it so! It is never too hot or too cold. It is the most perfect place in the world." She really meant it. She couldn't wait to go to Monticello every year, and was always the first one there. She had her large house in Brooklyn, but her favorite place was here in Circle Ten. She smelled the flowers here better than anyone else did and watched the birds wake up in the morning.

In the evenings she sat on her porch till late at night and watched nature go to sleep. Only when she was overcome with exhaustion would she go to bed. She didn't need much sleep.

Irene and Carl and the others locked their doors at night. Shirley never did. She slept with her doors wide open. Only the screen door was shut, but it was never locked.

Shirley had vices too. She was a compulsive gambler. She worked hard for her money and would say, "I don't buy a lot of clothes or jewelry or furs, even though I can afford them. I get pleasure from gambling." She felt justified in spending her money that way.

She also liked to play cards. She played with men for high stakes and sometimes lost a lot of money. But on the rare occasions when she won, she would take her friends out to an expensive restaurant. Her generosity was unending.

Shirley and Paul had three children, Betsy, the oldest, and Donna and Charlie, who were twins. Even in raising them her generosity took over. She let them do whatever they wanted. She didn't understand that children needed guidance. She herself had grown up in a home where her parents were busy 12 hours a day trying to make money and had had little time for their children.

Shirley grew up in a vacuum cleaner store, where she helped out and did what she wanted. By the age of 12 she was playing cards with adults and smoking cigarettes. But Shirley had a superb sense of values. Her basic character remained unblemished and she had a wonderfully sensitive and devoted nature. She loved her mother with a passion and never did anything that would hurt her. That's why she felt that she could trust her own children the same way. That was her mistake.

Shirley's and Irene's children grew up together. Betsy, who was the oldest, was about Alice's age. Donna and Charlie were twins, about five years younger than Betsy. All of them had been adopted. They were all beautiful children. When Alice was 6 months old, Shirley and Paul got Betsy. Irene was with them to pick her up. She was a tiny baby, very delicate and had been born with a dislocated hip. Shirley and Paul took loving care of Betsy and her hip was corrected. By the time she was a year old she started to walk. Alice and Betsy played well together and spent a lot of time with each other.

Shirley and Paul adopted Donna and Charlie when Betsy was about 5 years old. Till then she had been the only child and a little princess, especially to Paul, who adored her. She could do no wrong. And Betsy was a very sweet little girl, smart and with a good disposition.

Irene and Carl got Terry and, as time went by, Alice, Terry and Betsy became good friends. How good these years were for Shirley. She worked in her vacuum store and she and Paul enlarged it and made it into a very profitable business. At home she had a family well taken care of by the maid, Gladys.

In the evenings, she played with the children before they went to sleep. Afterwards, friends would come over or she and Paul would go out. These were happy years.

The children were growing up and it was time to send the older ones to school. Irene and Clare took Alice, Ruth and Beth to P.S. 20, a public school nearby. It was 1964 and the school was picketed by mothers who opposed integration. Children from different areas were being bused into their neighborhood. Irene and Clare went through the picket lines and enrolled the girls in kindergarten.

Shirley and Paul decided to send Betsy to a private school called the School of Ethical Culture. They had to pay tuition for Betsy and a bus picked her up every morning to take her to school.

Terry was only 3 years old at the time and stayed home with Irene. She was a very good child and became a real companion to Irene, who took her everywhere while Alice was in school. Terry was interested in everything Irene did and tried to help her in her own way. She went shopping with her mother for food or clothes. At home, she played while Irene cleaned the house or prepared food. When it was time to pick Alice up from school, Terry came along.

When she was 5 years old it was time for her to go to school too. She adapted quickly to the new situation and became the teacher's pet. "She is so dependable," her teacher would say to Irene on Open School Day. "She is such a help to me. I love her."

Alice went on to the first grade. She was a very good student. But she had problems with her tonsils and often ran a high fever and had a strep throat. Finally, there was no other choice: her tonsils had to come out.

Milo advised Irene to have this done, but Irene was afraid. She loved the children so much. "What if something goes wrong?" she asked Milo fearfully.

"Nothing will go wrong," he answered. "Don't worry so much. Alice is sick too often."

The appointment was made and Irene took Alice to the doctor's office. Alice was never afraid of doctors. Her tonsils were removed. There was a slight complication when Irene, who sat with her after her operation, noticed that her breathing was impaired. She called in the nurse, who removed blood that was accumulating in her throat. After that everything was fine and, several hours later, Irene took Alice home. Alice ate her ice cream and never complained.

Irene was so happy to have this behind her that she made a party for all the children and mothers on the block.

Two years later Terry's tonsils came out because she had large adenoids which affected her speech. This time Milo made arrangements in the hospital. Everything went smoothly but Terry suffered for a week with bad pain in her ears and couldn't eat. When she felt better, Irene made a party again.

Sometimes Terry and Alice fought. Terry, being younger, had to accept certain things and, being a child, didn't fully understand why. Especially that she was getting bigger than Alice and wanted to tell her what to do. On the block there was only one girl Terry's age and the two of them played well together. Terry was always a devoted friend and she carried this attitude into adulthood.

Alice spent most of her time with Clare's children, Ruth and Beth. To them, she could do no wrong. They spent most of the time in Irene's house and Terry played with them as well. Even though she was two years younger, Terry was very mature and fit in well with the older girls. Sometimes Betsy would join them, but somehow she didn't get along too well with Ruth and Beth.

Time passed. Anna, Irene's sister, wrote that Michael, her husband, had lost his job. Anti-Semitism in Poland was growing steadily and they realized that they could not stay there. Michael worked for the government in the capacity of vice-minister of industry and trade and he couldn't get an exit visa. He knew too much and the Polish authorities didn't want to let him out. Also, he was a member of the Communist Party and the United States wouldn't grant him a visitor's visa. However, Anna, who had visited Irene twice before, got a visitor's visa. She came alone and left Michael behind. Her son and his family were still in Poland too.

When Anna got off the plane, she looked very bad and her first words were, "In Poland it is like the times of Hitler." She came to live with Irene and Carl. Irene was happy to have her sister with her but she knew that they must immediately begin efforts to bring Anna's family to the States. She went with her to the Immigration and Naturalization office, where Anna applied for a permanent visa. She was told that this could take a long time.

In the meantime Michael tried to leave Poland. He was finally able to about eight months after Anna had left. He went to Rome, where he applied for an American visa. Anna received her green card and immediately applied for a visa for her husband. She had a right to do that.

But Michael had to stay in Rome a whole year before he could enter the United States. Anna's family also came to New York. Four people couldn't all stay with Irene.

As usual, Shirley came through with a solution. Her parents spent the winter in Florida and their apartment was empty till April or May. She suggested that Anna's son and his family move in temporarily, until he found a job.

It took Wilus four months to find a job, during which time he and his family stayed in Shirley's parents' apartment. This was a tremendous help as Irene and Carl couldn't afford to rent an apartment for them. Wilus got a job on Long Island. Shortly afterwards, he bought a house there. His wife, Olga, became pregnant and had a baby girl.

Chapter 26

The Tragedy

Carl received an unexpected telephone call from his brother Leo: "Mark has had a heart attack and is in a hospital in intensive care. I don't know the details, but you know that Mark has gained a lot of weight over the last few years and he has been smoking heavily. He's also had a lot of trouble at work."

Irene and Carl could not see Mark until his condition became stable after a few days. When they went to the hospital Mark was much better, but he sounded very bitter.

"Imagine what happened," he said. "My boss came to the hospital, fired me on the spot and took my car away from the hospital parking lot." He held an imitation cigarette in his mouth, as the doctor had forbidden him to smoke.

"I have part-time work from another man who pays me by the hour. I am writing patents for him." He tried to sound optimistic.

Carl thought for a while and said, "If you want, you can work for my company. We are doing chemical work but I think you will be able to make yourself useful. You can start as soon as you get out of the hospital and feel better."

His son, Mark Jr., visited him a few days later. A heated argument ensued. Mark Jr. accused his father of not being a man and letting Bonnie, his wife and Mark Jr.'s mother, go out openly with another man.

After convalescence, Mark started to work in Carl's company. Though the company was small, Carl was fortunate in having gotten some government production orders for storage batteries. Mark's mechanical abilities were now needed. He became friendly with Ray, the production manager, and things seemed to be going smoothly. Then tragedy struck.

Hilda phoned Carl, "It's Mark Jr., something terrible has happened; come immediately!"

"What happened; tell us." Both Irene and Carl were petrified.

"We don't know, he had an argument with somebody at school, went home, went down to the basement and hanged himself." Hilda was crying.

Irene and Carl drove over as fast as they could. They found Bonnie hysterical; Leo and Hilda were trying to calm her. Mark stood immobile as if turned to stone.

"What happened, what happened?" they asked . "I came home around noon to make lunch for Mark Jr. I didn't see him so I went to the basement; he was hanging there," sobbed Bonnie. She had called the police and they cut the rope and tried to revive him, but it was too late.

"He had an argument with somebody on a motorcycle in the schoolyard," said Mark. "Then he went to a store and bought some recording tape. The whole thing looks fishy to me. Maybe the guy on the motorcycle followed him and killed him." Mark was angry, "He didn't kill himself. Why would he buy a large roll of recording tape if he planned to kill himself?"

"Let's go to the police and find out," suggested Carl. But the policeman in charge was adamant:

"He killed himself all right; we have no suspects. The fact that the man on the motorcycle looked like a hippie does not make him a killer. Did you know that Mark Jr. had moved into the basement before he died?"

They went back to the house and examined Mark Jr.'s car. There were tire tread imprints on the hood and roof of the car as if a motorcycle had driven over it. They reported this to the police. But the police didn't change their story.

"We'll never know the truth," Mark said. "He has taken the secret to the grave with him." He was in control of his emotions, but one could see that he was suffering gravely. "He left rolls of taped telephone conversations," he continued. "It will take me days to listen to them, but maybe I'll find an answer there."

Mark Jr. was buried in a nondenominational cemetery. His school friends were there and they whispered to each other, but when asked what they knew, they clammed up and wouldn't say anything.

Mark ran through all the tapes of the telephone conversations. In one of them Bonnie talked to her lover, "I'll aggravate Mark so much that he will have another heart attack, and I'll be free to marry you." He thought, Mark Jr. must have known about this conversation.

Chapter 27

Proxy Fight

In 1972 Polymer was doing well. Paul was excited about the company and had big plans for it. The first step was to take the company public. This meant issuing shares to the public with the approval of the government. He found a lawyer who was very knowledgeable in this field. He arranged everything in a short period of time and Polymer became a public corporation. Carl and Paul became the principal shareholders, with an equal number of shares. The company obtained finances and was growing.

After half a year Paul came to Carl with a proposal. "Carl, let's use the name Polymer for Flicker Vacuum Cleaner Company and my other companies as well, and let all of them become part of the public corporation. I will be the chairman of the board of the whole conglomerate and you will remain the president of Polymer."

Carl stiffened. He loved Paul but he knew that Paul was a gambler in business and that his aim was to become a millionaire at any cost. Carl saw Polymer being used for risky business and he could not agree to that. They had a heated argument and Paul told Carl that he would wage a proxy fight and take over the company.

At that time Carl's Aunt Eva was visiting from Israel. She had come to see her son Uri and his wife Carmela and was staying with Irene and Carl for a while.

When Carl came home after his fight with Paul he was extremely agitated. Irene and Eva tried to calm him down.

"What can be done," asked Eva "to prevent this proxy fight?"

Carl answered, "I would have to buy enough shares to have more votes than Paul."

"How much money would you need?" asked Eva.

"I can't even figure it out. We don't have that kind of money."

Eva persisted, "How much money would help you?"

Carl hesitated, "I suppose I would need $25,000."

"I will give you the money," she said.

Irene and Carl looked at each other, flabbergasted. "We cannot take that kind of money from you," said Irene. "We could never return it."

"Don't worry," Eva said. "You will have the money. Relax, Carl."

She went to the telephone. Carl and Irene watched in silence and admiration. She was a master on such occasions. She phoned her bank and, to the surprise of Irene and Carl, the $25,000 check arrived the following day. Eva had proved to be generous and magnificent.

Now Carl bought additional shares of the company. He also hired a lawyer, who advised him to have the board of directors approve an option for Carl to purchase a large block of shares of Polymer.

When Paul found out about this he dropped the proxy fight. He came to Carl's office and admitted defeat, "I have 80,000 votes and I could get more." But he really needed 200,000. "By the way," he continued, "would you be willing to pay for my lawyer?"

Carl thought for a moment and asked, "How much is it?"

"Eighteen hundred dollars," Paul answered, showing him the lawyer's bill.

"OK, I will pay," Carl answered, remembering what he had learned at school about Abraham Lincoln. After the Civil War he had offered a hand of reconciliation to the vanquished Confederacy.

It was a time of hostile takeovers and leveraged buyouts and Polymer Research Corporation was challenged by proxy fights four more times in the next five years. It was able to weather each storm because of the loyalty of the shareholders and the company's staff, not to mention Irene's help and Carl's perseverance.

Chapter 28

"Acute Depression"
by Shirley Genoa

March 1979

A person who suffers from this condition is naturally down. That does not mean you act or appear that way. In fact, you learn to affect these thoughts by diversion—whatever drives them out or stops them for a while.

People like me work beyond any normal drive. Up until my divorce and the onset of so many responsibilities, I used to run; I was always going somewhere, because when I sat still the thoughts would come.

Others would say - so spirited, so humorous, so whatever, but it was basically a coverup, not just for them but mainly for myself. There was a lot of cynicism in my humor and it helped. People liked to laugh and they liked me for making them laugh. It was a way of bringing pleasure and taking away some of the seriousness.

I was born and spent my childhood during the Depression, 1927–1934. Psychologists say that the first seven years establish a vision of the future for a child. Something is formed by the age of seven.

My world was sad and gray, just seeing things as they really were. My home was filled with worry and fear and the ever-present need to get by. It wasn't a world of girls and boys, of joys or toys. Children were not indulged and they were reminded that they were lucky just to have heat and food.

One had to work to make sure he could give his family these luxuries. Our home was serious and insecure. The motherly comforts that make a child's world brighter and more stable were not really forthcoming. My mother had to take over the reins as provider since my father, who in the early years, when he would carry his own sewing machine to work in the factory, had been injured. It was up to her to find a way to make a living for her family.

There were trials and tribulations daily. It was then that the fear, insecurity and sadness set in, which, I'm sorry to say, remain all your life.

Later you can forget temporarily or relieve these feelings, but they are your basic makeup. It's not the scene that stays in your memory, but the feelings are permanently engraved on your personality. I remember trying to tell my mother funny stories in the hope that it would make her laugh. My pleasure came from seeing her less sad.

She was a determined lady, a hard worker and a good provider. When, years later, she had to retire because of ill health, I watched her give love and attention to her grandchildren and I saw another facet of this remarkable woman. It's a shame she didn't have the time or freedom from all those responsibilities when her own children were small. It would have been marvelous.

On the other hand, in retrospect I had a liberated mother in 1927, and I think that because of what I heard and saw from her I was able to survive my own difficulties. I am quite sure that, had I not been exposed to such a person and such strength and endurance, I could never have imagined how to pick myself up when I was knocked down to the count of nine.

Times got better and my adult life, by about 30, started to be what I had dreamed about. We had our own home (I was very impressed that the bedrooms were upstairs). It was a row house (attached) but it represented a new world to me.

As these comforts became available, I felt overwhelmed and guilty about having what my parents, who had struggled their whole lives, never had.

I tried to enjoy my life, but the guilt was too much to handle in ordinary ways. I became attracted to a group of people who were survivors of the Holocaust. I felt a strong emotional pull toward them and whatever they represented. We are still friends after twenty-seven years. I seemed to be able to get closer and to understand these people better than my American peers. My friends were oblivious and shallow compared to this group. We had parties, good times, get-togethers and became very involved in each others' lives.

The guilt I spoke about before was ever-present in that I always felt that something bad was going to happen. A person simply cannot live in peace while his inner feelings keep giving messages of impending doom.

For the next eight years my life moved forward. Business was expanding. We were growing and we now had three children and a larger home. The picture of happiness.

The new home and I were from different worlds. I had a special room for my parents but my fears grew greater. I developed acute claustrophobia and, without realizing it, my marriage was going bad.

It took me years before I realized that my marriage was over.

Chapter 29

My Impressions

The following chapter was written by Herta, Carl's cousin.

July 1979

It was about one year after my arrival in United States that I met Shirley and Paul Genoa. I was barely beginning to adjust to my new life, and Shirley and Paul were the first Americans to whom I could relate on a personal level. Coming from a traditionally European background, I had never met such a couple. Looking back now, what amazed me most about them was their total equality. They worked together, spent time together, had fun, talked. Shirley expressed her opinions or preferences freely, as Paul did his. She was never obsequious, he never "the boss." Shirley, unlike so many Americans I came to know later, showed great interest and compassion for our experiences during the war. Perhaps it had something to do with her background, although I rather suspect that it was her personal emotions and her ability to become involved in somebody else's life beyond her own little world.

Shirley was the daughter of immigrants from Poland. Like so many before them, they came to America without money and, through hard work, started a small vacuum cleaner business in Brooklyn. They lived in an apartment over the store and, since the hours left for leisure and rest were few, it did not really matter how fancy it was. The main thing was working and making a living—and hoping that things would be better someday.

Shirley's mother, as was true in so many European marriages, was the driving force behind this effort of necessity. Because there was nobody else around who could help her, she began to turn to Shirley. Shirley was 8 years old when she started to give estimates in the store and make deliveries on her bicycle. Later she admitted to having been embarrassed by offers of "tips." She was the owner's daughter! When she was old enough to get a license, she drove the delivery truck. While doing all this, she learned. She understood the business and she liked it too.

Something very important must have happened to her in her early childhood. She grew up with the knowledge that a living was earned through hard work. This may not sound very impressive today, but one must remember that forty years ago, girls were brought up to think that, if they were nice and coy, somebody would come along to support them. Shirley did not go the traditional route long before many women began to think differently. This is an important, if not the most important aspect of her life. There was not always a man to take care of you.

Shirley and Paul met at Coney Island. He was collecting money at a stand where she was playing. Paul was handsome in a rugged way, extremely personable and outgoing. The kind of a man who, could make you feel you were the only person he wanted to see. Shirley had more to offer. She was bright, witty and charming, with depth, sensitivity and tact.

They fell in love and got married. A little later Paul joined Shirley's family business and they began working together. Neither could "think small," and I imagine that together they brought great enthusiasm to their endeavors. Paul, of the two, was the dreamer, with Shirley being the "brain" and the realist. Together they had style whatever they did, even spending their last dollar with the flair of millionaires. They did become successful and built up a big business.

Life separated us. I did not know what the Genoas were doing. After many years of silence, I received a phone call from Shirley, who wanted to talk to me. She was spending the summer in the country and, upon hearing that I found myself between jobs, asked me to visit her and discuss a project she had in mind.

I was interested to hear about it and I knew that being with Shirley guaranteed no boredom. But something had happened to Shirley, something intangible that had caused her manner to change, her laughter to become less frequent, her warmth to be restrained. She had changed a little in appearance, but it was apparent from the start that something as powerful as an earthquake must have happened in her life to have left such scars. She must have been very, very hurt. There was an invisible sign that read, "No Trespassing." I was cautious, but I cared and maybe she knew it. We talked.

Shirley and Paul had indeed succeeded in life. The business had grown and expanded. They had a large manufacturing plant, interests in other companies, real estate and a beautiful home. They had adopted three children and, since Shirley was a working business partner, there was a staff at home to take care of the children and the house. This was all right with Paul, then, because he had never worked without Shirley and he needed her. But he suddenly became critical of her as a mother. She could do nothing right. The Shirley he married was never a "homebody." She was a born businesswoman, just as some people are born with talents for painting or writing.

Perhaps the children did, indeed, undermine the marriage. Every relationship between a man and a woman has some kind of secret ingredient that makes it work. Theirs functioned on the basis of equal partnership, of personal freedom, of working together. Shirley brought with her the business aspect of their life; her drive and knowledge were the very substance of it. Paul knew this.

The marriage began to deteriorate. These things don't usually start with a bang, just a little thing here or there. They fought quite a bit. One day Paul asked Shirley to relinquish her rights to the business and stay home. In an effort to save her marriage, she acquiesced.

She became a housewife. She took care of the children. She bought new dishes for the table, new clothes to please him. She lunched with friends. But she became bored. His demands increased. Shirley's old father had to be moved from their house to a nursing home, which I am sure broke her heart.

Sometimes, in situations like this, one needs to regain a sense of normality and security. I am glad we were not working in a cold office. I am glad Shirley was such a good hostess, making fresh coffee every morning, making it possible to talk like old friends.

We began to talk about the agony of her divorce, which became inevitable after what had happened. She found herself totally alone, alienated from mutual friends who couldn't believe that Paul could have behaved in such a manner. He fought her with every means at his disposal. He also fought in a man's world, with the law on his side.

New and shocking experiences awaited Shirley. She met lawyers who called her "babe" or "sweetheart." Agreements were changed overnight, and she was treated like a half-wit. Her pride was hurt. For twenty-four years she had worked alongside her husband as an equal partner, and now was left with nothing and no law to protect her.

As Julia Perles, who practices matrimonial law in New York, says in an article in the New York Times, "There are cases that have come to me where the wife worked and earned as much as the husband. Her money was used to run the household, his to acquire assets which were held in his name but with the understanding that they would be for the benefit of both. If she divorces after many years of marriage she's left high and dry. She won't get the assets and she won't get much alimony either because the courts will take into consideration her earnings and earning potential."

Shirley needed an attorney to represent and help her with her own attorneys. The renowned law firm of Louis Nizer had disappointed her. They had handled many divorce cases, but here was not a woman fighting for alimony, but a business partner demanding half of what they had built together. Nothing belonged to her, as would most certainly have been the case with two partners. Whatever she was claiming as justifiably hers had to be fought for and eventually "given" to her.

This was the most demeaning and humiliating aspect of the divorce settlement, where all past accomplishment had been erased and she had to accept what the attorneys and the law decided she was entitled to.

When I asked Shirley, "Didn't you fight for support for yourself?" she said, "No, I just wanted a chance to make an honest living." The law certainly has a double standard when it deals with women.

The problems Shirley had to face were numerous and of such magnitude that I have difficulty sorting them out. Each one of them alone was sufficient to bring a strong person to the breaking point. They included:

1. Emotional problems.
2. Dealing with three suddenly insecure children.
3. The property settlement.
4. The daily necessity of asserting herself in a male-dominated environment at work.
5. Her frustrating experience with her own lawyers.
6. The unfairness of the law itself.
7. Alienation from some of her friends.

Though we have come a long way in recognizing that emotional stress is not a shame, and that seeing a psychiatrist does not mean that one is crazy, if a woman in Shirley's position admitted to the world that she could not cope, wouldn't she be accused of insanity? Wouldn't her statements to her attorneys or male subordinates be discounted simply because she was once considered emotionally unstable?

Of 114,000 corporations with over 20 employees, ninety-three are headed by women. Shirley Genoa was one of them. She was president of a $3 million a year corporation. Yet, even in her own business she had enemies. She had hired competent people for the vital position of controller, but every one of them felt that by withholding important information from her, they could gain more power. "They didn't tell her more than the minimum necessary." Problems were relayed in a distorted or altered way in order to protect the men and challenge her authority.

She had never realized that, when she and Paul had worked together, he had been a protective wall between her and the male business world. Bankers were not accustomed to dealing with women heads of corporations, and Shirley encountered difficulties.

Shirley's inability to entertain customers outside the home began to have a negative influence on the company's relationship with its customers. As a businesswoman she could not "entertain" customers. Men were uncomfortable going out with a woman who paid the bill. She attempted to give dinners at home, but this did not work. Out-of-towners coming to New York wanted to go out to restaurants and theaters, not to someone's home, especially a woman's home. This was never an issue when Paul was around.

Home life was a major problem, if not a disaster. Shirley's three adopted children had lost a parent for the second time. They needed full-time care. For months Paul could only be reached between 9 to 5; no matter what emergency may have occurred; he was adamant about this. The children needed therapy, guidance and, most of all, attention. When Shirley encountered a crisis at home, she had to neglect the business. A "but you weren't there" attitude developed at work when things went wrong. Her employees, trying to prove that a woman could not run a business, used every opportunity to cover up mistakes they had made, which she detected anyway.

The Woman In Court

One would assume that in a situation like this, a woman could find protection in the law. This was the most disappointing revelation. The court had preconceived ideas about a woman's rights, and the "burden of proof" rested on her shoulders. She had to prove that her high salary was earned, not arranged for tax purposes by her husband. She had to prove that she had been an equally contributing business partner. Louis Nizer says, in his book on divorce, "In all fairness, the woman should be compensated for the flower of her youth." The court would understand that, be more sympathetic, accord alimony. But the division of property acquired from Shirley's work, efforts and brain was too much to ask for. So Paul got most of what they had owned, leaving her with one business, of which he retained the assets of the building.

This business was the sole source of income for her and the children. Paul tried to undermine it. Everything was automatically his, so he must have thought that too much was given to her. Shirley, in fact, became so brainwashed that there were times when she came to doubt her rights.

A Hungarian joke says, "If one person tells you you are a horse, laugh at him. If two people say so, start thinking about it. When a third person tells you you're a horse, go and buy yourself a saddle."

At the age of fifty, Shirley had to face a different world than Paul did, but she was not defeated.

Chapter 30

Michael

Michael was dying. His face looked delicate, his skin transparent and yellow. He had cancer of the liver. His high, domed forehead, hinting at his unusual intelligence, glistened with perspiration. The usually penetrating look of his deep-set light green eyes was blurred. The doctors at the Presbyterian Hospital in New York tried desperately to save his life, but they were helpless.

Michael had first had cancer of the colon a few years ago. He had noticed blood in his stool, but hadn't wanted to worry his wife Anna and concealed it. Finally, when he saw no improvement, he went to a doctor. Tests revealed that he had advanced cancer of the colon. An operation was performed. The biopsy showed that the cancer had already spread into the lymph nodes, a very ominous sign. After several years Michael started to feel pressure in his lower abdomen; for a long time the doctors could not find anything wrong. They thought it was a stomach condition. Finally, a new doctor diagnosed it as secondary liver cancer resulting from the previous illness. Michael was put on chemotherapy and for a while he seemed to be all right. He responded to the medication, although he lost his appetite and started to lose weight.

He was staying with his son Wilus and daughter-in-law Olga on Long Island when suddenly, one morning, Anna noticed that his skin and body looked yellow. Anna called Irene, who, together with Carl, rushed to Wilus' house in Smithtown.

Though neither noticed any change, Olga and Anna called Michael's doctor who told them to bring him to the hospital immediately. He was rapidly losing his strength and, in spite of the doctors' efforts, he was dying.

The whole family gathered around him. There was Wilus and Olga, Anna, his grandchildren Bronek and Julek, Irene and Carl and his sister Rose. Milo, his brother-in-law, came with his wife who hadn't seen the family for years. She came to see her dying brother-in law.

When Olga and Anna had washed his emaciated body the evening before, Michael had turned to Anna and said, "I am not afraid to die."

The doctors avoided him, to Anna's dismay. "Why don't they

come when we need them? Why don't they do something?" she cried. But there was no remedy for Michael and the doctors knew it. The following night he died; freed by death from further suffering.

Michael had been born in Boryslaw shortly before the outbreak of the First World War. His father was killed in that war, leaving his wife with three children and penniless. Though she somehow managed, there were times when Michael could not go to school because he had no shoes. He was very capable and started to tutor other children to help out at home. Finally he graduated from high school and went to Lvov, where he was admitted to the Lvov Polytechnic. He studied chemical engineering as one of a very few Jewish boys who were admitted to higher education in anti-Semitic prewar Poland.

One Saturday he was working in the laboratory when a group of Polish hoodlums entered the building of the Polytechnic. Armed with clubs spiked with razor blades, they charged into the room. His Polish, gentile school friend Yurek was in the room with him and, seeing what was happening, grabbed a bottle of sulfuric acid.

"If you take one more step and try to harm Michael, I'll pour this acid on you!" he hollered.

"Are you defending a Jew?" one of the attackers asked in amazement.

"He is my friend and I won't let you harm him. And I'll report you to the dean," he said. "I know you, you are students too; you should be ashamed of yourselves."

Surprised by his determination, they left slowly, shaking their heads in disbelief. Why would a Christian defend a Jew? A Jew-lover. But they never molested him again.

Michael graduated from college, but as a Jew he could not get a job in his profession in Poland. He got married and, putting together the resources of his brother and his in-laws, he bought a small nonproducing oil well. The well was drilled deeper and struck oil. Things started to look up, as the well began earning enough for all of them.

On September 1, 1939 war broke out between Poland and Germany. Poland lost and was divided between Germany and the Soviet Union, according to a secret agreement. The Russians occupied the eastern part of Poland, including the oil fields of Boryslaw. Michael greeted their arrival with relief, even though his oil well was taken away from him and nationalized, alongside with all the private property of other people. He had been sympathetic to socialism before the war, hoping that Communism would give the Jews a chance to better themselves. After all, he thought, the confiscation of private property was applied equally to everyone Jew and gentile alike.

Michael worked hard and lent all his enthusiasm to the new ideals. A child was born to his wife and things were going as well as one could expect, considering that a war was raging in the outside world. In Poland things were relatively peaceful.

But the peace did not last. After two years, a war erupted between Germany and Russia. The Germans attacked and overran the eastern part of Poland in a few days. They rapidly approached Boryslaw.

Michael was fully aware of the mortal danger the Nazis represented to the Jews in general and the Communists and their sympathizers in particular. He decided to run away with the retreating Russian army. He asked his wife to join him but she refused. With a little child and her old parents, she felt that she would not be able to bear the hardships of such a trip. Michael reluctantly left his family behind.

He traveled deep through Russia as the Russians retreated and finally wound up in Orsk in the Ural Mountains. A petroleum refinery had rapidly been built there to supply gasoline for the Russian military aircraft and Michael was hired immediately as an expert. To be sure, the conditions were atrocious, but they were equally bad for everybody. All they ate each day was a slice of bread and a salt herring. Since they had no refrigeration, Michael would put the herring outside the window in the freezing Siberian cold and cut a piece off each day.

He worked very hard; after all, he knew that he was contributing to the effort to conquer the hateful Nazis. Fear and worry about the fate of his family gnawed constantly at his heart. The news filtering in from the other side of the front was unbelievably grim. The Germans were exterminating all the Jews. It was impossible, he thought. Nobody could do such a horrible thing. These must be rumors. But worry kept him awake at night.

His refinery was personally praised by Stalin for its outstanding work, no small distinction in a country in which Stalin was considered the Supreme Being.

A contingent of Ukrainian workers was brought to the refinery to perform menial jobs. They were hungry and covered with dirt after a long trip. It was easy to see that they were not Jewish because they were crossing themselves with their hands after every few words. Michael approached them and eagerly inquired about his home town and the fate of the Jews under the German occupation. The Ukrainians were conspicuously silent on this subject, avoiding his eyes. Michael stopped asking them questions, realizing that they were unwilling to talk. However, he offered them what little food he had and invited them to his tiny room on the refinery grounds, where he lived with other refugees.

As soon as the Russian troops liberated Boryslaw, Michael asked the management of the refinery to give him a pass to go visit his family. Permission was given reluctantly and only after he gave them his solemn word that he would return.

He boarded an unheated freight train (the only available transportation) and headed home. As he approached, rumors of German atrocities got louder and more specific. Whole Jewish communities had been eradicated by the Nazis. In Kiev, the capital of the Ukraine, tens of thousands of Jews had been machine-gunned in a suburb bearing the little-known name of Babi Yar.

When he finally got home in October 1944, his worst suspicions were justified. His wife, son and in-laws had been brutally murdered by the Germans. They had rounded up all the Jewish inhabitants of the town, locked them in a synagogue and set it on fire. His house was now occupied by his former neighbors. When Michael approached them to find out the details of his family's fate, a group of men armed with axes came out to meet him. One of them said, "We know who you are and why you are here. You want to get your property back." When Michael denied this and told them that he didn't want anything except to find out what happened to his wife and child, a man said, "You'd better leave right away; otherwise we're going to kill you."

Now he was all alone. His brother and sister had been transported to Germany to unknown concentration camps and he didn't even know if they were alive. He thought about returning to Orsk permanently. Then somebody told him that his schoolfriend Anna was in Boryslaw with her child. Anna had lost her husband under the most tragic circumstances. Bronek Rabinowicz, whom she had married before the war, had tuberculosis and became incurably ill during the war for lack of proper nutrition and because of the horrible living conditions in his hiding place. When Anna left to see her sister Irene, who was living in another hiding place, he committed suicide. He knew that his situation was hopeless and he wanted to ease the burden resting on Anna's shoulders.

Michael had liked Anna very much since high school and now the two people met again. After a short while Michael proposed to Anna and offered to adopt her son. Anna didn't know what to do. She had loved her deceased husband very much and the wounds were still fresh. She asked her younger sister Irene what she thought about it.

"Your life is finished," said Irene. (Anna was thirty years old). "The life of your young son is important and Michael will be able to provide for him."

"But my emotions are dead," said Anna. "After all this I cannot love anyone."

They got married and, in spite of what Anna had thought, she learned to love again. Michael loved her very much and was very good to her and the child. After a while she fell in love with Michael.

Eastern Poland was given to Russia in the agreement at Yalta between Stalin, Churchill and the ailing Roosevelt. The two westerners had very little choice. Poland was already occupied, or would be shortly, by Russia and large pieces of eastern Europe would be lost for years to Russia's slavery in disguise.

The indigenous Polish population left for western Poland and Michael, Anna and Wilus left too, going to Ligota, near Katowice, where Michael was given the position of director of an oil refinery. At that time, Carl was working as an assistant director of the refinery and Michael became his superior. Anna's sister Irene came to Ligota too, and through them Irene and Carl met. They fell in love. But, while Irene and Carl left Poland because of the rise of post-war anti-Semitism, Michael was determined to work hard to help rebuild the war-devastated country of his birth.

When Michael found out the whereabouts of his brother, he left immediately for Vienna, Austria. There he found his brother in a hospital with one leg amputated. The Germans had put the inmates of a concentration camp under a train, presumably as protection against an air attack, and then started the train, killing and maiming many of them. Michael's brother was lucky; he hadn't been killed but his leg was cut off by the wheels of the train. Michael brought him back to Poland, where he nursed him back to health.

Meanwhile, he was rapidly advancing in Communist Poland, and he moved his family to Warsaw, where he eventually became vice-minister in the Ministry of Trade. His family had a beautiful apartment in the city, rebuilt after being completely destroyed by the Germans during the last days of the war.

Michael traveled often on official business. Once he got stuck in an elevator as he was trying to leave his house. A neighbor knocked on Anna's door, saying, "Mrs. Dichter, your husband is stuck in the elevator."

Anna was unperturbed. "That's impossible, my husband is in Cracow; he's there on business." And she returned to her household chores. Half an hour later, another neighbor knocked on the door, "Mrs. Dichter, your husband is stuck in the elevator."

"That's impossible," answered Anna again.

"But I saw him myself in the elevator and he asked me to tell you."

This time Anna went to the elevator and found her husband sitting on the floor. He had been waiting for help for hours.

On another occasion, Michael was sent to China to conclude a trade agreement. He was able to get favorable terms; however, when it came to translating the agreement, the Chinese insisted that the contract have the same number of words in both languages. They were afraid that otherwise it could have a different text and they might be shortchanged. This proved to be a formidable task, as the two languages were entirely different.

Weeks passed in useless haggling over the use of this or that word in the agreement, and Michael yearned to go home. He didn't like the local Chinese food and missed Anna's home cooking. He had the idea of teaching his personal servant to make potato pirogen and, after a while, the man could do it very well. Michael finally had a dish that reminded him of home and the Chinaman was enthusiastically turning out Ukrainian pirogen by the dozen.

Finally the translators were able to prepare a contract that had the same number of words in both languages and Michael returned triumphantly to Poland. But his deal was not appreciated at home. For example, the tea which China was now providing for the entire country was green, and the Poles were not used to drinking green tea. The Russian Communists who ruled Poland during the Stalinist era saw that Michael had concluded a better deal than they had and, in their paranoia, they accused him of scheming against them. This was during the height of Stalin's Terror in the 1950's and the consequences could have been dire for him. He was summoned to Moscow to explain himself. Michael was a master at explaining his point, and luckily was able to convince them that no malice against the Soviet Union was intended.

In 1953 Stalin died and the iron grip he had had on the countries of eastern Europe started to loosen for a while. The Polish puppet government fell and was replaced by a more independent regime. Michael, who had been working devotedly day and night trying to help rebuild Poland, was relieved of his duties amidst false accusations and insults.

"They lied and spat on me," he complained bitterly years later. "I kept telling them, 'Let's forget about the politics and let's rebuild the country,' but they wouldn't listen to me." His attempts to defend himself were ignored as the Poles strove to get rid of anyone who was connected with the fallen pro-Russian government and especially Jews.

For six months Michael was without work. Finally, he was offered a job as the director of the Polish Petroleum Institute, a prestigious position suited to his prewar and war experience. He performed brilliantly for ten years. In 1967 the Polish people openly celebrated Israel's victory over the Arabs in September. This was not out of love for the Jews: the Polish people hated the Russians and, since the Russians supported the Arabs, they in fact had suffered a defeat and the Poles gloated over it.

However, Russia's perfidy was underestimated. Seeing anti-Russian sentiment riding high, they started an anti-Jewish campaign in Poland, spreading all kinds of fantastic rumors. The most ridiculous was the accusation that Poland was going to be attacked by Israel. Poland didn't even have a common border with Israel. But the Polish people were very anti-Semitic and were eager to believe any rumor directed against the Jews. They began to fire Jewish workers everywhere. Demonstrations against the Jews were organized by the government and the naive Poles went around shouting anti-Jewish slogans. They didn't realize that Russia was really trying to divert their attention from their real oppressors, the Russians themselves.

Wilus, Michael's son, who was a professor at the university, was fired from his job and decided to emigrate to the United States. The government now accused Michael of delivering faulty lubricant formulations for automobiles to the petroleum refineries and sabotaging Polish workers. They forgot that the Polish workers had no cars. The lubricant formulations were secretly sent by his accusers to West Germany for testing. After a while a glowing report arrived and Michael was vindicated. But by that time he was totally disillusioned by duplicity of Communism and its masters.

Anna came to visit her sister in New York. Her first words were, "It's like a concentration camp. The situation for the Jews in Poland is like during the German occupation during the war." When Carl heard this he said, "You're not going back to Poland. We won't let you."

Anna had visited the United States several times before and Irene and Carl had tried to persuade her to stay for years, but her husband and son were in Poland. Now, with her son leaving with his wife and two children, she agreed.

Anna had begged Michael to leave Poland, but he would never consider it. Now he saw that she had been right all along and decided to emigrate to the United States. It was not an easy task. Michael had been a member of Communist Party for years and even though he returned his party card, the American Government looked upon him with suspicion.

It took Irene's energetic pleading with her congressman and a long wait for a visa in Rome, Italy for Michael to finally be allowed to come to the United States and rejoin his family after being separated from them for more than two years.

Carl was eager to help him. He confided to Irene, "I wonder how Michael would feel if I hired him. I would be his superior now; before, he was my superior in the oil refinery in Poland."

"Maybe it would be better if Michael tried to find a job somewhere else," answered Irene thoughtfully. "Then, if he comes to you and asks you for a job, he won't resent the fact that you are his boss."

As it turned out, Michael did start working for Carl's company and, thanks to an honest effort by both men, things worked out very well. Michael worked for the company till the end of his life. He quickly adjusted to the American way of life and loved his new country.

He was a keen observer. "You know, Carl," he once said as they went for a walk, "the black people here spend all the money they make. They buy a lot of things and this keeps the economy going." He tried hard to justify to himself the fact that capitalism worked while Communism was failing, and he became completely disillusioned with the ideas of Communism, though he never said so openly. He had gone through the entire cycle, from young, enthusiastic Communist to the mature man totally disappointed by the inefficiency of that system and its brazen abuse by the Communists for their own greedy goals.

Yet he never talked critically about it. He knew a lot of secrets, having had a high position in Communist Poland, but he kept silent even in the United States. Only once in a while did the truth about the horrible excesses of Communism come out, mainly through Anna.

She talked about the endless hours Michael had devoted to his job, going to the office seven days a week, eighteen hours a day. Once, after elections, he didn't come home for three days and nights. Together with other government officials, he was falsifying election returns in order to show that the population was unanimously in favor of the Communist regime. In fact the vote had been overwhelmingly against Communism, but to produce such returns during Stalin's regime was tantamount to being sent to Siberia or worse.

Chapter 31

Mark's Death

Mark was now working in Carl's company, and at first everything seemed to be working out well. He was made vice president with a salary second only to Carl's. Carl showed him how to bid on government contracts and Mark also learned how to solicit research contracts. He gave very good presentations to prospective clients in the private industry sector of the company. But his original enthusiasm was disappearing quickly. He started to slacken in his work and an important government contract was lost because of carelessness. He had also begun to go home early.

He once said once to Leo, "Carl doesn't know how to run the company. He should leave the running of the business to me." Leo advised him, "If you are not happy, you should leave and find yourself another job."

Meanwhile, the company was awarded a large research contract with Gulf + Western. Mark could be useful. But he joined the project reluctantly. His heart was not in it and he started to openly criticize the company. He said to one new employee, "So now you too will be working for this shitty company."

The man reported this to Carl, not realizing that they were brothers. Though Carl was shocked, he didn't do anything.

The company went public and was able to expand its activities using the funds obtained from the sale of stock. Mark was now making a very good salary, but he was obviously unhappy. His wife Bonnie decided to divorce him and married her boyfriend of many years. Mark was bitter. He said to Carl's daughter Terry, who was now working at Polymer, "We're the black sheep of the family."

The company was soon challenged by a proxy fight. It was important to keep the company working smoothly, so Carl went to Mark's office and asked him not to take time off, and to arrive at and leave work on time. Mark got furious and started to scream at the top of his lungs, "I am not a worker. I can come and go whenever I want to!"

Carl ran out of his office, with Mark following him yelling, "I'll take you to court, I'll sue you!" as the other employees watched in silence.

With the children growing up, Irene now had more free time and Carl suggested that she come to the company and see if she could find a niche for herself. She began to organize the marketing department and, seeing that Mark was slackening in his work, suggested that they work together.

"I'll give you the leads and you will give the presentations," she said. Mark agreed and, for a while, things seemed to return to normal. But he became visibly unhappy and uninterested in his work. So when Carl got a call from an employment agency, asking if he would be interested in an executive position, he suggested to Mark that he apply for the job.

"If I want to find another job I won't need your help," Mark replied stiffly.

"But you are very unhappy here; I think you should look for a job in your field," said Carl helplessly. "I'll give you a month to look for another job and two months' severance pay."

"I should get seven months' severance pay," Mark said, "one for each year that I've worked for the company," and he ran out of the office.

Mark finally left and began to work in the place Carl had originally suggested. Then, when Carl bid on another government contract, he discovered that he was being underbid by an unknown company. A check on the new company revealed that it had been organized by Mark and one of the employees of Polymer while Mark was still working at Polymer. At the same time Carl got a summons informing him that he was being sued by Mark for inadequate compensation and age discrimination.

The suit was dismissed in court, but Carl agreed to pay Mark's lawyer's fees.

Mark devoted most of his free time to his second, surviving son, Scottie. Every day after work he would take him to a rink where Scottie would practice skating, because his dream was to be a hockey player. Mark also traveled to Colorado, where he donated money to amateur skating events and enjoyed the recognition he received. He became very heavy and could no longer skate much himself, but he loved to watch the events. There he met a young, divorced woman named Lisa, a nurse with three children. They married, but again Mark did not invite his brothers to the wedding. He did not tell the bride his religion, nor did he tell her of Carl's existence. Carl's name would betray his religion. When Lisa complained to Hilda and Leo that she didn't know her new husband's religion, Mark forbade her to pry into his past. In this area he behaved as if the war were still on and he was still hiding from the Germans on Christian papers. Or maybe he had come to the conclusion that being a Jew was not safe, having experienced some of the horrors committed by the Germans. Being a Jew meant danger, humiliation and death.

The first year of the marriage was bearable, but soon problems began to appear. Lisa agreed before the wedding that her children would live with her first husband, but eventually the two teenage girls moved in and this created a lot of friction. Scottie especially was very unhappy and overwhelmed by the sudden appearance of two additional children. Gradually, Mark and Lisa drifted apart and Mark started to spend more and more time in a little office he had rented for himself. He became extremely obese and could hardly tie his shoelaces.

Things weren't going well at his job either. He pretended to be working, but it was obvious that he didn't. The older president of the company, who liked and valued Mark, retired and the new, younger management had no special feelings for him. They moved Mark out of his office into the factory, where cold air blew on him from the front and hot air from the machines in the back.

One Sunday morning, Mark was sitting in his little office preparing some samples for a private customer who was supposed to arrive around noon. Suddenly he lost consciousness and fell to the floor. When the client came Mark was still unconscious. He was taken to the hospital and put on a respirator. But he was brain-dead. Mark was 62 years old when he died.

Leo and Hilda were the first to arrive at the hospital. When they entered the room, Mark was breathing heavily on the respirator, as if asleep. They called his name, begged him to wake up, slapped him on his face and yelled, but to no avail. Leo cried now aloud.

When Carl and Irene arrived at the hospital, Mark appeared to be sleeping peacefully, his troubles behind him. He had finally escaped his tragic and unhappy life. Nobody could harm him now, nobody would ever call him a dirty Jew again.

Carl looked at Mark's hands. They were large and his fingers unusually thick. He thought of "Hansel and Gretel." The old witch kept the boy in a cage and fed him in order to fatten him up and eat him. Every day she would ask him to show her his finger to see if he was fat enough to be eaten. The witch had finally gotten Mark, Carl thought.

There was no change in Mark's brain function. He had suffered a massive brain hemorrhage and help had come too late. With his wife's consent, the doctors decided to take him off the respirator and he died.

Scottie was there too. He was confused and didn't know what to do. He didn't want to live with his stepmother. He disliked both her and her daughters. But a lawyer advised him to stay in the house to claim ownership, since Mark hadn't left a will.

Carl took him aside and offered to help: "Please let me know if you need anything. I'll be more than happy to help you, if I can," he said. But Scottie was very bewildered, besides being shocked by his father's death.

Everyone came to the chapel a few days later to pay their last respects. Not many people were there aside from his immediate family: Scottie, Carl, Irene, Leo and Hilda. The owner of the company where Mark had last worked came with his daughter. She was the new manager of the company, along with her husband.

Carl introduced himself, "My name is Carl Horowitz; I'm Mark's brother."

Their conversation revolved around Mark's childhood. Scottie, who overheard the conversation, must have deduced that he was Jewish. He didn't remember Carl from his childhood and now he was frantic, "I am not Jewish, am I?" he asked. Somebody said, "No, but your father was a Jew." Scottie was quite distressed, but Lisa was unperturbed, "I don't mind," she said. "I would have liked to have known you while Mark was still alive."

Mark was buried in a non-denominational cemetery next to his son, Mark Jr. Scottie delivered a eulogy at the graveside, "My father was a good man and I loved him very much," he said almost apologetically, as if being a Jew was a fault. He waited for Carl on the way out. He wanted to know a lot about Carl, whom he didn't remember at all. A long conversation ensued and Carl was sure that a closer relationship would develop; he invited Scottie to his house. But Scottie never came to Carl's or Leo's house, giving evasive answers when invited. Thus all contact with him was gradually lost.

Chapter 32

Shirley's Death

On August 1, 1984 Carl sat down in the evening in his kitchen in Brooklyn to read a book. It was Wednesday and he had just finished his dinner with his sister-in-law Anna in her apartment. He was lonely. Irene had left for the Circle Ten Bungalows in Monticello with Gisa and Lynn that morning to spend a day in the country with Shirley. Shirley was staying there for the entire summer and was running her company over the phone.

Irene usually went there on weekends with Carl. This time, however, she decided to go on a weekday without him. She felt an inexplicable urge to see her friend.

"You're coming because Gisa is going to be here," Shirley had said. "No, I'm coming to see you," Irene answered honestly. Shirley was pleased when Irene arrived in Monticello. She loved her dearly. Shirley had just gone through a long bout of internal bleeding from a stomach problem, and was taking hormones to counteract osteoporosis, from which she suffered greatly. Her doctor had warned her not to take them because she had an enlarged heart that would be at risk of a heart attack. But her pain was so excruciating that she ignored her doctor's warnings.

"I don't care, as long as these pills take away the pain," she said when Irene begged her not to take the hormones.

Carl was reading a newspaper and getting drowsy when the telephone rang. He hadn't been expecting any more calls that night. Irene had called already; it was now 8 o'clock. Irene was on the other end of the line. She was in a panic and her voice was desperate: "Carl, Shirley is dying, what shall I do? Please help me!"

"What are you talking about? What did you say?" Carl shouted.

"Shirley is dying. She is unconscious. I've tried everything possible to revive her but nothing has helped. Please tell me what to do." she cried.

"Irene, try again, you know what to do better than I, but do something!"

Carl was talking incoherently. Irene hung up and called back 15 minutes later. She cried, "Carl, Shirley has just died. I tried to revive her but I failed. I could not help her."

"How did it happen?" Carl felt as if he were choking.

"We went out to dinner in the afternoon and afterwards we walked with Shirley to her bungalow. You know, she could hardly walk, but she was happy and said she had had a wonderful time with all of us. We went to change our clothes and were going to go back a few minutes later to spend the rest of the evening together. She said, 'OK, I'll wait for you and watch some television meanwhile.'

"Lynn was the first one back to her bungalow. A minute later she ran out screaming, 'Irene, come quickly, something terrible has happened! Something is wrong with Shirley.'

"I tried to save her but I couldn't. We called the ambulance and they tried to revive her, but they said that nothing could be done and pronounced her dead."

"Irene, please calm down. There is nothing you can do. You did everything possible to save her life."

"Carl, you have to notify her sister Ceil. She is in a bungalow colony in Monroe." Irene gave Carl the name of the colony, and he got the telephone number and called. When he told Ceil what had happened, she started to sob, "My sister, oh my sister, she is dead!" He heard the voices of people trying to calm her down.

When Irene called again she was more in control of herself: "The emergency people told us that even if they had been there earlier, they couldn't have saved her. She died instantly. Imagine how much presence of mind Terry had. She took Shirley's pocketbook, which was standing there open with a lot of money inside. Terry closed the pocketbook and brought it over to our bungalow. After all, there were many strangers around. Ceil and Willie came over and we gave it to them."

By now it was close to midnight. Carl went to bed and tried to fall asleep, but he couldn't. He lay in the dark bedroom with his eyes open. So many wonderful memories were going through his mind. He remembered when they met Shirley and her husband Paul in the Grand Hotel in the Catskills in the summer of 1952, thirty two years ago. Irene and Carl went for their first vacation in the United States after they came to this country four years ago. They were sitting in the Casino of the hotel watching the show. A hypnotist was performing his routine act and a number of people became hypnotized and were called to the stage. A young blonde woman standing on the stage caught their attention. She was not pretty but she was very attractive and had a peaches-and-cream complexion. She always gave an impression of a clean, freshly scrubbed person which she really was. She didn't have a good figure but had very shapely legs. The expression of her face was alert and clever.

She marched on the stage and sang school songs under hypnosis as ordered by the hypnotist while Paul, her husband, was laughing hysterically in the row behind them. Irene turned several times back, annoyed by his loud laughter. Paul was sitting right behind them. He was tall and handsome with brown eyes and regular features of his face. His light brown hair was combed straight back in pompadour style with lots of pomander holding it in place. His whole person emanated charm and friendliness.

Next day they got acquainted. Carl met Paul at the chess game at the swimming pool and Irene met Shirley at the card table where Shirley was playing a hard game of poker with the men. They became instant and lifelong friends.

They spend weekends with each other, first in the hotel where the girls stayed for two additional weeks. The men met every evening in the city and then came for the weekends together to the hotel to join their wives. After going back to New York, the two couples spent almost every evening with each other after work and stayed together till early morning hours only to wake up a few hours later and go to work.

It seemed like they didn't have enough time to tell each other about their lives, families, plans for the future and fun. And they did have fun. Carl and Irene had fun for all those years of war and sufferings, for their lost childhoods and tragedies. Shirley and Paul seemed to enjoy watching all the moments when they made their new friends happy. They took Irene and Carl to restaurants and they insisted on paying the bills, even though they didn't have too much money themselves.

For Irene and Carl still fresh from Europe and after-the-war poverty, it was unthinkable to go to restaurants to eat. Each time it came to pay the bill, Paul insisted that he will pay, and when Carl protested feebly he would say, "Don't worry, it comes out of the business."

They did everything together. They played miniature golf till wee hours of the morning, they went on picnics together in the spring and in the summer they went to the Grand Hotel, where the girls now stayed together for the whole summers while the men commuted for the weekends to them. They bought houses together on Fillmore Avenue in Brooklyn almost next door to each other.

Both, Irene and Shirley couldn't have children of their own. When Irene and Carl adopted a girl Alice, Shirley and Paul adopted a girl too. Shirley named her Betsy Irene. Then, Irene adopted a second girl,

Terry and Paul brought home a pair of twins, Donna and Charlie.

Shirley and Paul started to expand rapidly her mother's vacuum cleaner business and moved out to a larger prestigious house not far away, owned previously by the wealthy store owners, Fortunoff's. The couples saw each other much less now because they were now preoccupied with their children.

Even when the two couples were preoccupied with their work and their children, they still saw each other on weekends. Every Friday night Shirley went to see Irene in her house and Carl would spend time with Paul, since they didn't want to leave the children with baby sitters.

Shirley's marriage to Paul had ended in a divorce. The divorce was bitter and caused a lot of harm to their children. Torn by their love for both parents, they became confused and unhappy. Betsy became a drug addict and drew one of the twins, Charlie, into using of drugs. Donna, the second twin, was the only one who didn't succumb.

Paul remarried after a while and created a new life, but Shirley loved him till her dying day.

Carl was turning and twisting in bed but could not fall asleep. So many memories were going through his mind, so many pictures parading in front of his eyes. He remembered the magical times that the four of them had had together. When Shirley and Paul got divorced, he knew that their friendship would end. Right after they separated, Shirley called Carl to her house alone, without Irene. She got into his car. "Carl, I want you to know that Irene and Paul were in love with each other," she said, coming straight to the point. Carl looked at her in disbelief. He trusted both Irene and Paul and tried to figure out what Shirley's motive was in making up such a story. She looked intently at him as if hoping he would react strongly, but he didn't react. He knew it wasn't true and he began to understand. Shirley, with her marriage in ruins, wanted to destroy his and Irene's too. He wasn't angry but he felt sorry for her. He went home and described the incident to Irene. That was the end of the matter. Carl knew that a chapter in their life had ended. He fell into a restless sleep.

At Shirley's funeral Carl delivered the following eulogy (written by Irene):

"Dear friends and family members,

"In deep sorrow we came here today to say good-bye to a wonderful person and a dear friend. How do you describe a friend of a lifetime?

"When we met Shirley for the first time thirty-two years ago, we noticed her right away. We had never met another person like her in our whole life. She was not tall and yet she towered over other people. She was not loud and yet her voice was always heard. She was not strong and yet she projected power and confidence.

"If the word 'unique' can be applied to a person, then it should be applied to Shirley. She was unique and extraordinary. She was hard-working and hard-playing, a businesswoman par excellence.

"She was willing to give all she had in order to succeed. Many times she would get up in the middle of the night and work until morning on a new business plan and she was happy when it was successful.

"But there was another side to Shirley, the human side, which all of us experienced. She knew how to create personal friendships with people because she was really interested in them. She loved people and she loved her family and friends dearly.

"She knew how to listen and how to give advice. Often, she would forget her own problems in order to listen to other people's problems. Shirley loved fun and she loved life. We were in this country a short time, greenhorns at that time, and Shirley introduced us to pizza and Coney Island, to miniature golf and to Brooklyn. We grew attached to her and loved her. Her porch in her country home was the first place to visit and she was the first to talk to. She had time for everybody and patience to listen to everyone. Her table was always laden with good food and she knew exactly what everybody liked to eat. She was at ease with a businessman as well as a cleaning girl, a scientist as well as a worker.

"We spent many wonderful days together over a period of many years. Shirley had time for friends and relatives, for business and fun. She was very clever and her advice was sought by many people in business and in private life. She was admired by everybody, loved by many and respected by all. She influenced the lives of many people, often without saying a single word. Her sense of humor brightened many sad occasions. She will be missed terribly by all of us, but we will always love and remember her.

"We will always have a special place in our hearts. She made our lives richer. Our lives will not be the same without her."

Shirley wrote her own eulogy on November 23, 1982 as if anticipating her premature death.

Eulogy By S. Genoa

She was valiant. She was down-burdened, fought and succeeded. Society, the law, her peers, family, everyone was against her—no one understood they were drowning with her, but their ignorance made her stronger.

How can you blame fools? There was no understanding. Her friends cheated her, blamed her, didn't want to listen. Her children abandoned her, hated her, cursed her for breaking their home—listened to bad stories about her, making her the evil one. The lawyers made mockery of her case: "Everything belongs to the man." Society agreed: it is his.

And she endured, she waited, she said less and less. She needed time—only time was her ally—to show the lies, the misjudgment and the people really responsible for all that happened.

The children came back, the family and friends understood enough (not fully) that here was a worthwhile human being, one who suffered and paid a big price for surviving.

A murder was committed but not by her.

Time—what's eight years?—I pity them not me, for I am able to see the workings and effects the system can impose.

They may never see the depth, or understand the difficulty and bravery of stepping over the line.

She cared for all those in her life; any bit of kindness was truly appreciated. And she totally forgave, and was willing to start fresh as her people were ready.

Her wisdom was partly hers, but largely supplemented by a much wiser mind, who gave to her the understanding that they act to the best of their understanding and not to blame them—be patient. Some will understand in time, others maybe never. She would have given up long ago without her faith in her.

Chapter 33

Giselle and George

Giselle lay in the hospital with cancer that had spread through her body; she was beyond any help. Her husband, George, was at her side. He wouldn't leave her for a minute. For the last five years George had taken care of his wife as her sickness got worse. He had forgotten about everything else. George was a very sociable and outgoing fellow, ready to travel 100 miles to visit friends, new or old. He liked to meet new people and make new acquaintances, but now Gisa was terribly sick.

Gisa had been born in the town of Stanislaw in southeastern Poland in 1925. She could not finish high school because war broke out between Germany and the Soviet Union. However, she was very clever and had a lot of common sense. She saw what was going on around her. Jewish people were being killed by the Germans. While working as a servant to a German family in her town she was approached by the head of the household: "Why don't you run away?" he asked. "Sooner or later you will be killed too."

"How can I run away without any place to go and without any documents?" asked Gisa.

"This is what you should do," the German explained. "Go to the authorities and volunteer to work in Germany."

"And what will I say when they ask what nationality I have?" asked Gisa incredulously.

"Tell them that you are Volksdeutsche (German national) and that your entire family was killed in an air raid," answered the German.

"And what about my documents, my Ausweiss or Kennkarte (I.D. card)?"

"Tell them they were destroyed in the air raid," said the man with a twinkle in his eye. "You have nothing to lose."

Gisa didn't waste any time. She included her best friend in this plan and they both reported to the nearest recruiting station as volunteers willing to go to work in Germany. It would have been impossible for a Jewish boy or man to do this. A physical examination would have revealed that he was circumcised, and in Europe only Jews were circumcised. Fortunately for women this problem didn't exist.

Thus Gisa and her friend, after undergoing a thorough questioning about their fictitious places of birth and Christian origins, were shipped to Germany to work as servants for a German family. They survived the war and, when it was over, Gisa found out that she was all alone. Her whole family had been killed by the Germans. She left the family for whom she was working and registered as a D.P. (displaced person) in an American refugee camp in Foehrenwald, Germany, near Munich. In the same camp there was a dashing young man who was the head of the Fire Brigade. His name was George. Blond and handsome, he immediately attracted Gisa's attention. She fell in love with him.

George was popular with women, but he chose Gisa. He saw in her all the values he was looking for: loyalty, sincerity and integrity. He admired her cleverness. They decided to marry and emigrated to America.

After they arrived in the United States, they got married in a modest ceremony. They were poor but they loved each other and were happy to finally have a family of their own as two children were born to them, Phyllis and Mitchell.

One day in the winter of 1949, as they were standing in the New York Association for New Americans, they noticed another couple. It was Irene and Carl. They had just come in from the bitter cold and it took them a while to warm up. George looked intently at Irene and exclaimed, "Nuska, is it you?"

"George!" called Irene, recognizing him. They hugged. They had known each other since childhood. Their home towns were not far from each other and George used to come to Boryslaw often to visit his family.

The two couples became lifelong friends. Carl liked George's sociability and friendliness and Irene and Gisa became good friends too. They saw each other often; they visited each other's modest apartments and they went together to parties and gatherings of friends.

One day, when their children had grown up and gone off to college, Gisa said to Irene, "What should I do now that the children are out of the house?"

"You should go to college," Irene replied.

"But I'll be 50 when I graduate," said Gisa.

"You'll be 50 anyway," said Irene.

So first Gisa went to high school and obtained a diploma. Then she entered college and, after three years, received a degree in social studies. George was bursting with pride. "My Gisa, the brains," he used to say with real admiration. She got a job in her field, first working for the New York Association for New Americans as an advisor to Russian immigrants, and then at a high school, working with mentally disturbed children. She won recognition for her work and was even called to testify in court in the case of a mentally disturbed immigrant who had killed his mother. She proudly read her report to the court to Irene and Carl.

But Gisa didn't stop there. She went on to graduate school and got a Master's degree. It seemed that her life-long dream of becoming an educated person was coming true.

Then tragedy struck. A routine blood test revealed that she had leukemia. The doctors were blunt and told her that she had, at the most, five years to live.

Everyone tried to console her and friends produced medical reports stating that a cure was at hand, but Gisa was a realist and didn't delude herself. She took the news calmly, and her only worry was whether George would be able to take care of himself. "He is so helpless, he doesn't even know how to make a cup of tea," she used to say. She underwent chemotherapy, which made her hair fall out. "You can wear a wig," suggested Irene. "I will go with you and we will choose a good one." Gisa took everything bravely.

Irene had bought a wig for herself too, just to make Gisa feel better.

Then she had a stroke which left her paralyzed and unable to walk. She underwent physical therapy to enable her to walk again. At her son's wedding she even danced a little, to the applause of all her friends.

In spite of every effort, her illness progressed unabated. When her white blood cell count got lower, she was taken to the hospital. The last time Irene and Carl visited her, she didn't even recognize them. She thought that Carl was an officer in a uniform. The next day she died. George was inconsolable.

Chapter 34

Letters To Gisa
My Wife, My Friend

Nov. 1988 (written by George after Gisa's death)

Do you know something, Giselle? For a smart broad, you were pretty stupid.

Why in the world did you get sick and die on me, not to mention on Kristalnacht? Couldn't you have picked some more "Jewish" disease, such as arthritis or even angina pectoris? No, it had to be leukemia; and if that wasn't bad enough, you had to get cancer of the breast and top it with a hysterectomy and a stroke, all this within five years.

One thing I'll say for you, you were some gutsy lady, with admirable courage. You made less fuss about leukemia than most people do about a cold.

Being married to you for almost forty years, I surely got to know you, but I was constantly amazed at the quiet courage with which you faced overwhelming odds.

I can't forget the time I picked you up from Mount Sinai Hospital after your breast operation. We were driving to our own Shangri-La, Circle 10 in the Catskills, and you said, "George, if you are tired, I'll drive." Do you remember how I cried? You worried about *me* being too tired to drive, *me*, who practically drives for a living?

I also remember just a couple of months ago, when you started to be in real pain, how you called for help in the middle of the night because you couldn't get off the toilet seat by yourself, and how I carried you back to bed. Later on you got dressed and insisted that I drive you to work. How I fought with you, saying that if you couldn't get off the toilet, how could you possibly go to work; but you insisted and I drove you to school. A couple of hours later you called and told me, quite nonchalantly, that, of all days, today the elevator wasn't working and you'd had to walk up four flights. How did you do it?

I also remember other, much happier times, when our kids were grown and you decided to go back to school, starting with a High School Equivalency Diploma and obtaining a Bachelor's degree in 2½ years. Yes, in two and a half years, when Phyllis, our daughter, whom

I consider to be a semi-genius (in her field only), took 3 years to get her degree from Wesleyan University; our son the lawyer was probably slightly retarded because it took him the full 4 years to finish a 4-year course at the University of Rochester. With that diploma you went to look for a job. You were interviewed by Evelyn Cohen of N.Y.A.N.A., and only after you got the job did you tell her that she and her husband, the former director of the D.P. camp in Fohrenwald, had been sitting at our table at the 30th reunion of Fohrenwalder. I am convinced that you would have gotten the job even without the interview, but no, you had to get the job on your own merits with no pull, without "protectzia" or "Blatt."

Gisa, I want you to know that you had a very nice funeral, if funerals can be described as nice. There were so many people; the place was jammed with all our friends old and new and everyone from the school system. Rabbi Halpern delivered the most moving eulogy about a woman of valor, adding a tribute to you written by your colleagues from work.

I am sure that you would have liked Rabbi Halpern because you were not too fond of Rabbi Hertzberg. You could never forget Hertzberg saying, "I kiss your hand, madam."

Yes, you never liked show-off people. Then let me ask you how come you married me? Boy, how vividly I remember back in 1945 in Fohrenwald, when I approached you for the first time, dressed in my officer's boots and riding britches. I grabbed your chin, shaking it slightly, saying, "Hi cutie, how about going out with me?"

I remember how outraged you were: "Mister, you have no manners, you are rude and uncouth; please get lost," and how I just kept laughing, totally amused at your discomfort.

Did you know that, despite the ex-soldier's bravado, I turned red when a girl just looked at me? I guess you never knew it, because I would never have admitted it.

Do you remember the beginning? The wedding that cost $75, our honeymoon in the Poconos, our place in the Bronx, our apartment in Manhattan, our trip to the Grand Hotel in Liberty, New York with Carl and Irene?

Do you remember Carl's car that had to be pushed, the same car that hit a policeman in front of our house? Do you remember meeting Shirley and Paul, what fun we had? Remember how Paul was shocked at the quantities of food Carl and I would consume? How young and carefree we were!

Your first and only miscarriage, your trip with Shirley to Detroit. And finally a beautiful girl, Phyllis. Do you remember how she used to shriek and jump off the high chair the minute I put my keys in the door. Then Mitchell, then moving to Englewood, New Jersey, the big, old house, the wooded backyard, kids learning how to ride a bicycle, Mitch being hit by a swing, rushed to the hospital. Later, moving to Tenafly, good schools, nice parks. Phyllis' Bat Mitzvah in June of '67, Mitch's Bar Mitzvah? I remember with pride Phyllis' graduation from high school second or third in her school. All awards in Russian, Spanish, English; remember me bragging to everyone that it was my daughter and you saying, "Stop it, please"?

What about all the summers in the Catskills, the Spector's Era, the Dingle Daisy interlude? We traveled, we saw the graduation of our kids from colleges and law school. Remember Phyllis' wedding, how we danced? You went to Mitchell's wedding in a wheelchair, but you went. You were there. Hardly three months later, we went to Israel, attending Manek's son's wedding at the Hilton Tel Aviv. Do you remember when the band started to play the "Rendevouz at Nine" (Umowilem sie z nia na dziewiata) and you said to me, "Hold me tight and we'll dance together"? By the time the band played our very favorite tango, "Jealousy," other men wanted to dance with you, but I wouldn't let them.

With all the "tsoris," we still managed to squeeze in another Mexican vacation, another trip to Israel and a summer in our enlarged bungalow—I'm sorry, I should have said, "our summer estate."

And then a series of visitors: Mary from Australia, Edna and Yacov from Israel and Miriam from England, but then you were already in the hospital.

I didn't know whether to curse or to praise the doctors. I wished that they could keep you well at least to our 40th wedding anniversary, January 2nd, you remember. I had prepared a nice surprise for you, a nice bauble that Moshioh had brought from Israel. I made my children a sporting proposition that the first girl to be born in our family to carry your name will inherit it, fair enough? Mitch and Sima have a good chance, because she is expecting, as you very well know. There is a rabbinical saying that when one "Neshuma" (soul) goes to heaven, another one comes down.

There is also a Polish saying that it is better to lose with someone smart than to find something with someone stupid.

I feel that our almost forty years together were good years overall, with the exception of the last five years. Even during those years you made it possible for me to continue.

And so, darling, you were buried in New Jersey in the same cemetery as Kathe, Dorothy, Joe Intrater, according to your wishes in a plain pine coffin dressed in the traditional Jewish shroud. Next to you there is also a place for me, but promise me not to snore this time. In time there will be more people and perhaps we will be able to play a good game of "May I."

I want to thank you for putting up with me for almost forty years, for the two most wonderful children, and they are such a joy. They are, indeed, your monument and they are so much like you, modest and unpretentious. And me—I'll just keep on bragging about them to whoever wants to listen.

I'll eat, maybe not your vegetable soup, but I'll eat and carry on for the two of us. I have to see the Bar Mitzvah and Bat Mitzvah of our grandchildren and maybe, just maybe, their weddings.

I promise I'll do my best. I miss you and so does everyone else from Circle 10.

Rest in peace.
Niech ci ziemia lekka bedzie.

P.S. I just want to include the tribute of your colleagues and out of so many letters and cards, a note from Carmen A. (your supervisor).

Farewell to Giselle

Yesterday, a rabbi said these words: "They are not dead who live in the hearts they leave behind." And for us, her co-workers at CSE in District 22, Giselle will ever be alive in our hearts.

The years we shared together allowed us to know this courageous, cheerful, dedicated and very special lady who became such an important part of our family. She made each of us a little better and a little happier just because she was Giselle. Indeed, Giselle, we will miss you, but we will always remember you. You will be in our hearts.

Dear George and Family

Never did I imagine I would be writing this note. Giselle was such a part of my professional life that I will miss seeing her and learning from her. She was a supervisor's "dream." She was so caring and yet so professional; she was dedicated and always willing to assume any task. I so enjoyed discussing cases with her; she was always right on target and always so full of understanding and compassion. Little did we know that she was able to be all these things while living with her own great problem. It is a regret we have that we did not know and perhaps would have been able to make her life simpler. But I guess this would not have been Giselle and the way she wanted to live her life.

From a personal viewpoint, she was a lady I considered my friend. We did not need to share a social life; we thought and acted similarly. I feel such a loss.

And how all of you must feel this loss, but what wonderful memories of such a loving wife, mother and grandmother. So dedicated to all of you and so proud.

Please accept the condolences that I must share with you. We will miss her, but she will remain in our hearts.

Sincerely,
Carmen Aquilon

We sat "Shiva" in our apartment. Many people came (standing room only). Some of these people we hadn't seen or heard from in years.

Mitch and I went twice a day to the shul to say "Kaddish." The kids stayed with me. Little Gregory was running all over the place looking for Nana. I told him that you had gone to work. That he accepted, because where else would you be?

Today, a week later, the "Shiva" period ended. Rabbi Halpern blessed us. "No more sorrows." I believe him.

Before we came back to the house, Mitch and I went around the block so that your soul could peacefully go to heaven.

I removed the towels covering the mirrors, because mirrors are the only things in the house that don't have any memory, only reflections. I tried to turn on the light on my side of the bed and one of the bulbs went out. It was the light out of my life.

Write to you soon.

Hi Pampucyk:

I didn't think I was going to write to you so soon, but I want you to know that last Friday I went to the bank safe and took out your jewelry, because Saturday I was going to see Phyllis and Mitch.

I spent most of Saturday afternoon playing with Gregory. I brought with me a set of dominoes and checkers. I tried to teach him how to play dominoes because he knows the numbers and can count to fifty.

Glancing over the box of Milton Bradley's dominoes, I noticed a sign in small print: "Ages from 7 to adult." Tell me, darling, am I pushing too hard? Before I left, as you wished, I gave the bulk of your jewelry to Phyllis (mink coat too). Not that I minded giving it to her, because eventually the kids would have inherited it anyway, but somehow I wasn't able to describe to her each piece how and when I obtained it, whether it was for your birthday, wedding anniversary or Valentine's Day.

Should I have also told her that some of the more valuable pieces I had to pay in several installments to our friend Mankin? Would the kids really care? I also stopped at Mitch and Sima's place and left them a few items. After all, she may be carrying your name.

The same evening I went to David and Wacka's for dinner. Dudek was ever cheerful and in his humorous way asked me, "I hope, George, you're not too hungry?" He was right, of course, my stomach was tight as a drum. The food was really good; Wacka is a superb cook, but I couldn't eat much. We talked and then talked some more. Coming home to an empty house, there was a new stack of mail waiting for me. Among others, a very nice note from Anna from the laboratory, the same one that drew your blood every two weeks. There was also another very moving note from Dr. Figur.

If I were cynical, and occasionally I am (not this time, however), I would say that he wrote it to soften the blow of the bill that his office sent. After all, he doesn't mail bills, he only sets the prices. I won't tell you how much the bill was because it may upset you. Since I always was hiding medical bills from you, I'll do it this time again.

Nevertheless, the note was a nice one and here it is:

Dear Mr. Lee:

I wish to express my condolences to you and your children. Having two malignancies simultaneously was too much to bear, but Giselle was a marvel. She had immense strength and came back to full activity after a stroke which would have made the rest of us give up. I am a better physician by having had the privilege of caring for such a warm, gentle and strong woman.

Sincerely,
Arthur Figur

There isn't much I can add. Tomorrow, Sunday A.M., Louise McCullough and her cronies are supposed to stop by and in the afternoon I will go to Blanche and Marion's for a Circle 10 meeting. The meeting will be held to discuss what to do with Shirley's bungalow. I shall vote for you because, after all, I always had your vote.

Love,
George

Monday, November 21, 1988

Hi:

I came across your wedding band, the same one we bought as a set before we had gotten married, some forty years ago.

Yours was almost brand new, because the ring was too tight and you usually wore other rings.

Mine, which I always wore over all these years, was well worn out. All the intricate design was hardly visible; all the sharp edges were gone. On the spur of the moment I decided to tie both rings with a black thread to put away in a safe.

I went to the car and couldn't start the engine. The battery was dead!

Are you sending me any kind of message? Or did the battery simply go dead because I had left the inside dome light burning all night after coming back from the Circle 10 meeting in an awfully heavy rain. I've called Polymer to ask someone to give me a boost to start the car. I glanced at my shoes; they were brown, but each shoe was from a different pair. Otherwise, I am fine. Don't worry, darling, I made it to the office on time.

Chapter 35

Uncle Herman

On Monday October 22, 1990 Carl picked up the phone in the office and dialed the number of his uncle and aunt, who were living in a Home for the Aged in Miami, Florida. His uncle was sick with bone cancer, diagnosed only three months ago and Irene reminded him to call every day. "Herman Gruber is 89 years old; one day it may be too late," she kept saying.

"I'll call him," he pleaded lamely, "but please join in the conversation. He likes you very much and it will give him pleasure to talk to you." This was true but the real reason was that Carl found it difficult to talk to his uncle. There were so many memories and there had been so much tragedy.

His Aunt Hermine picked up the phone. She recognized his voice immediately. "Carl, your uncle is dead, he committed suicide," she said bluntly.

Carl was shocked. "How did it happen? When? Why?" he showered her with questions. There was a cold sweat covering his face and shivers ran up and down his body.

"He asked me to go down to get him a newspaper and when I left he went onto the porch and jumped down from the eighth floor." Her high-pitched voice was full of despair but surprisingly calm and collected.

"When I wanted to go back, the people in the Home wouldn't let me," she continued.

"When did it happen?" Carl pressed.

"On Wednesday, last week."

"Why didn't you let us know? Today is Monday. We would have come to pay our last respects and to keep you company."

"It all happened so fast and I was in shock. I didn't know what was going on around me. The funeral took place right away," she said, trying to justify her behavior.

Irene was sitting next to Carl and realized that something terrible must have happened. After Carl got off the phone, he repeated the story to her. "We must go there," she said. "Let me call her." She dialed the number and talked to Hermine for a while. "She doesn't want us to come now," she said after hanging up. "She wants to get used to being alone."

Carl sat petrified in his chair as thoughts raced through his mind. He had known his uncle since childhood. When Carl was 7 years old, his uncle was already a grown man of 29. Uncle Herman had been very handsome, with regular features, black hair and green eyes under black eyebrows. Carl remembered him sitting with his friends in the "salon" in his house on Old Zniesienie. He remembered how they had all worn spats, which at that time were the latest fashion; Carl had been very impressed by them. Uncle always brought gifts of money and chocolate to the three boys, his brother's sons, and they adored and admired him. He would give them 5 zlotys each, at the time a considerable sum of money.

Carl's mother had introduced Herman to her sister Fela and a courtship had followed. There was talk of their getting married. Fela was a strikingly beautiful girl, ten years younger than Herman, with flaming red hair and a stunning figure. She left to study pharmacology in Vienna, where she lived with her married sister Susan. She wrote love letters to Herman. Then, Herman met Hermine. She came from a wealthy family; her father was a successful lawyer in Lvov and gave her a substantial dowry. On the other hand, Fela had no dowry. Her father, an impoverished farmer, could not afford any. After a short courtship, Herman married Hermine.

Carl's mother Amelia, Fela's older sister, was heartbroken. She had hoped that Herman would marry Fela. She wrote an urgent letter to her in Vienna, telling her what had happened, telling her to break off the correspondence with him. She spoke about it a lot at home and Carl heard all the conversations; he started to think less of his beloved uncle.

The newly married couple moved to Warsaw, where Herman got a well-paid position in a bank. At that time, Carl's father Nathan lost his job and was unemployed for two years in crisis-ridden prewar Poland.

"Ask your brother to help you," Amelia would often say to her husband.

"He cannot help us. He told me all his money belonged to his wife," Nathan would answer. Uncle Herman now visited them seldom and didn't bring any more gifts for the boys.

"He knows that you have no work; he should help you. At least let him give you some money towards the boys' tuition," Amelia insisted.

"He knows we don't have any money." Nathan kept silent.

Carl overheard these conversations late at night when his parents thought he was asleep. He was heartbroken. His uncle was a fallen idol. He developed a resentment towards him. He could not forgive him for not helping them. After all, Uncle Herman was rich and they were poor. He had bought an apartment building in Warsaw while they had no money at all. Yet he wouldn't help them.

Amelia used to travel to a resort town in Otwock, near Warsaw. Carl was a sickly boy and she would leave him there for the summer with another Hermine, the wife of Amelia's brother Meyer. Amelia met Meyer clandestinely because her father had forbidden her to see him. He had broken off relations with his son because Meyer was a gambler. On these occasions Herman also came in order to see his sister-in-law.

They were sitting on the grass in the hotel's garden when an ant walked onto Herman's back.

"Uncle, an ant is crawling on your back!" exclaimed Carl.

"She is so small and I am so big," Herman answered good-naturedly. "Besides, how much can an ant eat?" he joked. He still could be the charming man Carl had known before.

Herman took them to his apartment in Warsaw. A baby had just been born and they had named him Richard. Herman told them proudly that he had just bought the apartment house in which they lived. Amelia asked him for help. Her husband (Herman's brother) had just gone bankrupt in the little grocery store he had inherited from his mother. Uncle Herman refused. "All my money belongs to my wife," he said, "and I cannot help you. I have no money."

Years passed and Nathan and Amelia's financial situation got worse and worse. They were now sending three boys to high school and could not afford to pay the tuition. Nathan was working as a clothing salesman and was earning very little. His monthly salary was barely enough to feed the family. True, they lived in their in-laws' house on the farm and didn't have to pay rent but there was no money left for anything else. Amelia took in sewing to help out.

In September 1939, the war broke out. Herman and his family were stuck in Warsaw under the Germans, while Carl and his family found themselves in Lvov, which was occupied by the Russians. A large number of Jews, especially young males, fled from the German side to the Russian, fearing persecution.

One day in the late fall of 1939, Uncle Herman appeared on

Nathan and Amelia's front porch. He was tired after a long walk and covered with dust. He had a backpack on his shoulders. Nathan and Amelia showered him with questions. "Where are your wife and child? Why didn't they come with you? What are you planning to do?"

"Let me answer one question at a time," replied Herman. "Hermine and the child are all right and relatively safe in Warsaw. There was talk that the Germans would kill Jewish men, so I ran away. Can I stay with you for a while?"

"Of course you can," both Nathan and Amelia said without hesitation. All the grudges and injustices were quickly forgotten. Uncle Herman stayed with them in their tiny apartment for two years without paying anything for room and food. He didn't have any money; this time it was true. Herman didn't know what was happening to his family. An impassable border now separated the Russian and German parts of Poland and letters took months to arrive. Most of the time they didn't arrive at all. Travel between the two territories was forbidden.

Carl marveled. Uncle Herman hadn't helped his parents when they were poor before the war. Yet when he was in trouble, he didn't hesitate to go to them and ask for help. They helped him without asking any questions or making any reproaches. It certainly didn't put his uncle in a better light.

On June 22, 1941 war broke out between Germany and the Soviet Union. Russia was totally unprepared and succumbed easily at the beginning. The Germans reached Lvov by June 30 of the same year, record time, having covered as much as 50 miles a day.

A horrible period of persecution, robbery and killing of the Jews began and lasted for three years. Shortly after the German occupation began, Uncle Herman announced that he was going back to his wife and son in Warsaw. Traveling for a Jew was still dangerous, but there no longer was an impassable border between Lvov and Warsaw, as the Germans had annexed Lvov to the already existing General Government. That's what they called the rump state made of what was left of Poland.

They lost all contact with each other as the winds of war buffeted them to and fro. Carl's parents, aunts, uncles and grandfather were killed by the Germans in ghettos and in death camps. He and his brothers survived, living as Christians under assumed names in cities where nobody knew them. (Their stories during the war are described in a separate book entitled, "Of Human Agony."

When the war ended, Russia, which had liberated Poland from the

Germans, created a totally subservient puppet regime in Poland. There was an immediate shortage of qualified government personnel and Herman got a high position in the Ministry of Finance. This enabled him to make a comfortable living.

Carl also got a high position as an assistant to Michael Dichter, the Director of an Oil Refinery in Ligota in Upper Silesia, which had been returned to Poland. There he met Michael's sister-in-law Irene and fell in love with her. Irene reciprocated his feelings and the couple planned to get married.

Carl was called to see his Aunt Fela, who was now living in Katowice and who had gotten him his position through acquaintances. His uncle was there too.

Herman came straight to the point. "I understand that you want to get married?"

"Yes, I do."

"Don't you think you're being too hasty? You are young and you should go to college. If you get married, that will be much more difficult. If you don't get married I'll take you to America."

Carl kept silent. He didn't know what to say.

The conversation continued and, after a while, Carl said good-bye and left. He knew he was not going to give Irene up no matter what happened.

Carl and Irene got married in Poland and soon afterwards emigrated to Germany. Uncle Herman emigrated too. He went to a D.P. camp and obtained the position of manager of a food warehouse. It was a lucrative position, since food was very scarce in Germany after the war.

Carl and Irene enrolled at the university while waiting for visas to the United States. They were very poor and often went to bed hungry. Aunt Fela came to visit them in Munich, where they lived. Seeing in what bad shape they were in, especially Irene, she invited them to her D.P. camp, where food was somewhat more plentiful, and for two weeks shared with them whatever little she had herself. They returned to Munich in much better physical shape.

Uncle Herman never helped them, even though he was much better off financially, and Carl couldn't help marveling at how history had repeated itself. His mother was right, he thought: Uncle wouldn't help anybody. Irene said, "He is the type of person who doesn't give anything and doesn't ask for anything."

Finally, Irene and Carl got their visas and became the first in their families to emigrate to America.

Some time later, Uncle Herman also moved to the United States. He struggled at first, but was finally able to become a stockbroker and got a job in a brokerage house.

Carl was studying to be a chemical engineer. Leo, his older brother, also came from Germany, where he had received a degree in electronic engineering. He looked for a job for four months. They all struggled. They lived in a poor section of Williamsburg in Brooklyn, where the resourceful Hilda, Leo's wife, had found cheap apartments for all of them. They saw Uncle and Aunt often, as they lived in adjoining apartment houses.

The youngest brother now arrived from Germany. He had stayed there with Uncle Herman and hadn't studied. Now, pressed by his brothers, he enrolled in night school in mechanical engineering.

"Your parents would be so proud of you boys," Uncle repeated often. "Two boys with college degrees and the third one studying to become an engineer too. It was the dream of their life for you to go to college and to study. How sad that they cannot see what has become of you now."

After a while, Uncle and Aunt moved to Queens, while Irene and Carl stayed in Brooklyn. Aunt Hermine invited them once in a while to dinner on a Saturday evening. They took a genuine interest in the progress their nephews were making and Uncle was bursting with pride. He was especially happy when Carl was made vice president of his company.

"Go to the president of your company and ask him for a big, fat raise," he advised. "Tell him to give you fringe benefits." He was full of enthusiasm and his happiness over Carl's successes was written all over his face.

He enjoyed telling the story of how he had outsmarted death and survived the war. "We were hidden in the house of a Polish family and we paid them for hiding and feeding us. This lasted for months until I used up all the money. At that time I told the man that I had no more money, but I had a house in Warsaw, and I gave him the deed to the house. However," he said with a twinkle in his eye, "I stipulated in the papers that he could get the house only if we survived the war. So the fellow did everything in his power to protect and hide us. We were now his investment guarantee."

"What happened after the war?" asked Carl.

"I gave him the house," answered Herman. "After all, he had kept me and Hermine in his house in hiding to the end of the war."

When Irene and Carl's 25th wedding anniversary came around, Irene reminded Carl to invite his uncle and aunt to the celebration. It was January 9, 1971 and Uncle had just turned 70 a few days before. After the anniversary cake was served, out came a cake Irene had ordered for Uncle's birthday. Everybody sang "Happy Birthday" and he was visibly touched. He had tears in his eyes. He hadn't expected this at all.

In the summer that year, Irene and Shirley went to the Catskill mountains for a vacation, while Carl and Paul visited on weekends. One day he got a call from his aunt. She and Uncle were staying in a summer cottage on Long Island and invited him to come for dinner that evening. Carl accepted. When he got there he was struck by the way his uncle looked. Herman was rested and sun-tanned and he looked like a young man, maybe 35 years old. He was full of life and energy and didn't walk but rather ran around like a young boy. Carl hoped that he would look and feel that young when he was 70. He could not help but think that maybe his mother was wrong when she complained about Uncle's behavior towards them. He thought that, in any case, it was ridiculous to hold a grudge for so long. It was time to repair the relationship with his only living older relative (besides Aunt Fela in Israel). Yet the feelings that had been etched on his heart during childhood lingered and, try as he might, they persisted.

Aunt Hermine informed him that Uncle intended to retire in the near future and that they planned to move to Florida.

In the spring of 1988, Irene and Carl flew to Orlando, Florida for a vacation. They had bought a house there a few years earlier. Irene's sister Anna and their friend Lynn came too. After a short stay in their house they proceeded by car to Miami to see Uncle Herman and Aunt Hermine, who were now living in a Jewish Home for the Aged.

They arrived in Miami in the evening and stayed overnight in a hotel. The next morning they asked Anna and Lynn to stay behind. It would be better if they spent the time alone with the family. Carl took a video camera to take their pictures.

They found the Home for the Aged in a bad area of the city, but the buildings were in good repair, surrounded by a fence, with several watchmen present. Uncle and Aunt occupied a small apartment. They had made generous contributions to the Home and were entitled to live there any time they wished. A year before, Aunt had been slightly injured in a car accident and they were afraid that if something serious happened to them, they would not get proper medical attention. Uncle was especially concerned about who would take care of his wife if he were gone. After all, he was ten years older than she. So he decided to exercise his option and move into the Home.

Carl and Irene had visited last two years ago, and Carl found them somewhat more frail, but still in good physical shape. Their minds were clear and lucid. They still went for walks in the enclosed area of the Home. Aunt, who was close to 80, walked more than Uncle, who was 89 years old.

The conversation centered around their health, activities, Home facilities and services. They seemed to be happy and satisfied with the conditions in the Home.

Hermine took Irene to their bedroom. There were pictures of a beautiful boy at different ages, from infancy to 10 years of age. "This was my son Richard," she said. They stood in silence, as if paying respect to the dead boy. "There was a selection during the war by the Germans. We were given a choice: either go to death with our son or give him away and save our lives. We agreed without saying a word. We gave our child away and stayed alive."

Suddenly, Hermine got up and went over to Irene. She took out a golden necklace and a bracelet from a jewelry box and said, "Irene, I want you to have these things. I want you to wear them so you will remember me." With tears in her eyes she proceeded a little awkwardly to place the necklace on Irene's neck.

Carl's eyes welled up with tears too. Thoughts from the past crowded his mind. During his childhood his aunt was wealthy but she was never willing to help his family. They were poor and his mother and father had turned to Herman several times. Uncle's standard answer was, "The money belongs to my wife. I cannot help you." And yet, when he was a bachelor, he had always brought them gifts and money.

As they were leaving, Uncle said to Carl, "I think often about your parents, Carl. Why were they killed by the Germans? Such good and innocent people. They never harmed anybody in their lives."

He spoke with feeling and intensity in his voice such as Carl had never heard from him before. He must have thought a lot about the past, how he had behaved towards them and how they, in return had behaved towards him.

When they left the old age home, Carl asked Irene, "Why did Aunt give you those expensive gifts?"

She replied, "They wanted us to have something to remember

them by. Aunt said to me, 'I want you to wear it' and I promised her that I would wear them often."

But Carl thought otherwise. Maybe she wanted to compensate them for all the times in the past when she could have helped them but didn't. After all, his uncle must have agreed to give them these presents.

Carl reminded himself of that terrible banging on the door at night fifty-eight years ago, when his uncle had come running to his older brother, Carl's father, to tell him the horrible news. Their mother, pregnant sister and her husband had been brutally axed to death by robbers. The robbers received light sentences: ten, five and one year, respectively. It was on the first page in all the newspapers and everybody was saying that these lenient sentences were given because they had only killed Jews.

All these thoughts rushed through Carl's mind and a wave of memories went through his head like a tornado.

And now his uncle was dead. He had committed suicide by jumping out of the window. True, he was incurably ill and didn't want to be a burden to his wife. And he was in terrible pain. But why had he chosen this kind of death?

He had so much joi de vivre in him. He was the last person in the world that one would expect to do this. Why, why? Only now did Carl realize that he had always loved his uncle very much, even when he had held a grudge against him.

Chapter 36

Irene's Poems

January 30, 1989.

In Memory of Basia Tabaczynska

My mind is racing through the years
Of my life gone by
My heart beats fast, I'm full of fears
My eyes are misty and full of tears
I fight the strong desire to cry.

My past comes clear, I see my friends
The ones who did much good for me
The ones who held out to me their hands
When from oppressors I had to flee.

I cry inside for losing them
Somewhere in the waves of life
I keep repeating each precious name
Each memory is sharp as a knife.

I know that some of them are gone
Forever gone from me
I can't do now what I haven't done
When my life was busy and I failed to see
The race of time.

Now it's too late to go back there
To my friends who helped when I
Really needed them in my despair
And jump the years gone by.

And Basia dear, you were my friend
Right to the end.

I sit down to write my regrets
And pray to God to my friends to be kind
To forgive them for their life's mistakes
When they were busy and out of their minds
Were others, who did good for them.

My heart is full of sorrow
I mourn my dear old friends
I fear to see tomorrow
For I see a life which ends.

August 15, 1989

As Life Is Going By

We go through many, many times
Sometimes we laugh or cry
Sometimes it rains or the sun shines
As life is going by.

We go through youth and suffer some
Sometimes we're bold or shy
We wait for miracles to come
As life is going by.

We reach mature and adult age
And we know how to satisfy
Ourselves, as we turn the page
Of life that's going by.

How sad it is to reach the old
Age, we thought we'll always be spry
But age is catching up, it's cold
As life is going by.

We all are born by God's will
And all of us will die
No one escapes the fate so real
As life is going by.

Monticello, 8/27/89

My Favorite Place

My favorite place waits for me
In lovely shade under a tree
A chair stands there under thee
And waits and waits for me.

A lovely day, a lovely sky
Here and there a cloud dancing by
The sun over me orange and shy
I so love to watch it passing by.

The day goes on, the children play
Their games are, oh, so sweet and gay
I watch them run, so that I may
Remember me, when I would play.

And now I go under a tree
Where my favorite place waits for me
I sit in a chair which stands in shade
And watch the daylight slowly fade.

Monticello 8/27/89

Day Is Done

The evening's here and day is done
As I sit on a porch and write
I feast my eyes on beautiful sight
In front of a cottage and enjoy the fun
Of watching nature in its purest beauty.

A part of the yard is light
And a part is dark
As the sun sets in the sky

And to sleep goes the lark
And the day is done, and the sun is gone.

Soon the lights of the lanterns
Which are in the yard
Will light, to emulate the sun
Oh, how silly it is to believe that they can
Be like sun, when the day is done.

The darkness comes so stark and cold
One cannot feel the warmth
Of the sun which went behind the sky
After riding earth back and forth
To end the day and bow before night
And go to other places, out of sight.

Tomorrow is another day
The sun will again come here
Everything will once again be light
The world will start anew and bright
And once more we will hear
The singing of the freshened lark who
Woke up to sun which came after dark.

1979

Youth

A child is born so very pure
Knowing not what his fate may be
Innocent of what he may have to endure
Will life bring him happiness or tragedy?

A baby trusts and knows no more
Than it should know in its mother's care
Who loves him and wipes the tears away
And who will always be there?

He grows and learns that young grow older
He won't accept it though
He grows taller and stronger and bolder
And that's how he should grow.

When youth is climbing up the hill
Each day holds promise like the sun
He strives and plans to live forever
His dreams don't end when night is gone.

And that's how youth helps man survive
Because he knows not that he'll grow old
He knows not this sad fact of life
Because he's strong and young and bold.

Adam

On the sixth day of creation
God looked and checked his work so fair
The world was beautiful and full of promise
Yet something was missing there

Said God "I alone shall enjoy the earth
No one else is here who can
See the beauty of my creation
Unless I create a man."

And so Adam was made to see work of God
He lived in heaven as the angels did
God gave him Eve and Adam was happy
Till the snake came and planted the seed of evil.

Poor Adam, he did what so many do
He ate the apple from the forbidden tree
Later; he was sorry, but couldn't undo
The wrong he did when his choice was free.

And so he had to leave heaven
Never again to return there
His life was to end when he did his share
Angels saw it all, but they didn't care.

Maybe they were a little sad
When God created Adam?
And now they were a little glad?
You bet!

No matter, the fact remained a fact
That God with Adam broke a pact
And I think Adam made a bad mistake
By not listening to God, but listening to snake.

Prayer for My Children

God give me strength to let them see
The light of right from wrong
And save them please from peril which
Might break them before they are strong

They are so tender, young and true
The world is so confusing today
Don't let them join the misguided few
Who have the tongue of snake and say

"Follow not the old ways
The good ways are new
We show you road out of maze
We give you the right cue

Our way is to live for now
Tomorrow may never be
On this we take a vow
So please yourself and be free"

Free from what my friend?
Free from future, yes, you'll see

For your life will quickly end
Your tomorrow will never be

So please oh God, please let them see
The light of right from wrong
And help their hearts and minds to grow
Kind and free and strong

    This is a poem written by Irene for Carl on their 25th wedding anniversary:

25 years old is our married life
It's a long, long time
25 years since I'm your wife
And you are a husband of mine.

How do you paint a picture of life
With all its happiness and sorrow
A lifetime since I became your wife
Or yesterday, today or tomorrow?

We had an eternity to look forward to
How very little we realized then
That moments of joy are precious and few
So let's catch them while we can.

This is to say "thank you"
And tell you that I am proud to be your wife
And that is the reason why
I'd like to forever share your life.

Thank you for years that passed
Let's have a long and happy life!
I wish you health and much success
I'm proud to be your wife.

A Certain Mood.

Music in the air
Music everywhere
Radios, phonos, singing, bands
People dancing, clapping hands
In the winter or in May
Music makes us hep and gay.

Music can be short and strong
Music can be light and long
Music could be dark and gray
On a long November day
Or colorful and very gay
When the children are at play.

Music is for young and old
Music is for weak and bold
In the stories we were told
Music was around the earth
Before words were ever heard
Before God made the man
So let's enjoy it when we can.

1971

This was written on the plane, on the first trip to Israel.

How beautiful and happy is our earth
When you look at her from the sky
It's hard to believe the cries I heard
Before I came to fly.

The cotton like clouds and peaks of a mountain
Alps, Switzerland and the Roman fountain
Rivers, oceans and map like lands
Become like dear and very close friends.

The joy so great
It's difficult to tell
How much God made
Besides heaven and hell.

And before us the greatest joy of all
Israel waiting with its secret places
I don't know how I'll feel at the Wailing Wall
And other sacred things
My heart speedily races.

3 weeks later coming back from Israel

We are coming back from the Promised Land
Our hearts are happy and gay
The camels on deserts of hills and sand
The Wailing Wall where so many pray
And put their wishes into the sacred stone.

Beautiful Jerusalem with streets so narrow
With thousands of stores standing side by side
Where Arabs catch tourists and a little sparrow
Becomes your most welcome and interesting guide.

You walk on history and you don't believe
That it is really you who are walking there
Upon the ancient ruins which geologists retrieve
And touching with your hands things sacred and rare.
Masada, so dignified and proud
A fortress which no one could reach
Still covered with a mourning shroud
You stand at her feet on the Dead Sea beach
And you cry inside for the bravest of men.

I once wore a Star of David on my hand
As a sign of disgrace that only we understand
Now I want to shout that I love my Land
And I am proud to be a Jew.

More about music

What is the one thing which everyone likes
Old people in rocking chairs and children on bikes
Young men going to work and girls curling their hair
It is music, music, music in the air.

There are all kinds of music we hear
Some is loud and noisy
Some is soft yet clear
Some is far away and other is near.

Music can make you so happy and gay
Like a little bird jumping lightly in the bay
Other music can make you thoughtful and sad
And make you remember things which were very bad.

Music is singing, music is bells ringing
Music is to dance or jump over a fence
When you are alone in a room
Music in the air takes away the gloom.

1973
This Irene wrote for Shirley and Paul's 25th Wedding Anniversary, which never came to be.

It is a joy for us to be
A part of your Anniversary
And celebrate and wish happiness that's due
To wonderful people like you and you.

You are so dear and close to us
That an occasion like this can't pass
Without us wishing you all the best
And health and wealth and all the rest
That goes with wishing.

And from the bottom of our hearts
We hope that we shall never part
From the both of you.

Let's stay together and join our hands
And let's be merry for we are friends
By our choice and love that's true
So, Happy Anniversary to both of you.

1973

It is a quarter of a century
Since you and I first saw New York
We looked at the Statue of Liberty
As the ship inched her way to the harbor.

It was a cold winter day
We were so young and full of hope
As "Marine Tiger" pulled into the bay.

We stepped onto the land of freedom and equality
Where our dreams dispersed into thin air
And were replaced by stern reality.

We were open wide to all which came
In this new world of ours
Nothing seemed hard, we could face together
Anything.... We were young!

1972

This was written by Irene to celebrate the furnishing of the Casino in Circle Ten which was done by the members themselves.

Shangri-la

There is a little town in the Catskill Mountains called Monticello. We all know the town, we have been coming here for years. But to me it is more than just another town, I love it. I call it Shangri-la because here is my little place in this world where I always feel young and most of the time happy.

Here I spend time with people who are close to my heart, who know me for what I am and like me just that way.

Allow me to say a few words for each of them. Please take it with a sense of humor. No offense meant—I love you all.

> Shirley's a gal you must admire
> The rare kind of whom you cannot tire
> She can drive you crazy winter and fall
> But when you need her, she's the greatest of all.
>
> Paul is a guy that's a pleasure to meet
> The successful kind which never meets defeat
> He is a guy with that certain spark
> Never angry, always smiling, happy as a lark.
>
> Blanche is a lady so wonderfully neat
> Good friend and neighbor and so very sweet
> She's a real darling, she will always do
> Whatever she can for me and you.
>
> Marian is a favorite with many a man
> A great fellow will help where he can
> Too bad he was in such a big pain
> But there's no denying it, he's a Calamity Jane.
>
> Gisella, the mother hen of our group
> She closely watches over her coop
> She's everyone's friend, good sport, good pal
> The kind that is an all-around gal.
>
> He's our president, we all know the guy
> When things have to be done, he doesn't ask why
> He's a real wonder as a host
> And will do his utmost not to leave his post.
>
> Wacka, o Wacka so likable and gay
> Always ready to make fun around her

And take away the gray
From a cloudy day.

David comes on Fridays tired evermore
Until he unwinds behind a locked door
But all in all he is very nice
And just loves to read everybody's Times.

Elaine is made of a different clay
Please let me tell you if I may
That you will never find a rarer treat
She's smart, she's fun and a little offbeat.

Joe's a fancy dresser, has a heart of gold
Brings babka and asks questions which make you gray and old
He's fun to be with, wish he could relax
And not worry so much about the future on rocks.

Carl I cannot describe as you all understand
Or I will get a taste of a man's strong hand
I am only joking, he's the good kind
To me he's the best, body, soul and mind.

I am the girl who loves you all
From early spring through winter and fall
I found a Shangri-la which my problems cures
You guessed who I am

              Respectfully yours

November 1993

              The enchanted cottage

Once upon the time there was an enchanted place in the woods.

In that enchanted place there were ten enchanted cottages, lovely white cottages.

In each of these cottages lived an enchanted family. All these families knew each other for many years and they liked being together.

Chapter 38

A Walk with Leo

April 13, 1991, was a rainy Saturday in Brooklyn. Leo and Hilda, Carl's brother and sister-in-law, were coming to visit them and Irene and Carl were waiting for them to arrive at noon from New Jersey. Irene was busy preparing food for the guests. She prepared their guests' favorite dishes for lunch. Hilda loved schmaltz herrings and Leo liked smoked fish and there was plenty of it besides cold cuts and cheeses.

Irene and Carl were planning to go in the beginning of May to Israel and Carl's thoughts were on the impending visit to his Aunt Eva who lived there with her children and grandchildren.

Carl wanted to bring Eva a copy of the book he wrote together with Irene describing the Holocaust and he felt that the book was incomplete and that it did not give enough attention to Eva. She saved his life, the life of his brothers and many other people from the Germans by her heroic behavior and Carl wanted somehow to express his gratitude to her. She saved his life and thanks to her he was now alive here in the United States. Her deeds during the war were heroic, yet she never bragged about them and very little was known about them. At that time her name was Eva although she was intermittently called Fela which was her real name before the war. Carl wanted to know more about her exploits during the war.

He was preoccupied with this idea already for quite a while but he didn't know how to write about her. Irene was very good in writing and Carl liked her lucid, direct method of describing things that happened. Carl even asked Irene to help him write about Fela, but somehow they never got around to do it.

Another problem was that Carl felt that he knew so little about his aunt and he simply didn't know what to write. Although he knew a lot about her deeds during the war and he knew how she saved his life by providing him with false Christian papers but he lacked many details about the things that happened. Suddenly an idea occurred to him. He will ask Leo about it. Yes, Leo had a much closer relationship with Eva during the war. May be he would be able to tell him about it. But it had to be done delicately. Leo didn't like to talk about the war. Each time Carl started a conversation on this subject in the past Leo would give him an evasive answer and it usually stopped right there.

Finally, Leo and Hilda arrived and after embracing each other and exchanging the welcoming pleasantries they sat down to lunch. The conversation was centered around their impending trip to Israel and their additional side-trip to Italy. Since Hilda and Leo were in Italy already they were giving them useful tips where to eat, what to see and the like.

Finally the lunch was finished and they moved to the living room to talk some more. At that time their dog Bambi started to bark and Carl got up to take him for a walk. Leo got up too and said, "I'll walk with you." They put on their coats and took an umbrella. It was now raining heavily. After they walked for a few minutes Carl asked, "Do you remember Leo how Eva gave us the papers to travel from the ghetto? How did you meet with her?"

Leo thought for a moment and said, "She brought us forged documents allowing us to travel from Lvov to Cracow. The names were omitted because she didn't know what assumed Christian names we will be able to get." In order to have a Christian name one had to obtain somehow a gentile birth certificate.

He continued, "I had my Polish friend type in the names later in the office since we didn't have a typewriter at home.

Seeing that the conversation is getting off on a tangent, Carl interjected quickly, "Please tell me, how did you meet Fela? She was outside of the ghetto as a gentile and it was dangerous for her to meet with the Jews."

Leo was visibly straining his memory trying to remember the details, "Aunt Susan helped me in that. She was hiding out in the city with Herta and was helping us by sending food."

"When did you meet with Eva?" Carl was pressing on. "The big pogrom or rather an organized killing of Jews took place in August 1942."

"It was before the pogrom," said Leo unsure of himself. "It could not have been. Our mother and Aunt Donna were already taken away by the Germans and I remember you told me that Aunt Eva was devastated by it," said Carl.

Leo tried to gather the facts in his memory, "It was such a long time ago, almost fifty years ago. It is possible that it was during that pogrom." Carl said, "I miss a lot of details about Eva. You were much closer to her than any one of us. You were her favorite."

"Yes, that's true," said Leo thoughtfully "but things changed over the years and now you are much closer to her and her children. I feel almost like a stranger." He continued, "I read your book. I feel that it is incomplete. You should write more about Eva and her heroic behavior during the war. After all she saved the lives of many other people besides ours."

Carl said, "I feel that we should show her gratitude for what she did for us."

"Yes I should show her gratitude," said Leo honestly "and I am sorry that I didn't."

It was raining heavily now and they both got soaking wet but they didn't even notice it. The poor dog got soaking wet too. By the time they got back home they were excited and stimulated by the conversation.

Irene and Hilda were concerned about their long absence. "Where were you so long!" they both exclaimed. "Oh, we were just talking about the old times," answered Carl happily. He felt as if a big stone fell of his shoulders. "You were walking in this pouring rain for an hour and talking?' asked Irene with disbelief. Yes. we were," answered Carl.

Chapter 39

Trip to Israel and Italy

In May 1991, Carl and Irene decided to go to Israel. The Persian Gulf War was over and the Arabs in general and the Palestinians in particular were down after siding with the loser, Sadam Hussein. They didn't expect any acts of terrorism against the victorious Americans and time seemed propitious to travel. They decided to stop over for a few days in Italy on the way back to break the jet-lag.

Last time when they were in Israel in 1987, it took them two weeks after the return to the U.S. to get over the effects of the jet-lag. They were walking like in a daze, sleeping during the day and not being able to sleep at night.

Carl wanted to see his Aunt Eva and her family. He also wanted to go to Yad Vashem, the Holocaust Museum to look for the names of his relatives and school mates. He lost all the contact with them during the war. He was especially interested to see what happened to his cousins Matthew and Ziggy, the sons of Aunt Donna. He had a faint hope that they might be alive.

Carl was going to Israel with apprehension. He was taking with him the manuscript of the book entitled, "Of Human Agony," which he wrote together with Irene. The book contained many mentions of Eva and Carl wanted to give it to her to read. He did not know how Eva will react to the book and to the way he described her.

He was also apprehensive about going to Yad Vashem. He knew that he was hoping against any possible odds, that any members of his family still lived. If they did he would have known about it for sure. After all, it was now forty five years after the World War II has ended and the dramatic reunions of people who lost each other were more and more rare. They were rare even at the beginning because so many people were killed by the Germans.

Irene was anxious to see her cousins, one of whom, Ann, had now Alzheimer's disease.

The excitement before the trip was high. They went to Essex Street on the East Side in Manhattan to buy electrical appliances operating at 220 Volts. This is the voltage existing in Israel. Essex Street is the only place where you can get them.

The trip itself was uneventful and they landed at the Ben Gurion Airport without a hitch. Carl loved to watch the Israelis. He felt warmth and kinship with the older people, recognizing their common origins in Europe. He saw in them people who reminded him of his parents, his uncles and aunts. He felt pride watching the young people too unaffected by the anti-Semitism and members of a proud Israeli Army. He remembered himself and his school mates when they were young. Denigrated by constant anti-Semitic remarks at school and on the streets of the city before the war, they themselves felt inferior.

The Polish Army didn't want them. They considered at that time the Jews as unfit for the army and as cowards. Today, the Israeli Army has the respect of the whole world and even the Polish people grudgingly admit it. Of course, they add quickly, the Jews learned it all from the Poles.

• • •

They were sitting in the dining room in the Sheraton Hotel the next day. Carl was enjoying the variety of food at the breakfast table. There were fresh Israeli rolls of all kinds, eggs any style prepared for you by the chef, all kinds of pickled and smoked fish and mountains of fresh tropical fruit. The conversation was light. Carl and Irene came together with Irene's sister, Anna, and their friend George. George loved to travel and it took very little to persuade him to go to visit his large family in Israel. He came with a lady-friend, Leah, whom he was courting. George's wife Gisa died two years ago. Also, their friend Charlotte came along. She wanted to visit her old uncle who was living now all alone and was in failing health.

Carl doesn't remember how the conversation turned back to the war-time. Lately, they tried to avoid this topic because it would immediately bring old painful memories. But Charlotte said, "Do you know Carl how I lost my father? I went with him in August 1944 to the barracks in Boryslaw where the last Jews were kept by the Germans. We were in hiding but my father said to me, 'I have to go to the barracks to get my friend out so I can hide him too. You,' he turned to me," Charlotte continued, " 'wait outside and I'll be back soon.' All of a sudden a commotion took place inside the camp, which I saw from where I was hiding. The entire compound was closed and surrounded by German and Ukrainian police. My poor father was trapped inside with the rest. They were taken under heavy escort to the railroad station and shipped to the concentration camp. I never saw him again."

There was a sadness in Charlotte's face as if it had happened only a few days before and not forty six years ago. It brought to mind a poem by Goethe entitled, "Die Ehre" (The Word of Honor), in which a nobleman is condemned to die for a crime he committed. He begs the king to let him to say good-bye to his family. But they live far away and the king is reluctant to grant him this wish, fearing that he will not return. The convicted man gives the king his word of honor that he will return, so the king lets him go and the nobleman goes home and says his last good-byes to his family.

When he starts on his way back to the place of execution, all kinds of obstacles beset him. He overcomes them all and reports to the king to be killed. The king is so moved by the man's honesty that he pardons him and spares his life.

No such pardon was given to the Jews, and there were many heroic deeds performed by nameless Jews.

• • •

Friday, May 10th, 1991

The next day, Friday, they went to visit Eva. They spent a lovely evening with her and her family. There was her daughter Nurith with her three children, Nir, Danni and Roni. Carl and Irene brought gifts for all of them and gave Eva the manuscript of their book.

Eva and Nurith prepared a delicious old-fashioned dinner which included gefilte fish the way Carl's mother had prepared it. Then there were home-made potato pirogen with two kinds of meat. The dinner was topped off with a delicious mousse cake prepared by Nurith. Finally, Turkish coffee was served.

Carl asked their opinions of current events. They were all supportive of peace talks with the Arabs and in favor of giving parts of Judea and Samaria to the Palestinians.

"If we don't give them anything we will certainly have a war," said Danni, a young, very intelligent girl. "But if we give them something we can hope that maybe there will be peace."

Uri, Eva's son, came after dinner. Carl liked Uri and always enjoyed talking to him. He was intelligent, well read and well informed about politics. Carl wanted to hear his opinion about the Palestinians. To his surprise, his opinion was the same. "Look, Carl," he said, "all the Arabs have to do is shoot a Scud missile once in a while, and life in Israel is paralyzed." The conversation drifted to business. Uri had a consulting civil engineering company and they were surprised to see how many similarities existed between their companies and in their approach to the problem-solving in business. They agreed to see each other again and talk some more.

Saturday, May 11th

They now visited Anna's family. Anna's brother-in-law and his wife lived next door to their married daughter Hela and her three children. Hela's husband Pinchas had become a hero during a recent attack by Palestinians on a busload of people traveling on a tour of Egypt. A terrorist had thrown a grenade into the bus. Pinchas, who was with the group, grabbed the grenade and tried to throw it out. It exploded in his hand, tearing off all the fingers of his right hand and riddling his body with metal splinters. He survived and his heroic deed had saved the lives of most of the passengers. Pinchas was a successful businessman and lived in a penthouse with a beautiful large veranda full of tropical trees and flowers.

The three of them, Irene, Carl and Anna, were taken before dinner to visit Hela's parents' apartment nearby.

Yulek was the brother of Anna's late husband Michael. Carl had met him before and knew about his tragic experience in the concentration camps in Germany. In the last days of the war the Germans had hidden the prisoners under a train which then started to move, killing and maiming many of them. Yulek's leg had been severed by the wheels of the railroad car.

Carl avoided Yulek, not wanting to talk about the tragic old times. He carried on a light conversation with Yulek's wife Victa. But an irresistible force drew him to Yulek and, before he knew it, he was talking to him across the room. He moved closer.

Yulek said, "You know, my daughter Hela was in charge of tours of young Israelis to Poland. They went to see the places where their parents had lived and where their grandparents had been killed by the Germans." Yulek continued with pride, "Some Polish anti-Semites made nasty remarks: 'Where were you Jews, in hiding during the war?' They didn't know that my Hela understood Polish. She answered, 'I understand everything you say. Don't worry, soon *you* will be buried.' "

Yulek continued, "Of all the nationalities in the concentration camps, the Poles were the worst."

Carl interrupted him, "What about the Ukrainians?"

"We knew that the Ukrainians were uneducated and beastly, but the Poles were civilized. Yet they would trade with a Jew, giving him a few cigarettes or a slice of bread for his last pair of shoes, and then kill him to take back the cigarettes. But I was young and strong," he continued, "and prepared to defend myself with the help of my friends. When they wanted to do the same thing to us we beat the hell out of them.

"The last ten months of the war, when I was in the concentration camp, were the worst months of my life," he continued. "When I tell people about it they don't believe me. Sometimes I don't believe it myself. I saw people so hungry that they killed each other for a slice of bread."

Carl interrupted him. "You can't really blame them. They were pushed to the wall by the Germans, who starved and tortured them. I knew a woman who was told that she would be killed if she didn't denounce another Jew. So she denounced me. Then, after a while, they arrested her again and she denounced somebody else under the threat of death."

Yulek grew animated: "Before the war ended, they put us all in a gas chamber, including me with my leg cut off by the train. They kept us there for days until the Americans came and liberated us."

Sunday Morning, May 12th

Visit to Andzia Katz

Irene, Anna and Carl took a taxi to a nursing home in Givatayim to see Andzia Katz who had Alzheimer's disease. It took the driver a while to find the place. Salka was there already, taking care of her sister and talking softly to her. Andzia was motionless in her bed. She was thin and her face was waxen. Her red hair was now completely gray.

"Look, Andzia, you have visitors," said Salka. "Do you recognize them?"

"Yes, I recognize them," said Andzia quietly, almost in a whisper. "It's Irene and Carl and Anna." She grew quiet.

"Aren't you glad they came?" continued Salka.

"Yes, I am," answered Andzia absent-mindedly," slipping back into her own world. Irene and Anna showered her with questions and soothing words, but Andzia didn't seem to hear and didn't answer. She just smiled.

Carl looked at her with emotion. He remembered meeting her in

Anna's house in Ligota when he was courting Irene. At that time she was in her late twenties, with a good figure and flaming red hair. She had accompanied Irene and Carl on their long walks and was always a welcome companion, bright, intelligent and openly approving of Carl's relationship with Irene.

Then tragedy struck. Andzia's boyfriend was killed by the Polish underground in some kind of vendetta. Nobody had known that she had a boyfriend. She had kept it secret, but now it all came out. She was heartbroken. When Irene and Carl left in the winter to go to the university she said, "It will be cold there in Wroclaw and you will have to cling to each other a lot." She said it almost in tears, still under the influence of her own personal tragedy, yet she wished to others something that had been denied to her.

Their ways parted. Irene and Carl left Poland after getting married and finally landed in the United States while Andzia emigrated to South America, where her sister lived. She married Ernesto, a very nice fellow whom she loved very much. She occasionally came with him to New York and always spent some time with Irene and Carl. They always had a lot to talk about, reminiscing about old times.

And now she lay listless on a bed in the nursing home. After the visitors left, Salka asked "Did you enjoy the visit?" Andzia replied in a monotone, "What visit?"

After the mostly window shopping they felt hungry and decided to have a bite. They noticed a deli and went in. "What should we have?" asked Irene.

Carl wanted the usual, frankfurters, but they were not on the menu. He was disappointed. He missed New York's Nathan's frankfurters. Resourceful Irene studied the listing on the wall and exclaimed triumphantly, "They have frankfurters; let's order three of them; no, four! Carl can certainly eat two of them. They are quite expensive, though—eight and a half shekels each. That's almost $4 for a frank."

They soon found out why the price was so steep. The frankfurters were huge and they could hardly finish them. Carl ate only one. Since they came wrapped in foil he wanted to return the unopened package. The clerk insisted on refunding his money. Carl refused, saying, "Please give it to somebody else or take it as a tip." But the man insisted, "You must take back the money." Carl finally gave up seeing that the man was simply very honest.

Evening: Shopping for silver on Ben Yehuda St.
Dinner in Dan Restaurant: Cholent and Baked Duck.

Monday, May 13th
AM Shopping for bathing suits at Gotex.
Lunch with Fela.
Dinner at the Twelve Tribes Restaurant in the Sheraton Restaurant. Nothing to write home about.

Tuesday, May 14th, AM

The Shuk

Irene, Carl and Anna were waiting in front of the hotel for Eva and Nurith. They were planning to go to the shuk, the equivalent of a flea market in New York.

Eva arrived in a car driven by Nurith. They went straight to the Carmel Shuk. They parked the car at a distance, since no traffic was allowed, and walked the rest of the way. Hundreds of stands lined narrow streets. Hawkers were advertising their wares, piled in veritable mountains on table stands. Shirts, skirts, pants, T-shirts, tablecloths and hundreds of other items were on sale. They walked slowly, pushing their way through, along with hundreds of other people, stopping occasionally to examine the merchandise.

They entered the food market. Tropical fruit of all kinds, askedinias, dates, figs and others were displayed in large quantities. Huge vegetables out of "Brave New World" greeted them. Large radishes and scallions, three times larger than in New York, amazed them; tiny green spring onions, which they hadn't seen since leaving Poland. Carl grew excited at the sight of each new item, greeting them with loud exclamations, like a child.

Eva bought apples and Carl could hardly wait to sink his teeth into one of them. They tasted like the apples he had eaten a long time ago in his grandfather's orchard. Further out, they saw fruit and vegetables artistically displayed on open bales of hay, while a band of new immigrants played Russian music.

Eva stopped at a silver stand and bought a pendant and earrings for Alice and Terry. Then they stopped at a sidewalk cafe and treated themselves to blintzes and oriental salad with feta cheese. For dessert they had an apple strudel made of fresh apples, which was absolutely delicious.

They topped it off with excellent Israeli coffee.

Tired but happy they returned to the car. "You should write about Tshudek in your book, Carl," said Eva. "He helped me send food packages to you in the concentration camp."

"You are right," replied Carl. "I don't know many details and I would appreciate it if you told me more about it."

"We have to sit down and write together. There are many things that ought to be on record," said Eva.

Wednesday, May 15th

Dinner With Uri and Dorothy

Uri invited Irene and Carl to an elegant Chinese Restaurant called "The Ribs." At first the atmosphere was very stiff but Carl was determined to keep the conversation going. Uri was separated from his wife Carmela and was going out with Dorothy. Dorothy looked older than they had expected. She tried very hard to make a good impression but somehow she didn't succeed. Uri didn't look happy either. They talked about old times, but Uri seemed to be preoccupied. After dinner Irene said, "Uri we would like to see you again."

Uri took them to a place were a Scud missile had fallen, "It fell inches from my office," he explained. "All the windows were broken except in my office." The large area was leveled to the ground except for a modern structure which had withstood the impact. "This was due to the modern way of building," Uri said. "And the windows in my office were double layered, I had installed them earlier so I could listen to music without the street noise. It came in very handy," he said with satisfaction.

After they parted Carl said, "I cannot understand how he could leave Carmela for this woman. Carmela is much prettier, she has a good figure and she's also very pleasant." Maybe he was prejudiced. Both Irene and Carl liked Carmela and were very upset by Uri's leaving his wife.

Wednesday, May 15th

A Day In Jerusalem

They left for Jerusalem at the crack of dawn. Manek Schreck, a friend of Charlotte's offered to take them there by car. There were four of them besides Manek: Irene, Charlotte, Anna and Carl.

A few days earlier, Irene had asked Carl why he wanted to go to Yad Vashem.

"Because I want to look for members of my family, neighbors and schoolmates who may have survived the Holocaust," answered Carl.

"But you know what happened to them." said Irene.

"No, I don't know about all of them. There were, for example, the two boys, Matthew and Ziggy, sons of my Aunt Donna. They ran away during the Holocaust and nobody knows what happened to them. They didn't look like Jews and may have survived. And there were my schoolmates. I want to see if any of them were left alive."

Irene, seeing how determined Carl was, had agreed.

• • •

They moved quickly up the hilly road to Jerusalem while Carl took moving pictures of the beautiful landscape. Manek played tape cassettes of music from Lvov for his guests. They arrived at Yad Vashem early in the morning and Manek took them to meet his friend, Dr. Ahron Weiss a historian and member of the Yad Vashem staff. Dr. Weiss, a short, plain man in his early sixties, received them in his office. "I only got back three weeks ago from Russia, looking for new materials on the Holocaust," he said. "I was in Boryslaw, and the guide directed me to an archive in Lvov. where I found thousands of documents about the Holocaust. I had to persuade the authorities to let me photograph them. It took me days to copy them with a portable xerox machine. Would you like to see them?"

Seeing the enthusiasm on the faces of his visitors, he left and returned with a pile of papers. "It took a lot of persuasion on our side to convince the authorities to let us see them," he said. "We told them, 'You don't need them and they describe crimes that you didn't commit.' So finally they agreed." A smile of satisfaction was in his eyes.

Carl watched him intently. He seemed to grow in stature as he spoke. The three women, all natives of Boryslaw, took the documents eagerly and started to leaf through them, looking for relatives.

They exclaimed excitedly as they found the names of fathers, husbands or friends who had perished in the Holocaust. Anna found the name of her first husband, Bronek, who had died during the war, and her heart pounded with pain and emotion. They found the name of their father, Jakub, who had also perished. Charlotte found her name on one of the lists. Irene found the name of her closest school friend.

Carl looked at them with a mixture of happiness and sadness. He asked the professor, "Doctor, I would like to see the computer lists of people from my home town, Lvov. Could you help me?" The professor made a few telephone calls and said, "The names are not in the computer yet, but I will take you to the Hall of Names and they will look them up for you."

The group started the long walk; halfway through, the doctor asked, "Would you like to see the new addition, the Children of the Holocaust Museum?" He took them to a cave and soon they found themselves in a chamber, in total darkness, containing hundreds of tiny dots of light. An invisible voice slowly recited the names, ages and places of birth of children who had died in the Holocaust. The effect was overwhelming and crushing. Finally they walked back into the daylight, stunned.

Inside the Hall of Names Carl handed in the names of his relatives and friends to the person doing the searches. But no trace of his family or friends could be found.

They had seen the rest of the exhibits on their previous trip three years ago and Manek was in a hurry; he had to deliver some documents to the Kneset. "Would you like to see our Parliament?" he inquired. They agreed eagerly.

After they went through the necessary checks they were permitted to enter. Manek seemed to know everybody and was liked by many members of the Kneset. He took his friends to the visitors' gallery. Arik Sharon was speaking. After a while they went to the cafeteria. Manek introduced them to everybody who passed by: Sheva Weiss, a member of the Kneset; Bibi Natanyahu, the Deputy Minister of Defense; Dov Olmert, the Minister of Health; Shaki Milo, the Minister of Police and Menachem Porush; the Vice Minister of Labor, with his majestic beard.

As they sat at the table having coffee, they noticed Arik Sharon sitting at the next table with his wife Lili and a group of people. Arik noticed them too. Irene and Carl walked over and Arik got up to greet them. "Why didn't you get in touch with me sooner?" he asked. "I'd like to invite you to my house. It's only an hour's drive from here." He continued, "How is Dita (his sister) and Milo (his brother-in-law)?"

Arik told the waitress to charge everything they ordered to his bill.

• • •

"Now I'll take you to the Eastern Wall," Manek said after a while. But the women were afraid and demurred. Carl would have liked to go and see the hustle and bustle of the vendors and the stores and stands lining the road Then Roni Milo, the Minister of Police, came over. After an introduction and a short conversation he warned the group not to go to East Jerusalem because there had been acts of terrorism by the Palestinians.

They went back to the car and Anna suggested that Manek show them Jerusalem. Manek drove around and took them through the Arab section, while Carl photographed everything, spellbound by the beauty of the city. Meanwhile, Manek took out his gun and put it at the ready as he drove through the narrow, winding streets of the Arab section. The hearts of his passengers pounded with fear.

"Jerusalem is a jewel of a city," exclaimed Carl. They all watched the buildings, old and new, built with the beautiful, honey-colored Jerusalem stone, the walls of the Old City built by Suleiman the Magnificent and the Tower of David.

It was getting late and they were emotionally and physically drained by the excitement and events of the day. On the way back to Tel Aviv Manek put on Russian music and they joined in singing happily. Carl was now photographing the beautiful vistas of nature and the Jewish settlements unfolding as they traveled downhill. They saw green forests on the Israeli side and barren hills on the Arab side of the West Bank.

"Why don't they let the Jews live in peace?" lamented Irene.

They arrived at the Sheraton Hotel and, after thanking Manek profusely for a wonderful day, returned, exhausted but happy, to their rooms in the hotel.

Evening. Dinner in a Russian Restaurant called Beriozka. Nothing special.

Thursday, May 16th

The Caves

Eli and Eva picked up Irene and Carl in front of their hotel at 9:30 in the morning. Eli had taken a day off from work to show them the caves. He drove along the highway to Jerusalem and turned onto a side road. The road was steep and winding. They stopped for coffee. The views from the heights were breathtaking. Then they continued along the winding road down towards the caves. Workers who had been digging up stones for a cement factory a few years earlier had come upon a huge underground cave filled with stalactites and stalagmites. It was now under the protection of the Conservation Department of the Israeli Government.

Eli parked the car and Eva disappeared down the stairs, anxious to pay the entrance fee for her guests. Now they had to wait for their turn to enter the caves, as a large number of Arab children were before them.

"How did you like our book?" inquired Irene. "Especially Carl's part?"

"There are many details missing," answered Eva. "For example, you didn't write about my monthly visits to the ghetto. I used to come to you once a month with bags of food for the family. Once, as I walked with Susan, I was stopped by the police. I had my Christian papers in order but the policeman asked me suspiciously, 'How come you speak German so well?' I told him that I worked in the German Forestry Department in Zakopane. Luckily, he didn't stop my sister, because they would have wondered why I was walking with a Jewess."

Carl interrupted, "I did not know many details about you when I wrote the book. I wish that you would tell me more. You were responsible for getting us out of the ghetto, but you planned it with Leo and he is reluctant to talk about it."

Eva replied, "I first got out Mark and Herta. I told them to meet me at the railroad station and bought them train tickets. It was important that this be done by me and not by them. Most of the escaping Jews were denounced to the police by the ticket clerks. We traveled to Cracow and I placed them for the night and had to go to the office to get false papers for you and Leo. I had asked my superior a few days earlier to leave me the keys to the office in case I came in late and had to sleep there. I had a night pass, so I could walk during the curfew, but Mark wouldn't let me go alone. He had a lot of guts," she said sadly, as Mark had now been dead for five years. She continued, "We went to the office and I forged the papers for you, stating that you were traveling on behalf of the Ministry of Forestry. Fortunately, the desk drawer containing the official seal was open so I could use it. I sent you the papers by mail."

Carl listened intently to every word she uttered, trying to engrave it in his memory. He knew that her words were a genuine testimony that he would not be able to get from anybody else.

It was time to go to the caves. They entered an anteroom, where a guide explained how stalactites and stalagmites are formed by droplets of water. The water seeping through the layers of lime dissolves it and drips in the cave. As the water evaporates, it leaves deposits of lime on the ceiling and floor of the cave. They grow slowly reaching each other like two lovers.

The group looked around in awe. In a dimly lit grotto, thousands of shapes seemed to leap at them. There was Moses with two tablets; then there was a huge ice cream cone with a cherry on top; now two lovers embracing, Snow White and the Seven Dwarfs; a mother with a baby; a monkey; and many, many others. Sometimes a stalactite and stalagmite missed each other. "We call it lost love," explained the guide. "The columns grow at a rate of 1 centimeter every five years and we now have some of our own, since the caves were discovered in 1968, twenty-three years ago.

They left the cave overwhelmed by the beautiful works of art created by nature and marveled about the infinity of time. It had taken 35 million years to create this phenomenon.

Next they went to Herodion to see Herod's palace. After driving for a while they saw a mountain with a flat top; the car could not go any further. They had to climb to the top of the mountain to see the palace."

Seeing the steep climb, Irene said, "I cannot climb that mountain."

"I'll stay with you," volunteered Eva.

"All right, then you two lock yourselves up in the car and Carl and I will go alone." While Carl collected his photographic gear Eli added, "Irene, here is a gun which you should use if the Arabs attack you. Do you know how to use it?"

"No, I don't," answered Irene.

"Then use a knife," he said, pulling out a long military knife.

"Carl, are you going to leave us here?" Irene said. "Please don't go."

He didn't. Instead they headed to Jerusalem. Eli took them on a tour of the city. Even though they had seen Jerusalem a couple of days ago, they still hadn't had enough and absorbed the views of the city like a man thirsty for water.

Eli took them to the Haas Memorial, where the Old City could be seen as if on the palm of one's hand. The golden dome of the Mosque of Omar was shining in the afternoon sun and Carl gazed at it and the Old City for a long time, mesmerized.

Chapter 40

Trip to Israel, (Continued)

Friday, May 7th

Visit With Fela

They were invited by Fela to lunch. Irene, Carl and Anna went by taxi. Fela prepared a delicious lunch of pirogen and dumplings filled with apricots and for dessert she served strawberries, cake and freshly brewed coffee. The conversation lingered on, first concerning the political situation and the events of the day in Israel. Then, as usual, it turned to old times. Fela and Carl reminisced about the house on Old Zniesienie, with its the orchard and fruit trees.

"You described everything in a dry and matter-of-fact way," said Fela. "You should include some more cheerful, or at least tragicomic, events."

Carl explained apologetically, "I didn't study writing and I don't know how to do it, but I feel that I am getting better as I go on."

Fela smiled. "Let me give you an example. I was in Lublin in Poland towards the end of the war, trying to transfer cyanide poison to some people in the ghetto. The poison was taken by the Jewish people when they were caught by the Germans and wanted to avoid the agony of death at the hands of their oppressors. All of a sudden, I was stopped by two Polish policemen, who arrested me under the suspicion that I was Jewish. They put me in jail and left me there for the night. I had to lie in my dress on the cement floor. There was no bed and mice were jumping all over me all night. An old prostitute offered me her shoulder to sleep on. 'Never mind my being a prostitute,' she said. 'You can still sleep on my shoulder.' The next day I was called into the warden's office, and he interrogated me and checked my identification papers. After a long while he finally said, 'You do not seem to be Jewish but with the Jews you can never tell.'

"This is the type of story you should write. They should contain humor so that people can laugh once in a while, not only cry. Your stories are very sad and dry."

"I agree," answered Carl, "but when I wrote my story, I would fall into a frame of mind as if I were in a trance. I was carried back to the old times and places and I lived through the events again. I wrote whatever came to mind without thinking about what form it would take."

The conversation continued around their house on Old Zniesienie. "Do you remember, Carl, when you got sick and your mother took you to a resort hotel to visit your Aunt Hanna?"

"Yes, I remember," answered Carl. "We met her husband there, Uncle Meyer."

"He was a handsome fellow," said Fela. "He loved me very much and let me participate in his experiments when I was still a child. He loved to tinker with tools."

"What happened between him and grandfather?" asked Carl. "They didn't talk to each other."

"Nothing happened, really," Fela answered. "He was a very active young man and used to go on hikes for days. Your grandfather once broke a cane on him."

"Fela, what year was my mother born in?" inquired Carl.

"She was fifteen years older than I," answered Fela.

"What year were you born in?"

"I was born in 1908."

"That means she was born in 1893." Carl felt relieved. It was important to him to know, although he didn't know why.

They stayed a while longer and it was time to go back to the hotel. Fela ordered a taxi for them. They said good-bye and went down to the street. Suddenly they heard a voice calling them. Fela came down quickly. She was holding an old piece of paper in her hand: "Carl, this is the letter you wrote me from the concentration camp." Carl took it from her. "I will make a copy of it."

"You don't have to. I am an old woman and I don't need it."

They got into the waiting taxi, leaving Fela behind. Carl unfolded the piece of paper, yellowed with age. The letter was dated January 1, 1945.

> Dear Eva:
>
> I am happy that everything is all right with you and that everybody is healthy. You cannot imagine how often I think about all of you. Thank you very much for the food parcel containing butter, bacon, sausage and 2000 zlotys. Please send me a pair of heavy socks if you can. I have only one pair and they are very light. I see Kw. once in a while and I am helping her out a little. The address of her daughter in Hungary is: (there came a street address in Budapest). In general, she is very depressed. Her other daughter feels all right. As far as our evacuation to Cz. is concerned, it may take place any day. We

do not know what it will be like there. Also, the possibility of contact from there is not known. In general, I feel fine and I am trying not to lose hope. It will be as God wants it.

Kissing and hugging you, I remain

>
> yours,
> Edward.

Edward was Carl's Christian name, Kw. was Carl's distant relative who was arrested with her daughter on Christian papers and taken to the concentration camp, Cz. referred to a labor camp in Czestochowa. The letter was addressed to Alicia Moskalska, Eva's gentile friend, as a precaution, in order not to endanger Eva.

Carl read this letter several times. At the beginning he could not remember the events, but as he thought more and more about it he recalled what had happened. A Polish messenger had smuggled the food package into the concentration camp and carried back Carl's letter confirming its delivery.

Saturday, May 17th

Lunch At the Hotel

Fela, Carl, Irene, Janka and her husband were sitting in the hotel coffee shop. Janka was Irene's friend from Boryslaw. Carl had met her before he married Irene, at which time Irene, always thinking about others and not herself, tried to match them up. Now, forty-five years later, they met again. Janka was married to a man from Lodz and was a mother and a grandmother. She proudly showed them pictures of her grandchildren. She had not changed as she got older. Carl wanted to know her opinion of the political situation. She was strongly in favor of giving some land back to the Palestinians. To Carl's surprise, the majority of people in Israel were in favor of making peace with the Arabs at almost any price. Hawks like Carl, who were unwilling to give back any land, were in the minority.

While Carl discussed politics with Janka and her husband, Irene talked with Fela.

"Carl told me that you were against our marriage," Irene said.

The two women were close and Fela did not take offense.

"No, I wasn't," she said. "I even told Carl to bring you and introduce you to me, but he didn't want to."

Carl broke into the conversation: "That's not true!" he exclaimed suddenly and immediately regretted his outburst. Trying to repair the damage, he said, "You called me to your home in Katowice. Uncle Herman was there with Aunt Hermine. Uncle told me that if I got married he wouldn't be able to take me to America." Thoughts raced through his mind but he decided to stop there and leave well enough alone.

After they finished their coffee, Carl and Irene said good-bye and went with Fela to their room. Carl tried to be especially attentive to Fela, feeling guilty about his outburst. The conversation continued, turning to Carl's grandfather and his disregard for money and business. Carl said, "During the Russian occupation I once went with Donna to Brzezany to get food. Some of our family were living there and they helped us buy food from the farmers. When we came back, I described how we had spent the money and grandfather was very impressed by my business sense. He thought I would be a good businessman."

Fela said, "You must take out a whole piece of your book. I did not convert. I went with Zygmunt Drohocki to Katowice and we had a civil marriage ceremony. That was the only place you could marry without a religious ceremony. True, grandfather warned me that the Drohocki family was stingy and that there would be problems. He knew them well. They converted to Christianity. Their Jewish name was Deiches and they were very rich. It was an opportunity for me; I was poor and my father had no dowry."

For a while they remained silent, then Fela said, "It seems to me that people get more selfish and wrapped up in themselves as they get older."

Carl disagreed. "I feel that I want to explore my past as I get older. I think about the old times more than I did when I was 30."

Fela said, "This trip has brought us closer together than anytime before."

Carl felt now closer kinship to her. He felt that the tension between them was dissipating. Many problems had been aired and many questions answered.

• • •

They were invited that evening to Manek Peled's home. Manek was George's cousin and he was throwing a party. His wife, Shoshana, had just gotten the news that she was free of cancer after a breast operation. They had been worried about the results of the tests for weeks and now they could breath easier.

Irene had known Manek since childhood. She used to take care of him when she was a young girl and he was a few years younger. After the war he had gone to Israel and later joined the army. He performed heroic deeds during the Six Day War. He flew a helicopter over the Golan Heights and directed the artillery fire. Afterwards he was promoted to colonel. Upon retirement he became a manager in a large plant and was rewarded for his work with a high salary and bonuses. He lived in a large expensively furnished house in Kiryat Ono, an exclusive suburb of Tel Aviv.

Carl, Irene and Charlotte spent a pleasant evening talking to the many people who had been invited. On the way back to the hotel Irene observed, "People in Israel laugh a lot." Carl added, "One should always smile. It helps you to make friends."

Charlotte said, "Yes, people laugh a lot here. But you have to have a reason to laugh."

Sunday, May 19th

Irene and Carl met Minnie and Hessie in the lobby of the hotel. Minnie, a lively blond woman in her sixties, had been in love with Milo before the war. But the war had separated them and Minnie married Hessie, while Milo married Dita. Milo must still have had some feelings for his old love because he asked Irene to call her up in Israel. Now they sat near one another after not recognizing each other at first. Carl asked Hessie his favorite question: "Do you think Israel should give back the territories to the Arabs?"

Hessie was hesitant to be drawn into a political discussion and answered briefly, "Yes, we should give them a part, but there is a question of semantics. We should give back, not give. It didn't belong to us in the first place. If we don't we will have no peace. If we do we have a chance."

Carl was surprised that so many people in Israel wanted to give the land to the Palestinians. After all, the government didn't want to and Israel was a democracy. If the majority of the people wanted something why would the government do the opposite?

While the women chatted, the two men turned to talk about Lvov, which Hessie and Minnie had visited not long ago. "Lvov is unchanged; it is still beautiful," said Hessie. "The public buildings and churches are well preserved on the outside, but inside they are in ruins. The staircases are in terrible shape and the plumbing doesn't work. Milk is sold in bottles stoppered with a piece of crumpled newspaper. However you can travel freely everywhere."

Carl asked, "Is there any danger in going there?"

"No, there isn't," replied Hessie. "We were invited to people's homes and they were very friendly. By the way, the Boryslaw Society is planning a trip to Lvov and Boryslaw in August and we are planning to go."

Carl exclaimed, "Irene, did you hear, they are going to Lvov and Boryslaw in a group, so it will be safe. I would love to go too."

Irene didn't share his enthusiasm. "I don't want to go there. It has nothing to do with safety. I want to remember the things as they were, not as they are now."

But Carl's imagination was working feverishly. He saw himself walking from the city on foot to his house. First he would walk through the village. No, he would approach the house from the railroad tracks. He would watch the hill on which it stood from the distance first. He would savor each step as the house got closer and closer. He would climb the steep portion of the hill and the house on top would suddenly appear. He would cry and laugh at the sight of it. He would touch the water pump in the center of the big yard in front of the house and look at the rooms where he spent his childhood with his parents, brothers and the rest of the family. He would go to the orchard and look at the fruit trees. He knew each one of them like a dear friend. The apple, pear, and cherry trees and tens of plum trees would greet him and wave at him in recognition. Then he would walk along the house, down to the village and up another hill next to the "tserkev." He would now see the railroad tracks from the right. He would look at the village houses on the left and the little old schoolhouse near the bridge over the railroad tracks. Then he would slowly walk over the bridge....

The words of his guest brought him back to reality. "We must go now. But we will see you at the Askara (Memorial Day) on Tuesday."

• • •

They had dinner at Nurith's house. Her apartment was full of people—her husband Eli, her children Danni and Ronni, Uri's estranged wife Carmela and her daughter Miki with her husband. The conversation was light and lively but mostly in Hebrew, and Irene and Carl could understand little. Delicious food was served, prepared by Nurith. There were vegetable dishes only, as required on the Shevuot holiday. Carl looked at the young Israeli people and saw beautiful, delicate Miki, who was studying business administration, tall, lean

Ronni, who was going to Hungary with an Israeli athletic team, and pretty Danni, with her long light hair who worked as a waitress at night to make extra money for college. What a beautiful youth, he thought; what a far cry from the stereotype of the Jew.

Monday, May 20

Morning. Shopping on Allenby St. with Eva.

Dinner in Eva's apartment, consisting of delicious mushroom soup, salads and meatballs. For dessert she served home-made fresh apple strudel and freshly brewed coffee.

Carmela came after dinner and they spent some time talking with her. After she left the conversation centered on Herta and a letter she had sent to Eva. In it Herta had said that the people who had treated her best at home were Donna and grandfather. Carl was hurt. He remembered his mother taking care of Herta as if she were her own daughter.

At that moment the television started to show Lech Walesa's visit to Israel and the conversation stopped. Everyone listened to Walesa's speech in the Kneset and heard him say, "We Poles did wrong to you Jews during the war and we ask you for forgiveness."

• • •

That night Carl had a dream about his mother. He was a child and she was catering to his younger brother Mark hand and foot and totally ignoring him. Carl felt unloved, lost and confused. He became resentful towards her. With each act of attention and love for Mark he resented her more until it finally burst into the open and he told her how he felt.

Carl woke up and could not calm down for a long time. He could now understand how it must have been for Mark, feeling unloved.

Tuesday, May 21st.

Breakfast with Regina and Salka.

Lunch With Eva

They went to Eva's by taxi. It was their last day in Israel and Eva had prepared dinner for them. As usual, the food was delicious; there was corn soup, meatballs, salad and apricot dumplings, Carl's favorite dish. Irene said, "You know, Eva, you are the best cook I have ever known and I don't mind telling everybody. I even say it to my sister, and she is an excellent cook herself." Eva smiled. Irene continued, "We both love you very much." Eva had tears in her eyes. "I love both of you very much too."

Carl was eager to learn more about his grandfather. "Eva, please tell me how our grandfather became a farmer. After all, the Jews in Poland were not permitted to own and till the land at that time."

"Your grandfather was an expert farmer. First, he worked on his mother's farm in Trosciniec, which was called Adamowka. Then he managed a farm in Ujscie Zielone for Baron Scheib. He had come to Lvov and leased the farm from the Baczewski family. They owned a whiskey factory and a lot of land."

"But why did they lease the land to a Jew?"

"They were Jewish themselves. Their name was Baczeles and when they converted they changed their name."

Anna interrupted. "In 1914, when the war broke out, did you run away to Vienna?"

"No," said Eva. "When the Russians approached we got ready to go and the carriages were packed and waiting. Then a little child said, 'I won't go.' That little child was me. I was 6 years old. And your grandfather said, 'If this little child doesn't want to go, we won't go.'"

Tuesday, May 21, Afternoon

Ascara

The group went to visit the Doctors' House on Kaplan's Street in Tel Aviv for Ascara. Ascara is a yearly remembrance day for the departed. The Boryslaw and Drohobycz Jews had gathered for a Kadish prayer and it had become a day of gathering and meeting of friends and relatives of the remaining survivors of the Holocaust.

Irene and Anna got very excited when they heard about this and decided to stay two more days in Tel Aviv to attend the Ascara. Carl agreed gladly, seeing how much they wanted it. They hadn't seen many of the Boryslaw people for years, sometimes as long as forty-five years.

When their taxi reached the place it was easily recognizable from the gathering of people in front of the building. They were immediately surrounded, embracing people they hadn't seen since childhood, laughing and crying. Each of them was introduced to Carl, who was busily shooting heartwarming scenes of reunion and remembrance. What joy and surprise, meeting friends and relatives not seen for so many years!

There were many men there who had been in love with Irene when they were young. Some of them still had feelings for her, to the dismay of their wives. Irene had been a beautiful girl, probably the prettiest girl in her town. She was still beautiful and Carl was very proud of her. One of her former admirers followed her every step while his wife tried in vain to steer his attention away. Another man who had been in love with her was not there. A search party was sent for him and he came running breathlessly to see her.

It was time for the official part of the Ascara to begin. Everyone walked into the auditorium on the upper floor of the building. Manek Peled presided over the meeting and sat on the dais with the historian Ahron Weiss of Yad Vashem and a few other people. After the introductory speech by Manek, the floor was given to Dr. Weiss. Carl videotaped everything. He could not understand much because the doctor spoke in Hebrew, but the tone of his voice and the few words that sounded similar to English made him feel he understood. It was an accusation of cruelty done to innocent people. From a once thriving community of thousands, a small group of people remained alive. No family was spared and everybody lost many of his loved ones. Doctor Weiss held lists he had just obtained from an archive in Lvov; they bore the names of people who had worked in Boryslaw and Drohobycz during the war. He read them out loud. Most of the people had perished, but a few people in the audience answered to their names, to the excitement and surprise of everybody.

Doctor Weiss shook the lists as if accusing the murderers who had killed so many of them. People rose to their feet. After he finished, a cantor recited a Kadish and sang El Mole Rachmim. The festivity ended with the group singing Ha Tikva, the Jewish national anthem. An announcement was made about a trip to Boryslaw and Drohobycz in August.

They said their many good-byes to everybody, hugging and kissing the same people repeatedly. They promised to come back the next year.

"Everybody recognized me!" Anna exclaimed happily.

"One of my former boyfriends was still running after me!" exclaimed Irene. "His wife was as jealous of him as she was forty-five years ago."

Manek drove them back to the hotel. "This meeting was the icing on the cake," said Irene. Everybody agreed.

Chapter 41

Italy

Wednesday, May 22

They got up at 5 o'clock in the morning and dressed quickly. A minibus took them to Ben Gurion Airport and they boarded a plane to Rome, Italy. Irene, Anna, Carl, George and Leah were going together. Leah and Anna had been to Italy before; the rest had not. After a few hours of flying over the Mediterranean the plane landed smoothly at Leonardo da Vinci Airport. They proceeded by taxi to the Ambasciatori Hotel, an old and respectable hotel in the center of the city. On the way Carl eagerly pointed to various buildings and asked the driver what they were. "San Pietro e Paolo, San Paolo, Palatino, Foro Romano, Sette Colli Romani, Piazza della Patria," answered the driver in Italian. Carl tried to memorize the names. From a distance he could see the Colliseum for a moment and he was awed by the sight. It seemed almost threatening.

They reached the hotel and found that their reservations were confused, but the hotel manager accommodated them, though at a high price. Irene enjoyed every moment.

They found an unassuming restaurant on the Via Veneto. The food was delicious, consisting of vegetable soup, lasagna, ravioli and wine. The American-style hamburgers ordered by Anna and George left much to be desired, but why order hamburgers in Italy? For dessert they had strudel and frozen strawberry pie.

"Let's see the Spanish Steps," someone suggested. After a short walk through narrow streets they arrived at the Piazza di Spagna and were only mildly impressed by a multitude of marble stairs leading to the Piazza. Hundreds of people were milling around.

"Let's go to the Fontana di Trevi," suggested Irene. They walked in its direction, stopping at tens of small shops along narrow streets without sidewalks. They were continually walking into cars and motorcycles, almost colliding but not quite.

The women went shopping while Carl and George stood watching hundreds of people passing by and hundreds of motorcycles zooming by in all directions. Italians seemed to be quiet and aloof, exactly the opposite of what Carl had imagined them to be.

A young woman approached them. She had two small children with her. She didn't know any English and pointed at her mouth as if trying to say that she was hungry. Both Carl and George reached into their pockets to give her change, at which point the woman moved closer to Carl. Her two children put a piece of cardboard against his chest and she reached for the wallet in his breast pocket with her hand masked by the cardboard.

Carl was horrified. The woman was obviously trying to rob him. His money, all his credit cards and his driver's license were in the wallet. In a moment he grabbed the woman's hand and pushed her away like a snake. He was in a cold sweat. His vacation had almost been ruined.

They now looked for the Fontana di Trevi and finally reached the Piazza della Patria, with a monumental structure erected by Mussolini. After asking several policemen and walking through a multitude of narrow, winding streets they finally reached their destination. To their disappointment, the Fontana was being renovated and was covered with tarpaulin. They had walked into a gift shop when they suddenly realized that Anna was missing. They were terrified. Anna had bad eyesight. How would she find her way around? After about 20 minutes of searching Anna walked nonchalantly out of a store where she had been shopping. She had been on the second floor all the time.

They found a taxi, bought some fruit and returned to the hotel. Carl's overall impression on his first day in Italy was negative, but he kept this to himself.

Thursday, May 23rd.

The Colliseum

Our little group began the day early. They ate a skimpy continental breakfast in the hotel restaurant. It consisted of coffee, fresh rolls, orange juice and jams, and was no comparison to the scrumptious breakfasts served at half the price in the Sheraton Hotel in Tel Aviv.

Soon they stood in front of the hotel trying to get a taxi. No taxi would stop for them even if it was empty. They finally had to ask the hotel clerk to order one. They were unpleasantly surprised by the abruptness and unfriendly attitude of the taxi drivers and pedestrians. Carl was still keeping his impressions to himself, but now they were all coming to the same conclusion.

They decided to go first to the Massino Hotel, which had promised to give them rooms at a lower rate over the phone. But when they got there, they saw that the rooms were small and uninviting. The difference in price was small, so they decided to stay in their hotel and prepared to go sightseeing.

They walked to the Colliseum and were surprised by the graffiti on the walls, "Yanqui go home!"

"Why do they hate the Americans?" asked Irene. "Maybe because the Americans always give," suggested Leah. "You often hate the person who gives things to you."

Soon they reached their destination. The huge ruins of the ancient arena loomed over them. They walked in silence down the stairs and thought about the early converts to Christianity, many of them Jews, who were torn to pieces by hungry lions right there. To Carl's surprise the floor of the arena was not flat, but consisted of a labyrinth of man-high partitions. Maybe they wanted to prolong the agony of the condemned by letting the lions chase them through the labyrinth, he thought.

There was a souvenir stand outside the Colliseum and Carl wanted to buy a replica of it, but the vendor didn't have one. Instead he showed them a beautiful replica of the Pietà, which he bought after Anna bargained down the price.

Anna suggested that they go to the San Pietro in Vincoli Church to see the sculpture of Moses by Michaelangelo. They went by taxi and then climbed the steps and entered the church. "Where is Moses?" Carl asked eagerly. He expected a small statue in front of the church. This was the impression he had gotten from the pictures and small replicas he had seen at home. Suddenly the statue of Moses appeared. He was sitting at the wall, almost in bas relief. He was huge and sat erect. The effect on Carl was overwhelming. He stood transfixed in front of it, taking video pictures. Moses seemed almost alive, straining to free himself from the stone in which he was imprisoned as if by magic. The expression on his face was that of a leader ready to give his people the laws that would bind them forever.

They went out and bought a small replica of Moses in marble. It was heavy and Carl carried his precious load carefully.

They proceeded to the Piazza di Venezia, with its numerous ruins of the old city and the magnificent Palace de la Patria built by Mussolini. Carl walked past the Forum Romanum, full of ruins that hinted at the splendor of old Rome. Statues of the Roman emperors greeted them. Carl could almost see the Roman citizens walking in their togas. But he was appalled by the graffiti on the statues.

For lunch, George found a ristorante on the side street. It looked tiny from the outside but it was spacious inside. To their surprise the food was excellent and not expensive. The minestrone soup was thick and tasty and the linguine with white clam sauce was the best Carl had ever eaten. The others were equally satisfied. And the coffee was strong enough to wake up a dead man.

"And now off to the Vatican," exclaimed Carl. "The Pope is waiting for us." Again they took a taxi and they soon found themselves in a large plaza leading to St. Peter's Basilica. They entered the cathedral and admired the statues of apostles and saints, the huge paintings on the walls and the frescoes on the ceiling. Then they saw the Pietà behind a glass partition on the right side of the Basilica. They stood there in awe of its perfection and beauty. The body of Christ, totally limp, was held by Holy Mary. In her face there was an expression of infinite pain over the loss of her son.

They were glad they had bought the replica of the Pietà earlier. Irene said to Carl, "We will build a shelf in the dining room to display all the statues we bought in Israel and Italy."

They walked over to the main altar, built by Bernini, and were moved by its almost mystical appearance and aura. Carl thought that he felt the presence of God there. It was strange for a Jew to feel the presence of God in a church, but wasn't it God's choice where He let Himself be felt?

To their disappointment the Vatican Museum and the Sistine Chapel were already closed. They decided to come again the next day.

The group rested in the large plaza outside the Vatican and treated themselves to double portions of delicious gelati on a cone. The vendor, seeing that they were tourists, tried to cheat them by giving back insufficient change.

After resting for a while they returned to the hotel. They were tired but happy and satisfied with the day's events. After a short rest and a call to the company in New York, Irene, Anna and Carl went for a leisurely stroll. They window-shopped for a while and went back to the hotel exhausted but happy.

Friday, May 24th

Shopping

A.M. Trip to the flea market called Mercato di Via Santo Giovanni near Via Appia Nuova.

Irene, Anna and Leah bought a lot of leather goods, shoes, pocket books, jackets and sweaters. George went to Milano on a business trip early in the morning.

Shopping on the Via della Croce in the afternoon.

They took a taxi to the shopping area and watched the crowd of people milling around. Hundreds of men and women were speeding on motorcycles in all directions, ignoring all the traffic rules. Carl remembered that in Tel Aviv everybody followed the traffic rules to the letter. The moment you got into a taxi, you had to put on the safety belt. Here nobody cared whether you put the belt on or not and the motorcycles and cars drove on both sides of the street, weaving to the left and right as traffic allowed.

Thousands of people walked on the narrow sidewalks, window-shopping. The women were dressed elegantly. The young ones especially showed off their shapely legs. The men were neatly dressed in suits. The women were not pretty but had good figures. The men were handsome and charming.

Friday night, May 25th

They ordered dinner through room service in the hotel. Irene, Carl, Anna and Leah were tired from the day's walking and shopping. They were waiting for George to return from Milan. They were disappointed with their trip. "The antiquities and art in Rome were interesting," said Irene, "and the city is beautiful but the people in general are indifferent to tourists. The 'Yanqui go home' graffiti were apparently scribbled by Communists, but that was no excuse. After all, graffiti can be removed or painted over if you care about your image."

George got back from Milan as they were ready to sit down to eat. "I got the contract and the money will be sent on Monday," he announced triumphantly. "That puts the icing on the cake," said Irene. They ate heartily "Tomorrow we are going to Florence and we have to get up early. Let's go to sleep now," said George, who was tired from the day's trip.

In bed, Carl said to Irene, "Rome is nice but the people are boring."

Saturday, May 25th

They got up early, dressed quickly and had breakfast in the hotel restaurant. "Take a jacket," said Irene to Carl, "you'll be cold." She was always mindful of Carl's weak lungs, since he had tuberculosis years ago in the United States and as a child in Poland. For him a common cold could develop into something much more dangerous.

"No, I don't need it, it's warm outside," he replied. But it was not warm as they stood outside trying in vain to hail a taxi.

They finally got a taxi, went to Roma Termini railroad station and bought first class tickets to Florence. They boarded the train and took the first available seats. A few moments later some people entered and told them that these seats were reserved and they would have to stand most of the way. Later some of the seats became vacant as people left the train and they were able to sit down.

It was 11:30 when they got to Florence and again they could not get a taxi. The tourist information office told them that it would only take 5 minutes to walk to the Academia, where the statue of David was standing. This was their main objective, and they wanted to see it before they got too tired. It took longer than 5 minutes but they finally got to the Academia. After passing a few other sculptures they saw David. He reigned over the exhibit like a king, attracting tourists like a magnet. Carl stood before him for a long time, admiring his masculine beauty, his steady, intense gaze at the invisible Goliath and his oversized hands holding the sling and the pebbles. The strong legs and steady feet of a shepherd supported his beautifully proportioned body. "This is the high point of our trip," said Irene. Carl agreed.

"Let's go to the Piazza Signoria," said Leah. It was nearby, with the Palace di Vecchio towering and a replica of David in front of it, overshadowing all the other sculptures. The real David stood inside to protect it from pollution.

The Uffizi Palace was next door. "We must see the painting of the Birth of Venus by Botticelli," said Carl excitedly. "We learned about it in high school. It is very beautiful." They entered a large building and climbed the stairs without realizing that there was an elevator. On the third floor they breathlessly entered a long gallery full of statues, which they examined perfunctorily.

"Where is the Birth of Venus?" Carl asked an attendant. He pointed to the next room. There she was, standing on a large seashell in the water. She was naked, with long hair partially covering the intimate parts of her body. Her face was half awake, as if she were just coming alive after a long sleep. Yet she was alert and curious about the world unfolding in front of her eyes and into which she was brought by divine intervention. The painting had a divine simplicity and beauty, produced by the hand of a master.

Carl looked at the other paintings. There was Spring, also by Botticelli, with Venus, three Graces and Hermes, the god of merchants. It was symbolic and beautiful, but Carl had to go back to the Birth of Venus and look at it again and again.

They left the Uffizi Palace exhilarated. "Let's have a bite," suggested George, who led them to a small restaurant on a side street, where they were treated to excellent food, starting with thick vegetable soup. Carl ordered tripe, different from the Polish tripe served in New York. Others ordered the equally delicious chicken and roast pork.

"Where should we go next?" asked Irene. Carl had a list Milo had given him and he read it to his friends. "Let's go to Ponte Vecchio and see the Florentine jewelry," someone suggested. They agreed and got there quickly. Now they knew how to get a taxi. You simply had to call the taxi service by phone. Trying to stop a passing taxi was useless.

The Ponte Vecchio was a bridge over the river Arno that was completely covered on both sides with jewelry stores, with a pedestrian passage in the middle. Thousands of shining necklaces, bracelets and other gold objects in the windows seemed to line both sides of the walk with a veritable carpet of gold. The women eagerly went from one store window to another, examining the jewelry and asking for the prices inside. They finally settled on a store where the prices were lower and started to select items for gifts. Irene and Anna bought presents for Alice and Terry, bargaining with the owner yet unconcerned about the expense. Carl enjoyed their generosity, their bargaining and buying.

It was now 5 o'clock and they had little time left. As they drove by taxi back to the Central Termini railroad station, Carl wanted to take a picture of an especially beautiful cathedral, but he missed it. The driver, seeing Carl's interest said, "Now you will see the Duomo." Carl prepared the camera and waited. On the left side a portion of the building appeared at the street's end. They looked at it with awe. It was magnificent. The driver turned the corner and, to their amazement, the Duomo continued with thousands of frescoes, adornments, statues and ornaments. The driver turned the next corner and the passengers saw the Duomo continuing for a long distance. It seemed endless to them.

They hurried back to the train and waited for its departure. Once on the train Irene suggested, "Let's have dinner in the restaurant car." They loved it. They sat at the windows watching the beautiful Italian countryside and dinner was served to them. They were happy and elated. The train was coming from Germany and the waiters were German: a young girl and a young man. Irene turned to Leah and said, "We've come a long way since Auschwitz and Dachau. The Germans are serving us now."

The waiters were polite and the people on the train were friendly. Italy had seemed to grow on them and they had begun to love every moment of being there. They got to Rome without realizing that 2 hours had passed. At the Roma Termini they got a friendly taxi driver. On the way to the hotel he obligingly offered to take them to the Vatican the next day. Even in Rome people seemed friendlier.

• • •

It was Saturday night and they had only two days left of their vacation. They were eager to see the Sistine Chapel tomorrow lest something interfere. They made arrangements with the driver to pick them up at 9 o'clock the next day, Sunday.

The Sistine Chapel

Sunday, May 26th

The group entered the Vatican from the back. There was a long line stretching for blocks, which they joined in the middle. Nobody objected. They entered the Sistine Chapel and had to climb a winding staircase three flights to the top. There they entered a long gallery with paintings on the walls, frescoes on the ceilings, gobelins, huge ancient maps and marble floors with mosaics. An enormous painting, The Liberation of Vienna by the Polish King Jan III Sobieski, by the famous Polish painter Jan Matejko excited them as if it were their own.

Their Polish roots were still strong, in spite of all the injustice done to them on Polish soil during the Holocaust.

Finally they entered a huge chapel with paintings on the walls. The ceiling was completely covered with scenes from the Old Testament, especially from the first book of Torah, the Creation of the World. There were God and Adam with their hands stretched out to each other but no longer touching. God's face was that of an older man with a beard. His outstretched hand and index finger radiated power and his gaze was fixed on his creation, man. Adam's body was limp and his hand stretched out with an effort, as if straining to receive life from God. Next to this was the Expulsion from Paradise, a scene consisting of two events, Adam receiving an apple from Eve with the snake wound around a tree trunk, and Adam and Eve being expelled from Paradise by an angel.

The chapel was full of people straining their necks upwards. Carl had begun to videotape the ceiling when a guard came over and asked him not to take any pictures. He was very upset, having traveled halfway around the world to photograph these paintings. The guard was just picking on me, he thought. He moved to another corner and started to videotape again. Now the guard became really annoyed and threatened him with something that Carl didn't understand. He angrily thought about the impolite Italians and wondered why he couldn't photograph. He was using his camera without flash and could not figure out what harm was done to the paintings by photographing them. Finally Irene, seeing how disappointed he was, solved the problem. She told Carl to sit on the marble floor and take pictures from there. Shielded by hundreds of tourists, he wasn't visible to the guards. For double protection Irene stood in front of him. Carl now photographed the ceiling without interference for five precious minutes and his happiness was complete.

On the way out Irene bought copies of the two scenes: the Creation of Man and the Expulsion from Paradise. It was now 11:30 in the morning and the Pope was due to give his Sunday sermon at noon. The group had to run along the walls of Vatican City to get to the front, where the Pope was supposed to preach.

"Imagine, we are circling an entire country!" said Carl. "The Vatican is a separate country inside Italy. They have their own government and the land belongs to them."

They reached the front square just in time. The huge area was filled to capacity with thousands of people. A few minutes later the Pope appeared in the window of a rather modest building. The people in the square applauded and the Pope started to speak in Italian. Carl couldn't understand a single word.

Irene said, "We've come a long way from Auschwitz, Flossenburg, Grossrosen and Belzec where our parents perished. Here we are now in the Vatican listening to a Pope." They both knew what that meant. During the Holocaust they would gladly have gone anyplace in the world to save their lives and the lives of their loved ones. But there had been no place to go and all escapes had been cut off by the Germans. Besides, nobody wanted them and no country would admit them. In their wildest imaginations they couldn't have dreamed that they would be visiting the Vatican almost fifty years later.

They now wanted to go to the Jewelry Exhibit in the Vatican, but no one knew where it was. Their inability to speak Italian was not helpful. Carl saw a statue of Venus similar to the one in Botticelli's Birth of Venus and, after bargaining with the salesman, he bought it. He had loved the statue of Venus de Milo since childhood and this one was close enough.

Next they went to the Piazza Navona, where they saw the statue of the Four Seasons and browsed among the stands selling original paintings by artists trying to get recognition. They finally settled down in a restaurant called Tre Scalini. While waiting for a table they were serenaded by an Italian musician playing the guitar and singing beautiful Italian songs. After dinner they decided to walk back. They bought a few beautiful oil paintings from the street vendors and happily went back to the hotel.

Monday, May 27th

Last Day in Rome, Shopping on Via Tritone

The group went shopping for "shmatys" (clothes) where Milo had sent them. He was right; they found clothes much cheaper and of good quality. By the time they finished it was 12:30 P.M. and the stores were closing for the midday siesta, which usually lasted till 2:30. They went back to the hotel to unload their booty: sweaters and wallets. Irene and Anna packed the suitcases for the trip. They were tired and they rested and slept a little. They were awakened at 4 o'clock by George, who called over the house phone in his "pure Italian," "Time to go eat!To their disappointment they could not find an open restaurant. Eating places didn't open until 7 o'clock in the evening. Finally George found a pizzeria. The spinach soup was excellent and the lasagna, canelloni and hamburgers were also very good.

But they were eager to go home now.

"I could never live here," said Irene.

Carl concurred, "We are used to life in the United States. I can't wait to have a good steak at Peter Luger's in New York. Besides, it is difficult to get used to another country, even if it is prosperous, like the United States. We had a very difficult time in the United States for the first two years."

They reminisced about the old days when they were young, poor and careless. They could stay up the whole night having fun and go to work the next morning. And they had a lot of fun in whatever they did after work. George and Leah told their stories too. Finally, Irene said, "I think I'll kiss the ground when we arrive back in the United States."

Both George and Leah had been wonderful companions. They were always in a good mood, cheerful and eager to help. This made the trip even more pleasant. As usual, George quickly made the acquaintance of the couple sitting at the next table. They were German and in their early seventies. One could see that the husband must have been good-looking and his wife very pretty. A friendly conversation ensued. On parting, the man said, "We had a wonderful time watching you, especially the beautiful ladies." Here he pointed at Irene, Anna and Leah. "And in my dreams I will kiss your hands. I am the son of Giacomo Casanova," he concluded half-jokingly.

The women were tickled pink. They all laughed heartily. "The man is a real charmer," said Carl after the couple left. The women were very flattered. It got cold and they went inside the restaurant and watched the last rays of sun falling on the people in the street.

Irene had packed everything earlier and now she and Anna collected odds and ends to put into their suitcases. They were tired and sleepy. Irene asked, "Are you ready to go back home?"

Yes, they were.

Chapter 42

A House In the Sky

Carl and Irene sat on the front porch of their house. It was their favorite place to rest after dinner, after a long day's work at the company. The evening was cool after a long, hot day in the unusually hot summer of 1991.

"You know, I went today to see where Shirley's house used to be," said Irene.

Carl was surprised, "You haven't been there since Shirley died. How does it look?"

"It's empty and covered with weeds," said Irene. "Shirley took it with her when she died. She loved that house so much."

It was a beautiful house in one of the choicest neighborhoods in Brooklyn. It stood on a large plot of land in the middle of a garden full of trees. All the rooms were on one floor. Inside there was a large, sunken living room with a fireplace, a spacious kitchen with a butcherblock table in the middle, an adjoining dining room a step above the kitchen. In the middle there was a corridor leading to a master bedroom and four bedrooms for children, guests and servants. Paul had had the garage converted into a children's playroom. There was a large backyard with a brick barbecue. Shirley's children, Betsy, Donna and Charlie, grew up in this house.

One day they got an excited call from Betsy. "Aunt Irene, our house has been torn down!"

"By whom?" asked Irene.

"I don't know," said Betsy, "probably the new owner. Maybe he plans to build a new house on that lot."

Carl jumped into the car and drove there alone, since Irene refused to come. When he arrived he could not believe his eyes. The house was gone. There was a smell of freshly turned earth and a bulldozer stood nearby. This must have happened recently, but everything was gone—the walls, the furniture, even the trees. Since there was nobody around, Carl entered the area now fenced off with pieces of plywood. He walked aimlessly on the fresh, soft soil. There was nothing there. Suddenly he saw a basket of dried flowers sticking halfway out of the soil. Carl picked it up and shook the dirt off. He wondered, How could a frail object like a basket of flowers survive the assault of a bulldozer?

He brought the bouquet back to Irene, who awaited him anxiously. She asked, "Is it true? Is there nothing left?"

"Yes, it's true," he answered. "The house has been torn down and the only thing left was this basket of flowers."

"But this was Shirley's favorite thing!" exclaimed Irene. "I must give it to Betsy as a memento." She called Betsy up but Betsy said, "Aunt Irene, keep the flowers. I'm sure my mother would have wanted you to have them. Tomorrow is Mother's Day and she always gave you flowers on the occasion."

A few months passed. Carl passed by the empty lot once in a while to see if any building activity was taking place. Foundations were laid down, indicating that a new house was being built. Once he saw Shirley's son Charlie standing there and crying, "My mom, my mom, I loved her so much and now she's gone."

After a while there was a telephone call from Betsy. "Uncle Carl, the man who bought our house has been killed. He was murdered. Maybe he belonged to the Mafia."

After that there was no change. The weeds grew higher and higher until they covered even the new foundations. Shirley had taken her house with her to heaven.

Chapter 43

Of Bedbugs and Lice

On a Friday evening, two days before the Jewish New Year in September 1991, Irene, Carl and Anna went to a restaurant , called Captain Quarters. They were joined by George and Leah and Lynn and Dave. The meal was excellent and abundant. "This is a blessed country," said Irene. "There is so much food here."

After the main dish, they were ready to order dessert, but Leah said, "Let's go to our house and I'll serve tea and cake." They accepted the invitation gladly.

"And I'm inviting everybody over for lunch tomorrow," added Irene. "We'll just go home for a minute to walk the dog and we'll join you shortly."

She and Carl drove to the house and Carl got out to open the door when he saw Irene greeting somebody. When he got closer, he recognized Wilus, who was passing through on a business trip. He had stopped by to see his mother and stayed overnight.

The next day Irene and Carl got up early to shop for food. They had to buy food for the promised lunch and prepare for the coming holidays. They bought a large whitefish, a container of pickled herring with onions, schmaltz herring and cheeses, such as Port Salut and Brie. They bought white and red seedless grapes, as well as corn bread in the bakery.

Back home, Irene prepared lunch for her guests. In addition to the fish and cheeses, she made a spring salad consisting of sliced cucumbers, scallions, radishes and cottage cheese.

Her friends came over, joined by Anna and Wilus, and they sat down to a table loaded with food.

Somehow the conversation got off onto the war, when the hunger and lack of food were in stark contrast to today's opulence. Carl said to Anna, "Please, tell them the story about the soup that you once cooked during the war. It's a classic."

Anna began, "It was during the worst hunger in the spring of 1943, and we'd had almost nothing to eat for months. We were in hiding and couldn't get any food. In addition, we had terrible lice and were bitten by them constantly."

Irene interrupted, "Anna was an expert in killing them with her fingernails."

Anna continued, "I somehow managed to scrape together some potatoes and vegetables, and the woman hiding us allowed me to use the kitchen at night, so that nobody could see us. I prepared the soup and put it on the table to cool overnight so that we could eat it the next day. When I looked at the pot in the morning I was horrified. The soup was full of bedbugs floating on top. They had been walking up the walls to the ceiling and dropping into the soup attracted by the heat. My stomach turned with disgust. Even though I was hungry, I would not be able to eat it."

Here she looked at her son. "But Wilus, who was 6 years old at the time, said, 'I am very hungry, Mom; I will eat it. Look, it's not too bad. You just have to push the bedbugs away.' "

On another occasion, Wilus and Olga came to visit Anna. As usual she prepared a special dinner and invited Irene and Carl. Carl liked Wilus and Olga. They were young, intelligent and well read, and they always had interesting conversations about literature and history. Occasionally they brought a poem or a story with them and read it aloud. This time, Wilus said that he wanted to read a poem. He read it with emotion:

El Mole Rachamim
by Victor Gomulicki

It happened in the backyard of a Jewish house,
On a summer evening. I sneaked in secretly.
Faith, instead of uniting, divides and separates.
A wave of black heads moved among the walls.
Itzek, the ragman was getting married to a peddlar's daughter
Guests and onlookers filled the backyard.
The place was ugly and the people ordinary.
A few awakened geese cackled in the barn,
Bedding was airing on the gallery railing.
An unpleasant smell of fried fish wafted from the kitchen.
Two acacias were dying of consumption in a corner.
The sky shone with stars like golden Sabbath candelabra;
There were no clouds in the skies
And the night was full of royal splendor.

Itzek stood under an old scarlet canopy,
In festive clothes, bathed in light and smoke.
He was a swarthy teenager, half-man half-child.
Love, among the Jews, grabs a man treacherously,
Leads him into the abyss with closed eyes
And throws him unexpectedly into women's arms.
The crowd consisted of common street faces,
People one sees daily at the market:
Peddlars, brokers, hucksters and porters.
Fever burned their bearded faces,
Gilded by the light of wax havdulas
(Candles, with flame clinging to flame
Like an archangel's sword woven with lightning).
Sometimes, foreheads bent down like ears of corn
Gibbering, but the rite did not seem to anyone
"Ridiculous solemnity"—as to Beaumarchais.
Itzek covered his face with a kerchief, and one of the crowd,
Not a priest, a plain man, only more pale
And more sad than the others, looking around,
Sang. A wedding song but not cheerful.
Two curly-headed boys seconded aloud,
And the whole crowd murmured half-wistful, half-wild.
I looked at this picture curious but cold.
Itzek, though shadowed by a light and smoky cloud
And somber, on garbage, like before an altar,
Was to me only Itzek, a poor ragman,
And there was nothing poetic in the others;
They seemed ordinary people who guard
Equally diligently their own breed like their faith and possessions.
In vain, their swarthy faces took a mysterious stigma
From the shine of the moon and from the flame of the candles;
No one attracted with an inspired or sad face.
Suddenly, the song stopped. As if spread far
Windows to the wedding hall opened with noise,
Where the bride, amongst the women,
Sat crying. Chazen raised his arms above her
(Chazen with shining eyes and a patriarch's beard)
And mentioned her father who died young
And who was missing today on the family holiday...
A great weeping arose and he, at the lamentation,

With women sobbing and arms twisting,
Began a song with a funeral note ringing:
El Mole Rachmim...
        First though swelled with tears,
The song flowed peacefully, bringing to Lord's feet
Heartfelt pain, held by the force of reason;
That's how a grown-up son cries on the father's grave;
Then, soaked in sorrow blowing from the graves.
Losing by sparks faith and hope,
Grew in power and captured by the pain confusion,
Melted in hot tears and woman's complaint.
Not one grave but millions of them
Became a loud weeper and crazy with pain
Ran to cry above old cemeteries,
Above Israel's bones, which are spread
All over the earth like grains of sterile sand;
About the sowing that will be meager,
About the graves overgrown with dead weeds,
About the dwarfed, weak children's souls,
About the long, long night of slavery!
Nothing could stop it; it ran like a stream,
When, after a storm, it changes into a foaming river;
The singer had sparks in his eyes and a shivering bosom,
A bare forehead, when he moved back his hat,
Ran with sweat—The song moved even an old grandmother,
Whom paralysis turned dead and a rock;
Her glassy eyes, half-dead, were sweating.
Everyone in the room was crying, overcome with great grief.
And when the chazen mentioned the holy Jerusalem,
Mother who, though shining with a white face from afar,
Was dead for ages to her firstborn children;
When he mentioned the heartless cruelty of fate,
Poverty, persecution, wandering, martyrdom
And the happiness lost forever, forever—
Pain became more real, heart's wounds bloodier.
In the room, the rage of despair breathed with a wild wind
And boiled over with a huge, hopeless scream...

I listened to the song with my bosom swelled with feelings,
And these people, complaining aloud to the Lord,

Proud of their great past, brave with a great pain,
Strangely grew in my eyes and became ennobled.
I did not see anymore the ugly spots on the canopy,
Itzek's dress and his name did not bother me anymore,
The dullness of these bearded faces disappeared for me
And I became like a man who. . . dreams while awake.
The backyard. . . No! it was a flowery valley,
Somewhere at the foot of Lebanon, climbing to the sky
Rustling with a forest of dark cedars, as if singing.
The moon poured streams of silver into this valley,
The sky covered it with a crystal bell,
The desert was breathing with hot breath,
And palms cooled with fans of fronds,
There was no hatred between heaven and earth;
The face of Jehovah gazed smiling from above
Blessing the valley, people and lambs;
Crowd of faithful whispered prayers and knelt before the Lord
The aroma of nard and sassafras wafted in the air,
The stream, like a snake, unfolded braids of silvery scales
And the stars shone like a golden Sabbath candelabra.

Carl was very touched by the poem. It addressed his longings and spiritual needs. He felt that the Jews had been mistreated and misjudged throughout the millennia. They were spat upon, tortured and killed. They were a people at whom everybody laughed. And yet they were not dirty, cheap or underhanded. They were clean, generous and honest. They descended from the most illustrious ancestors, who gave the world the Bible, the prophets and leaders in every field of endeavor.

Carl felt the hunchback he had carried for many years straighten out. He could now walk tall and erect. His cup overflowed.

Chapter 44

Hiding Under A Bed In Boryslaw

The next three chapters contain a story that was written in Polish and given to the author by Wilhelm Dichter (Wilus). Carl translated it into English and the credit is given to Wilhelm Dichter of Tewksbury, Massachusetts Carl had asked Wilhelm on numerous occasions to write about his experiences during the Holocaust. He felt that the impressions of a 6-year-old child would be invaluable, and he knew of no other description of war atrocities by a child. Children simply did not survive the war. They were usually torn away from their mothers and killed. And the chances of a woman's surviving with a child were reduced a hundredfold compared to those of single individuals. Wilus was reluctant to write anything about this period and claimed that he didn't remember anything because he was too young. But Carl did not believe it and he kept insisting. Finally, in November 1992, during Carl's visit with Irene and Anna to Wilus' house in Tewksbury, Massachusetts Wilus gave him a 48-page pamphlet written in Polish:

"Hiding Under A Bed In Boryslaw."

1. The Happy Times

My grandfather lived with Milo and Nusia in Wolanka on the outskirts of Boryslaw. I remember their old house, which could be entered through the backyard. A doghouse stood there and a tree grew. The dog ran around tied to a line strung between the house and the tree. His name was Lis; later he disappeared somewhere without a trace. My mother would pull me by the hand up a few wooden steps to the veranda and open the kitchen door. Each item there was neatly in its place.

My grandmother was short and somewhat bristled up. She wore a black dress buttoned all the way up. A small white collar stuck out. She had black hair and black eyes, just like my mother and me. She spoke to everybody in German except me.

She had grown up in Vienna. Standing on the third balcony, behind the last row of chairs, she had listened to the music coming from the deep well of the stage. She adored opera and Prater. She saw the city, where the Jews were happy, from a little car on big wheels. "The Danube is flowing with milk and honey," she reminisced later. She played a mandolin and sang waltzes with my future grandfather. She gave birth to Milo one year after the wedding. The war broke out while she was carrying Anna and the men were taken to the front.

The Russian offensive inundated Galicia. Jews from small towns ran away to Vienna out of fear of pogroms. My grandmother said to her injured husband in the military hospital, "The Germans are too cultured for these Russian savages."

"Civilization will take care of everything," Grandfather consoled her.

Those were tough years but others suffered just the same; this kept her spirits up.

Life became more difficult when her husband came back from the war. The empire collapsed and poverty drove them out of Vienna. They got out at the railroad station in Boryslaw and waited with their bundles until somebody from their large and hungry grandfather's family came with a horse and buggy and picked them up. Slowly they became more prosperous. Grandmother started to help Grandfather's sisters, who had married poor men. She did it behind his back. She squeezed hard-earned pennies into their hands and sent Milo and Andzia to them with baskets of food on holidays. She remade an old overcoat for Grandfather's niece, whose stepfather had gambled everything away. Andzia cried because she wanted a coat too.

"She is 17 and has to look nice," said Grandmother. "You have time."

Another girl was born after a few years, but she didn't live long. In spite of the fact that Nusia was born shortly afterwards Grandmother did not get over it for a long time.

A mandolin was hanging on the wall in the living room in Wolanka, next to a wicker etagère. Volumes of a German dictionary bound in green leather stood there. Its smooth and always cold pages were covered with gothic letters. I turned the pages slowly, looking for pictures and photographs. German pilots, hanging under the zeppelin in a rope gondola, shot at planes. The planes, with colored wheels and wings, buzzed around like wasps. The pilots, leaning out of the gondolas, pressed the triggers of machine guns. They could fall down at any time into the dark night crisscrossed with searchlights. The war was terrible. My grandfather was a paramedic in the artillery division. His photograph in an Austrian uniform with medals on his chest hangs on the wall.

After he came to Boryslaw, my grandfather was employed as a

bookkeeper in an oil company owned by the French. He earned good money and saved every penny. Since he knew the science of bookkeeping, he decided to open his own business. He resigned from his post and opened a hardware store on Wolanka. All kinds of merchandise, bought with money borrowed from the bank, appeared on the shelves: hammers, door locks, kerosene lamps and spray guns for cockroaches. It looked as if the bell had tolled for the old hardware store across the street, which had stood there since time immemorial. But a depression came and people stopped buying. The old store, vegetating as usual, survived but grandfather went bankrupt. The oil company took him back. He kept repaying his debts for years and paid up the last penny owed shortly before the war broke out.

Grandfather was gray, had a trimmed mustache and looked through wire-rimmed glasses. He wore snow-white shirts with stiff collars. Before he left the house, (he was always going somewhere) he would stop at the doorstep and wipe his shoes, which shone like a mirror, with a flannel cloth. Then he would flick a speck of dust from his lapel and open the door. At home, women treated him with respect.

Grandfather and Milo looked as similar as two drops of water. They had wide faces, strong chins and gray eyes. They didn't shy away from anybody. They sat on chairs as if they were horses. Even their voices sounded the same. But they fought with each other constantly. Milo, with a violin under his arm, went once a week for music lessons. Andzia would tiptoe after him and Grandfather told her to watch her brother.

"Andzia, they have pictures from America in the photoplasticon," Milo would say.

"Dad will kill you. I beg you, let's go to the lesson."

"No, I won't."

"I'll tell father."

"Just try..."

They watched three-dimensional photos through brass-rimmed glasses. Andzia pretended that she was not looking and came home petrified with fear. Grandfather would beat Milo up with a strap when his adventures came to light. Milo would disappear, roam the streets and come home early in the morning. Grandfather would be waiting: "You will study to be a doctor. It is the only profession for a Jew in Poland."

Milo's friends, Jews, Poles and Ukrainians, either fought bloody battles or got together and made life miserable for somebody else.

Once, during a lesson on ancient Rome, they brought frogs into the classroom.

"Samuel Mandel! Leave school and don't come back without your father!"

Milo wrote a poem ridiculing the teachers. For this and the frogs he was left back for another year. When he graduated, Jews were not admitted to medical school. He went to Prague but ran out of money and had to return. Unemployment and boredom reigned in Boryslaw.

Andzia graduated from high school. The band played a waltz at the prom. A tall, lean man, elegantly dressed and wearing a silk tie, crossed the room. He had light hair and green eyes. Andzia realized that he was walking towards her. Her heart beat fast and she stopped flirting with the boys. The stranger bowed to her. Andzia looked up. Black-haired and black-eyed, a head shorter than he, she stretched out her damp hand. She stepped on his foot while dancing and turned red with embarrassment. "I had never met anybody as handsome as your daddy," she would say later. He walked her home early in the morning. It was snowing and there was no wind. He wore a coat with a beaver collar and a peaked hat.

"Do you like skiing?"

"Yes, very much."

"Let's go to the mountains on sleds. We will come back to Boryslaw on skis...."

"On sleds? That's expensive?!"

He laughed. "Can I visit you at home?"

They said good-bye at the door just like in the movies.

Grandfather was waiting at home.

"Who was this gentile?" he hollered and swung his hand at her.

"Bronislaw is a Jew!" She shielded her face with her hands.

"No Jew has the name 'Bronislaw.'"

"Yes, he has, he has," she started to cry.

Bronek was five years older than Andzia. He worked for the largest oil company in the city and was making three times as much money as Grandfather. Everybody addressed him as "Mr. Engineer." Grandfather checked everything out and Andzia invited Bronek to the house. He looked like Gary Cooper and was charming. The older Mandel girl had won a ticket at the lottery. Dressed elegantly, she looked at herself in the mirror before going to a dance. Milo made faces and sang, "Miss Andzia has a day off, and she wears a stylish dress."

The wedding took place after graduation. They took an apartment on Panska Street in the center of Boryslaw. A one-story house stood inside a yard. The kitchen and maid's room were to the left of a corridor. To the right there was a series of white-painted rooms: the dining room, living room and bedroom. One could see the police building across the street from the house.

I was born nine months later. I slept in a baby carriage that stood in front of the house. A maid and a nurse peeked through the window. A huge St. Bernard, belonging to my father, basked in the sun nearby. My mother loved to stroll from the yard to the street holding my father's arm while he pushed the carriage. That part of Panska Street had a sidewalk, street lamps and stores.

A well-to-do Mr. Unter, my father's uncle, lived in Drohobycz (one had to go there by horse carriage or train). He managed an orphanage for Jewish children. I remember a room on the second floor of a red brick building. They brought me there from the hospital shortly before the outbreak of the war. I was screaming, which hurt my throat. They promised me as much ice cream as I wanted before they removed my tonsils, but I only got a little bit on the tip of a teaspoon.

Mr. Unter had three children, Julek (who, like Milo, was to become a doctor), Teresa and blind Maciek, who made brushes. Teresa fell in love with Milo during his visit to Drohobycz. Then Mr. Unter gave Milo money and sent him to Italy with Julek. The Italian cities overwhelmed Milo. He would walk along the streets surrounded by sculpture and paintings. In one yard he saw a huge foot sculpted in stone. He lifted his head to see the rest of the statue but it wasn't there. Only the foot had survived.

When I was 1 year old my father contracted tuberculosis. In a few months he was dying. My mother always dreamed of going to Lvov in an express train. Now, finally, she went there to take her husband to a lung hospital. There they gave him an edema but it did not succeed. They applied it for a second time and immediately sent him to a sanatorium in the mountains in Worochta. Would Bronek survive? Nobody knew. Had she done anything wrong? The baby cried. The St. Bernard barked and scratched at the door because he wanted to go for a walk. Who would pay for the apartment and the servant? Grandfather wanted her to sell the apartment. Mother dismissed the maid and gave the dog away.

"I have enough money for a year."

"And then you will go begging," despaired Grandfather.

"Bronek will return."

What about the child? Would he get T.B. too? He had to eat a lot. She pushed spoonfuls of farina into my mouth and I spat it out in anger. She started to spank me. Grandfather hit her again.

"Don't hit the child!"

"I'll tell Bronek!" she cried angrily.

A miracle happened. God answered Mother's prayers. After a year, Father came back. He was cured. He looked pitiful but he still looked like an actor in an American movie. Life returned to normal. A new maid appeared at home.

One day Father was playing solitaire and I was sitting next to him in a high chair. Mother brought out a frying pan with scrambled eggs and parsley. I didn't want to eat and closed my lips tight. Finally she lost patience and, with one motion, threw the contents of the pan on my head. I screamed in fear. Father dropped the cards and grabbed her by the hands. The pan fell on the carpet. Mother tried to free herself and clean the carpet, but he kept holding her firmly.

"Andzia, he is a little boy."

"I wanted him to eat and be healthy."

"He will eat later. He cannot now."

Father's friends used to come on Thursdays to play poker. At first, Mother didn't like it, but later she learned to play poker and loved those Thursdays.

"Will there be a war, yes or no? Two cards."

"Yes, there will be and Germans will get a shellacking. One card."

"Well? Nothing."

"The British will bomb Berlin. Three cards."

"The French will enter the Ruhr or will get here through Rumania. I'll give five and five more."

"We have enough soldiers ourselves. Ten and show your hand."

War hung by a thread for a long time, but nobody anticipated what happened. Young, smiling Germans entered the police courtyard on motorcycles while the mobilization was still in progress. They stood at the water well, drank and looked at maps. After they left, the streets were deserted. The Russians were coming. For a few days nobody came out. The clatter of horse hooves on the sidewalks could be heard. The Cossacks avoided the streets paved with cobblestones. They came on small horses, peered into our backyard and entered the courtyard of the police building. After them came soldiers with ruby red stars on peaked caps and civilians in semi-military outfits who spoke at meetings. The annexation to Russia was approved by votes taken at the movies. Crowds marched with flags in the streets. A loudspeaker played a song about three tank soldiers fighting four Samurais. Panska Street was renamed Stalin Street (everybody continued to call it Panska Street). The police building was taken over by the N.K.V.D. People were arrested at night. The streets were empty. Father and Grandfather were getting food rations at work. The maid disappeared. Portraits of bearded, mustached men were hung in the preschool building. On the anniversary of the revolution I recited in Russian,

> Dear leader comrade Lenin
> You are buried in the ground
> But when I grow up
> I want to serve your party.

    I had a friend from the backyard who was one year older that I was. His name was Marek Bernstein. Mother said that he was a brat. Marek played in the backyard all day and only went home when he was hungry. I followed him and copied him in everything. Our backyard was separated from the others leading to Panska Street by a high wooden fence. Going along the fence, we would go to the back where the fields started. Oil wells stood there looking like peasant women with large heads. The drilling towers were made of three wooden poles driven into the ground and were joined at the top. Marek would stand at the fence and pull up the sides of his short pants. Then he would lean backwards and a stream of amber urine would flow over the fence. Once I tried to outdo him and leaned back too much. The stream flowed too steeply upwards and fell back on me like rain.
    According to the Russians, the apartment on Panska was too big for us. Therefore, our grandparents, Milo and Nusia moved in with us. This way we at least avoided living with strangers. The oil companies were nationalized and organized into a cartel. The alphabet was changed. Only the numbers remained the same. Grandfather still filled his books with beautiful handwriting like print. He hated the Russians: "Illiterates! Curs! They steal and lie!"
    Nusia was dancing as a Cossack at school. I didn't see her on stage but I remember her in a colorful peasant outfit. She jumped on her left foot in a red boot, holding the right one in the air and pulling up the second boot.
    "Mom, give me a kerchief because I'm going to be late."
    Grandmother put the ironing iron on the oven and brought over a

warm kerchief with tussles. Nusia threw it over her shoulders and ran out of the house. She was 17 years old and beautiful. Her big green eyes made the boys nervous. They carried her bookcase to school and back. Grandfather was worried: "Only gentiles! Aren't there any Jews in Boryslaw?"

"School is for everybody."

"If anyone crosses the door of this house he will be thrown out."

"And if he comes to do homework?"

"Don't be smart!"

Kopcio appeared towards the end of the Russian time. He conducted a dance orchestra. He was older than Nusia and lived with his mother on a poor Jewish street. He had black hair, which he stroked with his thin, delicate fingers. He smoked and looked at Grandfather with anger.

"I can assure you that a lot of money can be made from dancing."

"This is not a profession."

"People like to dance."

"Andzia and I go to dances," said Father, playing solitaire.

"Don't mix in," whispered Mother. Don't you see how brazenly he talks to Father? He follows her everywhere like a dog."

Kopcio brought chocolates. Only Nusia ate them. His visits, however, became rarer. Finally he stopped coming.

Milo and Julek Unter did not return to Italy after their last vacation in Poland. They received their doctor's diplomas in Lvov. Milo married Teresa and moved with her to Panska Street. Here Romus was born. A short man smiled oddly when called for the circumcision. After the procedure, he carried a tray with a bottle of alcohol and a piece of blood-stained cotton.

The Russians mobilized the doctors in the summer. Milo came home in a captain's uniform and soft leather boots reaching to his knees. His belts squeaked. Teresa cried and her tears fell on Romus, whom she was holding in her arms.

I stood with my father in my parents' bedroom and looked out to the street. The sky was covered with black smoke from the burning oil wells. Soldiers marched along the street leading deep into Russia. Milo and Julek were among them. Suddenly, lightning tore the sky. Deafening thunder followed. Father grabbed me by the hand. We were thrown deep into the room until we hit the opposite wall. The Russians had blown up the power plant to prevent it from getting into German hands.

2. On Panska Street

A mob of men appeared on the street after the Germans entered. Soon the same thing happened in our backyard. The screams of beaten people curdled the blood in our veins. Some strangers stormed in and took Grandfather and Mother. Grandmother, Nusia, Teresa with Romus and I remained alone. Father stayed in the office; he was afraid to go into the street.

Mother came back after a while. She was petrified. They had found piles of murdered people in the basements of the N.K.V.D. building. The pogrom was in full fury on the streets. Jews were beaten with clubs and forced to wash the dead. They put a pail on Mother's head and ordered her to use her blouse for rags. A woman spat in her face, "Go and wash those you killed!"

Nusia's former high school friend, who was now a Ukrainian policeman, escorted Mother from the N.K.V.D. courtyard. However, Grandfather, as a male, was now in mortal danger. Our women muffled their cries of desperation so as not to attract the attention of people in the street.

After two days it started to quiet down. I saw Grandfather through the open door. He was breathing heavily, as if after a long chase. Blood from a wound on his forehead had solidified on his dirty, sweaty face. He was wearing a stained vest on his almost naked body and supported himself with his hands against the window frame. He reeked of carbolic acid. It was a strange and horrible smell. His glasses were missing and he was staring at nothing. Then his legs slowly caved in under him. The women ran to help him. The doors were closed shut. He cried out in pain several times when his acid-drenched pants were pulled off. When he stood in a large washbasin filled with water in the middle of the room, I saw that his buttocks had been burned.

A quiet descended after the pogrom. Grandfather, who still could not sit, said, "I know them. Germans do not kill. They need us as much as the Poles and Russians did. Bronek and I have already been told to report to work. If they trust us, nothing will threaten us.

"What are you saying!" said Father quietly. "They almost killed you."

"Those were Ukrainians. They would love to slaughter us with knives. The Germans have a real war on their minds."

Confiscations started. Jews were ordered to turn in their radios, watches and jewelry. Father had a Phillips radio. He sat with his ear at the set and rotated the dial. The news from afar was bad. The Germans were halfway to Moscow. Summer turned into autumn. We did not know Milo's fate.

"He didn't even have time to enjoy his baby," cried Teresa.

"Milo is a doctor," said Grandfather. "Russians take care of their doctors because they have so few of them."

"What shall I do?! Milo will kill me if something happens to Romus."

Father threw the radio and watches into a bag and took it to the Jewish Committee. Mother hid the jewelry. The white rings from their wedding bands remained on the hands of the grown-ups.

Next, they demanded furs. Mother's gray fur coat hang in the closet in the parents' bedroom. Whenever she opened the closet I got ready to touch the fur.

"You can stroke it. It's beautiful, isn't it?"

Grandfather brought two suitcases from the basement. In one he folded Mother's fur coat, with its big fox collar. In the other he put a beaver collar taken off Father's coat. The fox collar was yellow, with big glass eyes. The fox held his tail in his teeth. Grandfather also packed rabbit hats with earflaps, muffs and leather gloves. Mother started to cry and curse the Germans.

"There's nothing to cry about," said Grandfather. One day we will buy everything brand new."

He took the suitcases and left. Father looked on, too weak to help.

After the furs the furniture was next. Before the war Mother had won $4000 on the lottery. With part of this money, she took her sister, brother and his fiancée to Truskawiec for a vacation; with the rest, she bought walnut furniture for the bedroom. The evenings in Truskawiec were warm and the aroma of fruit trees wafted in through the open doors of the resort hotel. I listened to Milo's story about a lady who had a bat tangled in her hair. It was impossible to get him out and they had to shave her head. Mother, Nusia and Teresa screamed because they were afraid of bats and I was happy that I had short hair. The furniture Mother had bought consisted of a bed with a beautiful curved footboard, an armoire in which a fur had once been, and two night tables. Polished, it reflected the light in the walnut tree rings.

The German who came with a member of the Jewish Committee liked the furniture. He opened the window, smacked his lips with appreciation and stroked the smooth surface of the bed with his hand:

"I'll bring the wagon and horses tomorrow."

He turned around and left with the Jew who had accompanied him.

I was awakened at night by the screams of Mother, Grandfather and Father. They were coming from their bedroom. I pushed in the great white doors and looked inside. Grandfather was shaking his hands over Mother's head: "You idiot! Do you want to get us killed?"

"If I can't have it then they're not going to either."

"Be quiet or I will. . . ."

"Father, please calm down and don't lift your hand to my wife." Father took scissors out of Mother's hand.

She looked small next to this tall man with green eyes. She pressed her face into his sweater and he bent down and kissed her hair. Grandfather and Father spent the rest of the night repairing the bed, which had been scratched up with the scissors. In the morning Jewish porters loaded the furniture on a platform, kicked at the horses and left.

Peasants' horse-drawn wagons started to cruise around Boryslaw. Couples sat in the drivers' seats. A peasant would stop the wagon, climb down with a whip in his hand and knock at the door. If he saw something interesting he would call his wife. If not, he would climb back, take the reins in his hand and drive away. They were timid at first. The women would stretch their hands out to the children. "God won't let them be harmed," they would say.

They would open their mouths in amazement. Money was not necessary. Jews were selling for kascha, onions and potatoes. The peasants competed with each other. Hunger was lowering the prices and the amount of merchandise was diminishing. There was no time for formalities.

"I'll give you a bag of potatoes but you must add chairs."

"No, not chairs, take the carpet."

"I already have a carpet, give me the chairs. You won't need them anymore. You can't take them with you."

The carts did not stop anymore; they only slowed down. Sometimes the peasants just waved their whips and hollered that they were buying everything. Sometimes a door would open because somebody still had something to sell.

The German mounted police moved into the clean scrubbed building of the N.K.V.D. When I moved the curtains in my parents' empty bedroom I could see soldiers in green pants and white T-shirts. They brushed their teeth and the white foam dripped on their chins and chests. A stream of cold water came from a water well with an iron pump. They dipped their heads and jumped back, laughing heartily. Mother told me to get away from the window. She installed black paper shades and pulled them down. It became dark and stuffy. I stopped going out to the yard.

Soon soldiers dressed in green uniforms appeared in our house. They were from Austria and they liked the Viennese accent of our women. Grandmother brought the photo of Grandfather that had once hung on the wall in the apartment in Wolanka: "My husband fought the Russians, just like you."

The Germans lowered their heads over the picture and examined the medal.

A soldier who admired Romus' blond hair and blue eyes asked him where his father was.

"He died," answered Teresa in Polish.

"He died," translated Mother into German.

The German kneeled down, took out a chocolate from his breast pocket and gave a piece to Romus. I moved closer.

"What would you do if they told you to shoot him?" asked Mother.

"An order is an order."

One day they said, "If something should happen, we will put a guard outside the door and we won't let anybody in."

The first action after the pogrom surprised everybody. Suddenly German soldiers in black uniforms appeared on the streets. The street exits were manned by Polish and Ukrainian policemen. Jewish policemen, wearing old military caps without the eagle emblems, stormed the apartments. They pushed women, children and old people out of their backyards onto Panska Street. A crowd surrounded by Germans walked down the street in the direction of the slaughterhouse and the railroad station. A second crowd stood on the sidewalks and looked. Children pointed their fingers at these Jews who tried to escape. We were hidden in the basement and we could hear talking and screaming through the cracks in the pile of coal. Our grandmother was not with us; she had run away to the other side to a neighbor who had a basement too.

A mounted police guard stood in front of our house. A drunken neighbor named Kruk passed by and said, "Let me in. They are inside."

The soldiers started to laugh.

Kruk brought over some SS men. "He says there are Jews here," said one of them.

"The house is empty. It belongs to the mounted police."
"Let us in!"
"No, it's not permitted!"
The SS men cursed Kruk and left.

On the second night, the pail that served as a toilet started to overflow. In the morning we heard the thundering boots of soldiers entering the apartment. They opened the cover to the basement and shouted, "The action is over. You can come out."

When Nusia ran to the other side of the yard, a soldier in green said to my Mother, "They took them all away. Your mother too."

We remained alone. Grandfather was sitting in a chair with his hands on Mother's head as she knelt in front of him. Nusia lay on the floor and cried. Father sat down next to her and pulled in his long legs.

"Maybe we'll get a letter," he whispered.
"They will kill her," sobbed Nusia.
"They will kill them all," added Teresa.

Marek Bernstein was taken with his parents. The talk was of freight cars loaded with dead and living people. I had seen freight cars during the Russian time; cows looked at us through the open doors. Now children choked to death under people's feet in similar freight cars.

The railroad workers spoke about the camp in Belzec. A train would enter. People were stripped naked and shoved into the washroom. There they were flogged with clubs and whips. In the washroom there was gas instead of water. The bodies were incinerated on iron grills in crematoria. Those who died during the transport were thrown outside and the cars were washed with streams of water. The railroad workers joked, over glasses of vodka, "The only way out for Jews was through the chimney."

The Jewish orphanage in Drohobycz had its own vocational school. Orphans unable to obtain anything better learned a trade they could use for the rest of their lives. Maciek learned how to make brushes. Mr. Unter believed that the Germans would surely take the invalids from the orphanage. So in order to save Maciek from a selection, he sent him into hiding for a lot of money. He was smart: the orphanage was liquidated during an action in Boryslaw. The children and staff were gathered in front of the red brick building in a yard surrounded with an iron fence. Even the families of the teachers and craftsmen who lived in the orphanage were gathered there too. They were arranged in a column by the Jewish police. There was a truck with soldiers in black uniforms waiting at the gate. One of them leaned out from the cab and gave a hand signal.

"Forward!" screamed the policemen.

The column passed through the gate and moved towards the railroad station as the truck followed slowly behind. They walked in silence carrying in their arms small children, the sick and invalids. Freight cars stood in a field far from the railroad station. The children walking at the head of the line stopped in front of their open doors, too short to reach the floor, which was above their heads. The policemen started to scream and hit them with clubs. Older boys tried to run away but were pushed back and hit with clubs. Adults and children climbed into the freight cars in a panic, the taller ones throwing in the little ones. When the policemen had finished their job, the Germans jumped out of the truck and, screaming, pushed them inside too. Then they locked and sealed the doors. The railroad men fastened the doors with chains, white steam belched from underneath the wheels and the train started to move. The Germans stood there breathing heavily and wiping the perspiration off their faces with their sleeves.

The Austrian soldiers from the N.K.V.D. building cried when they were sent to the front. A peasant turned in Maciek, who had been hidden in a wagon full of hay. The Jewish Committee announced the creation of a ghetto. It was not far from the street where Kopcio lived with his mother. There were many people on Panska Street without furniture. Mattresses, coats and pillows lay on the floors next to cold, tiled stoves. Empty hooks protruded from the walls of the pantry. There wasn't even a crumb of bread in the kitchen. Maciek, his hair as white as straw, sat on the floor with his hands on his knees. When Teresa spoke to him he smiled but he didn't turn around. He was Nusia's age. She lay on her cot with her face turned to the wall.

"Mom, mom, take me with you," she whispered.

One day Kopcio came. Nusia got up and talked to him in the corner of the room. "Don't go to the ghetto, it's a trap! They'll transport them all. First the women and children and then the men. We all have to die. Don't you understand? Come with me and I will save you. I have a place in the village where nobody will find us. I have enough money to last through the war."

"I don't want to live without my mother."

"I love you."

"I won't leave my father and Andzia."

"Don't delay; I can't wait long."

Grandfather, who knew Poles at work, found a family willing to take Romus. He assured them that the child looked very good and wouldn't say anything because he didn't talk yet. They had six children and figured that he would go unnoticed. They told the neighbors that they were taking in a relative's son. Then they came to Panska Street to see him. Teresa did not say a single word. They took money and jewelry. Romus was put asleep with chloroform and a woman carried him away in a heavy fabric kerchief.

"If none of us survives," said Grandfather, "Doctor Samuel Mandel, my son, will pick him up after the war."

I was not present when Romus was taken away. I noticed his absence only on the next day, when I awoke and got out of the bed I shared with my mother. Everybody was lying on the floor. Teresa was following me with her eyes.

"Where is Romus?" I asked.

"Romus is safe," she answered in a dead voice.

Father ran a fever. His eyes glittered, there were red spots on his cheeks and he breathed rapidly through half-open lips. His cough grew worse and worse. He would lurch forward, grabbing his chest with his hands as if he wanted to tear something out from inside. His cough would turn into wheezing and gurgling and he would spit into a jar and rest for a long while, holding onto a window sill.

"This is the end, Andzia. It was the same before the edema."

"You'll be healthy." Mother kissed his hands.

"Children, don't be afraid. It will be more peaceful in the ghetto. They'll give us something to eat."

"Dad, you'll see how well I will feed him."

I still did not know where Romus was. I pulled at Mother's sleeve but she paid no attention to me. I went over to my father.

"Don't go near your father," Mother exclaimed.

"Please move away; you may get infected," said Father.

Midday passed. I drank water from a tin cup. Suddenly somebody pounded on our door with his fists and hollered, "Pogrom!"

Mother grabbed me by the hand and ran out of the house. Nusia followed us. We ran along the fence to the end of the backyard and then across the fields to the stream. The ground was soft after the rain, and the grass shone with dew. Our feet sank in softly and came out sloshing. Dirt sprinkled our faces and ran into our perspiration. Mother lost a shoe but she continued to run.

"Andzia, your shoe!" hollered Nusia and she turned around. "Oh my God! The Germans!"

A German sat on a horse on top of the field from which we were running and shot at us. We didn't hear the shots. Mother was jumping through water puddles, carrying me in the air.

"Mom, I can't run anymore."

We crossed the stream on rocks and continued to run uphill. Our yard disappeared and so did the German on the horse, and we continued to run. Mother slowed down only when it started to get dark. Letting go of my hand, she straightened her fingers with difficulty.

"Mom I want to lie down."

"Andzia, let us rest."

In the evening we dragged ourselves over to our unpainted block of apartments. Shivering with cold, we approached the wall to read the apartment numbers in the stairwell. Nusia knocked on the door.

"Who's there?"

"Andzia and Nusia Mandel."

A young woman opened the door. Her husband was standing behind her. "My God," she exclaimed.

Chapter 45

Hiding Under A Bed (Continued)

3. At Janka

The people we had run to on Panska Street had a room with a kitchen on the main floor. During the day, Mother and Nusia would sit in the corner of the room while I lay under the bed. Neighbors who came to see the lady of the house were entertained in the kitchen. We used the urinal that stood next to me under the bed. I would turn on my stomach and put the urinal under myself. Mother and Nusia would crawl under the bed and take the pot to their corner. At night, the owner would bring a pail, open the window and leave us alone. Then he would take the pail to the bathroom, which was located in the corridor and served several apartments. The owners slept in their beds and we slept on the floor.

Father came after a few days to take us to another apartment. We left in the middle of the night and sneaked close to the walls. Finally the walls ended and trees without leaves took their place. The sidewalk disappeared. Little houses, surrounded by fences, stood far from the road and dark fields stretched in between. The night was black. There was no moon or stars. Father, tall and lean in a long coat and peaked cap, looked like a silhouette cut out of black paper. Mother was holding onto his arm and pulled me along. Nusia walked behind us.

"They separated us in the backyard," Father was saying.

"Father, Teresa and I were taken to the ghetto and Maciek was taken to the slaughterhouse, where they were being gathered for a transport." He started to cough. We stopped so he could rest. Nusia was sobbing.

"Where are we going?" asked Mother.

"You and Wilus to Janka. Nusia will go to Tabaczynski."

"I want to be with you."

"You will come to the ghetto when he is safe." He motioned at me with his head.

Tytus Tabaczynski had been in love with Nusia since they were children. He could not, however, cross the threshold of her house. Although Grandfather was impressed by this son of a wealthy engineer who lived in a villa and drove to work in a horse and carriage, he considered a marriage between his daughter and a non-Jew to be out of the question. Tabaczynski had to hide during the Russian rule because he had been threatened with expulsion to Siberia. The whole family moved into the villa. Tytus' feelings for Nusia had not changed.

Tytus came running to see us right after the pogrom. Grandfather was lying on his stomach with towels on his burned buttocks. The boy stood at the bed, pale as a ghost, not knowing what to say. After the second pogrom, Grandfather asked Tabaczynski for help.

"Miss Nusia can come to us whenever she wants to," said the engineer.

There were rooms in the attic of the villa where the servant, cook and nurse had lived. Nusia got the nurse's room. She sat on the made-up bed and stared at the wall. She did not talk to Tytus. Books that he had brought from his father's library remained where he had left them.

"She will get sick," said Mrs. Tabaczynski to her husband.

"Unlucky child," sighed the engineer.

"She refuses to eat."

"To Palestine or Madagascar, but not to death. . . ."

"What are you saying?"

"I am thinking aloud."

One night, somebody knocked at the door. Tytus opened it. A lean, black-haired man stood before him. He stroked his hair with his fingers and said, "I am a friend. I came to see Miss Nusia."

They went upstairs. Nusia rose when she saw them and smiled at Kopcio. Tytus swallowed and left them alone.

"I can't wait any longer," said Kopcio.

"Will you be good to me?"

"I love you."

Janka lived with her father in a tiny house in a deserted area. Her father worked for the same company as Grandfather. He would come home late, take off his clothes, which were soaked with petroleum, and wash himself for a long time in a wash basin. Janka would pour water from a jar onto his head and hands. He would put on a fresh shirt, pants and slippers with open backs on his bare feet. While eating dinner he would tell his daughter what he had seen that day. Then he would roll a long cigarette and light it. He slept in a small room which he could enter through Janka's bedroom, where I was staying. Janka was an old maid. Petite, she had a sweet face, moist lips and eyes full of compassion. She limped because her right leg was short, a result of tuberculosis of the bone. She had warm and delicate hands and spoke slowly and calmly: "We have to pray to convince God, and who can do that better than a child? Don't cry because you are alone. Your father is sick and your mother has to be with him. It's not bad here. The food is skimpy, but at least we have some potatoes. My father knows old Mr. Mandel very well and can't praise him enough. One day you will be like him."

I listened to Janka from under the bed. I saw her legs when she limped to the kitchen and closed the door carefully. I felt like a cat or some other hiding animal. Invisible, I observed everybody who came into the room. I would turn slowly from one side to the other so that the floor would not squeak. Freshly scrubbed, it smelled of soup. The aroma lingered for a long time especially between the cracks in the boards. I was hungry and I would put my nose close to the floor and inhale carefully through my fingers (so as not to inhale the dust and sneeze) into my nostrils. Every sound could betray me, especially when Janka was talking with somebody in the kitchen. I would get drowsy out of boredom. But I was deadly afraid to sleep. I could moan or, even worse, scream and somebody would hear it. When my eyes closed I turned on my back and pressed them against the boards on which the straw mattress was resting. I would think about those who had died or been hidden like Nusia. I always remembered the lullaby she used to sing to me:

> Beautiful fables, enchanted fables
> My old gray nanny was telling me.
> About a scary dragon, a sleeping beauty,
> And how a band of knights fought.
> I cried bitterly when she finished
> Begging her, please nanny, tell me more.

I was most fearful of children. I was convinced that if I left Janka's room, they would immediately recognize me on the street and denounce me to the Germans. Grown-ups might show compassion, but children—not. I dreamt all the time that I was running away from them. I would run blindly, further and further until I stopped because my drowsy imagination could not invent what would happen next. In the shadow under the bed I saw my skinny legs in white socks.

During the day I heard the voices of birds behind the windows. They were uninteresting to me. I was waiting to hear the voices of those who would come for me.

Grandfather, Father and Teresa were in the ghetto. Grandfather was working as a bookkeeper for the petroleum cartel. I don't know what Father and Teresa were doing. Mother was staying here and there. She would sneak out of the ghetto to be with Father and then run away to Janka to avoid the selections in the ghetto in which women and children were being taken away.

When we were together, she would lie down on the floor next to me and talk to Janka who leaned out of bed: "Bronek coughs all the time. He has no strength for work."

"He will recover after the war."

"He contracted tuberculosis before he could even walk," she said, pointing at me. "I prayed to God and he got well."

"Mr. Bronek is so handsome. He looks like a lord."

"He always ate a lot of cheese, eggs and meat. Now, with the hunger, everything has opened up again." She looked up. "God, what have I done.?"

"Every woman would like to have a man like him."

"I have no more strength, but who will take care of him?"

(Who was she thinking of, Father or me?)

Grandfather would show up once in a while and bring money. Janka's father greeted him in the kitchen. He would take out a bottle and two glasses, pour out the vodka carefully and hand it to Grandfather: "Poverty is terrible. Money has no value."

"The Germans are taking a beating."

"They should drop dead and quickly, because we cannot last too long."

They drank heartily and grandfather would come over to us, We sat near each other on the bed. Grandfather told us about people who had hidden behind a false wall in a room. Huddled close to each other, perspiring and stinking of urine, they waited for hours in silence for the pogrom to end. A mother choked her baby to death when it started to cry. (I decided not to cry in a similar situation.) He told about a giant German who told the nurse in a Jewish children's hospital to hold the children in her arms and then killed them with a gunshot.

I never saw the ghetto. I imagined it as a large square made of beaten clay, surrounded by wooden houses. I dreamt that I was running to the square. A huge German in a black uniform lifted me up. Mother was begging him not to do anything. The German laughed as he gave me back to her.

The Jews tried everything to save their lives. At dawn, columns of men left the ghetto. Each one had an armband with a star and a document stating that the Germans needed him. They drilled for oil, made saddles and gun holsters. But that was not good enough. Gradually, they were transported in cattle cars to a place from which nobody returned or was heard from again. Those who did not wear armbands hid with Poles or Ukrainians. They hid in attics, basements and in the last room down the corridor, far away from the window. They sat in stables under the manure, in barns and wells. They ran deep into the forests that blackened the Carpathian Mountains and waited for the Russians. When they were discovered, they were killed on the spot or sent to a transport.

Oh, how I wanted to live! I was running away like a cat from dogs. What did it matter that the dogs caught somebody else and tore him to pieces? I did not cry over those killed. But I did not know whom I could depend on. Mother and Grandfather could be killed, or abandon me in order to save themselves. Janka, under whose bed I was lying, could denounce me out of fear or for money.

Mother said in a whisper, as if talking to herself—and it did not hit me at first what she was talking about, "Poor Romus. What have they done with him?"

Only this and nothing more. Finally, I understood that Romus was not alive any more. That night I could not fall asleep for a long time and, when I finally succeeded, I dreamt that a German grabbed Romus by his little leg and smashed his head against the tie beam of a railroad car. The scene was so real that, when I awoke in the morning, I was not sure if it had been a dream. I asked my mother how Romus had died. She looked at me reproachfully: "Why do you ask; don't you know?"

I was scared that what I had dreamed was really true. But I did not return to the subject, being afraid that with more questions I will irritate Mother and speed up her leaving the ghetto. I started to complain about being alone all the time. Mother got even angrier: "Stop already! Bronek is so sick!" Unexpectedly, she started to cry and hid her face in her hands. "Do you want to end up like the other children? You don't realize how fortunate you are."

Mother had seen Romus a few weeks earlier. He had not recognized her, but wanted to sit on her knees all the time and, when she was leaving, he started to cry. Shortly afterwards, one of the neighbors, a woman, informed the police that Romus was a Jewish child. A mustached policeman banged on the door with his fist and opened it without waiting for somebody to answer. The head of the neighbor peered out from behind his broad shoulders: "Where is this Jewish bastard?"

Seven children surrounded the woman in the kitchen. She put her hands on them like a mother hen and pulled them to herself.

"He is the one," said the neighbor, pointing at Romus.

"Son of my relative, I swear to God!" insisted the housewife.

"You are lying," hollered the neighbor.

The policeman stood with his legs apart, bent down and pulled the string holding the diaper. The diaper fell to the floor. Romus laughed and grabbed the policeman by his mustache.

"Little prick circumcised," said the policeman endearingly.

"And she swears still," hissed the neighbor. "She has no fear of God!"

The policeman took Romus with him. They locked him up in a cell with several Jews who had been caught outside the ghetto. After a few days they took them all to the railroad station, put them in the freight car and locked the door.

Mother left the ghetto again. Since I had not heard about anybody being born in a long time, I thought that maybe parents were killing their infants. Lying on my back I stretched the skin of my penis. As long as I held it, it looked all right. But as soon as I let go the telltale head would appear. They had cut it too short. I had no chance.

Mother came running over at dawn, perspiring and out of breath. This time she almost collapsed. Two women, washing their laundry in the river, had pointed her out to the Germans surrounding the ghetto: "Catch her, she is Jewish!"

They took Teresa away in that pogrom.

"I tried to push her after you," said Father later. "She could still have caught up with you." Father had screamed and begged her to run away, but she did not care about anything anymore.

When we started to run out of money (and nothing indicated that the war was going to end soon), Grandfather arranged for another, rich Jew, who had money but no place to go, to pay for our hiding place. Janka and Grandfather agreed to take in young Szechter along with mother and sister.

They went into the attic and paid for themselves and for us. During the day I would forget they were upstairs. At night, Szechter would go down the squeaking stairs, bringing the pail back and forth and taking food to the attic. I couldn't see his face because Janka would turn off the carbide lamp to avoid showing the shadow of a strange man in the paper shuttered window. One could hear steps and the sound of washing in the attic.

"The Szechters are not as refined as you," Janka would say. "I can't complain; they sit quietly; but the young one scares me."

The entrance to the roof began to open during the day too. Szechter would go down a step or two and Janka would wait for him at the top of the stairs. They would talk for a long time. One day Janka's father said to Grandfather, "I have only Janka in the whole world and nobody else. All I want is her happiness. She is good but she limps and nobody wanted her. What kind of a life is it, living with an old father? Szechter says that he loves her even though he is younger than she. What should I do? Baptize him? I am afraid to bring the priest here because somebody might see. Janka wants to go to bed with him but she can't when your grandson is lying under it. I'm not throwing anybody out, God forbid, but please find yourself another place."

4. At Sprysia

Mother and Janka cried as they said good-bye to each other. Janka's father wad working the night shift. The Szechters sat in the attic. We left in the dark of night, Mother and Father pulling me by the hands. My legs were buckling. We walked uphill to Tustanowice until we found ourselves above Boryslaw, which loomed in the darkness. We saw Panska Street dividing the town in half. Trains with large tanks stood at the railroad station; lamps flickered by the oil wells.

It was still dark in Tustanowice. Groping, we reached the barn where Mr. Turow was waiting for us. He pushed us inside and locked the entrance. We climbed up on a rickety ladder. Farm animals lay beneath us. The smell of horses, cows and manure mingled with the smell of hay.

"Here are some apples." Turow left a basket of apples and went down the ladder.

These were big golden Delicious; their juice flowed down my chin and onto my fingers. The aroma of an apple was stronger than the smell of hay, cattle and manure. I ate the core and took another one.

"Remember when you broke a ski and we rented a sled from the farmer?" Father asked Mother. "We were warming ourselves at the stove and the housewife gave us golden Delicious just like these."

"I loved riding in a horse-drawn sled under a fur."

"You complained that it smelled bad."

"Because it was not properly tanned."

Silence reigned all around. Everything was asleep in the forest, the barn, Turow's house, the village with farms spread far apart.

Suddenly the light on the boards seemed to flicker and it started to get lighter. The horse moved below and hit the ground with its hoof. Through the slits we saw a young woman coming in to milk the cows. She lifted her head and looked up. Did she know about us? Turow led the horse out and pulled a cart out of the barn. A boy climbed the ladder with a pitchfork and started to throw down the hay. I was afraid that Father would start to cough.

We were very tired but we dared not sleep during the day. Late at night Turow brought us boiled potatoes and apples. Then he took us downstairs to the bathroom in the bushes. Only then did we climb back upstairs and go to sleep.

On the third night we left to go to Sprysia. Father left us there and went back to the ghetto.

Sprysia was a Polish woman who had married a Ukrainian and did not have an easy life with him. He drank and beat her up for any reason. During the Russian time he disappeared without a trace. Since then, she said, she had no man to take care of her. She lived with her mother and kept Jews. We had been waiting at Turow for the previous Jews to leave.

Sprysia's house had two floors. It was surrounded by a wooden fence with flower beds stretching along the street—without flowers this time of year. I only remember the second floor. There was a small room with a red floor, a bed and a night table. Opposite the bed on a wall with a window, a picture hung representing Christ in a white shirt. His face was covered with light and soft hair. Father had the same kind of hair. Sometimes I touched him with my hand. Christ was looking upwards with a painful smile and a teardrop fell from his eye. He held his hands in front of him, folded in prayer, and between them his heart appeared, coming out of his chest.

A door connected the room to the attic. A mattress lay there covered with a blanket and red pillows, with feathers sticking out. Next, there was a pail covered with a board, a pitcher with drinking water and a cup for drinking.

In the evening Sprysia would bring food and fresh water from the well and empty the pail. She was somewhat taller than Mother and when she talked to her she looked above her head.

"A piece of onion or sauerkraut, please," Mother would say. "My teeth are getting loose."

"Onion?"

"And a blanket. It's very cold."

"A blanket?"

"Yes, a blanket."

"My mother remembers that you had a St. Bernard before the war."

"Yes, yes," answered my mother with a smile.

"It must have been very expensive."

She made the sign of the cross before leaving: "Jesus, please help us, don't forget us."

Grandfather had found Sprysia, but Kopcio, who was hiding somewhere with Nusia, was paying her. Sometimes we got a letter from her. Mother would read it a few times and then, holding it in her hand, say "Kopcio is an uneducated man, just like Szechter. Before the war a Mandel girl would never have looked at him. The world is upside down. We are paupers and we owe him our lives."

Mother was always cold, mostly her hands and feet. During the day, she gave me her hands to warm. It took a long time. Her fingers, usually white, would regain color slowly. At night I held her feet.

"You always have warm hands," she would say with admiration.

"I don't get cold."

The ghetto was being liquidated. A few hundred Jews were left. They were placed in the barracks that once housed the Polish soldiers. The rest were transported to a camp. Grandfather and Father survived. Those who were left had no illusions about their future but they thought that they would be able to run away.

Mother's teeth started to ache and she moaned incessantly. She swelled up and tears ran from her eyes. Sprysia told Janka's father about it and he informed Grandfather. They took Mother to the barracks at night. Father was waiting in the corridor before the entrance to the room where the dentist stayed. They embraced each other and cried. Grandfather pulled Mother away and pushed her inside.

"Please, sit down in the chair." The dentist lit a small lamp.

Men were lying on cots all around. They slept in their clothes or looked on without saying a word.

"The dentist looked into Mother's mouth using a flashlight. "Which one hurts you?"

"One of these."

"I will pull all on this side."

"All right."

"You understand that I have no anesthetics?"

The pain split her brain. She couldn't see or hear. She fought for each breath, sucking in the air. When the dentist finished Grandfather leaned over and said, "Andzia, we have to go back. It's dangerous here."

We had gotten very thin during the last months. Shadows appeared where the skin had sunk into the bones. Our eyes became immobile. Our hands, from hunger, lack of work and soap became delicate and dark. They reminded me of spiders, ready at a moment's notice to run away.

Grandfather came over from the barracks one cold autumn night. He knocked in the agreed-upon way on the window downstairs: first three times and then twice. Mother ran down the stairs and let him in. We went to the attic, which had no window, where we could safely light a small lamp. We wore winter coats and shawls. Grandfather brought us a roll with butter wrapped in a newspaper, and coffee with milk and sugar in an empty vodka bottle. He told us that Father was very bad. Even if the doctors in the barracks could give him an edema, it would still be too late.

Hunger was commonplace. Medicine was unavailable. Mother started to cry and begged Grandfather to bring Father to us.

"Bronek will never agree to that. A child and a sick husband. No, that would be too much!"

"Then we will go out onto the street!" Mother threatened.

"Are you insane! Sprysia won't take him."

"Dad, please arrange it with her."

"And if he dies? What will you do?"

But Mother did not want to listen. Grandfather sighed, opened his coat and scarf, unbuttoned his shirt and removed two linen bags tied with strings from his neck. He gave one to Mother and held the other in his hand. Loosening the strings, he removed a bag made out of waxed paper. He moved it close to the light and we leaned over the lamp. The smell of carbide irritated our noses. A white, fine powder, reminiscent of powdered sugar, was inside the bag.

"This is morphine. It's enough; take it in the mouth and swallow it with saliva. You will lose consciousness immediately. Death doesn't hurt." Grandfather spoke slowly. "But don't do anything foolish," he added after a moment.

Mother's face lit up. Pushing back her hair, she pulled the string over her head and hid the bag under her blouse. She embraced Grandfather and kissed the sleeves of his coat. He stepped back. "Watch it, or you will spill it. I can't get any more of it." He wiped his eyes and with a damp finger lifted my head. "You must not smell it or touch it with your tongue. You can't spit it out." He handed the second bag to Mother.

She hung it on my neck as she had for herself. After that I kept checking it to see if it was in place. In reality, I could not have lost it, but I was afraid it might disappear.

Father arrived at night, exhausted by the long walk. Mother helped him climb upstairs. Once in the attic, he lay down on the mattress and breathed heavily. Mother undressed him bit by bit and washed him with a wet towel: hands, chest, stomach and legs. She covered the washed parts with a blanket. Father was very skinny and long. His head, with its blond hair, was tilted backwards and his eyes were closed. Mother kneeled and put her hands under his head. She lifted it gently upwards. He opened his eyes. She held a cup of milk to his mouth.

"Milk?" wondered Father.

"Sprysia brought me some."

"What about him?"

"He drank already."

In the morning Mother sat beside Father and watched him draw the head of a horse with wild eyes. A few strokes with a pencil: mane, reins, horse's neck, saddle, knight's legs in iron leggings. He could start at any point and move forward wherever he wanted. A sword at the saddle, forearms and a hand in a glove. He drew quickly. A lance, wings at the arms and hooves in a gallop.

"A hussar! I could never do it," laughed Mother.

Father turned the page towards me, but I was sitting too far away to see the hussar. I moved to the head of the mattress.

"Don't come near me!" Father held me back. "Hand him the page." he turned to Mother.

He had changed a lot since I had seen him last at Turow. His face was yellow and crumpled. His forehead and cheeks were wrinkled. He lay on his back, covered with blankets and a coat, with hands spread out to the side. He kept his right hand on the pillow. When he had a coughing spasm he sat down, took a pillow and pushed it into his face. His whole body shivered and jumped to the side. His clenched fingers were visible on the pillow. Above, his wet hair shook. The sound of his coughs came indirectly from his chest and reminded me of hammer blows. Father choked and wheezed. Finally he put the pillow away and spat into a jar. He covered it with a paper cover and put it on the floor next to him. He collapsed on the mattress; heavy drops of perspiration poured down his face. Mother emptied the jars into a pail, checking to see if there was blood in the sputum.

Once, when Father started to cough, Sprysia came in. She crossed herself and gave us a blanket from downstairs.

"Mr. Mandel didn't tell me that your husband was so sick."

"Oh, here, in peace, he is getting better. His strength is coming back."

"Jesus, don't forsake us."

In the morning I was awakened by Mother's crying. Light was seeping in along the edges of the paper shade. The window looked like another picture on the wall, hanging next to Christ's. I got up from the bed and tiptoed to the door. Mother was in the attic with Father. She begged him not to leave. She did not want to stay alone. "God will have mercy on us." Father kept saying that she must not ruin her life and the child's.

"Accept that I am dying. What will you do with my body? They won't take me to the cemetery. They will kill you. They will shoot Sprysia too. I must go back to the barracks."

"No, I beg you, don't!"

"We will say good-bye. Forgive me. Father will help you."

He stopped to rest. Mother stopped crying and lay quietly next to Father with her hand on his chest. She seemed to fall asleep. Father was breathing noisily. Later he started to moan in his sleep. Then Mother got up, kneeled at the mattress and started to pray.

Grandfather came again at night. The door downstairs opened and closed. Grandfather's boots and Mother's bare feet could be heard on the stairs. We sat next to Father in darkness because we could not light the lamp. Voices came from different directions.

"Sprysia is throwing everybody out."

"Andzia and the child too?"

"Yes."

"She wants more money?"

"No, she is afraid."

"What will happen now?"

"You will go to Mrs. Richter on Panska Street. Nobody will search her because she has a brother who is Volksdeutsche. Bronek will go with me to the barracks. Hurry. The moon is getting brighter."

Chapter 46

Hiding Under A Bed (Continued)

5. At Mrs. Hirniak's

We spent a night at Mrs. Richter's. Her brother ran over the next morning with the news that they had been spotted going out through the gate. Governor Frank had arrived at night and a military parade was being prepared on Panska Street. Mrs. Richter panicked and sent her brother to Grandfather. When he arrived she demanded that he take us away immediately.

"Please, have mercy!" begged Grandfather. "They will catch us right away." However, when he saw that nothing could be done, he made a quick decision.

"We will go. We will walk far apart, you behind me and he at the end. Look straight ahead at all times."

"Where are we going?"

"To Mrs. Hirniak."

A crowd lined the road on Panska Street. They stood on their toes in slippers with their heels off the ground. There were boots soaked in oil with socks sticking out. The band was playing: drums, tubas and cymbals. Orders were barked: right foot up, left foot down! Barefoot children approached the shining helmets of the soldiers. It was empty further down along the road. There were stone-plated sidewalks with holes filled with sand. Little pebbles lay on squares drawn with chalk. We walked along, stepping quickly on the squares: Grandfather, dressed in a coat and hat, Mother in a babushka and I in a peaked cap to cover my eyes. If somebody called after me the others would disappear without turning their heads. I was losing track of Grandfather, who knew the way. I could follow my mother more easily, but it seemed to me that those were not her legs, but somebody else's, and that I had gotten lost. My knees ached and my neck stiffened with fear. The streets gradually became smaller. There was not a living soul anywhere. Everybody had gone to Panska Street. We walked without getting closer to each other until Grandfather disappeared through the gate of a house.

It was a brick house, dirty and old. The walls were stucco with peeled holes. The roof was patched with wood and tar paper. Pieces of broken glass and plywood stuck out from blackened windows. Dampness and the smell of urine reeked in the corner stairwell. Wooden stairs led to one apartment, under which there once had been a meat store, now boarded up with wood. Mrs. Hirniak lived utterly alone.

One more kitchen, room and attic for us. We climbed through a trap door in the wall in the direction of the light. Above an unmade cot was a beam supporting the roof. I bent down so as not to hit it with my head. An empty iron pail, with a round wooden cover, awaited us.

Grandfather returned to the barracks and we remained alone. Mrs. Hirniak had big, blue eyes above rosy cheeks. She tied her hair tightly with a colored kerchief, but a tress was sticking out in back. Stroking my face with the back of her hand, she said that she had once wanted to have a girl.

"Such a tiny one," she showed, her fingers lifted up.

"I'm sure that you will have a daughter," Mother assured her.

Mrs. Hirniak was pleased and patted me on the face.

In the morning she went out and was gone all day. We sat alone with Mother on the floor. She talked about Father: "Nobody in Boryslaw was more handsome than he was. You can ask whoever you want. But what for? You know it very well."

Meanwhile, I could not remember Father without tuberculosis.

"I can't get to the barracks," Mother complained. "He is all alone."

"He is with Grandfather."

"It's not the same. But Father will bring him to us when things get bad. The Russians are already under Tarnopol." She looked at me carefully. "You are scratching your head too much. Maybe you have lice? I'll have to ask Mrs. Hirniak to give me some kerosene."

She spoke about Grandfather: "When Bronek is with us, Father will go into hiding."

She talked about Nusia: "Nusia is safe. Kopcio loves her and he has money. If not for him, we would have died a long time ago."

"Where are they?" I asked.

"In a well."

Soldiers came to visit in the evening and Mrs. Hirniak came home to receive them. She knew some of them and others introduced themselves politely. Sober or drunk, there was always "love." The men hit the wall behind us with their elbows and knees. Mrs. Hirniak laughed or cried when she was sad. She gave what she had and took what they wanted to give. Then they made love more quietly and spoke to each other in Ukrainian or German, although Mrs. Hirniak did not know

German. The men would light the lamp and show her pictures of their wives and children, and they tried to make her smoke cigarettes. Sometimes they remained till the morning. We knew the voices and habits of those who returned. We tried to visualize how they looked. Once she would not let a lover in because he had brought a dog that could smell us. They both yelped by the door but it didn't help.

In time, soldiers started to come during the day too. They did not behave charmingly any more because they were drunk. They would throw off their boots and belts, which had buckles with the inscription, "God is with us."

They hit the bottoms of the bottles. The corks popped and bounced off our wall. They gurgled their vodka and made love right away, loudly and with enthusiasm. Sometimes, however, they would stop and listen to the noise coming from the sky, just as we did behind the wall.

"Damn Russians!"

They would lose their good humor, pick up their belts from the floor and leave.

One night, when Mrs. Hirniak was away, Grandfather brought Father, who fell on the cot, breathing heavily. He exhaled noisily, his lips parted. I wondered where he got the strength to come. Mother was happy. Soon the Russians would come and the miracle in Worochta would repeat itself.

Grandfather kneeled on the other side of the beam: "Everything is a matter of time."

"Dad, please hide now," Mother said mechanically.

"I have time. If something should happen, the Germans at work will warn me."

"Daddy, don't go back to the barracks."

"I won't be able to help you if I hide."

We kissed him and Grandfather left.

Mrs. Hirniak used us for money and our testimony. The Russians were standing near Tarnopol. The Germans were fleeing Boryslaw, but without her. She did not want to die. She reasoned that if she saved Jews, the N.K.V.D. would forgive her for sleeping with Germans. Although Grandfather had told her about Father's sickness, he had done it so that she did not really understand anything. Now she realized that she'd been tricked. She could not get rid of Father, dead or alive. Now she also prayed to God that the Russians would come as quickly as possible.

We figured everything out. And everything led to a dead end. Condemned to our fate, we were parting in silence. Mother and I still had some strength left, but nothing could be done. Father looked at the beam above his head all the time. Sitting on the cot, I almost touched his long legs under the cover. Once he told me to stand up because he wanted to know how tall I was. I lifted myself with difficulty (I moved mostly on my fours).

"He looks like Milo," he said to Mother. "At his age I was taller and I had blond hair."

Mother motioned to me to sit down. He lost the sight of me and grew silent.

He coughed all the time, but mildly. The jar smelled stronger than before. Mother lay next to him saying that if she was going to get infected by him, she would have gotten sick a long time ago. Their conversations were short. Father wanted to go out to the street, but Mother would not let him. I looked at them all the time. I did not ask for anything because I could not get anything. I slept or I was sleepy. I dreamed that I was in the attic at Mrs. Hirniak's. Thus there was no difference between reality and dreams. If only Grandfather could take me away from here.

Mrs. Hirniak came at night with a kerosene lamp. Her hair, unbraided, fell on her nightgown. The flame puffed like a torch when she turned up the wick in the tin can.

"Somebody wants to see you. He says his name is Tabaczynski."

Father asked Mother to prop up his pillow. Skinny and huge, he sat on the cot. Mother stood near me. An older man walked in, bent down and extended his hand to my father, but my father was unable to lift his hand. Mother paled. The guest straightened out and said in a whisper, "I am Tytus' father; he was a schoolmate of Miss Nusia. I am bringing the money that Mr. Mandel could not collect. The barracks were liquidated yesterday. They say that they were taken to work. Please accept my deepest sympathy."

Mr. Tabaczynski looked at us in silence and then asked Mother if she wanted to write to Nusia.

The landlady lowered the wick and put the lamp on the floor. The flame crawled in the glass and gasped for the air. Mother picked up a notebook and pencil lying next to the mattress. She looked for an empty page, but there were drawings on all of them. She started to write:

Dear Nusia!

Mr. T. is here. The barracks were liquidated. Maybe they took them to work and Father, with his knowledge of German, will get a job in the office. I begged him to hide. He kept saying that he has time. The Germans promised to warn him. Without him there is no hope. Bronek cannot get up any more.

Andzia

I don't remember Mr. Tabaczynski leaving. Maybe he was never there?

I dreamed that I was walking in the barracks on my toes so as not to wake anybody up. It seemed to have happened yesterday so it was not too late. Grandfather stood in an empty room with his head high and talked to God: "Take care of them because I don't know what to do with Bronek. For this reason I shall not hide."

He lifted his hand to his ear and listened.

"Grampa!" I hollered. "They'll kill you!"

"No, they won't. . . ."

"You've already had your behind burned with carbolic acid. Button up your shirt because the ribbon is showing!"

"We'll meet after the war."

He winked and disappeared. I was not sure if he himself believed what he said. I opened my eyes and sat up on the floor near the cot.

"Maybe Father couldn't take it any more." said Father to Mother.

"Father would not leave us."

"No, he wouldn't."

A letter came from Nusia. She wrote that she would kill herself if she didn't see my mother. She urged Mother visit her. Moszek, who was hiding out with Nusia and Kopcio, would come to pick her up Thursday night.

It was very far. (We did not know, of course, where the well was.) The visit to Nusia was planned separately by my parents and me. My parents thought that Mother would go to see Nusia, spend two days with her and come back on the third. I decided not to let her go alone. Death might come without her. With her it probably would too, but I was less afraid of it.

Mother wanted to take something for Nusia, but we had nothing. She smiled and talked about Thursday, arranging her raven-black hair: "I don't even know how Nusia looks now. She was still a child the last time I saw her."

Moszek came early in the morning on Thursday, not at night as we had expected.

"Can we walk during the day?" Mother wondered aloud.

"Go!" sputtered Father.

"I'll be back in two, three days."

I watched Mother put shoes on her bare feet. I did not believe that she would ever come back to Mrs. Hirniak's. My legs sagged under me when I got up. I held onto the beam with my hands and stood above my father with my eyes closed because I felt dizzy.

"I will not stay here alone! Take me with you!" I was shrieking in fury.

"Andzia," wheezed Father.

Mother looked at him: "I won't see you again."

"Andzia, be careful."

"I'll see you Sunday."

She fell to her knees and bent down so deeply that she hit the floor with her head near where Father was holding out his hand.

"God! What have I done?!"

"Go." He was stroking her hair with his fingers.

"I'll just see Nusia and come back."

"Mother, Mother!"

"Take him along," said Father.

"But how? He can hardly walk!"

"Please, don't worry." Moszek bent over her. "I'll carry him on my back."

6. In The Well

I sat on Moszek's back as if like on a horse, holding onto his forehead. He walked briskly and Mother literally ran next to him. People were still asleep and the streets were deserted. A huge red sun was shining straight into our eyes and I felt it warming my face.

"Let's just get out of town," said Moszek.

First there were streets with twisted houses and spots of gardens, and then there was nothing, only grass and trees.

Sometimes the town was covered by hills. We always walked along the forest, where we could hide in an emergency. Moszek's head was covered with sweat and I had to wipe my hands with my shirt to avoid slipperiness. Had God accepted Grandfather's offer and would take care of us? I reminded myself of how Father bared his teeth when he coughed and I was overcome by the fear that this time we would fail. We could not be lucky all the time.

We heard flies buzzing in the distance. Moszek said, "These are Russians. They fly and look down from above. They are preparing an offensive."

"Why did they stop at Tarnopol?" asked my mother with regret.

"They got tired and are resting, but they will move again soon."

"If only they get here in time."

I looked for the planes but I did not see anything. Moszek stopped in the forest, took me off his back and lay me on the ground. I started to worry that they were going to leave me here alone, but they sat down too.

"How is Nusia?"

"She cries and fights with Kopcio."

"About what?"

"He tells her to correct what he is writing, then he doesn't let her change anything."

Mother was surprised: "What is he writing?"

"The Diary of Boryslaw Jews."

"Those that are dead?"

"And those that are still alive."

We heard the sound of engines, which mingled with the noise of the trees. I lay with my face in the grass; big green stalks dangled over me. Suddenly the earth thundered as if something fallen on it, and we heard an explosion.

"A bomb!"

When the Russians had dynamited the electric power plant, the noise had been much louder.

We got up, but we couldn't see anything. When the noise subsided, Moszek put me on his shoulders and we continued to move along the edge of the forest. Soon it was dark between the trees. I dangled and fell asleep out of hunger, fatigue and boredom.

"Don't sleep because you get heavy."

I woke up when Moszek stopped. We were in the middle of an apple orchard. A candle burned in the window of a cottage behind the tree but nobody came out. Evidently Moszek was not afraid of anybody here.

"Here we are," he said.

"What luck!" came the voice of a woman from below the ground.

"Nusia!" screamed Mother.

"Andzia!" Aunt's voice reverberated in the water.

Before us, surrounded by a stone wall, stood an abyss of a well. We went underground. Moszek took me off his back, holding my hands, and moved me over the cement wall. He slowly started to lower me down into the well. I smelled moss inside.

"Dangle your feet so that Kopcio can catch you," bellowed Moszek from above.

Kopcio's hands locked onto my feet. Moszek let me go and I was pulled in through the hole in the wall of the well. Kopcio pushed me inside into a completely dark hole. I fell on Nusia. Her face was wet. When Kopcio pulled Mother in Nusia jumped over to her. They kissed each other and cried. Moszek, who could not go down to the well by himself, called the landlord. Kopcio told him to keep quiet.

"Well, how is your sister?" asked the landlord.

"She is very tired," said Nusia.

"She can rest now."

The landlord lowered Moszek and wished them a good night.

"Good night, Max."

Drenched with perspiration and tired, we lay or sat on the clay floor, which would fill with water during the rain. A strong smell of soil and roots permeated everything. A few rays of sunlight in which the dust could be seen penetrated the holes in the stones during the day. If somebody moved, an eye or ear suddenly became visible. I wondered how Nusia looked, but I could not see her clearly. She wore a bra, a white slip and panties. She talked little and slowly. Mother whispered something to her but I could not hear anything.

Kopcio, in a white shirt open down to his belly, was writing something in a school notebook. Next to his bare feet lay round tin boxes from films in which he was keeping his notebooks. He complained that the writing disappeared because of the humidity.

"Who will read it?" asked Mother. "Jews don't exist any more."

"Those who ran away to Russia will return."

"A handful."

"There are Jews living in Palestine and America."

"They don't speak Polish."

"I'll translate it into Hebrew and English."

Kopcio became enthusiastic: "In these notebooks everybody will survive. Romus and him too." He pointed at me with his finger.

"Leave him alone."

"What am I doing to him?" objected Kopcio.

I dreamed at night that I was a girl. Marek Bernstein did not want to play with me. I bounced like a balloon but he always turned away and I could not see his face. Suddenly, he disappeared. The wind was turning me slowly on the grass and then on the sand in the backyard, where squares were marked with a stick. It blew me in the direction of the oil fields. I flew higher and faster.

And suddenly Mother's scream: "It's a lie!"

"Murderers!" bellowed Max from above.

The sun was falling through a displaced stone and shone on us, intertwined and tangled like snakes. Mother was pulling away from Nusia, trying to push her hands away from her mouth.

"It's a lie!" she wheezed.

"You hanged him with a tie! The police are looking for you!"

"Max, calm down," pleaded Kopcio.

He leaned outside and it got dark inside.

"Who allowed you to bring this bastard?!" foamed Max.

"Pull me out. I'll explain everything to you."

Kopcio started to disappear into the hole. His feet moved through the hole and it got light again. Not for long, however, because Moszek pulled back the stone.

Mother was breathing heavily. Her hands hung down far from her body. Nusia let go of her and started to stroke her hair with her stiff fingers.

"I don't want to live," said Mother clearly.

"Bronek would have died anyway."

"I have no reason to live."

"What about him?"

Kopcio had a long conversation with Max, who had come in a panic from Boryslaw, where he had been selling apples. A stray Russian bomb had hit a house and uncovered the attic where a Jew was hanging from a tie with his knees touching the floor. They had cut him loose and taken him to the Jewish cemetery. The Police thought that he had been killed by other Jews. Mrs. Hirniak had disappeared.

Max was afraid that his well was too full. He was also very angry because he thought that Mother was coming alone. He calmed down only when Kopcio gave him money and promised that he and Moszek would find another hiding place.

"When?" asked Nusia.

"Soon."

Mother cried. Bronek would still be alive if she hadn't gone. She gave me her potatoes.

"Eat something," implored Nusia. "You give him everything."

Kopcio got excited: "Don't argue with her! Can't you see he's already eaten everything?"

"I want to die," said Mother.

"You should have died before you came here."

"Be quiet!" hollered Nusia. "How can you talk like that?!"

"Peace!" ordered Moszek. "Have you all gone crazy?"

Father must have bent down under the beam because otherwise he wouldn't have had enough space. He threw a tie (he had a yellow tie) and made a loop like a shoelace. He wound the loose part around his neck and made a second loop. He jumped (where did he get the strength?) and pulled up his feet. The tie tightened and he lost consciousness.

I touched the place between my neck and where the ribbon hung. I did not feel anything. I did not want to think about his fear; grown-ups were afraid of the same things children were. Father did not have time to pull us into the grave with him. We'd slipped out! They wouldn't find us in the well.

Yet I was afraid to gloat because the situation had changed completely. Father was now in heaven, bigger than Grandfather, who was fighting for his life somewhere. Bigger even than Kopcio, who had money and did not like us. I wanted to believe that Father had hanged himself for us, because he loved us and we loved him. I started to pray to him: "Daddy, please make me live. Or don't let it hurt. Help Mom, Nusia and Grandfather and everyone I love."

"What are you saying?" asked Mother.

"Nothing."

At night we would go to the top. Once, when they were pulling out Nusia, something big fell into the water. Mother screamed in fear.

"Be quiet, it's a stone."

"Give me your hands," she said to me.

"Are you holding him by his legs?" asked Moszek from above.

"Yes."

Pulled by my hands, I was a bird and could not drown.

The time broke and tore like a spider's web between trees in a garden; it hung from a branch and couldn't be seen. We peeled it off our faces with our fingers. It was fleeting and disappeared without a trace when we shook it off our hands. The gnarled branches looked like women holding their heads with their hands. We ate ripe apples like those at Turow's. From closeup in the moonlight, they seemed to be made of silver. We pressed them and picked the soft ones. Bitter pits burst between our teeth and dissolved in the juice. The Russians would be here before the apples fell from the trees.

Kopcio and Nusia were smoking one cigarette, covering the flame with their hands. They whispered to each other or jumped away in anger. The smell of smoke stayed in the well afterwards.

We couldn't even be happy when the Russians finally moved forward from Tarnopol. The darkest night arrived. Nusia thanked Kopcio for saving Mother and me. She begged him to be careful.

"I'll send you a letter when Max comes for money," said Kopcio.

"Nusia," Moszek said in parting, "I'll come back if you need me."

"Moszek! You are so kind."

Mother spoke to Kopcio: "I don't know how to thank you." She shook my arm.

"Don't wake him," said Kopcio. "Let him sleep.

It was not crowded after they left. Drops of water started falling into the well; a heavy rain followed. A white mist seeped in. At first it was silent; only after a few hours did Mother and Nusia begin to talk. They called on each other as witnesses: Do you remember, do you remember? Nusia talked about the people she loved and Mother about the people who loved her. They were the same people. Grandmother, Grandfather (mother whispered something in German), Father, Romus, Teresa, Maciek and Mr. Unter. Together they waited for Milo, who was the third witness. Max brought a letter from Kopcio. Nusia, on her knees, moved left and right, with her bare back and slip straps hanging from thin shoulder blades.

"What does he write?"

"That it's near."

"Does he still have money?"

"No, he doesn't."

Mother started to get a toothache like the one at Sprysia's. Crying with pain, she took my bag, loosened the ribbon and moved to the light the bag made of waxed paper into the light. She touched the powder with a finger moistened with saliva and smeared the gums around the sick tooth. She sighed with relief and dabbed it again.

"Andzia, be careful!"

"I know what I'm doing," gurgled Mother, and fell to the floor. Nusia leaned over her and put her ear to her chest. Mother was moaning.

"Sleep well." Nusia lifted her head and gathered her hair in the back.

I lifted the waxed bag from the floor and tightened it but my hands were shaking and I couldn't feel anything. Mother slept for two days. When she woke up she started to cry, realizing where she was. She wanted to sit but she got dizzy and nauseous. Nusia fed her cold tea made of apple peels.

Now nothing could stop the Russians. The sky over the garden shone with light. We heard canons and the sound of thunder got louder. At dawn we were awakened by Max's screams as he came running towards the well. We ran to the stones, our hearts pounding wildly.

"The Russians are here! You can come out."

"Please pull me out," whispered Nusia.

Max pulled her out, then Mother and me. The wet, blind eye of the well looked straight into the sun. Worms crawled out through the cement.

"We must get the tin boxes out," whispered Nusia.

"Speak louder," said Max.

"The boxes with the notebooks."

Chapter 47

A Literary Soirée

March 15, 1992 was a cold and wintry Sunday. Alice planned to go with Irene and Carl to a literary soirée. Her parents had just published a book entitled "Of Human Agony," describing their life during the Holocaust. Alice arrived at 3 o'clock; they went to pick up Anna and proceeded to the Williams Club in Manhattan.

When they got there, attendants were busy preparing the reception room. Then the invited guests began to arrive. Some of them were their friends. The publisher, Moshe Scheinbaum, had invited the others. Carl's brother Leo came with his family. Milo, Irene's brother, was there too.

Everyone was talking and helping himself to wine and hors d'oeuvres. There was coffee and delicious French pastries on a separate table. People came over to Irene and Carl to introduce themselves and congratulate them on their book.

The room filled up quickly. There was a sudden excitement when General Sharon, the Minister of Housing in Israel, arrived with his wife Lily and his entourage. Only Irene, Carl and the publisher knew that he was coming. They had kept it secret for security reasons. After a little while, everybody was invited to take a seat in the auditorium. Irene and Carl's friend Bill Fern began to introduce the speakers. The first was Professor Zvi Kollitz. He elaborated on the part of the book in which the Polish people collaborated with the Germans. He pointed out that gentile children were playing right outside the Warsaw ghetto as it burned during the Uprising. He concluded that there should have been an Eleventh Commandment: "Thou shalt not trust."

The second speaker was Professor Howard Addelson. He congratulated Irene and Carl on the book and he said that the public needed a book like theirs. It would serve to awaken the conscience of the people and prevent another Holocaust from happening. He was very expressive and eloquent.

The next speaker was a person everyone was waiting to hear Minister Arik Sharon stepped onto the podium. He described how he had met Irene and Carl when they first came to the United States. He had been a young soldier when he visited them in Brooklyn. He also spoke about the need for books like theirs. The audience responded to his speech with enthusiasm and applause.

Bill Fern asked Irene to say a few words. Irene thanked Mr. Sharon and the other speakers:

"I didn't start out with the intention of writing a book. I have two daughters, Alice and Terry, and I love them as all parents love their children. I very seldom spoke to them about my experiences during the war when they were growing up. One reason was that it would be hard for them to understand. The second reason was that I didn't want to appear to them as a hero or superhuman. I survived the war when so many perished. The truth is that I was no hero.

"I am here today because of a series of coincidences and good luck. I started to write down separate stories and, before I knew it, these stories started to come together. Carl started to write about his experiences too, but he will tell you about it himself.

"This is how we wrote our book."

Bill then called on Carl, who had not prepared a speech. He didn't like reading from a prepared text because he felt that reading did not reflect a person's true feelings. With his poor eyesight, his reading of speeches left much to be desired.

As if guessing his thoughts, Bill said, "Carl, you don't have to speak if you don't want to." But Carl felt a strong urge to speak. Something pushed him to do it. "I *will* speak, Bill," he said firmly. He went over to the microphone and looked at the audience, which looked back expectantly.

"General Sharon, members of my family and dear friends!

"People ask me why we wrote this book. Books about the Holocaust are not popular any more. People don't want to read these horror stories.

"I wrote this book to sanctify the names of my poor family who died for no reason at all. They never harmed anybody in their lives."

Carl felt the words coming not from his mind but from his heart.

He continued:

"When somebody dies, we know when he died and we know when to say a prayer for him. Irene and I went to a rabbi after the war and asked him to set the date for the yearly prayer for the departed. The rabbi asked us, 'When did your parents die?' We answered, 'We don't know.' Then the rabbi asked us, 'Where are they buried?' and we answered, 'We don't know.' "

There was a bitter note in Carl's voice. He paused for a moment and looked at the audience. It appeared to him that the floor of the room had moved down and the people in the room looked smaller, as if they were farther away. He felt as if he were standing on a much higher podium in front of them.

"People ask us, 'How come you did not defend yourself? Look at the young Israeli heroes. See how courageous they are, defending their country? Why couldn't *you* fight like they do?' My answer is, 'We were surrounded by enemies. We didn't have any arms except our fists. The Germans wouldn't have known who was Jewish and who was not. We looked exactly the same as the rest of the population. The Polish people knew us and pointed at us and denounced us to the Germans. The Polish people stabbed us in the back. Sometimes, in desperation, a Jew would grab a gun from a German soldier and kill him. The Germans would torture him and gouge out his eyes. Then they would kill him, his entire family and hundreds of other innocent Jews.'

"By writing this book we built a monument to our loved ones. A Roman poet once said:

> Exegi monumentum Aere perennius.
> (I built a monument that is stronger than brass)

"People think that we were heroes for surviving the Holocaust. They think that we were wise and smart. We were no heroes and we were not smart. If, by divine intervention, we survived the Holocaust, then we have a moral obligation to bear witness to the cruel injustice that was done to us and our loved ones. This book will forever bear witness to the inhumanity done to us and our families. Nothing will ever be able to destroy this evidence."

Carl stepped down from the podium. There was a silence in the audience. People were visibly moved. Several of them came over to him and congratulated him on the speech. Then Leo, his brother, came over to him and said: "Carl, we are very proud of both of you today. Our mother would be proud of you if she were alive."

Chapter 48

A Visit to Hilda and Leo

It was a cloudy, cold day in April 1992. In spite of the fact that it was the end of the month, it was still cold every day. Spring was late this year. The flowers and trees were starting to bloom, but they seemed hesitant, as if they didn't believe that spring was here.

Irene, Carl and Anna were going to visit Hilda and Leo in Bridgewater, New Jersey. They brought along Hilda's favorite schmaltz herring. Carl took a beautiful, illustrated book about Lvov, his and Leo's home town.

Carl dreamed of visiting Lvov, but Irene was afraid: "It's dangerous to go there," she kept saying. "Besides, you will be very disappointed when you see it. The people whom you knew aren't there any more. Maybe even the house doesn't exist after so many years. After all, fifty years passed since you left home. Why can't you keep the past in your memory the way it was then?"

Carl knew that it was true. His whole family perished in the Holocaust. Even the gentiles who lived in his hometown were transported to Siberia by the Communists during the Stalin era. But an irresistible force drew him back to his place of birth.

A number of people, among them their friends, were now going to Poland, Ukraine and Russia to visit their places of birth.

Even a group of their friends from Boryslaw and Drohobycz was organizing a trip of their own. The political situation was calm and the relations between the United States and the newly created states of Ukraine and Russia were warming up and there was no danger to go there.

Carl's desire to go to his hometown was whetted by these events but Irene was holding out steadfast against it. "I want to preserve in my mind the picture of my home the way I remember it," she would say. "I don't want to see how it looks now. It probably changed beyond recognition and it would only break my heart seeing it."

After an hour's drive they arrived at Leo's house. Carl gave him the illustrated book about Lvov and Leo was visibly pleased.

Hilda served delicious cold cuts, cheeses and home made tuna fish salad, which was her specialty. After lunch they sat down in the living room and started a relaxed conversation. Hilda started: "We are planning to go to Europe this fall. We will go to Lvov to see Leo's home there and to Beuthen where I lived and where Leo and I met."

This idea was not new to Carl as Hilda mentioned it on their previous visit. "Which way are you going there?" asked Irene.

"Oh, we'll fly to Berlin and there we'll rent a car and travel by highways to Prague, Vienna, Budapest, Lvov, Cracow and back to Berlin. From there we will fly back to New York." Carl was sitting quiet not saying a single word.

"How long will it take?" asked Irene.

"About two weeks," answered Hilda.

"I have a better idea," said Irene. "Why don't we fly to Berlin and then go by car to Munich. We studied there and I would like to see it once again. From there we can go to Cracow and Lvov, and then to Boryslaw from there."

Carl couldn't believe his ears. Irene was going to Lvov! "I'm going too," he exclaimed quickly as if afraid that she may change her mind.

"I want to go too," injected Anna, "but I would like to go to Warsaw. I lived there for a long time."

"Then we will need a large car," said Hilda, "and it will cost more money."

"We will share all the expenses with you equally," Carl reassured her fearing a slightest snag in the unfolding plan. Now he had the two people with whom he wanted to share his trip the most: Irene, his wife and Leo, his brother.

"Let's go to Warsaw too," Irene was getting more enthusiastic by the minute.

"Let me get the map" interrupted Leo. "We have to plan the itinerary carefully and in proper sequence." He brought in the map of Europe and spread it on the coffee table. They were all poring over it.

After some deliberation they decided to drive from Berlin to Warsaw, Cracow, Lvov, Budapest, Vienna, Prague and Munich. "We will be there for the Octoberfest," said Hilda. "From Munich we can fly directly to New York."

They were all excited now, talking at the same time.

"We can take side trips wherever and whenever we want to."

"When are we going?"

"In September," answered Hilda with authority. "It will be after the children's vacations and the highways won't be crowded any more. During the summer the roads are jammed."

They were all very excited now, making all kinds of plans and suggestions. Carl was the happiest of them all. He never expected the conversation to turn this way. He was only afraid that Irene shouldn't change her mind.

Chapter 49

A Letter from Poland

The letter presented below was sent to Irene by her high school friend. It was translated from Polish by the author.

The man who wrote it was highly intelligent and educated Pole. His views on the attitude of Polish people to the Jews are authentic and very revealing.

Katowice, August 10th, 1992.

Dear Irene:

I wrote to you in autumn 1991 and have had no communication from you for a whole year. I hope that you were not insulted (it's not in your nature). I explain it simply by a lack of time or forgetfulness. I have tried to write to you for a long time, mainly for the following reason: Titus, whom I visited in Cracow often, persuaded me to read your and your husband's memoirs of the war. Titus assured me that you had no objections to making them available to me. He convinced me to read them because of my considerable knowledge of the subject. True, I was not in Boryslaw during the war and I could not know everything. I was in Boryslaw for the first time since 1939 in 1958.

If I allow myself to give my views, I hope they will be of interest to you. I hope that you accept my opinions in a friendly spirit. If you don't like something I apologize right now and ask you to point it out to me (that would be best). As far as I know, my family was friendly with the Rabinowicz's and their relatives. I tried to bring my children up with tolerance and respect for other religions and nationalities. One of my daughters married a Swiss and another married a boy from a evangelical (protestant) family who identified himself as German (they live in Berlin). My own views are known to you.

I. Relationships: Jews, Christians, Poles.

I believe that the Christian religion is a continuation of Judaism (the word Judeo–Christian is very appropriate). We believe that Jesus Christ (which means Savior, Messiah) is the Messiah of whom the Torah speaks (which we recognize fully and who as a man was a Jew) and whose execution was carried out by the Romans (not by the Jews).

We recognize the Ten Commandments as the most important thing God gave Moses. That's why the anti-Jewish position of pseudo-Christians is the biggest nonsense. On the other hand, the most important Christian law, that you have to revere God and treat your neighbor as yourself, also says how to behave. I would like to add as a footnote that "Islam," which developed on the side, somehow does not convince me. I have, however, a great respect for Hinduism and Buddhism. Today, even the official position of the Catholic Church (the main sector of Christianity) is similar in these matters. It recognizes officially that one can achieve religious goals not only in the Catholic religion or other Christian religions, but also in the Jewish religion and even in other religions. It also allows mixed marriages. As far as I know, the Jews are trying to preserve their identity by preserving their religion, because otherwise nothing would protect them from assimilation during the thousands of years in the Diaspora. But I think that today certain modifications are necessary (e.g., people are usually surprised by Israel's denying citizenship to a Catholic–Jew, Rev. Rulfeisen, or condemning mixed marriages, which are thrown out of the Jewish community. Poles and Jews lived together throughout the entire history of Poland. The Holocaust's result was that there is only a handful of authentic Jews among the Poles. Large numbers emigrated (I do not count those assimilated totally as Poles). Can anti-Jewishness exist under these conditions? (I am deliberately not using the term anti-Semitism because, besides the Jews, the Arabs are Semites too). Not only can it exist but in fact it does exist and one can say with dread that it is spreading. There are small but very active groups that spread arguments which are very perfidious. They start with the Jews: Marx and Lenin (Lenin's mother was a Jewess) guilty of everything including communism. Of course, they do not speak about the first super-oppressor, F. Dzierzynski, who was a Polish nobleman. They continue to stress the role the Jews played in the Communist government (especially in the secret police–security service). They believe that, again, power is in Jewish hands, that the Jews are involved in all the biggest financial scandals in Poland (e.g. the embezzlement of several hundred million dollars and escape to Israel by Bagsil and Gasiorowski; nota bene, if I could give some sensible advice I would suggest that Israel extradite them to Poland). They accuse Walesa and Pope John Paul II (K. Wojtyla) of being crypto-Jews because, seemingly, of their friendly attitude towards the Jews. If, God forbid, there is an explosion of discontent, it can be easily predicted that history will repeat itself.

Unfortunately, similar movements develop in Europe and North America and the worst situation is in the former Soviet Union. The situation will be made worse by ignoring it. Religious - nationalist battles in Yugoslavia or the Soviet Union are a proof of it. It is, of course, different for an individual to be responsible for the whole nation or religion but there must be a decision taken to eliminate it everywhere and in everybody.

II. General Problems of Your Memoirs

I read your and your husband's memoirs with great interest. I empathized especially with your suffering. Truly, God saved you. I think that Poles, maybe, did not go through such a scale of suffering compared to the Jews. But the Nazis and communists had a similar plan for the globe. In return for all this, as the first allies they were sold into slavery to Stalin by Roosevelt and Churchill, along with half of their territory. The pogroms of Poles by the Communists had even greater scope and frequency (of 2 million Poles taken away in two years, half of them perished. All the suspected officers were murdered, etc.) One could ask a rhetorical question: which other nationality helped the Poles? I have only heard of sporadic instances. But I consider scandalous the behavior of collaborators, policemen (also in the ghetto), denouncers (e.g., one that pointed to your husband in Cracow, or Dauerman, described in your memoirs).

In your and your husband's memoirs, the Polish people came out looking not too bad because you preferred them to the Ukrainians. I also know that you were the only one who enrolled in the Polish, not the Ukrainian, class in the years 1939–41. You also were hidden mainly by Polish people. Finally, as a result of a change of borders, you emigrated to Poland, as did other couples unknown to you. You remember the Polish language. What is visible in your memoirs (besides the lack of help) is your stubbornness in fighting for life. I also consider it an important feature that Polish couriers delivered to the Americans and the British exact data about the German extermination of the Jews and they did not even react (didn't they behave similarly in the case of Katyn?). An armed resistance would make sense only if it were total, but ruthlessly shooting Nazis (including their families) because only this would have impressed them and gotten results—would it be right?

Today, I look without emotion at the problems of nationalities, religion, politics, etc. I see that everybody should be taken to account for deeds and not views or opinions.

III. Details of Your Memoirs

A number of descriptions in your memoirs are not fully clear: Why did your refusal to join the Komsomol save your life? What happened to Lolek? I think it would be good to describe the conditions in Boryslaw, e.g., water, sanitation, electricity, heating, the market etc. Also, many people in Boryslaw suffered emotionally during the "funeral of Poland" in 1939 (an ugly propaganda spectacle). Correction: There is no oil refinery in Ligota; there is one in Szopowice.

Forgive me for my long story. Once again, I ask you not to be insulted by my opinions. I feel that I am a friend of you, your family and your nation. But I am a realist and I think that one has to draw conclusions, act but not abandon one's principles.

And now at the end, a short report about myself. In the last few months I have visited Titus many times. He lives in difficult conditions. He has remained the lone tenant of an old building, on the third floor. The gate is mostly locked; there are no doorbells or telephones. He needs help, to begin with. Maybe he also deserves recognition from Israel for saving Jews from the Nazis (for which he risked his life). In the beginning of May a brother of Z. (28 years old) died tragically in a car accident. His funeral was exactly five years after that of my daughter. Was it merely a coincidence? I had kidney trouble and "gave birth" in pain to a large kidney stone (at the moment, I am avoiding an operation). Otherwise there are no changes; we are trying to survive. In general, the situation does not change and nothing gets better. It is very hot here. Please write something. In connection with your approaching holiday of New Year's, may I wish you all the best and, especially, health. Heartfelt regards to you, your husband, your family and friends.

Tadeusz

Chapter 50

From Prince Lvov To Michael Roth

October 13, 1993

After their trip to Poland and Ukraine, Carl had received an envelope from Herta. It contained a letter she had received from Lusia Skalka of Lvov, from their part of the city in Zniesienie. Lusia wrote, "I am surprised that you did not forget our conversation. I never thought that you would remember it. One does not forget good people. They never harmed anybody and they treated their neighbors well. We remember life during the war very well and what the war did to people. Those dirty Germans have destroyed many people without any reason...."

Herta had sent Lusia a letter and some money, but Lusia thought that Carl had sent it. It was now almost three months since their trip to Poland and Ukraine. Carl decided to call Olek Reisman in Lvov. He was concerned with the progress of the monument they were erecting in Zniesienie at Roth's Mountain. The last time he had spoken to Olek, two weeks ago, he was told that a document from the city's archive was needed. They had to confirm the residence of Roth's family before the war. Now Carl asked Olek about the status of this matter, as Olek was in charge of the project.

"I was told that your name was found in the archive," Olek said, "but the file is incomplete. Most of the documents have been transferred to Warsaw." Carl knew about that transfer. Years ago, when he requested a copy of his birth certificate from Lvov, he was referred to Warsaw. Anna had taken care of it for him when she was living in Poland.

Olek had written to Warsaw and was waiting for confirmation from the archive there. He continued, "By the way, the city did some preliminary archaeological explorations on Roth's Mountain. They believe that the city of Lvov originated there. They object to the word 'because' in the inscription on the monument."

Carl remembered that the inscription was supposed to read, "This place is called Roth's Mountain *because* Michael Roth lived here with his wife Esther and their children." The possibility of an important archaeological discovery made the city officials sensitive to the implications of such an inscription.

Carl asked, "What should we do?"

"Just eliminate the word 'because' to read: 'This place is called Roth's Mountain. Michael Roth lived here with his wife Esther and their children.'" Carl agreed. "I have another question," said Olek. "What was your Grandfather's occupation?"

"He was a farmer," answered Carl. "He tilled the land that he leased from Baczewski, the owner of the land and of the liquor factory."

They decided to speak to each other in a week.

Carl put down the receiver and looked at Irene who sat near him at her desk in the office. Irene had heard only his part of the conversation. He repeated what Olek had told him. "You know," Carl continued, "I always imagined that a landlord or a prince lived on top of the mountain. There was a very old house standing there, built out of huge, hewn stones. It was a hundred, maybe hundreds of years old. We lived in the newer house across the yard. It was built out of wood. The old house was occupied by the help during our time. But in the olden days, the old house may have been the residence of a landlord.

"The city was founded in the thirteenth century by prince Lvov and it may have been right there that he founded the city."

Carl was very excited.

"It was a custom in the olden times for the nobleman to live in a fortress on top of a hill. The villagers, like those in Zniesienie, lived below. They tilled the fields around the landlord's residence and paid him taxes, since the land belonged to him. During enemy attacks, the villagers would hide inside the fortress and the nobleman and his soldiers would defend them. After the enemy left, the villagers would go back to their fields and rebuild whatever the enemy had destroyed."

Irene wanted to know how Carl's grandfather had come to live there. "My grandfather loved Israel, which was Palestine at that time," answered Carl. "He believed that Jews should go back to the soil and till it as in biblical times. He went to Baczewski, whose ancestors were Jews too. Grandfather leased the land from him and part of the payment was in dairy products delivered to Baczewski's family." Now Carl reminisced aloud: "Herta's mother, as a young girl, worked in Baczewski's office and met her future husband, Marcus Hausknecht, there."

Carl was excited. But he was also humbled by the events that were now unfolding. He thought, If only my grandfather had known about this.

A week later Olek provided the following information: Roth's Mountain had been proclaimed "The Zniesienie Memorial Park." According to officials, it dated back to the tenth century and was at that time venerated as a holy mountain. A statue of a pagan goddess named "Baba" had stood there and people went there pray to her.

As the days passed, Carl grew increasingly impatient. The promised permit from the municipal government of Lvov had not arrived. And then, a fax: an official permit from the city for the erection of the monument with a seal of approval, signed by a city official. Carl was elated. He called Olek to thank him. Olek promised to hire an architect to design the memorial.

Chapter 51

The Autumn Leaves

Irene and Carl decided to go to Monticello one sunny day in the fall of October 1993. They wanted to meet with the builder who was enlarging their newly acquired second bungalow in the Circle Ten bungalow colony. They left early in the morning. The trip started uneventfully. Suddenly Irene exclaimed, "Look at the beautiful colors of the leaves!" Carl did not pay much attention at first. He was busy driving the car.

Irene was watching the scenery and getting more and more excited. "Carl, please look at the variety of colors on the trees." Carl looked around. They were driving along the New York State Thruway and the road was lined on both sides with thousands of trees, each of them with differently colored leaves. Some still had their original green color; others were yellow, red, carmine, cerise, cherry, crimson, maroon, pink, ruby, scarlet and vermilion. They were intermingled forming a truly breathtaking vista of colors.

Carl remembered a famous poem entitled, "The Steppes of Ackerman," written by the poet Adam Mickiewicz. He had been expelled from his native country by its Russian occupiers and traveled through the Russian steppes to his destination in the Crimea. Carl started to recite the poem but Irene interrupted him, "Please look at the scenery, it is so beautiful. I have never traveled through this area in the fall and I have never seen a sight this beautiful. I imagine that the Garden of Eden must have looked like this. This is how it must look when you enter Paradise. I expect to see the snake tempting us with the forbidden fruit any minute. Maybe God created these colors so, when he looked down, he could say, 'Look how beautiful my earth is.' "

The countryside grew hillier as they approached the Catskills. Carl was excited now too. "Look, Irene," he exclaimed, "that tree over there is actually violet, and this one is purple. Suddenly they reached a gradual curve in the road leading to the right, bypassing a large mountain. The mountain standing in front of them seemed to be on fire, glowing red in the light of the sun.

The words of the poet were ringing in Carl's ears:

I sailed the dry ocean's universe,
My carriage dips in green weeds and, like a boat, wades
Among the waves of rustling meadows and flowers' deluge,
I pass by the coral islands of red thistle.

It's getting dark, there's no road nor landmark.
I look to the sky for the stars to guide my boat.
Over there, a cloud shimmers? is it the Morning Star rising?
No, it's the river shining, it's the lamp of Ackerman.

Stop!—how silent!—I hear the wandering cranes,
That could not be seen by the falcon's eyes
I hear a butterfly rocking on the grass blade,

A serpent touching grass with its slippery chest.
In this silence! I strain my ear so hard,
That I could hear a voice from my homeland.
Go on, no one's calling!

    Carl didn't write poetry but he had a strong appreciation for it and had several favorite poems. Unfortunately, most of them were in Polish. He decided to translate some of them into English. One that especially fascinated him he had first heard at a school contest in poetry recitation. His high school presented a few poems by Polish poets. One boy even memorized a poem that was several pages long and he plodded through it with the help of an audience that helped him out whenever he forgot something.

    Then a boy stepped on the stage. He was from the so called "Jewish high school." He started to recite a poem entitled "Locomotive" by a Polish–Jewish poet, Julian Tuwim. Tuwim was not popular among the Polish literati, even though his poetry was excellent, because he was Jewish. His works were not read Polish by students. Thus Carl, who was attending a so called "Polish high school," hardly knew him. The poem was presented beautifully and Carl was enchanted by it.

    Now, many years later, he managed to get a tape of the poem and decided to translate it into English, trying to reproduce its onomatopoeic effect as much as possible.

Locomotive

by Julian Tuwim

A locomotive stands at a station
Heavy and huge. It drips with the sweat of greasy oil.
It stands and heaves, gasps and fumes.
Heat spews from its infernal belly;
Huff, it's so hot, puff, it's so hot,
Huff, it's so very hot, puff it's so very hot.
It hardly gasps, it hardly heaves
And yet the stoker shoves more coal in its belly.

Wagons have been attached to it,
Big and heavy, made of iron and steel
And many people are in each wagon:
Cows in the first one, horses in the second,
In the third only fat people sit,
They sit and eat fat sausages.
The fourth wagon is full of bananas;
In the fifth are six pianos;
In the sixth, a cannon, oh how big!
An iron beam lies under each wheel.
In the seventh, oaken tables and chests,
In the eighth, an elephant, bear and two giraffes;
The ninth has only fattened-up pigs,
In the tenth, coffers, boxes and crates.
There are about forty wagons;
Who knows what else is in them?

Even if a thousand athletes came
And each of them ate a thousand cutlets
And each strained as much as he could
Still they couldn't lift it, it's such a big weight.

Suddenly a swish, suddenly a whistle;
Steam goes puff, wheels go in motion.
The machine starts on tracks sleepily,
Jerks the wagons and pulls with an effort;

And turns, wheel after wheel turns
And speeds and runs faster and faster

And knocks and clatters and rumbles and rushes.
Where to and where to and where to? straight out.
On tracks, on tracks, on tracks and o'er the bridge;
Over hills, through a tunnel, over fields and forests
And rushes and rushes to get there on time;

To tact, to tact, to tact, to tact. . .
So smooth and light it rolls far away,
As if it were a light ball, not steel,
Not a heavy machine heaving and panting,

But a trifle, a joke, a little child's tin toy.
Where to, and how to and why does it run?
What is it, what is it that pushes it on?
That rushes and knocks, huffs and puffs, huff puff?
It's the hot steam that put it in motion;
The steam from a kettle through pipes and to pistons,
From pistons to wheels pushing on both sides.

They rush and push and the train is rolling.
Steam presses and presses and presses the pistons;
The wheels rumble and knock
Knock knock, knock knock, knock knock. . .

Chapter 52

A Conversation With Leo

October 17, 1993

Hilda and Leo were coming to visit that weekend and Carl was very excited. He wanted to find out how Leo had arranged their escape from the Lvov ghetto in 1942. As far as Carl was concerned, Leo had saved his life.

In preparation for their visit Irene bought three schmaltz herrings, which were Hilda's favorite food, and many more appetizers, fruits and cakes. She planned to serve them veal and pork chops the way they liked them.

As usual, Hilda and Leo were very punctual, arriving shortly before noon on Sunday. They all sat down to have lunch and the conversation was lively and pleasant. After a while, Carl suggested to Leo that they go for a walk.

"Leo, do you remember when we ran away from the ghetto?" he began.

"Yes, I remember, it was sometime in September 1942," answered Leo.

"It was on September first."

Leo continued, "I remember cooking vegetables for the family and for Herta and Oswald."

Carl remembered those beans and carrots cooked in plain water. He had been so hungry that he had even drunk the water in which they had been cooked in. But this was not what he wanted to know.

"How did you get in touch with Fela? We had no telephone," he asked.

Leo answered, "Well, I was going every day to the same place where Herta's mother worked in the city. She was planning an escape to the Christian side for herself, Herta and Oswald. Fela came to her from Zakopane and we discussed the possibility for our escaping too. I knew from Genek Vertyporoch that we would all die unless we ran away.

"This was after our mother was taken away to the Belzec death camp?"

"Yes, it was," answered Leo. " Fela was working in the German

Forestry Department and was able to give me several blank travel permits with an official stamp and signature at the bottom." He continued, "My friend, Mrs. Ziegler, helped me then. She was working in an office and could use a typewriter to fill in the blanks. She could also use the telephone and probably called Fela in her office in Zakopane to tell her when we would be arriving in Cracow. When we got to Cracow, as you remember, Fela and Ala were waiting for us and they took us to Zakopane. Mark and our father went to Warsaw the same way. Fela couldn't have too many people coming to her. That would have looked suspicious."

Leo was modest in his account, giving credit to others but not to himself, yet Carl thought that Leo had done most of the work. Leo had never really gotten credit for what he had done. He had saved Carl's life but he never said so.

It started to rain and they had to go back home. Leo turned to Carl.

"Are you going to put this in your book?"

"Yes, I will," Carl answered.

"Then I'd better be careful what I say," said Leo with a twinkle in his eye.

Chapter 53

Shirley, Where Are You?

After work Irene and Carl went to eat at the Floridian Diner. It was a cool but pleasant evening in October 1993. A few minutes later they were joined by George and Leah.

They ordered their favorite dishes: French onion soup, baked halibut and fresh water trout. The waiter brought the salads. While putting the dishes down, he overturned a saucer of milk. It spilled onto Carl's jacket and pants. Carl jumped up and started to wipe it off.

"Be a sport," whispered Irene, afraid that he would flare up. But Carl was not angry. "Don't worry about it," he said to the waiter, who was apologizing profusely, "I will have it cleaned."

"They should pay for the cleaning," said George.

"No, I don't want them to pay," said Carl.

"That reminds me of Marian and the buttermilk at the Grand Hotel," said George.

"What happened there?" asked Leah.

"Well, we sat at the table and we all ordered buttermilk," started George. "Just as the waiter arrived with the tray full of buttermilk, Marian got up and upset the tray. The buttermilk spilled all over him."

Irene interrupted him: "I am reviewing the new book Carl and I wrote and I am now reading the part where we met you, George and Gisella. The four of us went to the Grand Hotel and met Shirley and Paul."

Carl wanted to say something on a different subject but some inner force told him not to interrupt.

"They were most wonderful people," said George. "Once Paul was wearing a beautiful, new suit and I admired it very much. He went into another room, changed clothes and came back a few minutes later holding the suit in his hands. He insisted that I take it as a gift and he wouldn't take no for an answer."

"They were both very generous," said Irene. "When Shirley bought you a gift, it was exactly what *you* liked. She took the time and effort to find out what you wanted."

"That's true," said Carl. "For example, Shirley knew that I liked to do crossword puzzles, so she bought me a few rolls of toilet paper with crossword puzzles printed on them."

"I like that idea," said Leah, smiling. "Maybe somebody should print jokes on toilet paper and sell it."

"She had so much personality," said Carl, "that everybody was always aware of her presence, even though she could hardly move around towards the end."

George said, "Every morning she had two pots of coffee brewing. Fresh rolls and appetizing were laid out on the table. We would wait in line in front of her porch to get in."

Suddenly Irene hit herself on her forehead and almost jumped from her seat. "Oh my God!" she exclaimed, "Do you realize what day it is? All day long I've looked at the calendar and I didn't realize it. Today is the 28th of October, Shirley's birthday." Irene was visibly agitated. "It *is* the 28th, isn't it?" she asked.

"Yes, it is," said Carl, "and Shirley tried to give us a signal. First he spilled milk to remind us of the incident at the Grand Hotel and now we've been talking about her all evening."

"Do you believe in life after death?" asked Leah.

"I don't believe in paradise and hell the way it is usually portrayed, but I believe that there is something after death, although I don't know exactly what," answered Carl.

Carl thought of an incident that had occurred in Monticello exactly one month after Shirley's death. There had been a sudden power failure and all the lights had gone out. Carl tried to restore the light by pressing the safety switches, as did the others in their bungalows, but to no avail. The place was now pitch black. However, to their wonder, the lights by Irene's bed and in Shirley's bungalow continued to work. They could not understand it. The next morning they called the electrician and he restored power. But nobody could explain why the two lights had stayed on. According to Jewish belief, the soul of the deceased person stays in the air for thirty days and then wanders away. Was that Shirley's last hurrah before going off into the great unknown?

For a while they sat in silence. They finished their dinner, and left. The moon was full and shining brightly. There were no clouds in the sky and the stars were twinkling. They went home, each deep in thoughts.

Epilogue

There is a story by Hans Christian Andersen entitled "Johnny." In it a young man named Johnny becomes an orphan when his parents die. He gathers the little money which his parents have left in a kerchief and walks out of the empty house into the unknown world outside.

There is a storm and he runs into a little chapel to escape the rain. A dead man is lying on a catafalque and two strangers are standing near him. They are highly agitated and are cursing the dead man. When Johnny inquires as to the reason for their indignation, one of them answers, "This man owed us money and now that he is dead, we will never get it back."

The other man adds, "Let's throw his body out of the chapel into the rain. He deserves it for cheating us out of our money."

Johnny says, "I have a little money here. Please take it all and leave the dead man in peace."

The two men take his money and depart quickly, leaving the dead man behind and shaking their heads in disbelief. Johnny straightens out the dead man's ruffled clothing, says a prayer and leaves. The storm has passed. He walks for a short distance when somebody calls after him, "I see that you are traveling alone. Do you mind if I join you?"

"I'll be delighted," answers Johnny and they travel together. They travel over many lands and Johnny grows very fond of his companion. The man does many things which Johnny does not understand. For example, when a swan dies, after singing a beautiful song, the man cuts off his wings and puts them in his bag. On another occasion they see an old woman passing by with a bundle of sticks on her back. Johnny's friend buys the sticks from her, paying more than they are worth. And when he sees a knight with a sword riding on a horse, he buys the sword from him. He seems to know something that Johnny doesn't.

The stranger likes Johnny too and protects him throughout their journey until they reach the palace of a king. The king has a beautiful daughter and Johnny falls in love with her at first sight. However the law of the country says that he can only marry her if he can guess her thoughts. Whoever can't guess correctly is beheaded.

Now, the princess is under the spell of a wicked wizard who has advised her to ask her prospective suitors to guess her thoughts.

The evening before the event, the king takes Johnny to a garden and shows him the graves of all the young men who have tried unsuccessfully to guess the thoughts of the cruel princess. When they failed to guess correctly, they were beheaded and buried in the garden. The poor king has tears in his eyes as he tells Johnny this story. "My daughter breaks my heart each time another fine young man is killed," he says. "Please reconsider your decision. I liked you from the first moment I saw you and I don't want you to be killed." But Johnny's decision is unshakable.

That night, Johnny's companion attaches the swan's wings to his shoulders and follows the wizard to the princess's palace. He whips him all through the flight with the sticks bought from the old woman.

When the wizard enters the princess's quarters, the stranger sneaks in and listens to their conversation. "I was whipped by a terrible hailstorm coming here," he complains. "Let's have a party. Tomorrow, after Johnny is killed, I will gouge out his beautiful blue eyes." Johnny's friend heard what the princess is going to think about on the next day on the advice of the sorcerer: "Think about my head tomorrow," the wizard tells her, "he will never guess." When the sorcerer leaves the princess's quarters, Johnny's friend follows him. He takes out the sword which he bought from the knight and cuts off the wizard's head. He wraps it in a kerchief.

He tells Johnny what the princess is going to think about. "When she asks you what her thoughts are, give her this package," he says. Thus, Johnny marries the princess after guessing correctly, and they live happily ever after. The evil spell of the bad sorcerer is broken and the princess becomes a good person again.

Johnny loves his companion very much and asks him to stay with them. But the man refuses, saying. "Do you remember the dead man in the chapel? When the two strangers wanted to throw him out into the rain, you gave them your last penny to stop them. I am the man you saved from being disgraced, and I wanted to repay you for your good deed."

Carl often thought about this fable. He considered himself exceptionally fortunate in having Irene for his wife. She was very intelligent and had helped him throughout their lives. She had persuaded him to go to college. She had convinced him to leave Poland. She had saved his life when he was in danger of dying of internal bleeding caused by an ulcer. She had encouraged him to go into business and helped him make a success of it. And she had helped protect the company from hostile takeovers.

Irene had always given him the right advice. Often Carl had not understood her premonitions and warnings and had rebelled. But she had always been right and he always agreed with her in the end. And he often thought, What have I done to deserve her and our life together?